THE FIRST FIVE YEARS OF LIFE

A Guide to the Study of the Preschool Child

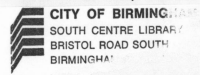

The
First Five Years of Life

A GUIDE TO THE STUDY OF
THE PRESCHOOL CHILD

Edited and partly written by
ARNOLD GESELL

With contributions by
Catherine S. Amatruda · Louise Bates Ames
Burton M. Castner · Henry M. Halverson
Frances L. Ilg · Helen Thompson

METHUEN & CO. LTD
11 New Fetter Lane, London E.C.4

First published by Methuen & Co. Ltd 1950
Reprinted four times
First published as a University Paperback 1971

Hardback SBN 416 32620 X
University Paperback SBN 416 18500 2

Printed in Great Britain by Butler & Tanner Ltd
Frome and London

CONTENTS

PLATES

The following plates, grouped as a separate section, will be found following page 58.

PREFACE

IT IS now fifteen years since the Macmillan Company published the predecessor of the present volume under the title: *The Mental Growth of the Preschool Child*. The subtitle was longer: *A Psychological Outline of Normal Development from Birth to the Sixth Year, Including a System of Developmental Diagnosis*.

This subtitle is recalled because it remains a fair description of the contents of the new volume, even though the text has been entirely rewritten and extended as a result of accumulated experience and investigation.

The last two decades are notable for the scientific and educational efforts which have been devoted to the first five years of life. As early as 1923 the National Research Council sponsored a Committee on Child Development to foster and coordinate the rapidly growing research in this field. More recently the establishment of hundreds of nursery schools as part of an emergency educational program has brought the problems of preschool hygiene into fresh relief throughout the nation.

The Clinic of Child Development has been in a fortunate position to share in what has become in America both a scientific and a social movement concerned with the welfare of young children. The social status of the preschool child has already undergone a revolutionary change; and this change has placed a premium upon a scientific understanding of his nature and needs. Too little is known about him, and there is always a danger that we shall presume on insufficient knowledge.

The present volume is written in a conservative spirit, and aims to broaden the approach upon problems of early psychological development. The subject matter is concrete and is addressed to students and laity, as well as to readers whose interest may be more technical.

The contents represent a true collaboration on the part of workers who have had both theoretical and practical interests in the applications of psychology and medicine to the protection of early mental growth. Professor Henry M. Halverson, who contributes the chapter on the motor characteristics of the preschool child, has made extensive studies of the development and mechanisms of prehension, and related motor phenomena. As Research Associate in Biometry, Helen Thompson, over a period of years, has given special attention to the normative and biogenetic aspects of early behavior development. She contributes a chapter on the genesis and growth of adaptive behavior. Burton M. Castner, as Clinical Examiner, has had considerable and varied contacts with early speech deviations and reading disabilities. He contributes the chapter on the development of language.

Dr. Frances L. Ilg, with basic training and experience in pediatrics, has been in charge of the Guidance Nursery and an associated clinical service. She and Louise Bates Ames, Assistant in Research, bring to bear a developmental point of view in the discussion of personal-social behavior. Mrs. Ames has also rendered valuable assistance in the preparation and correlation of the manuscripts for other chapters of the present volume.

Dr. Catherine S. Amatruda, as Research Pediatrist, in charge of the infant outpatient service of the Clinic, has had diagnostic and advisory relations with a wide diversity of infants and young children. She has drawn upon this practical experience both with normal and atypical conditions, in the two chapters dealing with the management and the clinical applications of the developmental examination. She also supplied the clinical data and many of the technical details summarized in the concluding sections which deal with examination records and arrangements.

It will be evident from the text that the preparation of this volume demanded a high degree of cooperation among the contributors, who met in repeated conference as a study group. They would be the first to acknowledge their indebtedness to each other, and to the rapidly growing literature which is only partially represented in the list of selected references. Genetic research, dealing as it does with continuous phenomena, is always dependent upon what has been done before. We wish therefore to express our deep sense of indebtedness to previous workers in the Clinic whose contributions have also been acknowledged in earlier publications.

As in previous studies, we have made use of the cinema for analyzing certain characteristics of behavior pattern. The cinema records of our Photographic Research Library have proved invaluable in perpetuating earlier observational data for subsequent comparative study.

We are greatly indebted to the generous long-range grants of the Rockefeller Foundation which have made possible a stabilized and systematic program of developmental research.

Our research has concentrated on the first year of life; but this very concentration has led us to a continuing follow-up interest in the subsequent years, particularly those which precede entrance to the elementary school. Previous publications from the Yale Clinic of Child Development have dealt chiefly with infant development. A major purpose of the present volume is to emphasize the organic continuity which binds the

preschool years with the period of infancy. Strictly speaking, that is bio-
logically speaking, the preschool years include all of the years between
birth and the sixth year molar. Our chapters therefore give due status to
the first year of life and indicate that identical principles of growth and
of guidance apply to infant, toddler, run-about, and school beginner.

A companion volume, *The Psychology of Early Growth* (Macmillan),
gives a month by month normative account of the developmental patterning of infant behavior from 4 through 56 weeks.

Our interest in the mechanisms of growth has apparently led us to
slight the problem of intelligence; at least we have made sparing use of
the term in the discussions of mental growth. We believe that the
widespread errors which come from a narrow preoccupation with the
psychometrics of intelligence can be corrected only by a broad and many-
sided study of the total process of child development. So-called intelligence or adaptive behavior is but one aspect of an intricate reaction
system, which is growing and which has grown.

Growth is a process of transformation which is especially active in the
preschool years. Moreover every child has a unique pattern of growth.
For these reasons we need versatile and various techniques, adaptable to
the observation and interpretation of the individual child. Such techniques
are needed in the fields of educational adjustment, parent and child
guidance, child psychiatry, and in clinical pediatrics. Under the present
trends of science, the potentialities of applied biology in the control of
human growth are so great that we have ventured a little prophecy in
the concluding chapter. As the. controls are perfected, the period of
infancy and early childhood will take on still more social significance.

It is hoped that the reader will not be too much disappointed if he
fails to find in the volume he now holds an inclusive ideology which
would explain the hidden forces and motivations of child behavior. We
believe that too little is known about the complex transformations of
early behavior to warrant an elaborate theoretical structure. First of all,
we must become acquainted with the process and products of natural
growth. Fortunately such acquaintance takes us one secure step nearer
to an understanding of the hidden mysteries.

ARNOLD GESELL

PART ONE

CHAPTER I

UNDERSTANDING THE PRESCHOOL CHILD

IN A biological sense the span of human infancy extends from the zero hour of birth to the middle twenties. It takes time to grow. It takes about twenty-four years for an American youth to reach the stature of maturity. For convenience one may think of this cycle of growth as a succession of four stages of six years each: (1) the preschool years, (2) the elementary years, (3) the secondary school years, (4) the preadult years.

We are now beginning to see this cycle of growth in its true perspective. Thus far, for sound social reasons, the middle twelve years have received most of the attention of the public school system. These are indeed important years for the transmission of cultural inheritance, but the demands of society and the findings of science are compelling us to see a new significance in the preschool years—the fundamental years which come first in the cycle of life and which therefore claim a certain priority in all social planning.

§ A. SOCIAL SIGNIFICANCE OF THE PRESCHOOL YEARS

Every eighth person in the population is a preschool child. There are in the United States sixteen million children under the age of 6 years, a total of about thirteen per cent of the population. In recent decades the proportion of preschool children has been diminishing; the proportion of aging and elderly adults is increasing. Families with no child or with an only child are more frequent. These populational trends are augmenting the importance of the preschool child.

The environmental conditions which surround the preschool children of the nation vary enormously. Many of these children are ushered into the world without the protection of medical service; many grow up without medical supervision, reared by parents who have received no guidance from the community in the most elementary principles of child care.

At the other extreme is the infant who is born in a hospital, safeguarded by medical supervision even prior to birth. This privileged infant is fed, weighed, bathed, sunned, aired, inoculated, examined, and re-examined at intervals, prescribed or periodic. When he is 2 years old an automobile transports him daily to a nursery school. At 5 he graduates into a progressive kindergarten. His mother has been trained to pay attention to his psychological as well as to his physical welfare.

Over 5,000,000 preschool children in rural, village, and tenement areas are underfed, underclothed, underhoused, and undereducated. About 75,000 children are enrolled in approximately 2,000 emergency nursery schools established through federal grants in aid. A similar number of children attend various forms of day nurseries, relief nurseries, and nursery-kindergartens. A few thousand attend laboratory nursery schools and tuition preschools. Only about one child out of four of eligible age attends a tax-supported kindergarten.

Some 1,500 institutions and 350 child placing agencies in a given year care for approximately 250,000 neglected and dependent children. Fully one-fourth of these are of preschool age. At conservative estimate, 65,000 infants each year are born out of wedlock. (One illegitimate birth for every thirty-five of the total population; one such birth in every sixty-one of the white population.) The death rate of these children is approximately three times that of other children; but those who survive create peculiarly intricate and exacting problems of social control. They make the most searching of all challenges to psychological understanding and diagnosis.

A Committee of the White House Conference on Child Health and Protection estimated the total number of handicapped children of all ages in the United States to be more than 10,000,000. Ten major types of handicap occur. They are listed below in an ascending order of frequency: (1) visual handicap, (2) epilepsy, (3) motor disability, (4) cardiac defect, (5) tuberculosis and pre-tuberculosis, (6) speech defect, (7) deafness and impaired hearing, (8) nervous and behavior disorders, (9) mental deficiency and subnormality, (10) malnutrition.

In the vast majority of cases the foregoing handicaps are either present at birth or arise during the first five years of life. To some extent the defects can be prevented; to a large extent they can be ameliorated during infancy and early childhood. Whether a handicap is classified as physical or mental, it inevitably involves problems of psychological understanding and of psychological guidance.

The great problem of physical accidents also proves to have a psychological aspect. Street and highway accidents, but more especially household accidents—burning, scalding, falls, poisoning, smothering, and play injuries—take a disproportionately heavy toll in the preschool years. Many of these accidents have their origin in controllable psychological factors in parent and child; many of them arise out of the limitations of the child's immaturity. Another reason, both social and personal, for attaining a better understanding of the preschool child.

The present volume is chiefly concerned with the normal aspects of mental growth. It makes no attempt to consider systematically the specialized clinical procedures necessary for the early diagnosis of the graver handicaps of child development. In the period of infancy and young childhood, however, it is not always possible to draw a significant line between normal and abnormal symptoms. Moreover, in early life defects are often veiled beneath a plausible exterior of "mere immaturity." Incompleteness, weakness, and inadequacy are overlooked; or they are too readily excused on the blind faith that the infant will "outgrow" his difficulties. Wishful thinking becomes easy when a defect is suspected. To reduce such errors of interpretation we need critical norms of development cautiously applied.

It happens also that errors are often made in the reverse direction. The normal is misinterpreted as abnormal. Under the spell of anxiety or of over-sophistication, parents impute dire meaning to symptoms of development which are really benign. They misjudge the child because they do not perceive his incompleteness, weakness, and inadequacy in terms of immaturity. This kind of misinterpretation is the most common of all. It can be overcome only by a more intelligent appreciation of the *process* of mental growth.

Then there are the uncounted everyday misinterpretations which all of us are bound to make because of sheer ignorance of the nature and needs of the child's psychology. We lack knowledge of the ways in which he grows and learns. We accept the fact that he is not a miniature adult, but we do not know enough about the traits which make him different from the adult.

A rational approach to the problems of child psychology can remove many misconceptions but it is not infallible. There is always a temptation to over-use new-found scientific data. For example, an excessive emphasis on the measurement of intelligence has tended to blind us to other very important factors in the child's economy. Individual differences in personality make-up, in emotional predispositions, and in innate growth characteristics demand more consideration particularly in children of preschool age. A superficial adoption of the doctrines of the conditioned reflex and of habit training likewise has led to faulty aims and methods of child care. Even the modern nursery school is too much influenced by a conventional psychology of learning and by the traditional patterns of public school organization. The preschool child is in danger of being regarded as a miniature school child.

The only corrective for this danger is an increased insight into the distinctive developmental needs and hygiene of the early years. There are profound social reasons why our understanding of preschool children should be deepened and humanized. The age period between one year and three years is peculiarly liable to misunderstanding and mismanagement. And between the ages of three and six there is the prospect that we shall once more use mental ages, intelligence quotients, and achievement tests in a pseudo-technical manner, prejudicial to the developmental welfare of the children concerned.

The nursery school movement as an educational and social experiment has yielded invaluable data relating to the preschool child. It would, however, be a mistake to propagate the nursery school as a subprimary addition to our present graded school system—as virtually another stratification to be administered like a schoolroom. Our public school system is already over-stratified. We must organize our social provisions for the preschool years in new patterns which will preserve the constructive forces of home life and vitalize parental responsibility.

This means that the problems of school entrance, of kindergarten and prekindergarten, and of the nursery school cannot be successfully divorced from the problems of infant welfare. Adequate protection of the preschool child demands continuous safeguards, beginning with birth and the prenatal period. From the standpoint of social control such protection can be achieved only through a coordination of medical supervision, parental guidance, preparental education, and special educational provisions in health and guidance centers. Social planning has already recognized the importance of housing, and the influence of favorable domestic surroundings on child life. Progressive housing programs may in the end prove a wholesome counterbalance to excessive physical expansion of the public school system.

These considerations all bear upon the subject of our chapter: Understanding the Preschool Child. It is difficult to separate cause and effect. However blind and impersonal social forces seem to be, it is certain that our understanding and evaluation of the preschool child will have a determining effect upon the form of the environment which is ultimately created for him. Psychology as a science makes a social contribution when it helps to specify the optimal environmental needs of the preschool child. Not even the architecture of a nursery school or of a child health center can be truly functional until we define the behavior characteristics and the developmental requirements of children of varying ages. An adequate understanding of the preschool child will promote favorable social provisions for him. A narrow application of psychological techniques will have an opposite effect.

§ B. GROWTH: A KEY CONCEPT

The hygiene of the preschool child must be conceived in terms of growth. This is pre-eminently true of his mental hygiene. His manifold

patterns of behavior grow so rapidly and undergo such ceaseless, continuous transformations, that there are few absolutes to guide us. We
must look for the principle of relativity which is inherent in all development. The ordinary concepts of habit, of intelligence, of mental abilities,
cannot do justice to his ever-changing organization. He is constantly
shedding habits or modifying them; his "intelligence" is a dynamic end
product of multiple, changing factors; his abilities are all relative to one
inclusive ability, namely, the ability to grow.

Growth, therefore, becomes a key concept for the interpretation of
individual differences. There are laws of sequence and of maturation
which account for the general similarities and basic trends of child development. But no two children (with the partial exception of identical
twins) grow up in exactly the same way. Each child has a tempo and a
style of growth which are as characteristic of individuality as the lineaments of his countenance.

Growth ceases to be a mystical notion or an empty abstraction when it
is put to work in a concrete way as an interpretive principle. The purpose
of the present volume is to outline the process and products of early
mental growth. This outline is drawn up with sufficient concreteness to
serve as a practical guide for the observation and the appraisal of individual children.

The following chapter (Chapter II) deals in an introductory way with
the nature of mental growth. It puts forth the thesis that mental growth
is a patterning process; a progressive *morphogenesis* of patterns of behavior. This point of view enables us to think of the mind in objective
terms as a living organic complex which assumes shapes and which pursues directions. We believe that such an envisagement of the mind as a
growing system puts us in a better position to observe and to comprehend
the determinants of the child's behavior. If we do not regard the so-called
psyche as a structured entity, we are likely to endow it with animistic
attributes, and to overlook the formative essence of the growth process.

Chapters III and IV offer a bird's-eye survey of this dynamic growth
process for the entire preschool period from birth to the sixth year. In
order that this survey may not suffer from vague generalities, ten successive age levels are separately considered, as follows: 4, 16, 28, 40, 52,
and 80 weeks; 2, 3, 4 and 5 years. The behavior traits and the maturity
status of a typical, normal child are characterized for each age. This
results in a series of psychological portraits.

In order that the portraits may be more readily compared, each sketch
briefly depicts in turn four basic fields of behavior: (a) motor characteristics, (b) adaptive behavior, (c) language behavior, (d) personal-
social behavior. This method of treatment preserves the advantages both

of a cross-sectional and of a longitudinal approach. The student who wishes to gain a continuous impression of any one behavior field (for example, language behavior) may select the ten sections devoted to this field and read them consecutively.

The period of infancy is included in this preliminary survey to emphasize the essential uniformity of the mechanisms of development at all ages. Fetus, infant, child are governed by identical laws of growth. Indeed, our understanding of the young child would be improved if we could realize that his problems of development are in their essential quality like those of early infancy.

From the standpoint of the mechanics of development, not only are the various ages similar, but the diverse fields of behavior are similar. Posture and locomotion, speech, adaptive behavior, and personal-social behavior are obedient to common laws. Accordingly it would improve our management of disciplinary problems if we could recognize in the field of personal-social behavior the same molding mechanisms which govern the development of creeping and walking.

There is a final important reason why the period of infancy should be included in our purview. We cannot do psychological justice to individual children of nursery school age unless we know more about the mental growth of these same children during the first two years of life. The time will come when nursery establishments will take account of the antecedent careers of their charges. An inclusive system of developmental supervision would begin with birth.

To enhance the concreteness of our developmental survey, photographic illustrations are included. These photographs picture the children of various ages, both in naturalistic and normative situations.

The child as a whole, having been portrayed in a series of sketches, Part Two concretely outlines specific areas of observation and of psychological examination. These areas, for convenience, are grouped in four chapters, corresponding to the four major functional fields of behavior already referred to. All told, some eighty behavior situations are considered.

Each situation is briefly described; the conditions for making observations, the procedures for administering the tests are detailed; the psychological significance of the situation is discussed.

The basic data consist of detailed records of follow-up examinations at 18 months, 2, 3, 4, and 5 years of the same children in the so-called "normative group" who had been studied at lunar month intervals throughout the first year of life. This group was carefully selected for homogeneity as reported elsewhere (39). Additional data were secured at intermediate and basic test ages for a more varied but normal group of children who were examined under clinical auspices. The incidence of behavior items for these two groups, expressed in percentages, is given in tables throughout the text, and in the Developmental Schedules reproduced in § 1, pages 319-343.

Each behavior situation, as now formulated for clinical and observational application, is described. The procedures for administering the tests are detailed; the psychological significance of the resultant observations is discussed with special reference to its developmental implications. The behavior trends and gradations for advancing ages are formulated in tabular summaries of genetic sequences.

This method of presentation, we believe, has several advantages. It makes for concreteness, succinctness, and convenience of reference. It emphasizes the growth factors in the child's behavior. It provides substantial source material for the non-technical reader as well as for the student of child development. At the same time it formulates the observation and test procedures with sufficient precision to permit clinical application by trained examiners.

A broad genetic approach of this character is necessary both for ordinary observation and for the more exacting tasks of developmental diagnosis. The only way in which we can escape the errors of mechanical psychometric methods is to bring to bear the critical correctives of developmental interpretation. The importance of such correctives is discussed in a separate chapter on "The Philosophy of a Developmental Examination," and in the chapters which deal with practical problems of clinical management and clinical technique (Part Three).

Our discussion of the simple (?) test procedures of a developmental examination calls attention to the varied meanings of the child's responses. These responses in the burgeoning preschool ages are profoundly influenced by maturity factors and traits of individuality. The formal psychological examination is regarded not as a series of achievement tests, but as a potent device for releasing significant behavior which at every turn calls for diversified analysis rather than a meager recording of successes and failures. Such analysis can be accomplished only by a deliberate application of developmental concepts and developmental data.

Every child has a unique pattern of development. So far as possible we must attempt to characterize the individual differences among children of preschool age. The concluding chapters of this volume deal with this problem. Even in the prodigiously complicated field of personality formation, growth factors are primarily determining. The individuality of the child as a person is reflected in his developmental career, and in his growth characteristics. Here as elsewhere Growth is a key concept.

CHAPTER II

THE NATURE OF MENTAL GROWTH

MENTAL growth is a rather elusive reality. Growth is a process so subtle that it cannot be perceived. And for ordinary vision the mind is utterly insubstantial. Yet the growth of the mind in its first years constitutes the subject matter of the present volume. How can we make this elusive reality less elusive?

First of all we must agree to think of growth not as an empty abstraction but as a living process, just as genuine and as lawful as digestion, metabolism, or any physiological process. We must also think of "the mind" as being part and parcel of a living organism. As such the mind has form, contour, tendency, and direction. It has "architecture." It is as configured as the body with which it is identified. It reveals this configuration in modes of reaction, in patterns of behavior. Mental growth is a process of behavior patterning which organizes the individual and brings him toward a stage of psychological maturity.

The metaphysics of the relationship between body and mind need not concern or confuse us here. We simply suggest that there are laws of growth and mechanisms of development which apply alike to body and mind. Growth is a patterning process whether we think of its physical or its mental manifestations. The embryologist is particularly interested in the transformations of bodily structure; the genetic psychologist, in transformations of behaviors. Both embryologist and psychologist investigate the shape of things to come and the shape of things becoming.

For example: The embryologist finds in the tiny human embryo at the fourth week of intra-uterine life, a pair of "buds" just behind the gill arches or neck region of the trunk. They are limb buds. They grow. Note the remarkable transformations of this pair of diminutive stumps. (1) Cells penetrate into the stumps causing them to elongate. (2) Some of these cells change into a skeleton or framework of three segments (future arm, forearm, and hand). (3) The outer segment (future hand) assumes the shape of a paddle. (4) Five lobes appear on the edge of the paddle. (5) A skeleton penetrates into each lobe and provides it with three or four bony segments.

Thus the paddle transforms into a five-fingered hand. Muscles and tendons attach themselves to the skeleton of arm and hand. Nerve fibers penetrate the muscular tissue; nerve endings ramify into the joints; end organs by the thousands, like so many sentinels, establish themselves in the sensitive skin which envelops the growing hand and arm.

Soon, very soon, this arm and even the fingers will make characteristic movements, spontaneous, reflex, and induced. The mind has begun to grow! For what are characteristic movements but patterns of behavior? And mental growth is a process of behavior patterning.

Even in the limb bud stage, when the embryo is only 4 weeks old, there is evidence of behavior patterning: the heart beats. In two more weeks slow back and forth movements of arms and legs appear. Before the twelfth week of uterine life the fingers flex in reflex grasp. Increasingly complicated postural movements take form: the trunk curves and straightens; legs and arms flex, extend, rotate; the head moves from side to side and up and down. By the time the embryo, now properly called a fetus, is 5 lunar months old, it has an astonishing repertoire of behavior patterns.

At this age the future infant is a foot in length and a pound in weight, but he is already far advanced in his bodily and behavioral organization. He is distinctly human in his lineaments. He is not unduly compressed by the confines of the uterus, but maintains a partially free existence in its fluid medium. His postural attitudes somewhat resemble those which he will assume in his bassinet. He makes lashing movements of arms and legs (quickening). His skin is sensitive and responds to stimuli. He even makes rhythmic movements of the chest—pre-respiratory movements in preparation for the event of birth, another five months hence, when the breath of postnatal life will rush into his lungs.

It is well to realize that even at this early age the fetus has attained such a high degree of behavior organization. It seems as if Nature hastens the growth of the organism as a safeguard against the contingency of premature birth. Fortunately, if the attendant complications are not too severe, an infant born eight weeks before normal term may survive and undergo a relatively normal behavior development.

The fetus at the age of 5 months is already in possession of twelve billion (or more) nerve cells which make up the human nervous system. This is the full quota, all that the individual will ever have. Many of these cells have already established functional connections among each other and with muscle fibers; many more cells, particularly those of the brain cortex, are still fallow. As the fetus grows, as the infant grows, and as the child grows, these nerve cells become organized into patterns of responsiveness, or into reaction systems. These neuron patterns determine behavior. They are influenced by the constitution of the blood, by endocrine hormones, and by electro-chemical regulators; but in a fundamental sense, the patterning of the mind is inseparably identified with the micro-scopic and ultramicroscopic patterning of nerve cells.

This neuron patterning pervades the entire organism. The fibers and fibrils of neurons proliferate within the extensive gastro-intestinal tract, the walls of blood vessels, the respiratory apparatus, the genito-urinary system, the sphincters of rectum and bladder, the mucous, sweat, salivary and tear glands, and the ductless glands of internal secretion. A vast network of autonomic and sympathetic neurons thus organizes the vege-tative and visceral functions.

Another vast network of sensory neurons supplies numberless sensitive areas in the skin and the mucous membranes, in the joint surfaces and tendons, and in a dozen special organs of sense. Motor neurons with innumerable collaterals ramify within the musculature of head, neck, trunk, and extremities. This network constitutes the sensori-motor system.

A third network of neurons concerned with memory, language, ideation, and with adaptations to past and impending experience, mediates the voluntary, symbolic, and imaginal forms of behavior.

These three neuron nets are in reality a single fabric, because the organism is an integrated whole and grows as a unit rather than by discrete installments. This single fabric preserves the unity of the organ-ism; it embodies and implements the psychological individuality of fetus, infant, and child.

It is permissible to speak of the individuality of the fetus, for even newborn infants display significant individual differences in their physio-logical processes, in their reactions to internal and extrinsic stimuli, in their patterns of feeding, sleeping, and waking activity, and in percep-tivity. These neonatal expressions of individuality are largely the end products of the primary mental growth which was accomplished in the long period of gestation.

The neonatal period lasts about four weeks. By that time the stump of the umbilical cord has separated and the infant is well advanced in his physiological adjustment to a postnatal environment. The period of in-fancy may be regarded as extending to the second year. Conventionally the years between two and six are known as the preschool years. They terminate with the eruption of the sixth year molar. With second dentition the child is usually ready for the elementary grades.

These conventional age periods are in a measure justified by distin-guishable differences in mental maturity. But from a biological standpoint, there are no sharp transitions in the continuum of mental growth. Even birth does not bring about a unique and abrupt transition, because *in utero* the fetus has already anticipated to a great degree the reactions of early neonatal life. He has been prepared; the very arrangement and relationships of his neurons have pointed to the future. In preliminary and provisional form these relationships were laid down by intrinsic patterning prior to and independent of actual experience. This preliminary prospective kind of patterning is mental maturation. It operates not only *in utero* but throughout the whole cycle of mental growth.

Environment inflects preliminary patterns; it determines the occasion, the intensity, and the correlation of many aspects of behavior; but it does not engender the basic progressions of behavior development. These are determined by inherent, maturational mechanisms.

Such mechanisms account for those characteristics of behavior growth which are universal in the species, and they also account for resemblances between human and infra-human growth. In all vertebrate creatures the general direction of behavior organization is from head to foot. The sequence of motor patterning in the human infant clearly reflects this law of developmental direction. The lips lead, eye muscles follow, then neck, shoulders, arms, trunk, legs, and lastly feet.

The tide and trend of preschool development may be outlined, tersely, as follows:

In the *first quarter* of the first year the infant gains control of twelve tiny muscles which move his eyes.

In the *second quarter* (16-28 weeks) he comes into command of the muscles which support his head and move his arms. He reaches out for things.

In the *third quarter* (28-40 weeks) he gains command of his trunk and hands. He sits. He grasps, transfers and manipulates objects.

In the *fourth quarter* (40-52 weeks) he extends command to his legs and feet; to his forefinger and thumb. He pokes and plucks. He stands upright.

In the *second year* he walks and runs; articulates words and phrases; acquires bowel and bladder control; attains a rudimentary sense of personal identity and of personal possession.

In the *third year* he speaks in sentences, using words as tools of thought; he shows a positive propensity to understand his environment and to comply with cultural demands. He is no longer a "mere" infant.

In the *fourth year* he asks innumerable questions, perceives analogies, displays an active tendency to conceptualize and generalize. He is nearly self-dependent in routines of home life.

At *five* he is well matured in motor control. He hops and skips. He talks without infantile articulation. He can narrate a long tale. He prefers associative play; he feels socialized pride in clothes and accomplishment. He is a self-assured, conforming citizen in his small world.

The psychological growth which is achieved in the first five years of life is prodigious. Both in scope and speed, the transformations of the preschool years exceed those of any other half decade.

The purpose of the succeeding chapters is to define the steps and stages by which the child accomplishes these developmental transformations. Our first task will be to characterize ascending levels of maturity in terms of typical behavior patterns. Such characterizations will provide a series of normative portraits outlining the directions and trends of psychological growth. In order that the lines of growth may be more apparent, each portrait will consider in turn four major fields of behavior, namely (1) Motor Characteristics, (2) Adaptive Behavior, (3) Language Behavior, (4) Personal-Social Behavior.

1. *Motor characteristics* include postural reactions, prehension, locomotion, general bodily coordination and specific motor skills.

2. *Adaptive behavior* is a convenient category for those varied adjustments, perceptual, orientational, manual, and verbal, which reflect the child's capacity to initiate new experience and to profit by past experience. This adaptivity includes alertness, intelligence, and various forms of constructiveness and exploitation.

3. *Language* embraces all behavior which has to do with soliloquy, dramatic expression, communication, and comprehension.

4. *Personal-Social behavior* embraces the child's personal reactions to other persons and to the impacts of culture; his adjustments to domestic life, to property, to social groups, and community conventions.

These four major fields of behavior comprise most of the visible patterns of child behavior. They do not, of course, fall neatly into separate compartments. The child always reacts as an integer. The underlying organ and instrument of his behavior it will be recalled is a single fabric. Our categorical classification, therefore, is simply for convenience, to facilitate observation and diagnostic analysis. Judgment is necessary to evaluate the psychological import of any given behavior. Behavior values overlap and they change with age. A behavior pattern may be regarded as "adaptive" at one age, and as "motor" at another age. The reactions to a behavior test may be observed and interpreted from two or more aspects at any given age. Take for example the test, *Draws a horizontal stroke responsively to demonstration.* First of all we may be interested to observe whether the child persists in making a vertical stroke or whether he has the motor maturity required for a lateral movement. This is a *motor* value. We may also note how intently he looks at the demonstration and how discriminatingly he begins and ends his stroke. This is an *adaptive* behavior value. There may even be accompanying verbal or emotional expressions which also have symptomatic value. It is evident that many behavior tests might be assigned to two or more categories. The classifications adopted in the present volume are for clinical convenience; but are not intended to obscure the fact that mental life normally is integrated.

Mental growth is a process of organization. It is synthetic and manifests itself in patterned wholes. All behavior items need interpretation because of the ever-present factor of developmental relativity. Unqualified psychometric ratings of behaviors as absolute abilities will prevent a sympathetic understanding of the young child's psychology.

The normative portrait sketches which follow attempt to call attention to the developmental contexts which color behavior at different age levels. The child's mind does not grow by simple linear extension. He has a persisting individuality, but his outlook on life and on himself transforms as he matures. He is not simply becoming more "intelligent" in a narrow sense of this much misused term. He alters as he grows. His personality sense, his appreciation of his own personal status, his assertiveness of this status, undergo profound developmental changes evidenced particularly in his personal-social behavior, but also in language and in "adaptive" behavior. The whole task of understanding the preschool child becomes more interesting and rewarding if we focus attention, not on his abilities, but upon the organizing processes of growth.

CHAPTER III

THE FIRST YEAR OF LIFE

THE developmental transformations which occur in the first year of life far exceed those of any other period excepting only the period of gestation. "The poor, new-born babe like a seaman wrecked, thrown from the waves, lies naked o'er the ground." But in the brief space of a year this helpless creature is on his two feet, cruising, prying, exploring. He becomes a complex individual capable of varied emotions, of flashes of insight, and of persevering stretches of effort. His personality and his diversified abilities at one year of age are the product of an extremely swift season of growth.

So multiform are these mental transformations that it is difficult to see them in proportion and perspective. Although the rate of development in infancy is extremely rapid, the process itself is no different from that which prevails in later years. In terms of process, the infant advances psychologically by the same steps which carry him forward in childhood and youth. The infant displays essentially the same kind of drive, the same fumbling power to profit by experience, the same proclivity to abstraction and generalization, in his progress from the known to the unknown, from the familiar to the novel.

The more minutely his behavior is examined, the more completely does it resemble in its dynamics the operations of the mature mind. Behavior development entails continuous interweaving of patterns and components of patterns. The organism is forever doing new things, but "learning" to do them in an old way—reincorporating at a higher level what it has already approximated at a lower one. The structure of the mind is built up by a spiral kind of cross-stitching. This process of reincorporation is mental growth. The methods of growth of the infant therefore anticipate and simulate those of later years. The infant is predictive of his later self. The characteristics of mental growth in the nursery school and kindergarten child are those of infancy.

The present chapter and the one which follows are designed to emphasize and to delineate this fundamental principle of continuity. The chapters consist of ten thumbnail sketches of ten advancing age levels from 4 weeks through 5 years. Because the rate of maturing is relatively so rapid at the outset it is natural that five maturity levels should be placed in the first year of life. These levels demarcate the neonatal period and four trimesters or quarters, subdivided on a lunar month basis. Five additional levels do similar justice to the next four years. By summarizing the behavior characteristics of these nodal ages, it is possible to glimpse the tide of development in its forward-moving continuousness. Adjacent age levels are referred to in the summaries in order to increase definition and to sharpen perspective.

The summaries are written in a somewhat informal style so that the total child rather than detached behavior items will come into view. To facilitate comparison, and to expose the leading threads of development, each characterization gives separate consideration to the four major fields of behavior, namely: (1) motor characteristics, (2) adaptive behavior, (3) language, and (4) personal-social behavior.

This arrangement, as already suggested, permits cross references from one age zone to another for any selected behavior field. It combines the advantages of a cross-sectional and a longitudinal approach. The total age level characterization furnishes a cross-sectional picture. But any given behavior field may be followed through consecutively from one age to another by selective reading. The studious reader may wish to read these summaries twice: first, age by age as arranged in the text; secondly, by behavior fields, reading in turn all the sections pertaining to motor characteristics (pp. 18, 20, 22, 24, 27, 30, 34, 41, 46, 52) and in similar sequence the sections for each of the other three fields.

The major purpose of these summary sketches is to provide a panoramic view of the entire preschool period. The sketches may also be put to practical and to clinical uses. The summaries then become standards of reference for estimating the maturity of the observed behavior in children of preschool age and of defective children generally or partially retarded at preschool levels. An approximate estimate is arrived at by the simple method of best fit. After the behavior picture of a given child has been recorded, this observed picture is matched against any one of the available age level portraits. With two or more such matchings, the examiner is in a position to decide which portrait as a whole or in part best fits the behavior picture which has just been under observation. He then makes a rough comparative estimate, shading up or down from the nodal age which has been selected as being the most appropriate.

These normative summaries are factual, but they are intended to be more than mere inventories. They are characterizations of maturity. It is hoped that they will enable the reader to conjure up an organic image of a child as a living whole even though this child must be portrayed as a somewhat generalized type. As the mind grows it changes in shape rather than in size; it is always personalistic and organic in make-up. In the following series of sketches we must not look for linear increases in a single intellectual function, but for progressive patterns of maturity. Nor must we look for static absolutes. In mental growth nothing *is*; everything is *becoming*.

§ A. FOUR WEEKS OLD

Of all infants, the human infant is at birth the most helpless. In a sense, he is not fully born until he is about 4 weeks of age. It takes him that long to attain a working physiological adjustment to his postnatal environment. Even so he may still show a certain precariousness of organization in fitful waking, in startle reactions, and in irregular respiration, also in sneezing, choking, regurgitation or vomiting on slight provocation. Such "instability" is relatively normal at this tender age, because the primary vegetative network of the nervous system is still only incompletely organized.

Frequently the neonate seems to be in a twilight zone between sleeping and waking. He is quasi-dormant. It seems as though sleep itself were an extremely complicated pattern of behavior and that it takes time for the rhythms of sleep and of open-eyed attention to define themselves. He is indeed growing so rapidly in all fields of behavior that he shows variations and fluctuations from day to day. He does not follow a rigid schedule in his spontaneous activities and cravings. He is ill-suited to an over-rigid routine.

The behavior characteristics of the 4-week-old infant, however, are in no sense chaotic or formless. They fall into their proper position in a genetic sequence. The following summary will suggest how certain 4-week-old patterns are developmentally related to those of the fetal period on the one hand, and to those of the 16-week-old infant on the other.

Motor Characteristics

The 4-week-old infant when awake lies on his back with head averted, usually to a preferred side. Only momentarily does he bring his head to a mid position. Almost invariably his arm is extended on the side toward which his head is turned. The opposite arm is flexed with the hand resting near or in the head-chest region. This combination of averted head, extended arm, and flexed arm is the so-called tonic-neck-reflex attitude (t.n.r.) which dominates the waking life of the infant for some twelve weeks.

Occasionally the 4-week-old infant bursts into startle responses, his head coming momentarily to the mid-line and all his extremities extending abruptly. Occasionally he lashes the air with more or less symmetric windmill movements of the arms. But the asymmetric t.n.r. attitude under-lies most of his postural behavior. Indeed, the t.n.r. is part of the ground plan of the total reaction system. In partial form it was present prenatally, helping the fetus to accommodate to the outlines of the uterine cavity. At 16 weeks it gives way to more symmetric patterns of behavior, but it is a precondition for the growth of these later patterns.

ADAPTIVE BEHAVIOR

The most active and adept muscles of the 4-week-old are those of mouth and eyes. A light touch in the mouth region causes the lips to close and then to purse; the head will also make seeking movements, particularly if the infant is hungry. Whether reflexive, deliberate, or conscious, this represents a form of adaptive behavior. Sucking and swal-lowing were within the infant's capacity even before birth.

The twelve tiny muscles which move and immobilize the eye balls are brought under increasing control in the neonatal period. The 4-week-old infant indulges in long spells of ocular immobilization and fixation. He stares vacantly and detachedly at large masses like windows, ceilings, and adults.

His visual field is delimited by the postural set of the t.n.r. attitude. He disregards a ring dangled in the mid plane; but if the ring is slowly moved into the field of vision, he will pursue it with combined eye and head movements, through a small arc of less than 90°. At 16 weeks he "picks up" the ring with his eye muscles, more promptly, and they operate more independently of the head in pursuit of a moving object.

However, at 4 weeks the picking up capacity of the eyes really exceeds that of the hands. Ocular apprehension precedes manual prehension. Both hands are predominantly closed (even when the eyes are open). There is no reaching out to grasp objects. Yet the patterning of prehension is well under way, for if one touches the child's hand (with the handle of a rattle) the activity of the arm is increased, and the hand either clenches or opens.

LANGUAGE

The 4-week-old infant is heedful of sounds. If, while he is busy with postural activity, a hand bell is tinkled, the activity ceases. This is a significant pattern of behavior, a kind of auditory fixation or "staring" at sound. At later ages the sound perception will become discriminating for things. He will listen to and understand the sound of footsteps. Yet later he will listen to and comprehend the sound of words.

Except for crying he is almost inarticulate. The intensity and manner of his cry vary with cause and circumstance. His vocalizations are meager and non-expressive, but he mews and makes small throaty noises, precursors of babbling.

PERSONAL-SOCIAL

The 4-week-old infant fixates transiently on a face that bends over into his field of vision. His own facial activity may subdue or slightly brighten on social approach, but a brief intent regard is the chief token of his "social" reaction. He may make a comparable response to the human voice. He tends to soothe when he is picked up and when he is snugly and warmly wrapt. He probably feels a dim sense of security from calm and assured handling. This tactile responsiveness and sense of protectedness must be set down as early genetic items which have social import.

§ B. SIXTEEN WEEKS OLD

At 4 weeks of age the neonatal period is drawing to a close. With each succeeding week the infant moves more deeply into his domestic environment. At 16 weeks he is already graduating from the cozy confines of the bassinet. He has longer and better defined waking periods; he may even demand social attention by fussing. His traits of individuality are becoming more obvious. Conflicts with excessive and untimely environmental pressures arise. His acculturation is well under way.

Developmental transitions are rarely sudden. Sixteen weeks, however, marks a turning point. It ushers in a period of rapid cortical organization which brings about important transformations and new correlations of sensori-motor behavior, particularly in the coordination of ocular and manual reactions.

MOTOR CHARACTERISTICS

The t.n.r. is losing its sway. The head is more mobile and comes more frequently to the mid-line. Arms and hands likewise, for their movements are in large part correlated with or even controlled by the position of the head and of the eyes.

The dozen directing muscles of the eyes have made enormous gains in the preceding twelve weeks, by virtue of an increasing network of neuron connections. Tiny as these muscles are, the grosser muscles of posture and prehension are becoming obedient to them. Accordingly, a ring dangled before the infant's eyes evokes massive movements of incipient approach, involving head, shoulders, and arms.

Legs and feet have a very subsidiary status, but there are anticipations of their future responsibilities. When the infant is held in the supported standing position, he extends his legs recurrently and sustains a fraction of his weight.

Trunk musculature is organizing. He enjoys propped-by-pillow sitting, and he enjoys holding up his head which no longer needs a prop. He likes to look around adaptively. This is a good illustration, by the way, of how a single behavior item (head control) may have a twofold significance—one motor, one adaptive.

ADAPTIVE

The t.n.r. is waning but during its ascendancy it served to channelize the pathways of visual attention. It led by gradual stages from diffuse and fleeting fixations on the extended arm to prolonged inspection of the hand. Indeed the 16-week-old infant looks intently at a rattle which he holds.

His hands will soon be ready (thanks to the ceaseless patterning of neuron networks) for grasp of the rattle on visual cue; even now his free hand comes toward the rattle as though to engage in grasp and manipulation.

Compared to the primitive window staring of 4 weeks, his perceptual capacities have gained prodigiously. Held in the lap, he will pay recurrent regard to a cube on the table before him; he may even detect a tiny 8 mm. pellet. He gives selective regard not only to his own hand but to the ministering adult hand.

LANGUAGE

The 16-week-old infant bubbles, coos, chuckles, gurgles, and laughs. These are fundamental productions of the oral and respiratory apparatus which will ultimately subserve articulate speech. More refined uses of this apparatus will appear in the varied vocal play which characterizes the next few months.

The 16-week infant is not, however, entirely engrossed with his own primitive vocalizations. He may turn his head on hearing a familiar sound. But even more significantly he pays heed to the human voice.

PERSONAL-SOCIAL BEHAVIOR

Face, hand, and voice of the mother—these fall within the ken of the 16-week-old infant. He "recognizes" his mother and other familiar attendants in numerous, inarticulate but patterned expectancies implanted through feeding, bathing, dressing, and expressions of affection. He is capable of a vivid smile on social approach and he may sober at the sight of a stranger.

He relishes a sitting position. His eyes widen, pulse strengthens and breathing quickens when he is translated from the supine horizontal to the seated perpendicular. His enjoyment probably goes beyond athletic satisfaction in his almost mastered head balance. This is more than a physical reorientation; it is a new social orientation. A comparable widen-, ing of horizon lies a year ahead when he will have command of his legs and will penetrate still deeper into his social environs.

§ C. TWENTY-EIGHT WEEKS OLD

Bassinet, crib, chair, pen, nursery, yard, kindergarten, school—this constitutes the environmental sequence which parallels the developmental progress of the preschool child. As the 16-week-old infant graduated from the bassinet, so the 28-week-old infant has graduated from the crib to a chair. He is becoming a sitter. He needs only slight support from the arms of chair or of mother. He will soon maintain independent seden-tary balance.

He is now so well adjusted on vegetative and postural levels that he can spend much of his waking time in active manipulatory exploitation of the physical world, its fixed furniture, its detached (and detachable) objects.

Motor Characteristics

The 28-week-old infant is chronologically and developmentally at a halfway stage on the way to a full attainment of the upright posture. At 56 weeks he will stand quite alone; at 28 weeks he sits alone, erecting his trunk perhaps for a whole minute.

With this improved sedentary balance his prehensory approach upon objects becomes less bilateral. He reaches for a cube promptly on sight, he grasps it with tilted hand, thumb participating in the seizure. He transfers the cube from one hand to the other and retransfers. This alter-nating one-handedness marks a significant motor gain over the bilaterality of 16 weeks.

Ocular adjustments are more advanced than manual adjustments. He can perceive a string, but is inept at plucking it. He gives consistent regard to a pellet but places his hand rather crudely over it and usually fails to secure it.

Adaptive Behavior

Although eyes are still in the lead, eyes and hands function in close interaction, each reinforcing and guiding the other. Whereas the 16-week-old infant is given to inspection of surroundings, the 28-week-old infant inspects objects. And if the object is within reach it is usually in his busy hands. Head became versatile in the previous trimester; hands become versatile in this one. Directly he sees a cube he grasps it, senses surface and edges as he clenches it, brings it to his mouth, where he feels its qualities anew, withdraws it, looks at it on withdrawal, rotates it while he looks, looks while he rotates it, restores it to his mouth, withdraws it again for inspection, restores it again for mouthing, transfers it to the other hand, bangs it, contacts it with the free hand, retransfers, mouths it again, drops it, resecures it, mouths it yet again, repeating the cycle with variations—all in the time it takes to read this sentence.

The perceptual-manipulatory behavior of the 28-week-old infant is highly active. It is not passive reception. It is dynamic adaptivity, fused with exploitiveness. If you wish, it is intelligence.

LANGUAGE

The 28-week-old infant crows and squeals. At 16 weeks he cooed, at 4 weeks he merely mewed! He has made progress since those small neonatal sounds which emanated from a throat that was used almost exclusively for alimentary purposes.

In the last twelve weeks he has indulged in abundant spontaneous vocalizations, producing vowels, consonants, and even syllables and diphthongs. He is almost ready for defined, duplicated utterance of *mu*, *ma*, and *da*, which lead to his first "words."

He has amassed a wealth of socialized acquaintance with specific persons in his environment, with their facial expressions, gestures, and postural attitudes, with routine domestic events. Into his own psycho-motor system he has incorporated responses in the form of motorized predispositions corresponding to these events, and their associated persons and objects. At present, however, he is more concerned with practical events, with physical objects, and with tones of voice and inflections, rather than with words. But all this practical experience is prerequisite to comprehension of words. In fact it *is* comprehension; that is, comprehension on the level of practical judgment.

PERSONAL-SOCIAL BEHAVIOR

The 28-week-old infant is relatively self-contained for reasons already suggested. Having acquired such a creditable command of eyes, head, mouth, arms and hands, he cannot give too much attention to onlookers! He takes keen delight in the exercise of his newly attained neuro-motor abilities. He can exploit a single toy contentedly for a long period in an extroverted manner. If he were too socially compliant he would refer and defer his activity too much to others. He can consolidate and correlate his developmental gains to better advantage by this independence. In this self-sufficiency he reminds us somewhat of the 18-month runabout who also is especially fond of his own devices. The most conspicuous difference in these two age levels is postural: 28 weeks is sedentary; 18 months is ambulatory; but both are much preoccupied with private enterprise for sound developmental reasons.

This does not, however, mean that the 28-week-old is an isolationist. He is constantly learning the elementary social context of domestic happenings, albeit chiefly in terms of their import to him personally.

But this is making him socially wise, for he is expectant and pursuant in his contacts with others. He has to lay foundations of concrete experience before he is ready for more complicated social reciprocity. He does not have sufficient background to be very heedful of words. He is not over-concerned with the strangeness of strangers if they do not disappoint his usual expectancies. But he cannot squander himself just now in exploring the social environment. He has more substantial matters in hand. It is developmentally fitting that he should remain somewhat self-contained. At least for a time.

§ D. FORTY WEEKS OLD

Forty weeks marks a transition to what is almost an epoch, since there are so many new and distinctive patterns of behavior emerging in the developmental complex. The supine position so acceptable throughout the first quarter of the year is now scarcely tolerated except during sleep. The 40-week-old infant speedily escapes from supineness by rolling or raising himself to a sitting position. He can also stand if he holds himself by the palings of his pen. He takes a new social interest in the household and even enjoys short expeditions into the outside world. He shows a new interest in words, both as receptor and producer. In prehension, manipulation, and investigativeness he gives many significant tokens of discrimination and elaborative behavior. Not only is he penetrating deeper into the family circle, but he himself is more fully adopted by that circle as a participating member. This is further evidence of important psychological transformations.

MOTOR CHARACTERISTICS

Forty weeks marks the beginning of the fourth quarter of the first year. The most distal outposts of the organism are being incorporated into the expanding nervous system—tongue tip, finger tips, and toes. In the first quarter, mouth and eyes; in the second quarter, head, neck, and shoulders; in the third quarter, trunk, arms, and hands; in the fourth quarter, legs, fingers, feet; such is the general order of advance of neuro-motor maturation and of functional emancipation.

His legs now sustain his entire weight, although independent balance will not come until the end of the year. Sitting equilibrium, however, is mastered. While sitting he can turn to the side, lean at varying angles, and recover balance. He can shift from sitting to prone and prone to sitting posture. When prone he retrogresses, rocks, or creeps.

Prehension shows new refinements; the index finger and thumb exhibit a specialized extension and mobility for poking, probing, and plucking. The volar pad of the thumb opposes the volar pad of the index finger.

Adaptive Behavior

The adaptive behavior at 40 weeks reflects new neuro-motor refinements in the mechanics of mastication and of manipulation. The lips approximate more adaptively to the rim of a cup; the tongue is used more effectively in the management of morsels, and in ejection. The 40-week-old infant can pick up a crumb with precise pincer prehension. He uses his inquisitive index finger to pry and to palpate. Thereby he gains new knowledge of the third dimension and of the textures of things.

He still brings objects to the mouth as he did at 28 weeks; in all probability his tongue now contributes more to the sensory experience of mouthing than it did at the earlier age; but the importance of the mouth as a sensory end organ is diminishing. He displays instead a strong digital and visual interest in details. He is sufficiently analytic to segregate a single detail for attention, and also to react in a successive and combinative way to two details or to two objects. In the presence of more than one object he manifests an awareness of more than one, a dim sense of twoness, of container and contained, of top and bottom, of side to side, and even of cause and effect.

His appreciation of these relationships is primitive, ambiguous, equivocal, embryonic. It is in no sense conceptual; but it is active and it denotes a remarkable advance toward that later form of intelligence which goes by the name of intellect and judgment. Genetically this discriminativeness has much in common with more sophisticated patterns of behavior; and it is far beyond the naïve single-mindedness of the 28-week maturity level.

Language

The distal expansion of the neuro-motor network is incorporating the accessory muscles of speech as well as those of mastication. Indeed, these muscles are to a significant degree identical. The increasing dexterity of tongue, lips, chewing and swallowing musculature, combined with imitativeness, favors articulate vocalization. It is not surprising that words emerge out of a matrix of feeding behavior, just as "razzing" intrudes itself even when food is in the mouth. Razzing is an audible sputtering brought about by activation of the tongue which is compressed between the lips. Tongue protrusion is another form of tongue play which has phonetic implications.

The 40-week-old infant is not self-contained. He shows a susceptibility to social impress. He tends to imitate gestures, facial expressions, sounds. He shows a responsiveness to his own name; he even "understands" No! No! Even though he is quite unequal to true comprehension of word meanings, he manifests a socialized responsiveness which will inevitably lead to speech. He already has one or two "words" in his articulate vocabulary.

PERSONAL-SOCIAL BEHAVIOR

The 40-week-old infant is fairly well established in the routines of everyday life. He sleeps through the night, takes two naps and three or four bottles a day. He is accustomed to solids, and accepts new solids if they are tactfully introduced. He feeds himself a cracker; he holds his own bottle.

He has a margin of energy for social contacts. Although able to play by himself for an hour or more, he likes to have people around. Even when he waves bye-bye he may prefer to have them remain. His new social responsiveness enables him now to perform nursery tricks like pat-a-cake. In the manipulation of toys he sometimes modifies behavior under the stimulus of demonstration.

He smiles at his own mirror image but he may show timidity when greeted by a stranger, particularly if the stranger does not respect his wariness and social sensitivity. This capacity to perceive strangeness is itself a symptom of more mature sociality.

§ E. ONE YEAR OLD

From the standpoint of development, the first birthday represents an intermediate rather than a culminating stage. The 1-year-old child is still perfecting patterns which came into the picture at 40 weeks and which come to further fulfillment at about the age of 15 months.

The 15-month-old child assumes the erect posture independently: he can walk alone; he can put a ball into a box; place a pellet in a bottle; build a tower of two blocks; scribble spontaneously, talk in jargon, communicate by gesture, use a spoon, and put on simple garments.

It is interesting to note that the 1-year-old child is just at the brink of all these abilities. They are then in a nascent or intermediate stage.

At 1 year we may sometimes wonder whether the infant is destined to be a quadruped or a biped, but if we bear in mind the behavior characteristics of the 15-month-old child, we can better understand the forward reference of his performance and conduct. Even quadrupedal locomotion proves to be a preparation for the assumption of the distinctively human upright posture.

MOTOR CHARACTERISTICS

The 1-year-old child can creep, often with great alacrity. He may creep on hands and knees, or on all fours in full plantigrade fashion. In spite of his creeping expertness he is under an irrepressible impulse to rise to his two feet and once he has assumed the full plantigrade attitude, he is almost ready for standing alone. He can pull himself to standing position unassisted, but ordinarily he does not achieve independent equilibrium until he is four weeks older. He cruises sidewise as he holds to a support; he walks but not without support. His prehensory patterns are approaching adult facility. His fine prehension is deft and precise, and he has almost acquired the capacity of voluntary release. The flexor or gripping component of prehension is now offset by an inhibitory extensor component of release. A comparable inhibitory control makes it possible for him to release a ball with a throwing thrust.

ADAPTIVE BEHAVIOR

The 1-year-old infant shows nascent appreciation of form and number. In a test situation, confronted by a round and a square hole, he shows a specialized perceptivity for the round hole. He can thrust a finger or a rod into such a hole. Utilizing his new-found power of release, he can place a cube into a container. He is beginning to geometrize space and is able to bring one object momentarily above another, a form of orientation which presages tower building. His manual orientation to spatial relationships also enables him to adapt his manipulation of a bottle so as to crudely expel a pellet. In the multiple cube situation he places one cube after another on the platform or table top. This is the genetic rudiment of counting.

His adaptive behavior reflects a new sensitiveness to imitative models. Although he brings a crayon to paper, his adaptive response is increased by demonstration of a scribble. His social ball play improves under the stimulus of give-and-take.

LANGUAGE

The 1-year-old infant displays a high degree of social reciprocity. He listens with new intentness to words; he repeats accustomed words under the stress of repetition and imitation. He is even beginning to suit action to words, surrendering a ball obedient to the command, "Give it to me." He may have added two or more words to his vocabulary and he tries to attract attention by a cough or squeal, if not by words. He approaches

4

his mirror image socially, often supplementing the social approach with vocalizations. Such vocalizations will soon lead to expressive jargon and a multiplication of articulate vocabulary.

PERSONAL-SOCIAL BEHAVIOR

The 1-year-old child has acquired considerable social status in the family group. Frequently he is at the very center of the group. He shows a significant tendency to repeat performances laughed at. He pleases himself thereby as much as he does his audience. Through such situations he begins dimly to feel his own self-identity which will become the nucleus of a growing sense of personality. He is now capable of unmistakable fear, anger, affection, jealousy, anxiety, sympathy. He may even be credited with an elementary esthetic sense. He responds to music. He likes single, repetitive rhythmically accentuated sounds. He may have a primitive sense of humor, for he laughs at surprise sounds and at startling incongruities.

In his domestic behavior he is becoming somewhat more self-dependent. He feeds himself with his fingers, he rubs the spoon across the tray and licks it; he expresses satiety by gesture. His bowel movements are usually regularized; he cooperates in dressing.

But his demeanor is not exclusively self-contained. It frequently assumes a social reference. If necessary, he takes vocal or other means to elicit attention. He displays considerable perceptiveness of the emotions of others and a growing capacity to influence and to adjust to these emotions. This is the adaptive aspect of the personal-social game of life. It is an indication of intelligence as well as of personality.

CHAPTER IV

FROM ONE TO FIVE

T HE tide of development deepens with age and in a relative sense it also slows down. As age increases it takes a longer lapse of time to attain a proportionate degree of maturity. It takes the infant twelve weeks to rise from a 24-week level of maturity to a 36-week level. It takes a nursery school child twelve months to rise from a 2-year level to a 3-year level. It takes a kindergarten child two years to advance from a 4-year to a 6-year level. In each of these instances the age interval represents a ratio of 2 to 3. There is some truth therefore in the paradox that the younger a child is the faster he grows old! Accordingly, five maturity portraits will suffice to outline the course of behavior development for the period from 1 to 5 years of age.

Development is so profoundly influenced by physiological and almanac age that it must always be appraised in comparative terms. No absolute units of measurement are available. A principle of relativity governs. To interpret the evidences of mental growth they must be perceived and judged comparatively. It is only by serial comparisons that we can hope to glimpse the continuous genesis in the patterning of behavior. To facilitate such comparisons the following sketches of maturity levels will repeatedly refer to a senior age and the adjacent junior age, designated by capital letters to suggest personal identity. To preserve continuities, the four major behavior categories will be summarized at each age level, as in the previous chapter.

§ A. EIGHTEEN MONTHS OLD

Many changes take place between 1 year and 18 months. The child gains from two to three inches in height, and as many pounds in weight; he may double his denture. So at 18 months he has a dozen teeth, is from thirty to thirty-three inches tall, and weighs from twenty-and-a-half to twenty-seven-and-a-half pounds. He sleeps almost as much as he did at 1 year—thirteen hours, or over half the day, but usually with only one nap instead of two.

He makes enormous gains in general bodily control. He also makes considerable gains in the fields of adaptive and social behavior. But the latter gains are rather less evident. Superficially they are often so sketchy that their developmental importance is not sufficiently appreciated. There is danger of underestimating the psychological complexity of this first difficult transition from babyhood to a more mature estate. The transition needs patient management and much insight. In many respects this is the most poorly understood period of early child development.

MOTOR CHARACTERISTICS

The most conspicuous difference between ONE and Eighteen is postural. Eighteen has gained at least a partial command of his legs, while ONE can barely stand without holding onto something for support. At 15 months the infant can attain a standing position quite independently; but not until 36 months does he have sufficient balance to stand on one foot. Eighteen hurries with a stiff, propulsive, flat gait, which is not true running but which is better than walking or toddling. He can seat himself on a child's chair with fairly accurate aim; he can climb into an adult chair. With help he can walk up stairs. He descends stairs unassisted, by the bump method, or he creeps down backward. But in floor locomotion he rarely resorts to creeping. For some time he has been able to push a chair around; now he can pull a wheeled toy as he walks. Such feats are quite beyond ONE who still travels best on all fours or on hands and knees, and has not yet fully attained the erect posture. But even during his first steps ONE may hold a toy as a surrogate support, thus bringing manual and postural behavior patterns into early coordination.

Manually Eighteen is deft enough to place one cube upon another on the first attempt. His prehensory release, however, is exaggerated and it takes repeated trials to build a tower of three. ONE can hold a single cube in one hand while he grasps for another; he may briefly poise one cube over another. But his adaptive release is crude; so he rarely makes a tower although he can, after a manner, "drop" a cube into a cup. Eighteen can throw a ball, whereas ONE rolls, projects, or flings it by a simple extensor thrust. Eighteen's elbow is more versatile and he can turn the pages of a book, albeit he seizes two or three folios with each sweep.

ADAPTIVE BEHAVIOR

The 1-year-old child is at the threshold of discriminating perceptions of space and form. He gives selective attention to the round hole in the performance box; fleeting heed to his own crayon marks; he brings the pellet to the bottle combiningly. He probes into the third dimension with index finger and rod. In his cube exploitation, and in his cup and spoon play, he displays a dawning sense of aboveness and verticality, and of container and contained.

To the 18-month-old child such discriminations are effortless and elementary. He has mastered, at a practical level, numberless geometric relationships in his physical environment. He knows where things are, were, go, and belong. Pictures which doubtless are mere blotches to the yearling are configured for him. He points to pictures of a car, a dog, a clock. He points to his nose, eye, hair, on verbal command. (If he could both introspect and remember, he would probably say that his perceptions of common things are much more individuated at 18 months than at 1 year—that is more disengaged from total postural set. But it is very unlikely that the percept or image of his nose or eye has a clearly defined discreteness.)

His sense of verticality, nascent at 1 year, has much matured, so he can pile two or even three blocks in vertical alignment. He imitates a vertical stroke. At 2 years he will attain a similar command of horizontal geometry, likewise reflected in his block building, paper and crayon behavior, and perhaps also in his self-feeding, for then he no longer tips up the end of the handle as the spoon enters his mouth.

The scope of his attention is undoubtedly wider than it was at 1 year. He has an interest in many and in more. He likes to assemble the many cubes into a pile or to disperse the pile into the many cubes. He likes to store and to hold four, six, or more cubes which are handed to him individually. In comparison, the 1-year-old is single- and serial-minded. The 1-year-old infant has a typical one-by-one pattern: he takes one cube after another and places it on the table or platform in a repetitive manner. This is a genetic anticipation of counting. The 18-month-old infant cannot count, but he has a vigorous interest in aggregates, and that also is a developmental prerequisite for a higher mathematics.

His perceptual maturity is reflected in the interesting way in which he punctuates his behavior. Although he is sketchy, mobile, and mercurial, he frequently gives evidence of reacting in terms of perceptually delineated episodes. He sits in a chair with a decisive *fait accompli* demeanor. He hands back the test material to the examiner with an air of *now-that's-over*. He waves *bye-bye*, not as a nursery trick but with a sense of termination. He also has a feeling for terminations and end results when he says *Thank you*, or reports that he has soiled or wet himself, or when he wipes up a puddle. This spontaneous interest in the *completion* of a chain of events is well in advance of the mere seriality of the 1-year-old. It is part of the developmental psychology of perception. It represents a stage of growth.

LANGUAGE

Language behavior embraces comprehension as well as communication. The 1-year-old infant is not very articulate. Ordinarily he can speak only one or two words in addition to *dada* and *mama*, and they have slight communication value. But he perceives in others and communicates to others a wide range of emotional states—distress, pleasure, fear, rage, vexation, affection, anxiety, etc. Much of his emotional expression is highly egocentric. He makes very meager distinction between himself and others. His vocalizations are only beginning to have a social reference. He makes a vocal as well as reaching approach to his mirror image; he has been known to cough to secure attention.

Eighteen similarly is self-absorbed but he makes much more frequent and diversified communications both by gesture and words. Often he boasts a vocabulary of ten definite words. He is articulate enough to say *eat* when he is hungry and *no* when he is sated. He accompanies the *no* with a shake of the head, but earlier he merely shook his head. He is now beginning to use words with and instead of gestures. He is even abandoning baby talk, preferring *thank you* to *ta ta*.

Three-word sentences must wait another six months. But at a preverbal level he has been for some time in a sentence and even a paragraphic stage of utterance, for he conducts expressive, inflected "conversation" by means of fluent jargon. For most children this jargon is a developmental matrix of speech.

His comprehension of the meanings of social situations is likewise on a jargon rather than an articulate plane. He senses the general import of familiar and even novel situations. (For example, he apprehends to a significant degree what you want him to do in the developmental examination, even though he understands very little of what you may try to *tell* him.) Yet he responds to simple commands like *Put the ball on the chair*, or *Open your mouth*. He recognizes many pictures which he cannot name. Words are only beginning to assume a free floating implemental status. But this imposes no embarrassment because he distinguishes only partially between himself and the things in which he is interested.

PERSONAL-SOCIAL BEHAVIOR

The 1-year-old child has a fragmentary sense of personal identity and almost no sense of personal possession. Eighteen is beginning to claim *mine* and to make distinctions between *you* and *me*. These distinctions are extremely elementary. He is ordinarily very content in self-absorbed spontaneous play and locomotor excursions. However, he may observe a newcomer, a child or adult, with concentrated interest. Even though Eighteen is playing independently he may cry if a companion leaves, or he may follow the companion. He also likes to do little errands of fetch and carry about the house. His satisfactions in them seem to be mildly social, mainly kinesthetic.

Temperament and recent experience greatly influence his adjustment to social situations, but in general he is rather resistant to changes of routine and to all sudden transitions. In comparison, the 1-year-old is apparently more amenable.

Eighteen is a nonconformist, not because of a propensity to rebel but because his stock of perceptual differentiations and embryonic concepts is so small and so precarious that he clings to his mental possessions as he clings to his mother or to an object in hand. For him, sudden changes are precipices. He avoids them by lying down, by backing away, by running off to hide, by screaming, struggling or beating the air. His defiance is self-conservative rather than aggressive. He strikes the air rather than the intruding person. When he becomes socially more mature he will slap the person.

The egocentricity of so-called resistant behavior at 18 months reflects the social immaturity of that age level. If the year-old infant is apparently more amenable it is because he is still more immature. The conservatism of Eighteen is, however, a normal condition of growth. His psychology generally demands gradual and gentle transitions. He cannot be reached by sharp discipline, by scolding, or by verbal persuasion. Words mean too little.

The negativity of the 18-month-old child has had exaggerated emphasis, because the adult has imputed contrariness to a type of behavior pattern which has developmental rather than emotional significance.

The sense of guilt in Eighteen is non-existent or very rudimentary. He is just acquiring voluntary control of his sphincters. He lacks strong compunctions concerning urine and feces because he lacks insight. At about the age of 15 months he began to attribute urinary puddles to his own behavior and used a summarizing word *after* the event. At 18 months or later he uses the word *before* the event, a symptom and medium of personal-cultural control; but he makes no verbal or intellectual distinction between the products of bowel and bladder.

His social insights are not much more brilliant than his perception of eliminative functions. He is self-engrossed (not selfish) because he does not perceive other persons as individuals like himself. *He* is the all encompassing individual within whom other beings take shadowy and inconstant shapes.

But he is making good his deficiencies. How? By unconscious mimicry and by dramatic impersonation. Even at 1 year he repeated performances laughed at and gave crude reproductions of combing his hair or of spitting or smoking! At 18 months such renderings are less crude; they are more imitative. Eighteen duplicates more completely what he sees. He pretends to read the paper. During the next year his imitative play becomes increasingly elaborate and frequent. By such emotional and perceptual reconstructions the other beings in his world become less shadowy and more detached. And so his egocentricity gradually lessens.

§ B. TWO YEARS OLD

In the preschool period the rate of mental growth is so rapid that every age seems to be an age of transition. Two years is no exception. But when ONE, EIGHTEEN, and Two are compared, the disparity between One and EIGHTEEN proves to be greater than that between EIGHTEEN and Two. One appears quite infantile in contrast with EIGHTEEN, whereas Two is in many respects an advanced and elaborated version of EIGHTEEN. Close analysis, however, discloses that the small differences between EIGHTEEN and Two have deeper developmental implications than appear on the surface. The developmental gain in language behavior is particularly significant. The 2-year-old gives many indications that he is becoming a thinking animal—entering upon a sapient estate which befits the erect posture which he has now more fully achieved.

Since the age of 18 months he has gained two inches, three pounds, and four teeth. (Height, 32-35 inches; weight, 23-30 pounds; dentition, 16.) He sleeps some thirteen hours and commonly has a nap of from one-and-a-half to two hours in the afternoon.

There is still a suggestion of primitiveness in his physical anthropology. His legs are short, his head large; there is a residual stagger in his steps, a spread in his stance, and a forward lean in his body posture. Perhaps Neanderthal man exceeded him in pantomimic symbolization, but the modern 2-year-old exhibits a precocity in speech which prophetically places him far in advance of primitive man. His emotional life likewise has great complexity, depth, and sensitiveness. It requires careful consideration, for his personality is acquiring difficult orientations at a time when his neuro-motor capacities are still very immature.

MOTOR CHARACTERISTICS

Two is decidedly motor-minded. His most numerous and characteristic satisfactions are muscular. He greatly enjoys gross motor activity. In this respect he is like EIGHTEEN, but he has made important advances in postural control. Two is more flexible at the knees and ankles, has a better balance and consequently can run, while EIGHTEEN propels himself with a wobbly, stiff, flat gait. Two no longer needs personal assistance in walking up and down stairs, but he has to shift into "marking time" at each tread. He can jump down from the first tread without help, one foot leading the other as he leaps. He can walk up to a ball and kick it on command. (EIGHTEEN simply walks up to the ball.) He can hasten his steps without losing equilibrium, but he cannot yet dart about, making short turns and sudden stops.

In his tastes he is to a great extent an acrobat, for he delights in rough and tumble play, both solitary and responsive. Joyful emotions he is likely to express with dancing, jumping, clapping of hands, screeching, and deep-seated laughter. His fundamental muscles tingle with kinesthesia.

His accessory muscles, however, are by no means idle. He can wiggle his thumb and his tongue. He likes to talk even when he obviously has nothing to say either to himself or to others. He "burbles on" with his new-found words as once he prattled in the crib and for comparable neuro-motor reasons. His oral musculature has matured. EIGHTEEN masticates with effortful attention; Two, almost automatically.

Manual control has similarly advanced. EIGHTEEN turns the pages of a book with swift sweeps, a few pages at a time; Two turns them page by page with modulated control and with improved release. EIGHTEEN builds a tower of three, Two builds a tower of six blocks. This is a mathematical index of the advance which has been made in fine motor coordination, both in the flexors of grasp and the extensors of release. EIGHTEEN cannot cut with a scissors. Two can snip. He can string beads with a needle. EIGHTEEN holds a glass of milk with two hands and somewhat precariously; Two holds it securely (often with one hand) and even nonchalantly, although the free hand remains poised in sympathetic tension. The spoon is tilted excessively as at 18 months but not until it is well in the mouth. Two seizes the handle with thumb and radial fingers and holds it supinely (palm up) as well as by overhand grasp. Two also remains seated for longer periods in a chair. By these fundamental motor tokens he certifies to an increasing readiness for domestic acculturation.

ADAPTIVE BEHAVIOR

Two builds a tower twice as tall as EIGHTEEN's. This denotes a real gain in span of attention. In spite of his fondness for bodily activity, Two can stick to confining tasks somewhat longer than EIGHTEEN. He conforms better to the table situations in the developmental examination. His memory span also has lengthened. He looks for missing toys. He recalls events of a yesterday, whereas EIGHTEEN lives much more from moment to moment.

The perceptual and imitative behavior of Two shows finer discriminations. At 18 months he readily matched round block and round hole. At 21 months he can insert a square block edgewise through the rectangular hole of the performance box. He identifies many pictures. He will soon be perceptually ready to make his first identifications of a few letters of the alphabet. He is beginning to make distinctions between black and white. Although he may use color names, he does not yet make color discriminations. He senses oneness *versus* many and more. He uses number words in accompaniment to serial pointing, a precursor of later discriminative counting.

The interdependence of motor and mental development is close in the 2-year-old. He seems to think with his muscles. He enacts what he sees and sometimes what he hears. He opens his own mouth when he hears about the wolf's mouth while listening to a fairy tale. This mimicry is also a characteristic of EIGHTEEN, but in Two it is more intimately related to words. Two often talks while he acts and he also acts what he talks. His developmental problem seems to be not so much to suit the action to the word as to get the word more fully separated from the action. By using them together he manages in time to put them more asunder. This is the ubiquitous process of disengagement or "individuation," operating at a psycho-motor level.

The ineptness he displays in folding and creasing a piece of paper illustrates at once a meagerness of directive imagery and the formativeness of his manipulatory geometry. He is not yet free to move his hands with versatility in different directions. His adaptive behavior is channelized (and delimited) by the lines of structure which have matured or are now maturing in his neuro-motor system.

His movement patterns show a new facility with horizontal maneuvers. EIGHTEEN shows a comparable facility in vertical control: he tends to imitate a stroke by a vertical movement; he builds a vertical tower of cubes. Two is beginning to imitate a horizontal stroke as well and he already builds a horizontal row of cubes, that is a train. In precision of coordination, train and tower make equal demands; but in configuration, the train is much more difficult. It requires additional neurological equipment. It presumes "two-year-oldness."

In infancy and early childhood it takes about six months of neurological growth before the child can do something distinctively new in his exploitation of cubes—as shown by the following genetic gradations:

Age	The something new
0 months	Grasps a cube on contact, but cannot see it
6 months	Grasps a cube directly on seeing it
12 months	Brings one cube over another
18 months	Places three cubes one upon another
24 months	Places three cubes in a row or train
30 months	Places a chimney cube on the train
36 months	Builds a bridge of three cubes

Two represents an interesting stage in the foregoing developmental sequence. It is an arresting fact that he must add a year of maturity to his stature before he can combine the vertical component of *tower* (*v*) and the horizontal component of *train* (*h*) into $h + v = bridge$.

Although Two is thus limited in his constructive activities by his motor make-up, he is already using this make-up as a thinking creature. At 18 months he pushed a chair about and climbed into it. This was an end in itself. Now at 24 months it becomes a means to an end. Two pushes a chair to location and climbs into the chair to attain an object out of reach. He is a deductive reasoner—at least on a massive-muscle plane. To what extent he rises also to a higher conceptual plane, his language behavior may indicate.

LANGUAGE

Articulate speech is in a stage of active nascency. The 2-year-old is burgeoning with words. He may have as many as a thousand. In some instances, however, he may have only a few words at command. Ordinarily jargon has almost entirely vanished, though under the stress of excitement with great tidings to tell, the 2-year-old may use jargon and words in almost the same breath. What has happened to the jargon of 18 months? It has apparently sunk into the subvocal, subconscious levels of functioning where it persists as an organizing substratum for the ordering of words, phrases, and inflections.

On an American average, the 2-year-old has about 300 words in his vocabulary, but they are for him of very unequal value; some are scarcely more than novel sounds, others do the duty of full sentences even when used singly. Names of things, persons, actions, and situations greatly predominate. Adverbs, adjectives, and prepositions are much in the minority. Pronouns, *mine, me, you,* and *I* are coming into use approximately in the order just given. While his sense of self is not as totalitarian as it was at 18 months, it is by no means sufficiently defined for conceptual verbalization. He is much more prone to call himself by his given name: "Peter slide down," instead of "I slide down." (Conversely he will understand you better in the psychological examination if you address him with a direct vocative, "Peter kick the ball," instead of "You kick the ball.")

With the same sentence he expresses intention and action, for while he slides he is quite likely to soliloquize, "Peter slide down." He may also elaborate to say, "Danny slide down," "Mamie slide down," "Peter slide down," repetitively and singingly. The soliloquy has become a chant. By such repeating with variations he not only practices the mechanics of articulation but he winnows out the salient parts of speech. "*Peter-slide-down*" is an organic unity from which *slide-down* must be disengaged (individuated). Jargon may have disappeared but not the singsong which often made his jargon musical. So he sing-songs his sentences.

He likes simple sound patterns, which indeed lie at the bottom of syntax and which belong to music and poetry. No wonder he enjoys Mother Goose which clinks and tinkles with 2-year-old sound patterns.

The 2-year-old likes to listen for reasons of language as well as of sound. By listening he acquires a sense of the descriptive power of words. Accordingly, he likes stories which someone else tells about himself and his familiar belongings. Then he becomes reassured of what the words mean, "Peter climbed his ladder." "Peter slid down the slide." He relives this in motor revivals as he listens. "I saw Peter slide, Peter saw me." Through such elementary locutions he begins to catch the meaning of transitive verbs; and the double reference of pronouns, whose meaning depends upon who does the talking. "I" means "you" when you say I. "I" means "me," when I do the talking. There is a bewildering paradox here, which it takes the 2-year-old some time to solve. No wonder he is confused. But in the long run, within another year, the pronouns and the transitive verbs with reversible subjects and objects help him to identify himself as "I, Peter."

He is most fluent when he tells his own experiences but he does not relate them in well-defined past tense; the past becomes present. He senses time and tide in terms of a succession of personal events. Here again words spoken to him will help him in due time to achieve a comprehension of *pastness*. Likewise with multiplicity, expressed by plurals; and with physical relationships (in, under, etc.) expressed by prepositions. His comprehension, however, does not depend upon vocabulary. It depends upon a neuro-motor maturity which in turn makes him appropriate suitable words. Two uses these words singly, in phrases, and in combinations of three or four as sentences. But he does not think or speak in paragraphs. Intellectually his highest achievement perhaps is his ability to formulate a negative judgment: "A is not B." ("A knife is not a fork.") This represents an extraordinary advance beyond mere rejection by head aversion, or a negational shake of the head. He is beginning to say *no* on the high plane of logic! It gives him genuine pleasure to match words with objects. A negative judgment expresses a new awareness of discrepancy when words and objects do not correspond.

PERSONAL-SOCIAL BEHAVIOR

One has only a fragmentary sense of personal identity; EIGHTEEN is beginning to claim "mine" without having a well-defined sense of personal possession; Two is beginning to use the word "mine" and to show unmistakable proprietary interest in things and persons. All in all, Two is still very much self-centered. He may even seem more "selfish" than EIGHTEEN because he has a more robust sense of himself. His use of differential pronouns, as we have seen, is rudimentary, but that he should use them at all indicates that in due time he will make clear-cut distinctions between himself and others. He recognizes and names himself when he sees his image in the mirror. He may even say, "It's me," but it is more characteristic of him to say, "See the baby," or "That's mother's baby." His mother is still very much part of himself, although she is undoubtedly perceived with more distinctness than at 18 months. When EIGHTEEN and Two are observed side by side in test situations, Two frequently refers objects to his mother in a quasi-social manner which is not characteristic of EIGHTEEN. When he plays with other children he defers chiefly to himself. He contacts his playmates physically, but his social contacts are few and brief. For the most part he limits himself to solitary or parallel play.

This is a natural condition of growth. If he were too socially minded he could not master the intricacies of parts of speech and of sentence structure. The meaning of the words must come primarily through himself and only secondarily through others. Ordinarily he has a wholesome restraint with respect to strangers; he is not easily led around; he follows his own devices. And yet he has acquired a creditable degree of conformance to domestic conventions. He helps to dress and to undress himself. He finds armholes in his garments; he pulls off leggings, and stockings; although he cannot untie shoe laces, he is beginning to take an interest in buttoning and unbuttoning. He uses a spoon without excessive spilling. If taken up during the night he sleeps without wetting his bed and daytime "accidents" are becoming rare. He makes verbal distinction between bladder and bowel functions, an ability which is correlated with his increased voluntary control.

His consciousness of the family group is displayed in different ways. He sometimes hides toys to be sure that he will have them on later occasions, reflecting a growing sense of possession. He shows affection spontaneously, that is, on his own initiative. He obeys simple domestic commissions: he gets slippers for grandpa. He laughs contagiously and even indulges in an elementary humor for the amusement of playmates or elders, making an abrupt gesture to create a socially incongruous situation. He shows symptoms of pity, sympathy, modesty, and shame. He may pout when he is scolded. He smiles at praise. He may show evidences of "guilt" when he has had a lapse of daytime sphincter control. He may hang his head "in disgrace," or he may instead accuse baby brother or the dog! This sense of guilt is probably not as profound as surface signs suggest, for the 2-year-old is something of a mimic and he readily dramatizes the emotional expressions of the adults in his social milieu. But even a rudimentary sense of culpability increases the hazards of his personality development in an over-disciplinary environment.

Dawdling is a characteristic of two-year-oldness which is somewhat inconsistent with a comprehensive sense of guilt. His dawdling probably represents a normal indifference to social requirements. He dawdles when motivation is low, or at mealtimes when tedious demands are made upon his motor coordinations. Dawdling is a form of deliberateness which may have a developmental function without being in any sense a vice or a weakness—a protective kind of negativism or filibustering.

Inconsistencies in the personal-social behavior of Two arise out of the circumstance that he is now making a transition from a presocial to a more socialized stage. He oscillates between dependence and self-containedness. His "negativisms" and his ambiguities are due to the same factors which create confusion in the use and application of pronouns. He has not yet made complete distinction between himself and others. But his dramatic play is much more elaborate than at the age of 18 months; it penetrates further into his cultural environment. Whether boy or girl, the 2-year-old is especially prone to dramatize the mother-baby relationship through dolls and otherwise. In a dim way he is beginning to understand this relationship which means that he himself is becoming somewhat detached from his mother. Only by increasing this detachment can he achieve an adequate sense of self. His ego, therefore, strengthens as his social perceptions increase. Such is the paradox of social development.

But even with his present immaturity he has a sense of status in the social hierarchy. He displays an unmistakable attitude of seniority toward EIGHTEEN. We have seen a tender 2-year-old girl bend over toward an 18-months-old boy and take him by the hand to lead him out of the observation room. She was somewhat awkward in the way in which she seized his hand. She soon lost hold of him. The scope of her attention proved less than her social attitude; she walked ahead alone, continuing to talk tenderly, unaware that she was leaving EIGHTEEN behind.

§ C. THREE YEARS OLD

Three is a delightful age. Infancy superannuates at Two and gives way to a higher estate. The transition is not abrupt but is evident in many quaint anticipations of maturity, serious for the child, amusing to us. Psychologically Three has more affinities with 4-year-oldness than with 2-year-oldness. He is not as knowing as FOUR but he is transcending the infantilisms of Two, indeed often indulging them by way of reversion rather than in his own proper character. His massive muscles are dominant enough to still afford him much pleasure; but he is most in character when his self-bound imagination makes an anthropomorphizing thrust into new realism of experience. Such a thrust was made by the boy (cited by Mitchell) who imagined himself a horse, while trotting by his father's side, and rationalized the incongruity, saying, "Little colts *do* hold their fadder's hands."

To understand the 3-year-old we must recognize his almost complete ignorance of the wide world beyond the nursery. This unsophistication accounts for his picturesque seriousness, his intellectual confusions, his boners. But his command of sentences is rapidly increasing; he has a strong propensity to reapply and to extend his experience; he is increasingly aware of himself as a person among persons.

All these factors combine to make age Three a nodal point, a turning in the upward path which leads to the kindergarten and elementary school.

MOTOR CHARACTERISTICS

Three like Two enjoys gross motor activity, but less exclusively so. He indulges in sedentary play for longer periods; he likes to use crayons and is interested in finer manipulations of play materials. He will, for example, work persistently at a puzzle box which imprisons a ball. And, having attained the ball, he prefers to re-solve the puzzle rather than to play with the ball. This reflects a change in motor interests, for Two would prefer to play with the ball.

Both in spontaneous and imitative drawings, Three shows an increased capacity to inhibit and delimit movement. His strokes are better defined, less diffuse, and less repetitive. Although he will not draw a man until he is 4 years old, he may make controlled marks, which reveal a growing motor discriminativeness. In tower building, likewise, he shows increased control. Two builds a tower of six or seven, Three builds a tower of nine or ten cubes. This increased command of coordinations in the vertical direction is apparently due to the maturation of new neuro-motor equipment, rather than to a prolongation of attention span. Although he has increased control of coordinations in the vertical and horizontal planes, he is curiously inept in oblique planes. He can fold a piece of paper lengthwise and crosswise, but not diagonally, even with the aid of a model. A similar ineptitude shows itself in imitative drawing. Nature has not yet matured the requisite neuro-motor girders for oblique movement.

Three is more sure and nimble on his feet. He runs with more smoothness, accelerates and decelerates with greater ease, turns sharper corners, negotiates sudden stops. He can go upstairs unaided, alternating his feet. He can jump down from the bottom tread with both feet together, whereas Two leaps down with one foot leading. Three likewise can jump upward with both feet as much as twelve inches. Three pedals a tricycle, while Two and Two-AND-A-HALF ride a mere kiddy-kar with primitive propulsion. An improved sense of balance, as well as the cephalocaudal advance, account for the new attainments. There is less sway and toddle in the gait of Three and he is much nearer to mastery of the upright posture; he can stand on one foot for a precarious second or more.

ADAPTIVE BEHAVIOR

In discriminativeness the behavior of Three far outranks that of Two. His discriminations, whether manual, perceptual, or verbal, are more numerous, more clear-cut. His motor coordinations are nicer. Accordingly he displays a new sense of order and arrangement and even tidiness. Give him four blocks to play with, he spontaneously tends to align them in a neat square of four. Lay out four blocks in a row, train-fashion, put a "chimney" on the block at one end, he likes to balance the arrangement with a symmetrical chimney at the other end. Although he ordinarily cannot name colors, he has an eye for form. He can match simple forms. He readily inserts circle, square, and triangle into the three-hole form-board even with reversal of position. But his perception of form and of spatial relations is still very dependent upon gross postural and manual adjustments. His finer oculo-motor cues are not sufficiently strong as yet to enable him to copy a cross from a model even though the cross consists merely of a vertical and a horizontal stroke. He must see you make these two strokes before he can duplicate the cross by similar strokes. Likewise he needs a demonstration of a bridge of three blocks. In another six months a model will suffice. For copying a circle, a model suffices even now. He needs a demonstration to add a chimney to the train which he could already build at Two.

All this means that Three is a transitional stage when many perceptual individuations are taking place. He is separating himself, his percepts, and his notions from a vast web of which he is a part and in which he is enmeshed. His flourishing vocabulary helps him to accomplish these intellectual disentanglements. He is forever naming things, with an air of incisive judgment. He voices his discriminativeness with "dis," "dat," "dere," "fix," "fits." These oft-recurring expressions register a process of classification, identification, comparison. His experimental application of words has a similar impulse. His frequent questions, "What is dat?" "Where does dis go?" reveal a tireless drive toward perceptual clarification. He is sensitive to the incompleteness of fragments ("Fix"). He recognizes the partialness of the halves of a severed picture and puts two separated halves together even when one half has been rotated 180°.

Such reorientation capacity bespeaks a more fluid mental organization, correlated perhaps with the greater flexibility and tentativeness of his manipulations. However, he retains some of the motor dogmatism of Two. He will persist in a non-adaptive motor pattern which FOUR would modify to meet the needs of the problem. Much of his practical geometry is still body-postural and not yet eye-manual. So he works with might and main in solving spatial problems which would yield to more delicate analysis.

Even so, fluidity of motor set is more characteristic than totalized reaction. Speak the right word and he will alter his motor set to suit the word. This represents an enormous psychological gain. Not only is he responsive to prepositions like *in, on, under,* but he will also conform to complex commissions related to his task. Readiness to conform to the spoken word is an outstanding characteristic of the psychology and maturity of the 3-year-old. This readiness should not be interpreted as being exclusively a social characteristic. It is part of the mechanism of intellectual development. It accounts for the charming seriousness of Three.

Language

Jargon at 18 months, words at 2 years, sentences at 3 years—such in outline is the order of growth. This outline, however, oversimplifies the developmental forces at work. Words at 2 years are different from words at 3 years. At 2 years, words are little more than lingual-laryngeal patterns, rooted in a total action pattern, or they are mere habit formations. Two acquires words. Three uses them. At 3 years words are more fully disengaged from the gross motor system and become instruments for designating percepts, concepts, ideas, relationships. Vocabulary is increasing at a remarkable rate, trebling since the age of 2 years, to reach an average of nearly a thousand. But the words of Three are at very unequal stages of development. Some are mere sounds to be tried out experimentally. Others have melody value or humor value. Still others are well-defined carriers of meaning. Many are in a larval state, but he has a growth method for bringing them to maturity. He indulges in soliloquy and dramatic play in order to hatch his words and phrases and syntax. He is both an actor and a talker and he uses acting to perfect his talking. He dramatizes the delivery boy, the plumber, the grocery store, and the physician's visit not so much from histrionic impulse as to create a matrix out of which he may crystallize spoken words and verbalized thinking. This combination of talking and acting often seems aimless and meandering. Many of his questions seem pointless. The chants which he improvises when he wakes in the morning likewise seem meaningless. But all

5

of this behavior takes on import when it is regarded as a developmental mechanism for achieving speech, for clarifying words.

Accordingly Three is less completely engrossed in action than Two, and the actions of Three are poised in more labile equilibrium. This enables him to suit action to word and word to action in his monologue. But words are also addressed to him. He learns to listen and he listens to learn. Sometimes a single word spoken by his mother instantaneously reorganizes his whole stream of activity, with startling suddenness.

When the word spoken by another has reached this magic transforming potency, the child is no longer in the lowlands of infancy. He has made a noteworthy advance in psychological maturity. The cultural import of this advance is so significant that the maturity level of Three appears to be a veritable mutation when compared with that of Two. In the field of language behavior, Three resembles Four vastly more than he resembles Two. But in actuality there is no mutation, for Two becomes Three by gradual genesis.

Personal-Social Behavior

You can bargain with Three. He knows with a clarity that was quite wanting at Two that he is a person and that you are a person. And he negotiates reciprocal trade agreements. He will sacrifice immediate satisfactions on a promise of a later privilege. His desire to please is typically so strong that he amenably meets most of the requirements of the mental examination. He usually remains seated in his chair awaiting the next behest. Should he leave, he will soon return, particularly if you do not interfere, but simply suggest that he must come back later. Often his cooperativeness is so positive that he will say with a smile, "Did I do it right?" This is not a bland docility. It is an active adaptiveness which makes the examiner feel that she is in truth an examiner and he, the examinee. She did not experience this kind of rapport when he was Two. Then she had to use tactics to manage an observational situation. Two's rapport was with the examination materials rather than with the examiner, and when she said, "Thank you," he echoed the words. Three accepts the same words in silence as part of a social transaction.

He uses words himself to express his feelings, his desires, and even his problems. He heeds words. Suggestions take effect. On request he will go on little errands in or near the house. He will place the milk bottle outside the door for his mother. He will heed her admonition to be careful not to break the bottle. He must have a sense of self and of status because he somewhat disdains such a simple, babyish commission as "Show me, where is your nose!"

But his sense of personal self and of other personal selves is imperfect and fragmentary. He makes smiling affectionate references to his mother which are highly socialized. On the other hand he may also direct angry attacks against a physical object, a chair, a toy, as though he were a savage animist. His emotional outbursts are usually brief; but he can feel prolonged anxiety and he is capable of jealousy. Acute jealousy may even cause him to roll on the floor, scream, and kick. A rival in the form of a new baby may arouse violent pangs of insecurity.

His emotional experience being relatively unintegrated, his fears often are highly topical. He may have a dread of rubber boots. He may tremble at the movement of a mechanical toy. He may suffer well-defined night terrors. There is a transient piecemeal quality to his emotional reactions.

He talks much to himself, sometimes by way of experimental word practice, but also as though to an alter ego, or to an imagined person. He ejects his own mental status into other people. Knowing the contagiousness of laughter, he tries to make others laugh by his own laughter. He notes the emotional expressions of others. His desire to please and to conform acquaints him with the social expectations of other people. His dramatic mimicry serves the same end.

But here, as elsewhere, Nature always strikes a balance. These socialized reactions are offset by many others that are egoistic and self-conservative. Although he takes a growing interest in playing with other children, he still likes solitary and parallel types of play. His cooperations are desultory, wayward, sketchy. This does not mean that they are superficial or worthless. His social nature grows bit by bit and these brief social experiences lead to fuller insight in time. He is beginning to understand what it means to wait one's turn. He is willing to wait and he will even share his toys.

By the age of Three the average child is well domesticated to the normal requirements of home life. He feeds himself and rarely needs assistance to complete a meal. He spills very little. He pours well from a pitcher. He may even show an interest in setting the table. His natural propensity to imitate and to conform ordinarily makes him obedient. Because of the new susceptibility to words he can be managed by distraction and to some extent by reasoning. His rebellions though violent are less infantile and less frequent. He gets over tantrums more quickly than at an earlier age. Thumb sucking is likely to occur only infrequently when he is fatigued or thwarted. When he wishes to resist he often uses language instead of the more primitive methods of pushing, biting, and scratching. He gives many other tokens of readiness to conform with cultural demands.

He shows greater interest and ability in dressing and und.essing, unbuttons front and side buttons, unlaces and takes off shoes and pants. Two cannot remove his pants; he can only push them down! This differential behavior item, normatively regarded, sums up a great deal. It well reflects both the postural and perceptual limitations of Two.

Three is beginning to sleep through the night without wetting. To a considerable degree he can toilet himself during the daytime. He still takes a nap of an hour or more but in going to sleep is less dependent upon solaces such as dolls and animal toys. His speech gives many evidences of conforming to cultural urge. He asks, "Is that right?" "Do it this way?" Often he asks of the adults questions to which he knows the answers. This is an experimental and practice type of questioning. So fundamental and natural is the trend toward cultural adaptation that marked persistence of behavior difficulties after the age of 3 years is suggestive of faulty functioning.

On a primitive and miniature level, the third year marks a kind of adolescence, a coming of age. Three is transcending the trammels of infancy, through his new command of words as tools, as vehicles of thought, and even as substitutes for blind rage and resistances. Words are also accepted as media of exchange. This socializes his behavior. Like the adolescent of the teens, he graduates into broader social life. But like this same adolescent, he does not always find it easy to cut from his moorings. He returns gladly to the comfort of parental protection after brief adventures in self-dependence. The outer world is full of wonders and strangeness. He has much to discover, much to assimilate, many generalizations to make. Problems of sex have not yet assumed great complexity, but he has numerous other problems of self-orientation. If he is constitutionally unstable, if his mode of growth is one of wide and erratic fluctuation, his inadequacies will now be revealed. Here again he reminds us somewhat of the adolescent of later years.

§ D. FOUR YEARS OLD

THREE was transitional. Four is well on his way. THREE, being transitional, is somewhat more quaint and naïve. Four is more sophisticated and even a bit dogmatic because of his amateur command of words and ideas. His verbal assertiveness may deceive us into crediting him with more knowledge than he actually possesses. His propensity to speak out, to produce, to create, makes him highly responsive to psychological examination. These interesting traits also make him more transparent to observation.

MOTOR CHARACTERISTICS

Four is a more facile runner than THREE. He is also more able to break up the regular rhythms of his stride. He can make a fair running broad jump and a standing broad jump. THREE's jump is usually limited to a downward and upward leap—another instance in which the motor command of the vertical dimension apparently precedes command of the horizontal. Four can also skip, at least after a lame duck fashion. But he cannot hop—much less hop-skip-jump in sequence. He can, however, maintain a one-legged equilibrium much longer than can THREE. He can balance himself on one foot for several seconds, and usually in another half-year he can hop. His improved body equilibrium is shown in his excellent performance on the 6 cm. walking board. He rarely has to step off with both feet to regain his balance.

Four likes to try motor stunts which are not too difficult. He enjoys accomplishment. This well-defined interest in feats and tasks is a somewhat new developmental symptom, which offers a clue to the psychology of the 4-year-old.

His new athletic feats are based on a greater independence of his leg musculature. Here, as elsewhere, the principle of individuation is at work. There is less totality in his bodily responses; legs, trunk, shoulders, arms react somewhat less in unison. This makes his joints seem more mobile. Whereas at 2 and at 3 he would merely toss or hurl a ball in a propulsive manner (with much torso participation), he can now swing back a more independent arm and execute a strong overhand throw.

He finds pleasure in feats of fine coordination as well. He can take a knitting-needle spear and thrust it with well-directed aim into a small hole, smiling with success. He can button his clothes and lace his shoes with ease. He gestures with more refinement and precision. In his drawing he may give concentrated attention to the representation of an isolated detail. His copy of a circle is more circumscribed than at 3 years, and characteristically is executed in a clockwise direction, appropriate to a more strongly entrenched right-handedness. In the manipulation of fine objects like the pellet, however, unilateral preference is not so dominant.

Motor command of the oblique dimension is still imperfect. Four cannot copy a diamond from a model, although he can combine a vertical and horizontal stroke into a cross. Between parallel lines a centimeter apart he can trace on paper a diamond-shape pathway. Imitating a demonstration, he can thrice fold a piece of paper, making an oblique crease on the last fold. This is a definite advance beyond THREE, in whom a neuromotor blind spot still obscures the oblique axis.

ADAPTIVE

A lamb was nursing. "What is the lamb getting from its mother?" The metropolitan 4-year-old who answered, "Gasoline," was more intellectual than appears at first blush. In a vague yet concrete way he knew that gasoline is a source of energy. Gasoline makes things, including lambs, go. Four has powers of generalization and of abstraction which he exercises much more frequently and deliberately than does THREE. THREE, to be sure, generalizes such relationships as *in, on, under,* etc.; he distinguishes between *one* and *many*; he seeks and finds resemblances among physical objects; but he does not ask the numerous and varied questions with which Four plies his elders.

These questions of the 4-year-old reflect not a hunger for information but rather an inveterate impulse to conceptualize the multiplicities of nature and of the social world. THREE is an enumerator, a designator. So is Four, but with a dim intent to generalize and to order his experience. He is even beginning to sense himself as only one among many. He is less circumscribed than THREE. He has a definite consciousness of kind, of his own kind. Once during a psychological examination he asked, "Do you spank children who don't finish?" A revealing question, which discloses that the 4-year-old realizes his equivalence with other children who come to the Clinic under similar circumstances. This realization denotes a fundamental noetic attitude which pervades his intellectual life and raises the level of his social life.

His intellectual processes, however, are narrow in scope. He has very meager comprehension of the past and the future, and even in stories he manifests very little interest in plot. He can count to four or more by rote, but his number concept barely goes beyond *one, two,* and *many*. He may have an imaginary playmate, but his communings with this companion are sketchy rather than organized. Even in his dramatic play he does not long sustain a role. He may, as *dramatis persona,* kiss his wife good-by as he leaves for his downtown office, but the next moment finds him fishing beside a brook. His questions often are equally kaleidoscopic; nevertheless they serve to clear up confusion for him

We underestimate the vastness of his *terra incognita* An intelligent 4-year-old, while building a playhouse, was heard to say, "Houses do not have tails." This lucid judgment was the sober product of an inquiring mind. Four has a busy rather than a profound mind. His thinking is consecutive and combinative rather than synthetic. Confronted by the two parallel Binet lines he says, "This is the big one; this is the little one"; he does not make one summary comparative judgment; he makes two consecutive judgments. Likewise in making an esthetic choice between pretty and ugly, he refers in turn to each member of the comparative pair.

He is so literal in this thinking that analogies when used by a storyteller tend to befuddle him, and yet out of his own motor experience he can create metaphors which are so fresh and startling that they suggest poetic imagery (to the adult!). When he listens to stories he is literally moved in a muscular sense, for he tends to re-enact in his body postures and gestures what is told.

There is a primitive mixture of symbolization and of naïve literalness in his drawings. A typical drawing of a man consists of a head and two appendages and possibly two eyes. The torso usually does not appear until FIVE. There is over-weaning interest in the individual parts as they are drawn. Unity may be achieved by making a circle to surround the parts.

When presented with an incomplete drawing of a man, he can supply three missing parts. If he supplies an eye, he comments, "Now he can see!" With similar literalness he represents the movements of a steam shovel through dramatic imitation.

He matches eight of the ten test forms. He imitates the construction of a five-block gate, inserting a keystone block diagonally. In his spontaneous play with blocks he builds in both vertical and horizontal dimensions, names his constructions, and sometimes exploits them dramatically. He likes to create and to produce by first intention. He likes to go from one thing to another, rather than to repeat. His mind is lively and covers much ground.

LANGUAGE

Questioning is at a peak at Four. A bright 4-year-old can elaborate and improvise questions almost endlessly. Perhaps this is a developmental form of practice in the mechanics of speech, inasmuch as the 4-year-old still tends to articulate in a somewhat infantile manner. His volubility serves to make him more fluent and facile.

Sometimes apparently he chatters along in order to maintain social rapport, and to attract attention. He also likes to play on words in a clownish way, particularly if he has an audience. He enjoys crude malapropisms and can perpetrate them for humor's sake. For example, "Cedar rabbits!" instead of "Cedar Rapids."

Why and *How* frequently appear in the questions, but Four is by no means always interested in explanations. He is more interested to note how the answers fit his own thoughts. He is, however, less apt than THREE to ask questions to which he already knows the answers. Much of his questioning is virtually a soliloquy by means of which he projects one verbal construction after another, concurrently rearranging his images and reformulating relationships. He is not building coherent logical structures, but combining facts, fancies, and phrases to strengthen his command of words and clauses. He makes declarations and running comments as profusely as he frames questions, using with aptness (and sometimes with marked ineptitude) such expressions as, "I don't *even* know that. You *almost* hit him. *Now* I will make *something* else; I can make something different. They are *like* the other one, *but* the other one is bigger. That one *too*." Such grammar, and such parts of speech, imply a considerable degree of relational and even abstract thinking. They are much more recondite than were nouns, verbs, or prepositions. The wonder is that Four acquires mastery over them so rapidly. How long did it take the race to achieve even the "simple" notion of *too*?

Four is verbal rather than verbose. He is also after a manner prolix. He tends to elaborate replies. "What scratches?" "A cat," says FIVE who knows that a responsive answer alone is desired. But Four names the cat and tells about his dog as well. Such associative thinking is a developmental kind of prolixity, pardonable in the preschool child.

The speech of Four is forthright. He does not like to repeat things. He says flatly, "I did that before." He has a certain crispness as well as garrulity. He can carry on long and involved conversations. He can tell a lengthy story, mixing truth and fiction. He can flounder as helplessly as adults do in discussions of war and crime. For example:

Arthur (age 4 years): "Soldiers are bad people. They kill others."
Betty (age 4 years): "Soldiers aren't bad. But if someone does something wrong, they shoot them. If some naughty person catches a bird, then the soldiers shoot them."
Arthur (unconvinced): "Well, if England catches a bird, then the soldiers shoot England."

No wonder that Bernard Shaw wanted to get us back to Methuselah. Part Five of Shaw's *Metabiological Pentateuch* is dated 31,920 A.D. Under this distant dispensation newborn children will be as mature as our youth now are at seventeen years, and these children will become adults (by present-day standards) at the age of four years. Our norms of preschool development will then need revision!

PERSONAL-SOCIAL BEHAVIOR

Four presents an interesting combination of independence and sociability. His self-reliance in his personal habits, his assertiveness, a certain "bossiness," his emphatic dogmatisms conspire to make him seem more stalwart and independent than THREE. During the examination he also displays a kind of maturity wanting in THREE. Four is much less apt to leave the table than is THREE, although Four may shuffle his feet and wriggle a good deal during the examination. Ordinarily he is quite willing to go into the examination room without his mother and during the examination there is much less smiling reference to the examiner. THREE shows much more tendency toward communicative smiling, due to a normal kind of social dependence which Four is now transcending. In reaction to the individual tests, Four goes about each appointed task more carefully; he has more drive; makes more uninvited comments; and may even pursue his comments and questions to such an extent that the examiner will find himself examined. This imparts to Four a pleasant if not always convincing plausibility.

In his home life he needs much less care. He is able to dress and undress himself with very little assistance, laces his shoes (but is unable to tie them), combs his own hair with some supervision, and brushes his own teeth. In eating he likes to choose his own menu; he can be very conversational without interfering with his eating. He needs little direction; indeed, he can even set the table well.

In many instances Four no longer naps during the day. If he continues to nap it is a long nap of one to one-and-a-half hours. He tries to put off going to bed at night but falls asleep in a short time and no longer needs to take things to bed with him. He sleeps through the night without having to get up.

Four goes to the toilet by himself and needs very little help. He manages his clothes without much difficulty. He likes to go to the bathroom when others are there to satisfy new curiosities which are awakening.

His play similarly reflects a balanced mixture of self-dependency and sociability. He takes less enjoyment than THREE in solitary and purely parallel types of play. He makes a greater number of social approaches and spends more time in social contacts with the play group. Associative group play rather than parallel play is characteristic of Four. He prefers a group of two or three children. He shares possessions brought from home. He suggests turns in play but he is by no means consistently orderly. Indeed, he often makes sudden "silly" sallies and purposefully perpetrates wrong behavior. But this is not so much because of antisocial impulses as it is to evoke social reactions in others. He enjoys evoking such reactions and can be very "bossy" in directing others. His dramatic play is less desultory and wayward than that of THREE, but it is often harum-scarum in its reckless changes of scene and of impersonations.

Four is talkative. His sentences are replete with the first personal pronoun. But many of these egoistic statements prove to have a definite social reference and social context. He is very good at supplying alibis: "I cannot make it because my mother won't let me." "I cannot make it because I don't want to." The significant fact is that he should be interested in alibis at all. Such interest is social. It denotes an awareness of the attitudes and opinions of others. His self-criticisms and self-appraisals also have social implications: "I am mad." "I said I don't know." "I said it too many times." "I have good ideas, don't I?" "I was very fast, wasn't I?"

"I put that nice, didn't I?" "Certainly I can make it." "Do you want to see how quickly I find the things?" "I know everything!" "I am smart. Am I smarter than you?" Four also criticizes others: "Mother, doesn't he talk funny?" "You mustn't say 'ain't,'" etc.

Despite his growing reasoning powers and his critical capacities, he is prone to so-called unreasonable fears such as fear of the dark, fear of old men, fear of a rooster, fear of feathers and pieces of cotton. Fears of this kind serve to remind us that Four is not so mature as his speech sometimes suggests.

Four is also reputed to be a fabricator. His fabrications, like his bossiness, his dogmatic assertiveness, his alibis, his rationalizations, and his clowning, all spring from a consciousness of social milieu and from maturing social insight. For the time being they may be regarded as developmental symptoms which usually have a favorable connotation. Because of his immaturity Four is unable to make realistic distinctions between truth and fable. His brave excursions into the unknown will in time supply him with adequate social orientations, if his deviations from the "truth" are not too clumsily handled by his superiors, who passed through a comparable stage of confusion when they were Four.

§ E. FIVE YEARS OLD

The period of early childhood is coming to a relative close at 5 years. The 5-year-old may not be ready for the technicalities or abstractions of reading, writing, and sums for another two years. But he is no longer tied to apron strings. He endures and even enjoys the separation from home demanded by a kindergarten. He is more self-contained and self-dependent than Four who is still deeply immersed in elementary explorations of the physical and social world. Five has a better understanding of this world and of his own identity in it. Society likewise recognizes a budding social maturity, and provides increasing opportunities for group behavior. Fascist governments have not found the 5-year-old too young to regiment in uniforms, to marshal in battalions preparatory to group behavior which will be required in later years. Five is more of "a little man" than Four.

Motor Characteristics

Five is more agile than Four and more controlled in general bodily activity. Five has a more mature sense of balance, which makes him seem more sure and less given to caution on the playground.

Four can skip in a lame duck manner. Five skips smoothly and jumps as well. He conducts himself with more self-reliant abandon. He can negotiate a 4 cm. walking board usually with a two-feet step down, or a one-foot slip. He can stand on one foot and even balance himself on his toes for several seconds or more.

These tokens of motor maturity, including a well-developed sense of equilibrium and an increased social adaptability, make Five a more ready pupil than FOUR in the teaching of dancing and of physical exercises and evolutions.

His spontaneous postural demeanor gives an impression of relative finish and completeness. Under wholesome conditions his postural attitudes show natural grace. Ease and economy of movement are present in his finer coordinations as well. He can pluck a dozen pellets one by one and drop them deftly into a bottle in about twenty seconds, typically with a preferred hand.

Five, in comparison with FOUR, shows greater precision and command of tools. Five can wield a brush for his teeth and a comb for his hair; he can wash his face. FOUR needs much more supervision than Five in these domestic duties. Five also dawdles less, partly because of his greater motor maturity.

Five likewise wields a crayon with greater assurance and definitiveness. He draws a recognizable man. His straight strokes show an increased neuro-motor command over the following axes: downward vertical, left to right horizontal, downward oblique. The vertical is most facile; the oblique, least. He has difficulty with the obliques required in the copying of a diamond, but he is quite equal to copying a square and a triangle. He shows interest and some competence in washing dishes. He keeps better time to music when he dances. Such motor abilities suggest that the neuro-motor system is now well advanced in its development. Musical prodigies may approach an adult level of motor virtuosity as early as the fifth year.

ADAPTIVE BEHAVIOR

The relative motor maturity of Five is reflected in the free, adaptive manner in which he solves simple problems involving geometric and spatial relations. He is not unduly confused by the problem of a diagonally cut visiting card, and reorients the two halves to make a rectangle out of the triangles. He solves the Goddard formboard with directness and dispatch, adjusting movement to perception, and rarely using the method of kinesthetic trial and error still frequently seen at Three and Four. He can insert in sequence a series of nested boxes, making immediate practical judgments as to succession and orientation.

Other characteristic abilities rest on a comparable perceptiveness of order, form, and detail. He is able to put his toys away in an orderly manner. His drawing of a man shows differentiation of parts with a certain completeness from head to feet. He adds eyes and even ears to an incomplete man. If he draws a flag, he delineates pole, stars, and stripes. He is realistic.

It is significant that in his play, he likes to finish what he has started. Four is much less sensitive to incompleteness and to inconclusiveness. Four may be rambling and prolix. Both in mentation and conversation Five shows conclusiveness and autocriticism.

In apprehension of number, also, Five displays increased discriminativeness. Whereas Four had concepts of *one, two,* and *many,* Five can intelligently count ten objects, and can do a few simple concrete sums within the magnitude of his age (5). And he can tell his age.

Sense of time and duration are more developed in Five. He can carry a plot in a story and repeat a long sequence accurately. He can carry over a play project from one day to another, which is correlated with a more vivid appreciation of yesterdays and tomorrows. He has a clearer remembrance of and interest in places remote. Furthermore, he can carry a melody. And when he paints or draws, an idea in the mind precedes the production on paper.

This relationship between idea and execution is much more ambiguous in Four who often draws first and names afterwards. Indeed, Four may supply two or three different names to the same drawing. The psycho-motor arc in Four is fluid and permeable in both directions. Five is more executive, more sensible, more accurate, more relevant, more practical. He is in these respects more adultish.

There is a vein of seriousness in Five which makes him less hospitable to fanciful fables and grotesque fairy tales than children of riper maturity who have a stable footing in realities. He is ready and eager to know realitie's, but is not equal to the double task of discrimination which excessive romancing entails. His method of drawing reflects the same realism. He aims at something definite with the first stroke of the pencil, whereas Four (like Polonius and the clouds) reinterprets his drawing as he goes along, changing designations to conform with the strokes *after* they are made. This difference epitomizes a significant gain in intellect. Add to this access of realism an increase of attention span, and many of the distinctive features of the psychology of Five are accounted for. Intellectually he seems well oriented, but close examination of his verbalized judgments and notions discloses amazing forms of immaturity in his thinking.

LANGUAGE

In speech, too, Five is much more grown up than Four. Five talks without infantile articulation. His answers to questions are more succinct and to the point. His own questions are fewer and more relevant. He asks questions for information and not merely for social intercourse or for practice in the art of speaking. He is no longer an experimental apprentice in this art, but makes serious inquiries, "What is this for?" "How does this work?" "What does it mean?" "Who made those (referring to test objects)?"

Parents are less annoyed by the questions of Five than those of FOUR because the questions are more meaningful. Five really wants to know. His questions and answers betray an interest in the practical mechanisms of the universe. He is a pragmatist. His definitions are in terms of use: *A horse is to ride; a fork to eat.* Fairy tales with excessive unrealities vex and confuse him. He is serious and empirical. His imagination is not so footloose as it was a year ago, nor as it will be a few years hence. Five has an ear as well as an eye for details. This shows itself in language. He can single out one word and ask its meaning, whereas FOUR would react to the sentence as a whole, without analysis of component words.

Language is now essentially complete in structure and form. Five has assimilated the syntactical conventions and expresses himself in correct, finished sentences. He uses all types of sentences, including complex sentences with hypothetical and conditional clauses. He uses conjunctions somewhat more freely than FOUR, but in general the relative frequency of parts of speech is similar to that of FOUR. Vocabulary is greater by several hundred words (1,500 at Four, versus 2,200 at Five, on an average); usage more accurate and much more elaborate. Five follows linguistic custom rather than the naïve movement of thought which determines word order in Two.

FOUR is rather more literal and concrete than Five. FOUR, having heard it said of a pair of gloves that "one" was as good as "the other," wanted to know which is the one, and which the other. Five might be capable of the required abstraction. The following dialogue also shows that Five has a bit of edge on FOUR when it comes to abstract cerebration:

> *Four:* "I know that Pontius Pilate is a tree."
> *Five:* "No, Pontius Pilate is not a tree at all."
> *Four:* "Yes, it was a tree, because it says: 'He suffered under Pontius Pilate,' so it must have been a tree."
> *Five:* "No, I am sure Pontius Pilate was a person and not a tree."
> *Four:* "I know he was a tree, because he suffered under a tree—a big tree."
> *Five:* "No, he was a person but he was a very pontious person."

The dramatic play of Five is full of practical dialogue and commentary which has to do with the everyday functions of business, kitchen, grocery store, transportation, garage. Bright 5-year-old children may even dramatize natural phenomena in which sun, moon, stars, wind, clouds, etc., figure as characters. There is a good deal of talk in these impersonations, —an effort to clear ideas and to capture relationships through words rather than to indulge make-believe. Even the renderings of death, killing, sickness, surgery, and accidents are factual instead of emotional in spirit.

The preoccupation with community situations in group play reflects an intellectual effort to understand social organization. But much of the talk is in essence a form of "collective monologue," and does not bear upon causal or logical relationships. Not until the age of Seven or later do such relationships figure in conversation. Genuine interchange of ideas remains limited. Although Five is clarifying the world in which he lives through a discriminating and even analytic use of words, his thinking is still so self-confined that he cannot suppress his own point of view even temporarily, in order to realize by reciprocity the point of view of others. He distinguishes his left and right hand in his own person, but not in other persons. He also lacks synthetic capacity. He will be Seven or older before he understands the simple mechanism of a bicycle and before he comprehends that pedals, chain, and gear are necessary to make the wheels go. He lacks the power of explicit reasoning. He makes no distinction between the physical and psychical; he confuses physical causality with psychological motivation. He is so egocentric (in Piaget's sense) that he is unconscious of himself, unaware of his own thinking as a subjective process separate from the objective world. Hence his animism. Hence an intellectual innocence which is profoundly primitive in spite of a deceptively mature facility in grammar and speech.

PERSONAL-SOCIAL BEHAVIOR

Within his capacities, Five is relatively independent and self-sufficient. One can easily imagine a self-operating Lilliputian village of 5-year-olds, which would require only a moderate degree of external control. Five is already mature enough to fit into a simple type of culture. (Perhaps it is for this reason that the adjective "adultish" characterizes him aptly.)

He is dependable and obedient in the household. Normally he gives little trouble in sleep, toilet habits, in dressing, and in the duties of everyday life. He shows interest in sweeping and in washing and wiping dishes. He is protective toward younger playmates and siblings. In under-privileged homes the 5-year-old frequently shows remarkable competence and responsibility in sharing the care of an infant.

If Five gets lost in a big city he can tell his name and address. He plays checkers with the policemen while he waits to be claimed. Adults may marvel at his "calmness." If he exhibits indifference in distressful and tragic situations it is because his emotional organization is limited by the self-engrossment which has already been noted in his intellectual reactions. He is innocent of certain complex emotions because he is still simply organized. But in less complicated situations he clearly displays attractive emotional traits and attitudes: seriousness, purposefulness, patience, persistence, carefulness, generosity, outgoing sociability, friendliness, poise, pride in accomplishment, pride in going to school, satisfaction in artistic production, pride in possession. He has a certain capacity for friendships. He plays in groups of two to five with new sociability. He also plays with imaginary companions. He is very social and talkative during meals. He quarrels rather less than Four. He can be spurred into increased activity under the stress of rivalry. But he shows a positive amenability and docility. A vein of politeness and tactfulness even emerges in his speech.

Tricycle and sled are favorite outdoor toys. Crayon and scissors have an increased appeal. His horizon is widening. He likes to go on excursions. Sometimes he even makes collections of objects.

Five, even more than Four, prefers associative play to solitary and parallel types of play. He definitely desires companions and enjoys group projects, requiring construction of houses, garages, switch yards, and city planning. Although he does not have a sophisticated appreciation of cooperation, he is sensitive to social situations. He likes clothes. He likes to dress up in masquerade. He likes to make an impression on his companions. He is also beginning to realize that these companions sometimes cheat in play. So he himself may develop mild deceptions and fabrications. He has an elementary sense of shame and disgrace, and of status. He is more conscious than hitherto of cultural and other differences in the two sexes. He is capable of anxiety and of "unreasonable" fears, but typically he is stable and well adjusted in his emotional life, as he is in his intellectual outlook. Self-assurance, confidence in others, and social conformability are cardinal personal-social traits at five.

CHAPTER V

A PICTORIAL SURVEY OF PRESCHOOL BEHAVIOR

BEHAVIOR has shape. The study of behavior is not unlike the study of anatomy, for both are concerned with form and configuration. In exploring the almost kaleidoscopic manifestations of preschool development, it is quite natural that we should call to our aid the actinic eye of the camera. The camera captures the visible profiles of child behavior, and gives us many hints of underlying attitudes, strivings, and satisfactions.

The illustrations in the present chapter were selected from a large collection of action photographs and cinema records. They delineate in outline the course of early mental development. The pictures are silent and the reader's auditory imagination must supply the sounds of objects and of voice which accompany the numerous activities portrayed. But the visible aspects of behavior pattern are made apparent, particularly if the pictures are studied in the light of the two preceding chapters. The photographs are seriated to build up an impression of the progressions and epochs of maturity. A composite page is devoted to each of the major age levels. Many of the photographs were taken under naturalistic conditions in the everyday situations of home, playground, and nursery school. Other photographs depict the controlled conditions of a developmental examination. Following is a list of the plates in the order in which they appear.

Plate I. A Neonate
Plates II & III. The First Year of Life
Plate IV. Eighteen Months
Plate V. Two Years
Plates VI & VII. Three Years
Plate VIII. Four Years
Plate IX. Five Years
Plates X & XI. Individuality in Infancy
Plate XII. Cube Behavior
Plate XIII. Adaptive Behavior
Plate XIV. Paint and Clay Behavior
Plate XV. Drawing of a Man
Plate XVI. Crayon and Writing Behavior

A PICTORIAL SURVEY

OF

PRESCHOOL BEHAVIOR

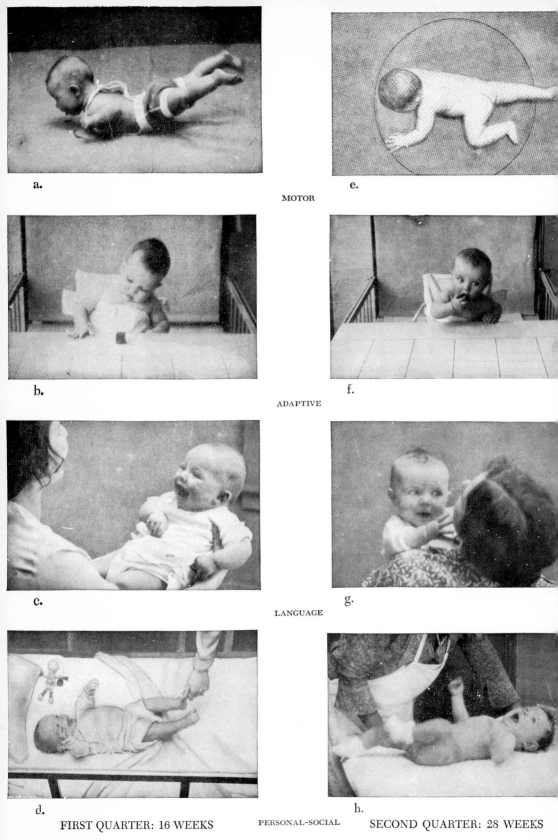

a.

e.

MOTOR

b.

f.

ADAPTIVE

c.

g.

LANGUAGE

d.

h.

FIRST QUARTER: 16 WEEKS   PERSONAL-SOCIAL   SECOND QUARTER: 28 WEEKS

PLATE II. THE FIRST YEAR OF LIFE: THE FIRST HALF YEAR

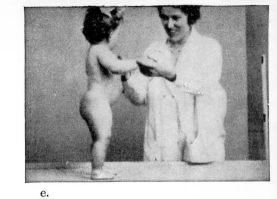

e.

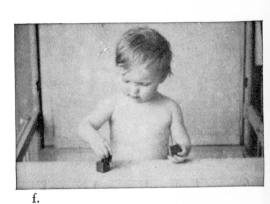

f.

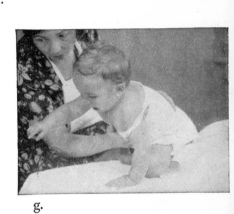

g.

THIRD QUARTER: 40 WEEKS   PERSONAL-SOCIAL   FOURTH QUARTER: 52 WEEKS

h.

PLATE III. THE FIRST YEAR OF LIFE: THE SECOND HALF YEAR

PLATE IV. EIGHTEEN MONTHS

b.

c.

f.

g.

e.

h.

i.

j.

k.

PLATE V. TWO YEARS

a.

b.

c.

d.

e.

f.

g.

h.

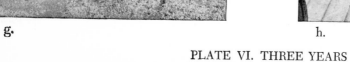

PLATE VI. THREE YEARS

a.

b.

d.

e.

g.

h.

j.

k.

PLATE VII. THREE YEARS

a.

b.

c.

d.

e.

f.

g.

h.

PLATE VIII. FOUR YEARS

b.

c.

d.

e.

g.

h.

PLATE IX. FIVE YEARS

a.

b.

c.

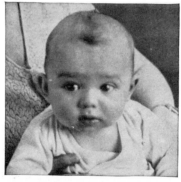

d.

A deep-seated motor trait of individuality. This child showed pronounced left-handedness.

    a) in manipulation (age 36 weeks).
    b) in spoon feeding (age 80 weeks).
    c) in block building (age 260 weeks or 5 years).
    d) in drawing (also age 5 years).

She draws a left-handed type of man pictured in E.

Two of the subjects whose individuality was studied in infancy and at five ye

PLATE X. INDIVIDUALITY IN INFANCY

b.

d.

f.

PLATE XI. INDIVIDUALITY IN INFANCY

THREE CUBES IN CUP

THROWS

FIFTEEN MONTHS

TOWER OF TWO

FILLS CUP

FAILS TRAIN

EIGHTEEN MONTHS

TOWER OF THREE

FAILS BRIDGE

TRAIN WITHOUT CHIMNEY

TWO YEARS

TOWER OF SIX

IMITATES BRIDGE

TRAIN WITH CHIMNEY

THREE YEARS

TOWER OF NINE

SPONTANEOUS BRIDGE

GATE

FOUR YEARS

TOWER OF TEN

PLATE XII. CUBE BEHAVIOR

PLACES TWO FORMS
EIGHTEEN MONTHS

PLACES THREE FORMS
TWO YEARS

IDENTIFIES THREE COLOR FORMS
THREE YEARS

ADDS LEG, ARM, AND EYE TO INCOMPLETE MAN
FOUR YEARS

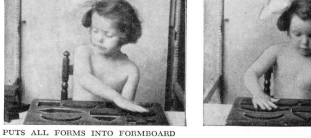

PUTS ALL FORMS INTO FORMBOARD
FIVE YEARS

PLATE XIII. ADAPTIVE BEHAVIOR

TWO YEARS

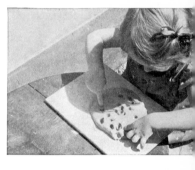

THREE YEARS

FOUR YEARS

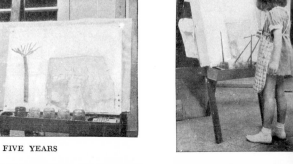

FIVE YEARS

PLATE XIV. PAINT AND CLAY BEHAVIOR

TWELVE MONTHS

EIGHTEEN MONTHS

TWO YEARS

THREE YEARS

FIVE YEARS

FIVE YEARS

SIX YEARS

PLATE XVII. STANCE AND THROW

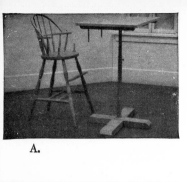

A.

B.

C.

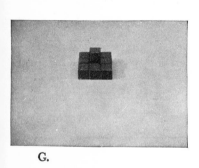

D.

E.

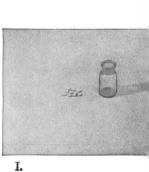

F.

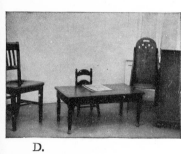

G.

H.

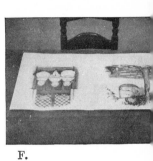

I.

J.

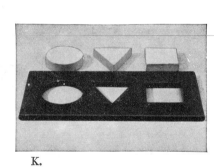

K.

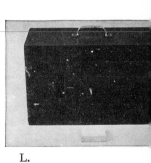

L.

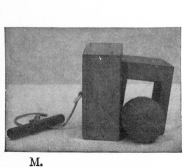

M.

A., B. High chair used at fifteen months and for older children unable to sit without extra support; examining table. Note method of attachment to chair. Height of table is adjustable.

C. Room arranged for examination with high chair.

D., E. Standard examination set-up.

F. Picture book on table.

G. Cubes.

H. Cup and cubes.

I. Pellets and bottle.

J. Paper and crayon.

K. Formboard and blocks.

L. Performance box and squa (facing child).

M. Puzzle box and ball (faci child).

PLATE XVIII. EXAMINATION EQUIPMENT AND MATERIALS

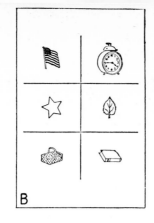
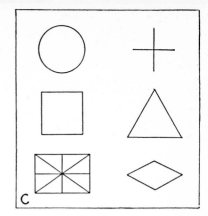

B

C

E

F

G

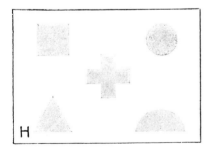

H

I

A., B. Gesell picture cards.
C. Geometric forms.
D. Incomplete man.
E. Blowing bubbles.

F. Humor card.
G. Garden maze.
H. Color forms.
I. Castner orientation card.

PLATE XIX. EXAMINATION MATERIALS

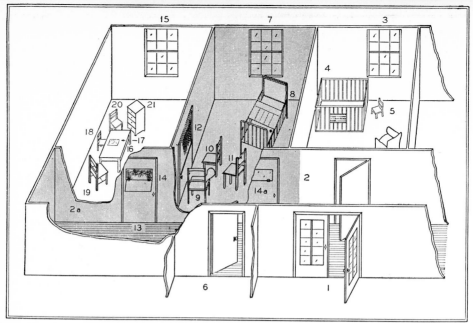

Diagram by Paul Hartmann

Diagram pictures a simple but effect setup for the developmental examination of infants and preschool children. The child enters at (1), passes through the hallway (2) which connects with the reception room (3) (and also with the bathroom at 6). The reception room is furnished with adult chairs and pen (4) and child's chair (5). The observation room (7) has been partially darkened by drawing the shade at the window. The recorder takes station in the chair equipped with writing arm (9). Observer is seated nearby, behind the one-way-vision screen panel (12) which communicates with the examination room (15), entered by the door at (13), equipped with one-way-vision window (14). The examination room is equipped with an examination table (16) showing the picture book (17) and child's chair (18) in position. The mother sits at the right (19); the Examiner at the left (20) with direct access to the examining cabinet (21).

12.

ONE-WAY-VISION DOOR
PANEL

8a.

OPAQUE ASPECT OF
PANEL

8b.

TRANSPARENT ASPECT
OF PANEL

PLATE XX. ONE-WAY-VISION ARRANGEMENTS FOR EXAMINATION SUITE

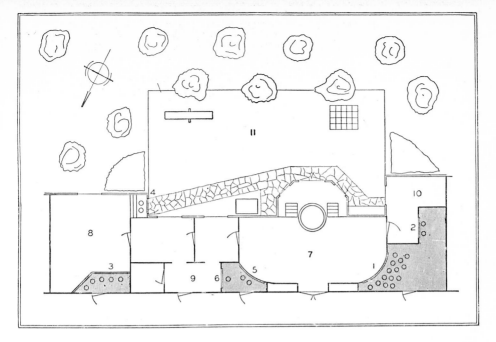

Diagram pictures general arrangements and appurtenances suitable for a guidance type of nursery. These arrangements provide for one-way-vision observation by individual students, parents, and large groups of observers. (1) Large observation alcove equipped with chairs of graduated size as pictured at (1a). This commands a comprehensive view of the playroom (7). (2) is an offset of the large alcove and gives a view of kitchen unit (10). Large observation alcove (3) gives upon junior playroom (8). (4) communicates with the play-yard (11). (5) is a small observation booth used by staff members and parents. It is equipped with a one-way-vision screen commanding the main nursery (7) and a one-way-vision *miroir diaphane " Argus " B^{te} France-Etranger*. Photographs picture: 3a. Seating arrangements for small group of

observers in an observation alcove; b3. Exterior view of observation alcove with wainscoting mural, screens camouflaged with light conventionalized cumulus clouds; 3c. Children seen by observers from alcove.

3b.   3a.

PLATE XXI. ONE-WAY-VISION ARRANGEMENTS IN THE GUIDANCE
NURSERY AT THE YALE CLINIC OF CHILD DEVELOPMENT

Plate XVII. Stance and Throw
Plates XVIII & XIX. Examination Equipment and Materials
Plate XX. One-Way-Vision Arrangements for Examination Suite
Plate XXI. One-Way-Vision Arrangements in the Guidance Nursery at the
      Yale Clinic of Child Development

The pictures may be analyzed for individual detail, or they may be inspected comparatively with projections both forward and backward. For the reader's orientation a few brief comments will suffice.

Plate I both symbolizes and delineates. It effectively suggests the immaturity and the promise of the neonatal period. It also portrays an individual—the sculptor's own daughter, three weeks old.

Plates II and III depict the four major fields of behavior and the four quarters of the first year of life. The pictures are selected to illustrate the increments of development which become apparent at approximately 16, 28, 40, and 52 weeks. These behavior increments can be best recognized by reading across the page. Reading a single column from top to bottom will convey an impression of a single age level.

Plate IV gives us an authentic suggestion of "Eighteen-monthishness." Very evident is the predominance of postural activity. This boy, who by the way reappears as a 5-year-old in Plates X and XI, is evidently enjoying the exercise of his maturing postural abilities: raking. trundling, leaning, squatting. Some of the activity is effortful because the postural coordinations are in a formative stage. His social contacts on sidewalk and yard are vivid but brief.

The pictures in Plate V register an unmistakable advance in general maturity. Gross motor activity is no longer so dominating. Hands and fingers are more busy. The attention to constructive activities is more prolonged. Play is self-contained, adults are taken more for granted. The 2-year-old is less naïve than the 18-month-old.

The 3-year-old requires a double spread to set forth the transitional characteristics of this age level. Plate VI portrays a diversified interest in both gross physical activity and in finer manipulation. The 3-year-old is well content with independent activities which bring into increasing utilization both fundamental and accessory muscles. Plate VII shows that he is also ready for a modest degree of group activity. The pictures give evidence of a rather evenly divided interest in individual play and in parallel play. Some cooperation, however, is evident, because he is able to take turns at play and the altercation over the express wagon was soon reconciled.

At 4 years (Plate VIII) cooperative play becomes very evident. It rises to heights of dramatic imagination. Activities are more complex.

6

Where the 2-year-old simply slides down the slide, the 4-year-old enjoys the ascent as well. Four is not overlogical. He blocks up the door and crawls through the window.

Plate IX. The 5-year-old is less sketchy in his play activities. He brings enterprises to completion. He is more serious, and also more logical. He is ready for constructive activities. Motor-wise he is so mature that he now shows considerable tolerance for sedentary occupations.

Plates X and XI remind us that the 5-year-old was once an infant. The individuality of infancy persists in countenance, in motor demeanor, and in personal-social characteristics. Each child at the tea party plays a distinctive role because he (or she) is in a behavior sense a distinctive individual. The process of growth has brought about remarkable transformations, but constitutional traits of individuality have remained intact. Girl A is still as left-handed and as engaging as she was in babyhood. Boy D was and is outgoing. Boy B was and is self-contained. (We shall refer at greater length to these boys in Chapter XIII, pages 296-308.)

The developmental advance of adaptive behavior from 15 months to 5 years declares itself in Plates XII and XIII. At 15 months cubes are cast overboard or placed in a precarious tower of two. The 4-year-old rears a tower of ten, and the 5-year-old shows mastery over ten different geometric forms, and while manipulating one is able to give anticipatory attention to a second.

Plates XIV and XV carry us into the field of artistic production, from the crude daubs and scribbles of the 2- and 3-year-old to plastic design and to graphic representations of houses and men.

Plate XVI reminds us that the preschool years are preparation for school. The adaptive manipulation of a slender cylinder for the second of the three "r's" proves to be a complicated motor act which requires a profound and gradual organization of postural, manual, digital, and ocular coordinations.

Plate XVII. Even throwing proves to be a more complicated performance than we had suspected. At 1 year the child is at the threshold of mere release. At 3 years he makes a crude hurling release, but only at the end of the preschool period does he succeed in mobilizing and focalizing this release with projectile efficiency.

Many of the growing behavior patterns of the preschool child can be most advantageously observed in naturalistic situations. But for economy of observation and precision of appraisal we need standardized stimulus objects and adequately controlled observation arrangements. Such objects and arrangements are portrayed in Plates XVIII to XXI. The examination materials and associated equipment are described in detail in § 5 to § 7, pages 351-359.

We do not wish to give too much advice to the reader, but it is suggested that the photographs of the infants and young children may profitably be scanned as well as studied in detail. Scanning, though more superficial, has the advantage of building up rapidly an impression of the sweep and trends of development. A more careful study of individual pictures should furnish suggestive detail concerning the changing outlines of behavior pattern. The reader will inevitably sense the distinctiveness in the individualities of the children who are pictured. Artist and scientist have a common problem: to capture this characteristicness, called individuality.

A reproduction of Paul Manship's sculpture of his infant daughter, therefore, becomes a fitting frontispiece to our series of photographs. This marble image is remarkable for its beauty and for its realism. And, it might be added, for its daring. When it was first shown in the New York Metropolitan Museum of Art it created a stir, and not a little comment from those who suggested that "so young an infant was not a fitting theme for a work of art." Rarely in the history of art has either painter or sculptor attempted to portray so young a child. We are told that even among the numerous and various representations of Christ there are almost none which present him as a very young infant. Manship's *Pauline*, therefore, is a unique artistic achievement.

Much of the charm of this marble portrait lies in its veracity. The subject is not over-idealized. If it is symbolic, it is so because it conveys an impression of a real baby at the age of three weeks. It even conveys, though of marble, a suggestion of action. There is a characteristic incoherent fanning of the fingers, one of which has touched the cheek which yields to the impress.

This marble portrait, as a discerning critic pointed out, shows respect for the nascent personality and records an aspect soon outgrown—"that air of infinite wisdom which vanishes when intelligence develops. . . . We may safely believe that so fresh and so vital a work of art will prove to be one of those which repay their debt to nature by opening many eyes to the interest and significance of natural things which they have never really seen before."

PART TWO

CHAPTER VI

MOTOR DEVELOPMENT

THE first five years of life are largely concerned with the elaboration of native reactions into a large variety of gross and fine motor skills. The interesting feature about the development of these complex movements is that their automatization increases rather than lessens their adaptability to new demands. The rate of improvement in any skill depends to a great extent on the capacity of the organism to anticipate the actual response by appropriate compensatory postural adjustments. Postural skills once acquired and mechanized not only permit greater freedom for adjustments to new situations but serve as an essential preparation for the development of the higher, more refined skills of later years. Writing, for example, is a highly specialized activity which can be successfully undertaken only when certain earlier acquired skills such as fine prehension and sitting balance are so well mechanized that they do not interfere with the writing activity.

§ A. THE ORGANIZATION OF MOVEMENTS

The early years of childhood may then be regarded as a period of integration and stabilization of basic behavior patterns fundamental to the development of the more advanced activities. Inasmuch as all movements entail adjustments of the organism as a whole to its environing conditions, all forms of motor behavior are actually postural activities. In this sense any form of locomotion or prehension is essentially a closely knit series of sequential postural adjustments.

It is our purpose therefore to discuss motor development in terms of posture. Posture may be static or dynamic. Static posture, or postural fixation, consists of those stabilized bodily attitudes by means of which the child achieves station and steadiness. It is concerned with poise, stance, and assumed motor attitudes of the body and its parts. Dynamic posture is concerned with translations and readaptations of postural set in the achievement of effective movements. By far the greater part of our discussion will center on the two main divisions of dynamic posture, viz., locomotion and prehension. The emphasis in our discussion will be on genetic sequences and interrelations of behavior rather than on age norms, so that we may more clearly indicate continuity of development.

Skills usually develop concurrently. Sometimes due to discouragement, supervention of another "drive," or other causes, skill in an activity may attain a stage at which there is no immediate observable improvement. At such times, and even during periods of rapid progress, the child may revert to a more primitive form of behavior to further his ends. Children, for example, frequently resort to creeping during the early stages of walking, and even later. They revert to early forms of prehension under a variety of conditions. Regression in these instances is a more or less temporary disposition to use an easier, or more adequate mode of behavior. Subsequent observations show that on renewal of the activity the subject has lost none of his former skill, for his abilities depend primarily upon the maturity of his neuro-motor system.

Many muscles, usually acting in groups, are involved in carrying out an apparently simple voluntary movement. Its course is determined by visual cues and by proprioceptive cues from the acting muscles. Groups of muscles also function as a unit in producing the component movements of a complicated activity. The component movements of one activity differ from those of another in accordance with the degree of similarity or dissimilarity of the activities. Walking and running, for example, have many component movements in common, whereas writing and jumping have very few. In the present chapter, activities are classified with respect to their objective similarity and genetic relationship. However, we are not unmindful of the fact that due to the overlapping of action patterns, some of the activities could just as well be placed within two or more categories, and for this reason, the categories are not mutually exclusive.

Our discussion deals chiefly with data obtained at the Yale Clinic, but information has also been drawn liberally from other sources (see References). The Yale data include both normative and cinema studies. The motor characteristics and capacity of a child are readily observed in a naturalistic and incidental way. His motor demeanor inevitably reveals itself in the way he deports himself, in the way he holds his head, "in the way he handles himself." His manner of sitting, standing, walking, running, gives an impression of the maturity and the competence of his movements.

If special abilities like jumping, balancing on one foot, throwing a ball, etc., are to be estimated, simple test situations are improvised. Procedures for such situations are specified at the end of this chapter. Careful regard must be given to all surrounding conditions when a motor ability is definitely put to test. Patterns of prehension and manipulatory performance may be observed in connection with drawing tests, cube behavior, pellet and bottle behavior, and other situations elsewhere described.

In the following survey, typical ages are italicized so that the reader may more readily note the age progressions in the maturing of motor abilities. Though ages are given without qualification, they are only approximate and must not be too strictly construed. The motor items which have the most normative usefulness reappear in the developmental schedules (see § 1, pp. 319-343). Maturity values for the first year of life are listed in greater detail in the normative tables of a previous volume (39).

§ B. UPRIGHT POSTURE

Head control. The first stage in the development of sitting and locomotion consists in gaining control of the muscles of the head and neck so that the head may not only be held erect but may also compensate for changes in bodily posture. The earliest steps in the control of head movements are revealed by the behavior of the infant in the supine and prone positions. Whereas there is little control of head movements at birth, at *16 weeks* the supine infant can rotate his head from side to side, and in the prone position he can raise his head so that the plane of the face is almost perpendicular. When the infant is supported while sitting, he can hold his head steadily erect. At *20 weeks* he makes adequate compensatory movements of the head as he is pulled from a supine to a sitting posture. At this age also he holds his head erect as he leans forward when supported. At *24 weeks* the muscles at the anterior end of the body are so well developed that in the prone position he can support himself on extended arms, hold his head easily erect, and rotate it.

Sitting posture. A study of the sitting posture of infants indicates that neuro-motor organization of the trunk proceeds in a head-to-foot direction. The general trend of development is from a uniformly rounded back to a straight alignment of the trunk. Up to *12 weeks* the back is uniformly rounded. At *16 weeks* this curvature is more restricted to the lumbar region. At *28 weeks* most infants hold the trunk erect, at least momentarily, and at *36 weeks* they hold it erect for an indefinite period. At 36 weeks also they can lean forward in reaching and regain the erect position. At *40 weeks* they can maintain balance as they turn to one side, and at *48 weeks* they can pivot about in the sitting position and lower themselves from standing to sitting by holding onto a support. This steadiness in sitting posture is further shown by the fact that at 44 weeks the infants can go from sitting to prone and from prone to sitting. In fact it is about this time that lumbar kyphosis is disappearing to be ultimately replaced by lumbar lordosis.

Developmentally, sitting represents a transitional stage between the supine and standing postures. When neuro-motor organization of the trunk has progressed to the stage when the sitting infant can pivot about and regain the upright posture after leaning forward, the legs can also fully support the body weight. However, lack of organic functional relationship between trunk and legs precludes standing.

Standing and upright locomotion. The behavior items in the developmental sequence of sitting also represent stages in the achievement of standing and upright posture. There are, however, additional items which also seem to be prerequisites to upright posture. Infants when held in the upright position frequently exhibit anticipatory standing and walking postures. At *16 weeks* the head remains erect and can compensate for body sway. At *20 weeks* the infant can momentarily support a large fraction of his weight. At *32 weeks* he can support his entire weight for short intervals. At *36 weeks* when held under the arms he can support his weight on his toes and maintain a standing posture, although he tends to bend forward at the hip joints.

It is interesting to note that stiffening the knees occurs before full extension of the legs at the hips. At *40 weeks* the infant can pull himself to his knees. He can also stand, holding onto a support. At *48 weeks* he can lift one foot while he supports his weight on the other, an immature anticipation of a 3-year-old ability to stand on one foot with momentary balance. At this age he also can pull himself to standing by holding onto the side rails of the crib. In standing he supports his weight on the entire sole surface.

The first half of the second year is marked by significant improvement in postural control. At *15 months* the child can attain a standing position quite independently. He counteracts body waver and sway by placing the feet far apart.

By *18 months* he has made remarkable progress. He has good sitting balance and can seat himself on a knee-high chair with difficulty, a feat which requires orientation of the body to the chair without the aid of vision. His increase in stability is shown by the fact that he has appreciably reduced the distance between his feet and can walk sidewise and backwards. Standing, however, requires great concentration of effort. He stands with both feet flat on the floor and cannot raise a foot except in walking. In attempting to kick a ball he merely steps against it. He steps both before and after throwing unless prevented, in which case he projects the ball with a simple forward thrust of the arm.

From *18 to 24 months* he makes great strides in the automatization of the standing posture. His stability is such that he attempts to maintain his balance on one foot as he exploits the other. At 20 months, for example, he can stand on one foot with help. At 24 months he tries to stand on a walking board 10 cm. high and 6 cm. wide. He can pick up objects from the floor without falling, hold objects without dropping them, and when shown how, can stand for a short time with his heels together. The degree of mechanization of the upright posture is further shown by the fact that he can run, kick a ball, walk up and down three steps alone, jump down a distance of twelve inches with one foot leading, and seat himself easily. Incidentally, it is noted that children of this age frequently step over the chair in seating themselves.

At 3 *years* standing requires little conscious effort. The child can easily maintain his equilibrium with his heels together. He runs and plays games with abandonment. He can erect himself from squatting and balance himself momentarily on his toes. At 30 months he attempts to stand on one foot, at 3 years he can hold this position momentarily, and at 42 months he can hold it for two seconds without help. His postural control at 3 years is so well developed that he can take walking and running steps on his toes, can walk a straight line, can walk backward a long distance, and is bold enough to attempt steps on the 6 cm. walking board. He can jump down from an eight-inch elevation and leap off the floor with feet together. He can also catch a large ball with his arms extended forward stiffly and throw without losing his balance.

From the time the child is able to stand independently, he is making increased use of the advantages of this posture. By the time that he is *4 years old* he has acquired strength, ease, and facility in the use of his legs which lend grace to his movements. He is rapidly becoming athletic and takes pride in attempting motor stunts requiring delicate balance. He can maintain his balance on one foot for four to eight seconds, and even longer. He can carry a cup of water without spilling it. He can jump down twenty-eight inches with feet together. He can walk the 6 cm. walking board part way before stepping off. He can crouch for a high jump of two inches and a broad jump of eight to ten inches. He can hop on his toes with both feet off the ground at the same time, seven or eight times in five seconds. He can also catch a large ball with the arms flexed at the elbows and even move the arms in accordance with the direction of the ball. He is also beginning to assume the adult stance in throwing.

At 5 *years* the child is quite adept in execution of complicated synergic muscular activities. He exhibits a greater ease in the control of general bodily activity and exercises less caution than at 4 years. Indications of his mature sense of balance are seen in his ability to stand indefinitely on one foot and to balance on his toes for several seconds. Whereas at 4.5 years he can hop only four to six steps on one foot, at 5 years he can hop a distance of sixteen feet and walk long distances on his tiptoes. He assumes the adult posture in throwing for distance.

At 6 *years* he can stand on each foot alternately with his eyes closed. He can bow three times successively and gracefully with the heels together. He can jump down from a height of twelve inches, landing on his toes only. He can hop fifty feet in nine seconds and make a standing broad jump of about thirty-eight inches and a standing high jump of eight inches.

§ C. WALKING AND RUNNING

Walking and running. At *20 weeks* the supine infant can roll over on his side by rotating the upper portion of the body and then flexing the hips and throwing the legs to that side. This accomplishment represents the first gross shift in body posture. At *28 weeks* the child can attain a crawling position and sustain the weight of the upper portion of his body by one or both arms. He can bring one knee forward beside the trunk but cannot raise his abdomen. Locomotion begins at about *32 weeks*. The child pivots about by means of the arms. He succeeds in raising himself to the creeping position at *36 weeks* but cannot progress on his hands and knees until *44 weeks*. It is at this stage that synchronization of contralateral arm and leg movements begins. Anthropometric measurements of postnatal development show that during the first thirty weeks there is a rapid growth in length and weight with only slight change in bodily proportions. From that time on the increase in stature is principally due to the growth in the length of the legs. Thus the increase in the ratio of leg length to stature begins at about the time the infant is ready to creep. Rapid lengthening of the legs continues throughout the period when the child is gaining skill in diverse kinds of locomotion. At *50 weeks* he is able to creep on hands and feet; the posture and movement of this all-four locomotion closely approximates bipedal walking.

Although incipient stepping movements occur during the first week, they are more marked and appear with greater frequency at about *16 weeks*. At this time also the infant pushes against pressure applied to the soles of the feet. At *28 weeks* he makes dancing and bouncing reactions when held in the upright position. Flexion and extension of the legs are accompanied by raising the arms. At *48 weeks* the infant cruises or walks, using support. The period at which infants begin to walk alone varies from less than a year to 18 months.

Instability of bodily equilibrium during the early stages of independent walking is counterbalanced by an exaggerated elevation of the arms, by a wide base support, and by a low center of gravity due to the relative shortness of the legs and to flexion of hips and knees. With the acquisition of substitute equilibratory responses, viz., appropriate movements of head, trunk, and arms, walking becomes easier. There is an accelerated increase in the speed of walking, a gradual increase in the length of the step, a decrease in the height, width, and angle of step, and a change from a full-sole to heel-toe contact with the floor. The arms are gradually lowered to relaxed suspension and move contralaterally with the legs.

The development of walking, as well as of other early motor abilities, depends on the ability to make appropriate bodily adjustments in response to visual cues and to proprioceptive cues from the muscles, tendons, and joints. In this connection the increase in the size and complexity of the cerebellum closely parallels postural development. This organ grows slowly during the first few months and attains practically its full size before the fifth year. The rate of growth is greatest during the last half of the first year and the first half of the second year. Thus its greatest increase occurs during the time when the child is rapidly gaining control of erect posture and manual and locomotor activities.

During the period between *12 and 18 months* walking replaces creeping as a means of locomotion. In spite of the difficulties involved, there appears to be a definite urge to assume the upright posture. It is not unusual, however, for the child who is fully capable of walking to resort to creeping or walking on the knees on frequent occasions. The child first walks with support. When he is led by the hands, his first steps are short and erratic and he depends largely on his support for balance. Gradually, however, he widens his stepping base and relies more and more on his own equilibratory capacity. During the first stages of independent walking his gait may be described as a straddle-toddle. He thrusts his head and the upper portion of his trunk forward and walks with his feet far apart (13 cm., according to Shirley [112]); using a full-sole step. His consecutive steps vary greatly in time and length and are characterized by out-toeing. The feet are raised relatively high. At *18 months* he is toddling. His steps are longer, the walking width is reduced to about 8 cm., and the stepping height has also diminished to a certain extent. He can now walk sidewise and backwards. He can go from walking to sitting and back to walking. He can pull a wheeled toy, push a chair about the room, and walk on the street if attended. He turns around poorly, however, describing a more or less circular path. He can creep up a flight of three steps (riser 6.5 inches, tread 11 inches) or walk up, if one hand is held. In both cases he raises the leading foot excessively high and then lowers it to the tread. He descends by backward creeping or by sitting bumps. He can obtain a ball from a table by climbing an adult chair. He can climb over a board 3.75 inches high and also get off a stool 10 inches high.

From *18 months to 2 years*, the child makes important advances in upright postural control. At 20 months his steps are quite uniform with respect to height, width, length (about 20 cm.), and time. Improvement in stability is shown by the fact that he has further decreased the width of the stepping base. However, he still uses the full-sole step. At 21 months he is beginning to run. He can walk up a flight of three steps alone, marking time, i.e., using both feet to a step, and walk down with help. He can also get down from an adult chair. At 2 years he walks steadily for a considerable distance if not hurried and shows considerable flexibility at the joints. The walking base is only 5 cm. He now uses heel-toe progression and walks in a hurried manner. He can rotate his head as he walks and shows some improvement in turning corners, although he cannot make short turns. He can walk both up and down a flight of steps, marking time, and climb on an adult chair to stand on it. He is able now to run little errands about the house.

Perhaps the outstanding achievement at this age is running. Whereas ability in walking involves anticipatory proprioceptive control over the movements of trunk and limbs, running is even more complicated and requires faster and more accurate timing of these movements. The inability of children to run when they can already walk may be due not only to lack of adequate postural control, but also to slowness of reaction time, viz., they lack the capacity both to anticipate the necessary adjustments and to make them with sufficient speed. Furthermore, running is more precarious to balance and requires greater flexibility and leverage of the feet.

During the period from *2 to 3 years*, walking becomes highly automatized. The improvement in the child's sense of balance is evidenced by a nimbleness of foot and an enterprising attitude which frequently actuates him to attempt stunts beyond his ability. He is becoming more persistent, confident, and daring. This confidence is in part due to the fact that he has a good command of the use of his feet. His progress during this period is shown by the following facts. At 26 months he can carry a chair by holding it under his arm against the thigh. At 30 months he can walk between straight parallel lines eight inches apart without stepping on them. He can also run and gallop and take short running steps on his toes. By the time he is 33 months old he can walk a straight ten-foot path one inch wide, stepping off only one to three times. He can also step-jump from a height of 18 inches and ascend a stairway with support, alternating feet.

He is apt to become somewhat knock-kneed at about the age of *3 years*, a condition which recedes rapidly during the following year or two. His shoulders are held more erect and the protruding abdomen is much reduced, due to the development of its musculature. Normal walking is characterized by uniformity in length, width, and speed of step. His step is longer than at 2 years and heel-toe progression is well incorporated into the walking mechanism. He can balance his weight momentarily on his toes and also negotiate a few short steps in this manner. He can walk a straight line, placing one foot directly in front of the other, and walks backward with considerable ease. He runs easily and smoothly with moderate control of speed.

He can walk up a flight of three steps without support, using alternate feet, and descend a long stairway alone, marking time (riser 6.5 inches, tread 11 inches). He can jump down twelve inches alone with feet together and twenty-eight inches with help. He can also ride a tricycle, using the pedals with great dexterity. This is the first instance of self-propulsion with the feet off the ground. He can walk between converging lines twelve inches apart at one end, and four inches apart at the other.

By the time the child is *4 years* old, he has acquired great steadiness of gait. He walks with long, swinging steps, in the adult style, getting the impulse for stepping from the same points on the foot as does the adult. He manifests greater mobility than at 3 years, and coordinates the movements of the parts of the body better in independent activities. He appears to take pleasure in stunts, i.e., whirling, swinging, somersaulting, etc., which greatly stimulate the semicircular canals. He balances well on his toes. He can carry a cup of water without spilling it, and walk, sitting on his haunches. He can walk a straight line three meters long and a circular path one inch wide, circle four feet in diameter, without stepping off in either case. He can make a running broad jump of twenty-three to thirty-three inches and also skip with one foot. His sense of balance is so well developed that he can descend a long stairway if supported, by alternating the feet; and if not supported, by marking time. He can negotiate the 4 cm. walking board (height 10 cm., length 2.5 M) in about 14 seconds, stepping off about three times. He runs smoothly, at different speeds, and can turn sharp corners and stop and go quickly.

At *5 years* the child can do all the things that he did at 4 years but he performs with greater facility and abandon and requires less super-vision. His activities are marked by ease, grace, and economy of move-ment. His keen sense of balance and versatility in the use of hands and feet show that he is about ready to engage in the more complex activities of later childhood. He can easily walk three meters on his toes without touching the heels to the floor at any time. He takes longer steps in both walking and running and normally exhibits greater alacrity in his move-ments than does the 4-year-old child. He can skip with both feet and march well, keeping time to music. He can make a running broad jump of twenty-eight to thirty-five inches and make a vertical jump and reach of about two-and-a-half inches. He can run the thirty-five yard dash in less than ten seconds and kick a soccer ball through the air a distance of eight to eleven-and-a-half feet. He can descend a long stairway or a large ladder alternating the feet. He negotiates the 4 cm. walking board in twelve seconds, stepping off not more than twice.

Items listed at 4 and 5 years are merely suggestive. They do not fairly represent the great variety of activities of which children at this age are capable.

By the time the child is *6 years* old he has developed in agility and strength to the extent that he can make a running broad jump of forty to forty-five inches, make a vertical jump and reach of three-and-a-half inches or more, run the thirty-five yard dash in less than nine seconds, and kick a soccer ball a distance of ten to eighteen feet. He can negotiate the 4 cm. walking board in about nine seconds, stepping off less than once per trial.

Walking boards. The walking boards were used with 3-, 4-, 5-, and 6-year-old children. There were four boards. The widths in order were 8 cm., 6 cm., 4 cm., and 2 cm. The 3-year group used the 8 cm. and 6 cm. boards; the 4-year group the 8 cm., 6 cm., and 4 cm. boards; and the 5- and 6-year groups, the 6 cm., 4 cm., and 2 cm. boards. Only a few children at 3 years attempted to walk the walking board with both feet. The others, not herein included, walked with one foot on the board and the other on the floor. The records of each age group, presented in Figure 1, show the average time required by each age group and the average number of errors committed by them in negotiating each of the walking boards.

The curves indicate that the speed of walking the individual boards increased, and the number of errors decreased, with age. On the average all groups showed an improvement in time of performance from the first to the third trial, and most groups showed a decrease in the number of errors. There is considerable variability in time of performance for all age groups at all four boards. This variability, however, appears to decrease with age. The figure also shows that, in general, the narrower the board, the greater the difficulty of performance and the greater the variability of performance in terms of errors.

A direct comparison of the speed and number of errors of the four age groups is available in the instance of the 6 cm. board. The fact that the six 3-year-old children took 15.1 seconds (average) to walk this board and that they stepped off on an average of three times per trial, is an indication of the difficulty they experienced with this board. The 4-year-old group negotiated the 6 cm. board in about two-thirds of the time required by the 3-year-old group and made only half as many errors. The 5-year-old group walked this board in only slightly less time than the 4-year-old group, but reduced the number of errors by 50 per cent. The average speed of the 6-year-old group was two seconds better than that of the

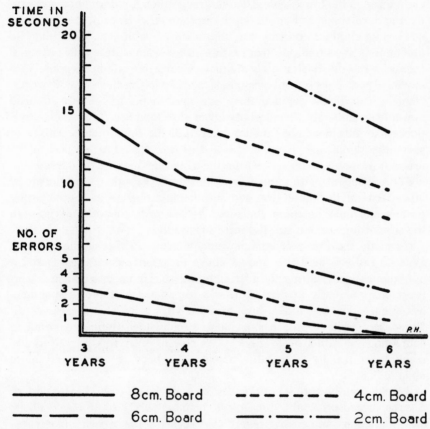

FIGURE 1. Average speed and average number of errors for the four age groups in their performance on the walking boards.

5-year-old group, and the number of errors was only one in seven trials. The other boards show similar trends with age.

Comparative scores for the girls and boys of the several age groups show that in most cases the girls walked more slowly than the boys and that on the average they committed more errors. The girls show a slightly greater tendency to improve in their performance in the three trials in both speed and number of errors than do the boys.

§ D. PREHENSION AND MANIPULATION

Reaching. No one can say just how distances appear to the unsophisti-cated eye of the young infant. The indications are that his perception of depth is the result of the gradual integration of visual and proprioceptive cues, through the process of trial and error. Although information concern-ing the development of visual depth discrimination is scant, investigations on young children indicate an improvement with age. According to McGinnis (85), visual localization is to some extent present at birth and improves rapidly during early infancy. Ocular pursuit in response to a moving light, objects, and persons is pretty well perfected at 6 weeks; whereas coordinate compensatory eye movements and fixational head movements undergo a somewhat slower development. True ocular fixa-tion apparently does not function well until the third month. This is of particular significance because it is at this time that directed arm move-ments in response to objects within the visual field are first observed.

The movement of the arm in reaching involves motor adjustments of other parts of the body. The activity effects a change in a pre-existing posture and must be counterbalanced by readjustments of body poise to the supporting surface and the force of gravity.

Normally the first reaching movements occur in the supine position. When a rattle is held four inches above an infant's chest, he regards it only momentarily during the first eight weeks. He makes small incipient movements as early as *8 to 12 weeks*. At *16 weeks* there is spontane-ous regard for the rattle, and arm activity is greatly increased. At *20 weeks* definite approach movements occur which frequently result in contacting the rattle. At *24 weeks* he is able to grasp it. Up to *28 weeks*, reaching is usually bilateral. Thereafter it becomes more and more unilateral.

Reaching in the sitting position first occurs when the child is supported. A cube placed on a table top before an infant of *12 to 16 weeks* elicits only momentary and passive regard. The regard shifts by twitchlike move-ments of the eyeballs, resembling the pursuit phase of optic nystagmus. These shifts in visual fixation are smooth and well controlled at 28 weeks. Even at *20 weeks* the child regards the cube actively and makes approach movements which usually result in contacting it. This is the first indica-tion of the intimate dynamic and developmental association between vision and prehension. At *24 weeks* he grasps the cube, manipulates it on the table top, and frequently lifts it. At *28 weeks* he begins to transfer it from hand to hand and resecures it after dropping it. Skill in manipula-tion develops rapidly from this time on.

The progressive changes in the patterns of reaching illustrate a proximo-

distal course of development. The early approach reveals a crudely functioning hand at the end of a poorly functioning arm, while the later
approach reveals a well-coordinated arm under the directing influence of
a fairly well-developed prehensile organ. Reaching at *12 to 20 weeks*
consists of discontinuous lateral arm movements in which the hand slides
on the table top, revolves clockwise above the table, or combines both of
these activities. At *24 to 28 weeks* the movements are more continuous,
the lateral deviations decrease as forward projection increases, and the
sliding and circular motions diminish. There is, however, a suggestion of
a momentary poising of the hand both before and after its forward projection. The transient suspension of the activity at these points may be
occasioned by the necessity for motor readjustment for directive reorientation of the arm, or against loss of bodily balance, or both. At *40 weeks*
reaching for near objects is a well-coordinated activity, although it still
lacks the fluency of the mature approach. At *60 weeks* reaching is accomplished by a smooth continuous movement with little or no spatial error
of the hand. Early inaccuracies of reaching movements may be due either
to imperfect visual perception of depth or to inadequate motor responses.

We have noted that early movements in both upright locomotion and
reaching are accompanied by marked lateral digressions of trunk and
limbs. This tendency to extend the lateral axis of the body may be in
part a precautionary measure against the loss of bodily equilibrium. It is
the function of childhood to straighten the course of the activity by
reducing to a minimum the number and scope of these lateral movements. The extent to which this economy of effort is effected is a direc
measure of skill in prehensory and locomotor activities.

At *18 months* reaching for near objects has become highly automatized.
This is shown by the nonchalant manner in which children frequently
approach the object. Their concern now seems to be centered on the
manipulation of the object after its prehension, rather than on its acquisition. Whereas at 1 year, reaching and grasping for near objects closely
approximates that of adults, the marked displacement of the child's center
of gravity necessary to obtain a distant object requires an extremely high
degree of neuro-muscular coordination for the maintenance of bodily
stability and for precision of approach and prehension. As a result we find
that up to 4 years, there is an exaggeration of one or more of the components of the prehensile activity which causes the behavior to appear
awkward and immature.

Although the child can easily sit without support at 18 months, in
right-hand reaching for distant objects he always places the left hand on
the table to balance himself. Up to 12 months children were required to
reach only 6.5 inches for the experimental cubes on the table top, a situ-

ation which involves but little leaning. In order better to determine the actual extent of neuro-motor organization of trunk and head movements, as well as arm movements in reaching, the cubes were at 18 months placed at a distance of 13 inches, which materially increased the difficulty of obtaining them. At this age forward leaning is combined with twisting the trunk and extending the arm, but these movements lack continuity of function and one or the other of them is grossly exaggerated. In right-hand reaching the twisting movement is usually accompanied by a strong list to the left which carries the head with it. Immature temporal coordination is shown by the fact that full arm extension and twisting of the trunk are later followed by further twisting and leaning. The fingers are fully extended fanwise, indicating a lack of proprioceptive adjustment of the digits to the size of the cube.

In spite of these limitations in control of bodily movements in reaching, the child can pick up a near-by pellet with thumb and index finger and drop it in a small-necked bottle. He can fill a cup to capacity with cubes, build a tower of three cubes after several trials, and turn pages of a book crudely. He can insert a key in a padlock and use a fork or spoon in eating, holding it with a palmar grip.

The *2-year-old* child reaches for the distant object with one hand, without supporting himself with the other, but lacks continuity of function of trunk and arm. The outstanding feature in reaching at this age is an exaggerated twisting of the trunk accompanied by a marked list to the left. At times he leans too far forward, at other times he places the burden of reaching on the arm, but appears unable to combine the two in an efficient manner. There is a tendency to bend at the waist and neck, as well as to lean forward from the buttocks.

He has, however, gained perceptibly in precision of movement. He can imitate vertical and circular strokes with a crayon, and can turn the pages of a book one by one easily. He can build a tower of six 1-inch cubes, and obtain a ball from a table top with a stick. He can imitate three or four simple movements such as raising the arms vertically, clapping the hands, putting the palms of the hands on the head, and revolving the hands around each other. He can fold a paper in imitation. He can pull off his socks and can find armholes in dressing.

At *3 years* the sitting equilibrium is good but is awkwardly combined with the reaching activity. The child now leans forward from the buttocks without bending at the waist and neck. Marked arm extension and trunk twisting, however, persist, causing a decided inclination of the trunk and head to one side. Improvement in the reaching mechanism and in the coordination of the functioning of this mechanism with vision is shown by the fact that he can trace a square, copy a drawing of a circle, and build a tower of nine or ten 1-inch cubes. He can catch a large ball with the arms fully extended once out of two or three times, although he makes little or no adjustment of the arms in receiving the ball. He can feed himself with little spilling of the food and by using both hands can pour water from a pitcher to a glass without spilling. He can also remove his pants in undressing.

Although sitting balance is well maintained at *4 years*, the child lacks poise in reaching. He leans forward with greater mobility and ease than at 3 years, but continues the exaggerated use of arm extension and trunk twisting which causes the head and trunk to list to one side. The free hand no longer plays any part in the reaching activity but remains down at the side. He can imitate or copy a circle and square, and fold and crease a paper three times on demonstration. He can touch the end of his nose with his forefinger on direction, brush his teeth, dress and undress himself with little assistance. He can catch a large ball tossed from a distance of five feet in one of two or three trials with the arms flexed at the elbows. He shows greater flexibility of arm movement than at 3 years by definite efforts at judging the position at which the ball will land. His movements, however, are restricted and inadequate and he depends more on his arms than on his hands in receiving the ball.

The *5-year-old* maintains an easy reaching balance. He combines reaching and placing objects into one continuous movement. Arm extension and trunk twisting are smoothly coordinated and, although the trunk inclines slightly to one side, the head remains erect. He shows much greater self-confidence than at 4 years, and performs with greater speed and precision. He can copy a square and triangle, and trace the diamond and cross paths without error. His improvement in ability is shown by the fact that he is now beginning to use his hands more than his arms in catching a small ball. He judges the trajectory of the ball better than he did at 4 years, and moves his hands accordingly, but frequently fails to catch it. He even attempts to receive it with one hand.

The *6-year-old* child has quite mastered the art of reaching. At this age movements of head, trunk, and arms are smoothly synchronized. He combines arm extension, leaning, and trunk twisting into an easy movement so that none of them appears in an exaggerated form. There is little or no lateral displacement of the trunk or head. He plucks the cube quickly but is very meticulous in placing it. He has gained in speed and steadiness of arm movement. He can fold a square piece of paper three times in eighty seconds. He can catch a ball tossed chest high from a distance of one meter with one hand in two out of three trials. This performance requires that he be able to judge competently the speed and trajectory of the ball and to react with unusual speed of closure. In this connection Johnson (65) has shown that the 6-year-old child is only slightly superior to the 5-year-old in steadiness of arm, but that they both are considerably superior to the 4-year-old child.

Grasping. Early grasping is reflexive. It is a two-component activity consisting of finger closure and gripping. Closure occurs in response to light pressure stimulation on the palm, whereas gripping is a static proprioceptive reaction to a pull against the finger tendons. Finger closure first appears at about 11 weeks in fetal life and is quite complete at 14 weeks. The gripping reflex appears during the 18th (prenatal) week and increases in strength up to the 25th week (Hooker [60]). The thumb is only feebly motile and does not participate in either closure or gripping. Although no observations have been made beyond 25 weeks, the strength of the gripping reflex undoubtedly increases throughout the prenatal period. The closure reflex apparently disappears at *16 to 24 weeks* after birth and is eventually succeeded by facile digital prehension. Its proprioceptive component attains its greatest strength at or soon after birth and shows no appreciable weakening until after about 12 weeks. It disappears after 24 weeks but vestiges of this "stretch" reflex are evidenced in the "phasic" reactions of the fingers of adults.

Voluntary grasping, like reaching, indicates a proximo-distal course of development. Early grasping consists of crude palming movements in which the three ulnar fingers predominate, whereas the thumb is practically inactive. This type of grasp is later succeeded by a refined finger-tip prehension characterized principally by thumb opposition, forefinger dominance, readiness for manipulation, and adaptation of finger pressure to the weight of the object. Digital mobility is manifested by such activities as poking, probing, and plucking. At *60 weeks* prehension is deft and precise. The child now has almost complete mastery over his fingers but not over his tools. In this connection the long-fingered child appears to enjoy certain prehensile advantages over the short-fingered child. Infants with long fingers are in general superior to those with short fingers in strength of reflex gripping. They later show greater dexterity and speed in voluntary prehension and in manipulatory activities which place a premium on precision of finger movements.

There is a significant change in the functional relationship of forearm and hand during the first year. For the first six months the forearm and hand extended in a straight line. At *1 year* the hand is normally flexed ulnarward at the wrist so that the angle formed by thumb and forefinger is in line with the forearm as in the case of the adult hand.

The prehension of simple objects in infancy leads to the adaptive use of tools in childhood. Normally reaching and grasping may be regarded as a single act. Already at 1 year the child reaches for objects not merely to grasp them but to use them. Furthermore, he seeks to secure a hold which is immediately adaptable for manipulation. He can lean forward to obtain an object at a short distance (6.5 inches) and regain the erect posture without materially disturbing his sitting equilibrium. However, we have already noted that when he is forced to reach for objects at a greater distance, he experiences difficulty in making the necessary postural adjustments. His reaching movements are much less accurate and as a result, in order to insure success, he resorts to a more primitive type of grasping, so that the object is usually displaced in prehension. The question then is, when can a child make postural adjustments which will enable him to reach objects which are quite remote but still within reaching distance. After 1 year therefore the cube and pellet were placed at a distance of 13 inches on the table top.

A review of the prehensile behavior at successive age levels gives a clear indication of the improvements in grasping and manipulation occurring during the early years of childhood. The child of *18 months* maintains a wide open hand until he contacts the cube. Although he secures it with good thumb opposition, his grasp is of an enveloping rather than a manipulatory nature. Furthermore, the cube is usually somewhat displaced during the act. In grasping the pellet the child first places his hand on the table at the right of the pellet and then very slowly curls the thumb and two radial fingers on it. As early as 18 months the child is bringing prehension into practical use. He is beginning to feed himself, build towers, scribble, pick up and place objects. He can hold four or more cubes at one time. However, in turning pages of a book he often takes two or three pages at a time.

At *2 years* his grasp of the cube and pellet has not materially changed. He can string beads with a needle, turn the pages of a book one at a time, turn a doorknob, snip with scissors, unwrap paper from candy, and unscrew the lid of a small jar. He can hold a glass of milk steadily with one hand, although he holds the other hand near by. In feeding himself he holds a spoon by the thumb and radial fingers, palm upward, whereas at 18 months he held the spoon with a palmar grip. He is beginning to hold a crayon by the fingers in writing.

At *3 years* he anticipates grasping during the approach by aligning the fingers for plucking the cube without touching the table top. He also grasps the pellet more readily and with the fingers more extended than heretofore. He is quite adept at picking up small objects such as the pellet and is beginning to handle the crayon in the adult manner. He can unbutton the front and side buttons of his clothes, but has great difficulty in buttoning.

At *4 years* he plucks the cube neatly, holding it mostly by thumb and medius. The index finger is frequently held aloof but in readiness for manipulatory activities. The pellet is usually picked up neatly by the thumb and index finger. However, he frequently substitutes the medius for the index finger, applying the latter only on manipulation. At 4 years his writing hold resembles that of adults in the general position of the pencil. The child can adapt his grasp to brush his teeth and button his clothes.

At 5 *years* he prehends both cube and pellet with great dispatch, frequently with the two ulnar fingers flexed into the palm in the manner of adult grasping. An interesting developmental change in grasping the cube is the gradual alteration in the lie of the fingers from a vertical to a diagonal direction. This change not only gives him a clearer vision of the cube, but is also a decided asset in constructive activities. At 5 years he shows great precision in the use of tools. He can brush his teeth well, wind thread on a bobbin, put matches in a match box, and make a little ball out of tissue paper. He can tie a bow knot (Montessori Frame G) and shows great improvement over his 4-year performance in buttoning his clothes.

Release. One of the most difficult prehensile activities to master in early life is voluntary release. The synergic pattern of release is the antithesis of the grasping pattern. In grasping, the extensors are inhibited; whereas in release, the flexors are inhibited, and in early childhood inhibition of the flexors is by far the more difficult. Cortical control over finger extension takes place only after reaching and grasping are pretty well perfected. Improvements in the ability to release objects can be observed in such activities as tower building, dropping pellets in a bottle, throwing, and performances with the formboard and performance box.

Release usually does not occur during the first half year. From *28 to 40 weeks* the infant can release objects only against a resisting surface. He transfers objects from hand to hand or releases them against the table top, or inadvertently drops them. Advertent release begins at about *44 weeks.* The infant can now voluntarily drop objects on the table top or floor. At *52 weeks* when he has attained considerable proficiency in dropping, he exploits his releasing capacity by putting objects on the table top or platform, by frequent attempts in placing one cube on another, and by occasional throwing. Difficulties in the release of objects may be observed throughout the first four years in activities requiring precision in placement of objects. In tower building, for example, it is the inability to release the prehended cube properly which causes the most frequent failures. The cube may be accurately placed in position but the tower will be thrown out of balance unless the contact of fingers and opposed thumb is broken simultaneously, or the movement of the hand is properly inhibited during the release. Difficulty in releasing small pellets in a bottle is experienced as late as 3 years.

Deftness of release improves rapidly during childhood and closely parallels the development of adaptive behavior. At 1 year over half of the children spontaneously insert the round block in its hole in the formboard. The activity, however, is accomplished by much forceful pushing of the block and is probably more incipient than deliberate. Two-thirds of the children will hold the pellet over the bottle but only one-half of them can release the pellet so that it will fall in or near the bottle. At 56 *weeks* most of the children can release the rod at the hole of the performance box, but only one-half of them succeed in dropping it within the box. In all of these combining activities, release occurs only in response to contact with a resisting surface.

At *18 months* the child puts the ten cubes in the cup but releases only on contact with the cup. He builds a tower of three staggered cubes after several trials and consumes much time in the process of placement and release. He drops the pellet in the bottle with difficulty and forcibly adapts the round block to the formboard. His adaptive prehensory release is exaggerated and crude. Although he can place, drop, and throw objects, these acts are accomplished by undue finger extension. Opening the hand is poorly timed with forward projection of the arm in throwing so that the ball is usually released either too soon or too late for good direction. In the latter case some of the forward momentum of the ball is lost.

At *2 years* he can place two or more cubes neatly in a row in imitation of a train, drop the pellet in the bottle on contact, and build a tower of six or more 1-inch cubes. He gives attentive visual regard to all of his performances. The tower usually has a strong right inclination and the cubes are poorly aligned. Although his hand is steadier than at 18 months, his hold on the cube obscures complete vision of the tower. As a result he has difficulty in bringing the prehended cube flatly onto the tower, in releasing the fingers simultaneously, and in withdrawing the hand. He presses rather than places the cube in its place on the tower, sometimes with so great a force as to cause the tower to sway or even to fall; and, as at 18 months, releases the cube by exaggerated finger extension. Placement and release require much time, frequently greater than 30 seconds per cube. The reluctant release appears to be due to apprehension of the fall of the tower on the removal of the hand.

At *3 years* the child can release pellets freely in the bottle and accurately place three cubes in constructing a bridge. However, he continues to force or pat blocks into the formboard; and in lacing his shoes, he frequently pulls out the lace on withdrawal of the hand. He can build a tower of nine or ten 1-inch cubes. Visual-motor coordination is much improved over that at 2 years. The cubes are slowly but more accurately placed, although they are usually somewhat staggered and rotated out of alignment. The hand now only partially obstructs the view, but the tendency to press the cubes into place and the unsteadiness of the hand on release indicate that tower building is still a difficult task. Both hands are frequently brought into play for steadying the tower.

The child of *4 years* releases pellets in the bottle with great precision and celerity. He can also lace his shoes with some difficulty, and deftly place the five cubes in constructing the gate. In building the tower, he holds the hand well above or to one side of the tower so as not to obstruct his view. His cubes are released without pressure and with just sufficient opening of the hand to permit its withdrawal. He has improved markedly in steadiness of hand and timing and deftness of release. He frequently uses both hands independently in building the tower.

At *5 years* the child shows marked improvement in speed, dexterity, and precision in the placement of objects. He demonstrates his discriminating appreciation of visual-spatial relations, ability in eye-hand coordination, and control of the mechanism of release by expert and almost perfect alignment of the cubes in tower building. He performs in a cool, deliberate, and confident manner, and unless he becomes careless, there is little risk of displacement on release. He can now lace his own shoes well and drop pellets in the bottle rapidly, frequently two or three at a time. In tower building he holds the cube by the finger tips at the upper right-hand corners so that he has a complete view of both cube and tower at all times. The cube is prehended and neatly placed in one continuous movement and then deftly released by a slight extension of the metacarpo-phalangeal joints without disturbing the tower. He sometimes erects two cubes at a time, holding one in the palm, and in fast construction may bring in his other hand to straighten the tower. Individual differences are marked. Some infants build rapidly, even carelessly, stopping only to make certain that the tower will not collapse. Others work very slowly and even take time out to view the results. The cubes are well aligned, but even at this age when tower construction is pretty well mastered, there is still a slight lean, usually toward the right.

The *6-year-old* child carefully aligns the cubes to build virtually a straight tower. His skill at this age is perhaps due as much to his improvement in visual-space perception as to improvement in the mechanism of release.

Throwing. Throwing is long-distance placement of objects. Instead of actually bringing the hand to the distant point at which the object is to be placed, the subject as it were projects the hand through the intervening space toward the spot by means of the object. Throwing involves visual localization, stance, displacement of bodily mass, reaching, release, and restoration of static equilibrium. Skill in throwing a ball requires a fine sense of static and dynamic balance, accurate timing of delivery and release, good eye-hand coordination, and appropriate functioning of the fingers, as well as the arm, trunk, head, and legs, in controlling the trajectory of the ball.

Ball playing is largely a social situation. In the laboratory the examiner rolls the ball to the young child, to determine to what extent he initiates a response. When good rapport has been established, the child is requested to throw the ball. The child first throws from sitting posture before he is able to stand independently. Normative records show that at 40 weeks he either retains his hold on the ball or releases it without definite reference to the examiner or to the goal. At 48 weeks he rolls or throws the ball. In fact, 50 per cent of the children actually succeed in projecting it toward the examiner. At 1 year, over one-half of the children definitely throw the ball; and at 56 weeks, they repeatedly toss or roll it to the examiner on request.

At *1 year*, throwing takes on a variety of patterns. The child rolls the ball or tosses it with an underhand, side, or overhand motion. Inasmuch as he cannot time its release, its course is usually very inaccurate. In the overhand cast he sometimes releases the ball above his shoulder and at other times fails to release it until he has completed the downward thrust of the hand. The throwing activity, in which the shoulder plays the major part, is confined almost entirely to the arm. The elbow and wrist display little mobility.

Although children at *18 months* have quite mastered the art of release as such, they have not as yet adequately incorporated it into other movements of the arm, such as tossing and throwing. The child now throws while standing. He is inclined to walk both before and after he casts the ball. Throwing consists of a forward thrust of the arm in an underhand, side, or overhand motion. If he is prevented from stepping, he stands facing the examiner with neither foot in advance of the other, cocks the arm above or near the shoulder, and delivers the ball with a full forward extension of the shoulder and elbow. He remains fairly erect throughout and neither rotates nor twists with the throw. He may on occasion lean slightly forward from the hips. Exaggerated finger extension and inadequate timing of the release causes the ball to be poorly directed. Some of the children throw the ball into the performance box and others drop it into the box after going through the motions of throwing.

The throwing posture has changed but little at *2 years*. In free throwing the child continues to take short steps both before and after delivering the ball. When he stands still and throws there is a slight body rotation with the forward thrust of the arm. Although he shows improvement in timing of the release, exaggerated extension of the fingers still precludes accurate direction of the flight of the ball.

The following itemized statements show how children of higher age levels throw a ball. All statements are in terms of throwing with the right hand.

Two-and-a-half years:

Is uncertain as to stance, showing great variations
Stands still, steps, skips, or runs with ball
Stands erect or crouches
Tosses or throws
Usually maintains weight on right foot
Directs ball poorly
Throws ball about five to seven feet
Throws a bean bag into a twelve-inch hole at a distance of three feet
Throws a large ball (diameter 5.2 inches) from three to five feet

Three-and-a-half years:

Has difficulty in acquiring preferred stance; hesitates before throwing
Faces straight ahead, neither foot in advance
Leans slightly toward left
Extends trunk in bringing ball above shoulder
Rotates with throw, by stepping or by sliding one foot ahead
Throws mostly with shoulder and elbow
Shows improvement in wrist movement and timing of release
Uses fingers to guide course of ball
Boys are superior to girls in ease of delivery and accuracy of direction

Four years:

Has acquired definite stance for delivery
Stands facing forward, neither foot in advance
Shifts weight to right foot preparatory to throwing
Leans forward and rotates body to left on throw
Usually uses right foot as fulcrum for the delivery
May shift his weight to left foot, or draw it back, or slide right foot forward
Throws ball straight ahead but with poor control of its height (inadequate timing of release)
Demonstrates a preferred hand in throwing by greater frequency in its use, greater accuracy and distance of throw, and better neuro-motor coordination in stance and delivery
Boys throw ball with horizontal motion from above or to right of shoulder
Girls throw ball from above shoulder with downward sweep

Five years:
  Boys
    Stance:

    Advances left foot
    Draws arm obliquely up to position in shoulder axis
    Rotates shoulder markedly, twisting and leaning to the right
    Lowers right shoulder, frequently crouches forward
    Shifts weight to right foot and extends left arm out laterally

    Delivery:

    Throws ball with horizontal motion around advancing shoulder at about
      shoulder level
    Accelerates extension of elbow and wrist just previous to release
    Releases ball when arm is fully extended
    After release arm sweeps across front of body
    Rotates and twists body toward left, raising right shoulder, then bends
      forward at hips and leans toward the left
    Shifts weight to left foot, raising right heel and rotating it outward
    Shoulder, elbow, wrist, and fingers well coordinated
    Legs function inadequately
    Throws a baseball a distance of about twenty-four feet

  Girls
    Stance:

    Appears uncertain as to stance
    Usually advances neither foot
    Supports weight sometimes on right foot, sometimes on left
    Draws arm obliquely up to over shoulder to a position back of shoulder
      or head, with elbow high at side.
    Extends trunk, lowers head, rotates and twists toward the right

    Delivery:

    Throws ball with forward and downward movement of hand, with
      forward and medial movement of elbow
    Holds wrist in dorsal flexion and then suddenly flexes it volarly and
      extends the fingers to release the ball
    Sweeps hand to left and downward after release
    Rotates and extends body, raises head, and then flexes forward at the
      hips and twists to the left
    Shifts weight to left foot or steps forward on right foot
    Throws ball principally with shoulder and wrist movement
    Trunk and legs, particularly the latter, function inadequately
    Throws a baseball a distance of about fifteen feet

Six years:

Boys

Stance:

Advances left foot markedly

Draws hand obliquely up to position at side and back of right shoulder joint

Rotates and twists body, and leans markedly to the right

Extends trunk and shifts weight to right foot

Flexes knees and raises extended left arm high at side

Delivery:

Throws ball as at 5 years

Moves body and throwing arm forward markedly, with great acceleration of arm movement and pronounced shifting of weight to the left foot

Steps forward with left foot at start of delivery, or slides right foot ahead as ball is released

Makes optimal use of shoulder, elbow, wrist, and trunk, and in some cases of the legs

Girls

Stance:

Differs from that of 5-year-old girls mainly in that in all cases the weight is shifted to the right foot

Holds ball in varying positions back of shoulder or in shoulder axis

Delivery:

Shows improvement over 5-year-old girls in the greater excursion of the arm and greater forward flexion at the hips

Steps forward with left foot before throwing in some instances

Sex differences. Sex differences at 5 years and 6 years were clearly evidenced both in the throwing stance and in the actual delivery of the ball. Among the outstanding differences were the following: (1) Boys advanced the left foot only during the delivery. (2) Boys held the ball at the right of the shoulder, while girls in general held it above the shoulder. (3) Boys utilized trunk and leg movements to greater advantage than did girls. Girls stood more erect in throwing than did boys. (4) Boys used the left arm to greater advantage in maintaining balance. (5) Boys shifted their weight more markedly than did girls. (6) Boys directed the course of the ball more accurately than did girls. On release boys held the wrist and fingers in almost a straight line with the forearm, whereas girls flexed the wrist sharply so that the hand was brought down almost at a right angle with the forearm.

Summarizing statement. The emergence of the mature throwing pattern is a product of slow development representing an economy in effort involving systematization and refinement of postural and perceptual mechanisms through the coordination of many specific fundamental patterns. Up to about 3 years the arm and shoulder joint are utilized to a greater extent than any other part of the body in throwing. The fingers, which at first functioned only inadequately, gradually assume a major part in directing the course of the ball. Trunk and finally leg movements are later incorporated into the throwing activity and take on increasing importance as they develop in scope and fluency. Up to about 4 years children throw with an overhand movement in which the hand describes a vertical arc. Later the ball is directed from the side of the shoulder on a more or less vertical plane. This change in the course of the throwing hand appears to be correlated with the act of shifting the weight from the right to the left foot, and is evidenced by boys at 5 years and by some girls at 6 years. Sex differences are apparent in throwing as early as 3.5 years and increase with age. At 5 years, for example, it has been shown that boys throw much farther and with much greater accuracy than do girls (Jenkins [63]). Throwing by the 5- and 6-year-old boys had many of the characteristics of mature throwing.

Manipulation of writing tools. The motor maturity of a child is revealed in the manner in which he uses objects as tools. One of the most revealing tools is the writing instrument in the form of crayon or pencil, etc. In accordance with the procedure detailed on page 140, a sheet of paper is placed on the table before the child, and a pencil or crayon with its sharpened end pointing away from him is then placed on the paper. The observer notes the manner in which the child picks up the pencil, adjusts it for writing, and operates it.

At *1 year*, the child can deftly grasp and manipulate long slender objects, such as a spoon or rod, with the finger tips. However, when he attempts to utilize the objects in poking, tapping, or brushing, he resorts to a more primitive and firmer grasp, holding the shaft enveloped in the palm. This type of grasp is also used on the crayon with its point projecting out of the radial aspect of the hand. The child wields the crayon by banging or brushing with a full-arm action in which lateral movements predominate. He raises his hand high and on lowering it frequently misses the paper and marks the table top.

At *18 months*, the child picks up and grasps the crayon with its butt end held firmly in the palm. He draws the point of the crayon across the paper largely by shoulder movements which raise the elbow upward and outward and lower it downward and inward. These movements alone determine the tilt of the crayon and cause it to be raised on the outward sweep. Banging is giving way to marking which is confined mostly to the paper. Scribbling is spontaneous at this age and is performed with great vigor in imitation of the examiner. The child for the first time makes definite strokes and differentiates between stroking and scribbling.

At 2 *years*, the child picks up the crayon by placing the thumb at the left of the shaft and the fingers at the right. He adjusts the crayon for writing with the aid of the left hand. Palmar gripping is giving way to awkward attempts to extend the radial fingers toward the point of the writing instrument. Some infants hold the butt of the crayon against the palm of the hand with the index finger extending down the shaft. Others hold the crayon crudely in the adult manner with the medius near the point and the index and thumb flexed sharply but higher up over the shaft. Writing pressure is exceedingly variable and scribbling movements frequently occur in which the crayon fails to contact the paper. The child definitely rests his hand on the paper in writing and confines his marks pretty well to the paper. Although his hold on the crayon is firm, he is beginning to manipulate the pencil with the fingers, and thus makes smaller marks than he did at 18 months. He can imitate vertical and circular strokes.

Children appear to take a peculiar interest in finger movements as early as 2.5 *years*. They restrict the size of their drawings and engage in activities such as stringing beads, building with blocks, and making writing movements in imitation of their elders.

At 3 *years*, the child picks up the crayon as he did at 2 years. In writing he simulates the adult hold by resting the shaft at the juncture of the thumb and index finger. The medius extends with its tip near the point of the crayon while the thumb opposes the index finger higher up on the shaft. There is a definite inhibition of large arm movements, as well as increased use of the fingers.

Four years represents the transitional stage in picking up the pencil. The child now places the index and medius at the left of the shaft and the thumb at the right. On lifting the pencil, he rotates its point under the palm toward him and adjusts it, sometimes with the aid of the left hand, for writing. In all cases the pencil is held with the tip of the three radial digits near its point with the medius more fully extended than the others. The paper is held in place by the left hand. The pencil is firmly gripped and moved by flexing and extending the fingers, although wrist movements are present. The writing is usually small and cramped. However, he handles the pencil with much greater facility than at 3 years and draws a much rounder circle. He can copy a cross and also trace the diamond path without committing more than two errors. He still has difficulty in drawing lines in the diagonal directions. In this connection it has been found that increase in accuracy of tracing is greatest between 3 and 4 years, and that children of 3 to 6 years experience about as much difficulty in tracing in one direction as in any other (Wellman 132). Four years is definitely the formative age in graphic representation. The child is beginning to represent objects in the way they appear to the adult. His drawings of a man may be crude but they have features which clearly identify them.

The *5-year-old* child is quite expert in handling the pencil. He plucks it from the table as he did at 4 years but with greater ease, and on raising the hand, revolves the point of the pencil clockwise in the manner of the adult and at the same time adjusts it for writing. The writing hold closely approximates that of the adult. The radial surface of the extended medius supports the pencil near its point while the thumb and index are applied at varying positions on the shaft. Marks made on the paper are generally confined to a small area. The child can now draw easily recognizable forms. He is quite adept at copying a square with pencil or with pen and ink. He can copy a triangle and trace the paths of the diamond and the cross without error. His fingers are much more nimble than they were at 4 years and he handles the pencil more adaptively and with greater precision. His control of finger movements is such that he will soon be writing.

The *6-year-old* child grasps and adjusts the pencil as he did at 5 years. His writing hold is similar to that of the adult, with the thumb and index flexed slightly more than the medius. Writing is accomplished principally by movements of the fingers and wrist and, as at 5 years, is confined to a small portion of the paper. The trend of his slow and labored movements is from left to right.

In summary it may be said that the course of development in writing is proximo-distal. The gradual decrease in the size of writing movements with age is paralleled by corresponding reduction in the number and magnitude of superfluous movements.

§ E. LATERALITY AND DIRECTIONALITY

Handedness. Eye-hand coordination improves with age and under normal conditions is accompanied by a gradual development of eye and hand dominance. The development of handedness, according to some investigators, depends on cerebral maturation. Thus the prevalence of right-handedness is due either to the functional superiority of the left side of the cerebrum over the right side, or to differential blood supply favorable to the left hemisphere. Other investigators ascribe the prevalence of dextrality to fetal position, social pressure, or superiority in structure of the

8

right arm over the left. None of these theories has been fully substantiated by experimental evidence.

Although it is quite generally believed that infants fail to show hand preference during the first few months of life, asymmetry of posture is indicated at birth by the prevalence of the tonic neck reflex attitude. This postural reflex, as is well known, has a pronounced effect on the position of the arms, but it also affects the position of the other extremities. The lateral posture of the head during the first months predisposes the infant to regard the activities of the hand which he is facing. Thus, in the first step in the coordination of eye- and hand-movements, indications of the preferred hand may already be present. Cinemanalysis suggests that the extensor arm as seen in the supine t.n.r. during the first sixteen weeks of life is the dominant arm (and hand) as determined in feeding, play, and normative examination situations at 1 and 5 years of age. Footedness and even eyedness are suggestively exhibited by the tonic neck reflex attitude. However, the relationship between the t.n.r. and handedness, eyedness, and footedness needs further study.

Records of behavior patterns in infancy indicate a differentiation in the amount of lateral activity by the hands, legs, trunk, and head. Lateral dominancy, however, appears to fluctuate, more or less periodically, from one side to the other. According to Giesecke (41), these fluctuations in lateral dominancy apparently occur at definite age levels, notably at 7 and at 10 months, but the degree of fluctuation varies from one individual to another and is inversely proportionate to the degree of dominancy. For the first four months lateral dominance is indicated by the greater frequency of use of the small muscle groups of one side. In older infants, hand dominancy is indicated by the preferential use of the hand in spontaneous activity as well as in reaching.

Most investigators agree that hand preference makes its appearance sometime during the second half-year of life, and that the preference becomes more marked after 18 months or 2 years. The present study in distance reaching shows that children of 18 months to 5 years maintain better bodily poise, reach faster and straighter, and grasp more accurately when the right hand is used than when the left hand is used. For example, in tower building the cubes are placed more accurately with the right than with the left hand. Other investigators show that increase in skill and strength is greater for the right hand than for the left hand in preschool children. Evidence at present indicates that ambilaterals tend to be retarded in early language development and also are likely to show other irregularities in development which, as a rule, disappear when strong unilateral dominancy has been achieved (Nice, 96).

Under normal conditions the child gradually adopts a unilateral use of the hands, thus realizing any physical advantage which may occur from the use of one hand instead of two. Even in the first year of life, in attempting to pick up any small object such as a cube or a bead, the infant grasps the object better with the fingers of one hand than with two hands. In addition, the use of two hands results in obscuring the object from view. Early in life the child tends to use one hand in the prehension of the object, and the other in an auxiliary role. For example, if the object escapes the grasp by one hand, the other hand may be brought in as a means of preventing its further escape. Infants of 20 to 32 weeks who are supported in a chair are frequently forced to reach with one hand because the other hand is required as an aid in maintaining bodily equilibrium. Furthermore, the infant also discovers that by leaning and twisting the trunk he can reach farther with one hand than with two. The tendency toward unilateral use of the hands is expressed during childhood by such activities as ball throwing, block building, self-feeding, drawing, writing, etc.

The determination of handedness in childhood is at best a very complicated problem. The numerous well-controlled studies have failed to yield definite information concerning either its origin or its development. Whether handedness is innate or due to factors in antenatal or postnatal life is not known. However, the problem is of such importance that it should be made part of every clinical examination. Studies in which hand preference is based on the frequency or amount of use of the hands should take into consideration that the hand used in any situation may be determined by a previous set, position of the examiner with respect to the child, the location of the mother if she is present, method of presentation of materials, and the posture of the child, i.e., whether he slumps to the left or right in sitting at the table. It is suggested that tests which place a premium on skill or precision of movement rather than on frequency of use or amount of activity may be most revealing for the early detection of handedness.

Hand preference was studied at 18 months and at 2 years at the Clinic by presenting the child with a crayon and paper and observing which hand was used in picking up the crayon and in writing (see page 140). The results seem to indicate that a large percentage of the boys show a preferential use of the right hand as early as 18 months in writing. There was no substantial increase in the use of this hand at 2 years. Only about 60 per cent of the girls used the right hand exclusively on the crayon at 18 months, whereas at 2 years all of them indicated a preference for writing with this hand. These results suggest that hand preference may be established at an earlier age in boys than in girls. The right hand was used exclusively for both picking up and writing by 68 per cent of the children at 18 months, and by 92 per cent at 2 years.

The records of eighteen of these children who were also available at 5 years and 10 years (see Table I) show that eleven of the children indicated a preference for the use of the right hand at all four age levels; four children who used the left hand once or twice at 18 months used only the right hand thereafter. One child, Number 7, whose records at 10 years indicate that he is right-handed, showed a mixed trend up to this age. In fact, his records at both 5 and 10 years show a tendency for frequent use of both hands in other situations than writing. One boy and one girl were definitely left-handed at 10 years. The boy indicated a preference for the left hand as early as 2 years, not only in writing but in other forms of manual activity, while the girl showed a left-hand dominance at 5 years.

TABLE I

INDIVIDUAL RECORDS OF THE HAND USED FOR WRITING AT 18 MONTHS, 2 YEARS, AND 5 YEARS. HANDEDNESS AT 10 YEARS IS ALSO SHOWN

| | Hand used in writing | | | | | Handedness at 10 years |
| | 18 months | | 2 years | | 5 years | |
	Trial 1	Trial 2	Trial 1	Trial 2	4 trials	
Boys						
1........	L	L	R	R	R	R
2........	R	R	R.	R	R	R
3........	R	R	L	L	L	L
4........	R	R	R	R	R	R
5........	R	R	R	R	R	R
6........	R	R	R	R	R	R
7........	L	L	R	R	R twice L twice	R
8........	R	R	R	R	R	R
9........	L	L	R	R	R	R
10........	R	L	R	R	R	R
Girls						
1........	R	R	R	R	R	R
2........	R	R	R	R	R	R
3........	R	R	R	R	R	R
4........	R	R	R	R	R	R
5........	L	R	R	R	L	L
6........	R	R	R	R	R	R
7........	R	R	R	R	R	R
8........	L	R	R	R	R	R

The results of these writing tests in general appear to indicate that whereas hand preference in some instances may be determined as early as 18 months or 2 years, predictions of handedness cannot in the present state of our knowledge be made with assurance until a later age.

Handedness at 3, 4, 5, and 6 years was studied in three different situations involving the picking up of ten pellets and dropping them into a bottle (for procedure see page 103). Although two of the groups were small, the results indicate that in the first situation, in which the child was permitted the use of either hand, there was in general no increase with age in the preferential use of the right hand. With the exception of the 4-year-old girls and the small group of 6-year-old boys, this hand was used about two-thirds of the time. The right hand was used exclusively by twice as many children as used only the left hand. The fact that the pellets were placed on the side opposite the hand used in the preliminary test may have influenced the results. Comparison of the results of the second situation, in which the child was permitted to use only the right hand, and the third situation, in which he was permitted to use only the left hand, shows that in general children worked with greater speed with the right hand than with the left hand. But there was a consistent increase in speed of performance for both hands.

Footedness. Only a few studies have been performed with a view to determining footedness in children. Ames (2) in a study of prone progression during the first year of life observed that foot dominance was exhibited as early as 42 weeks of age, when the child creeps on hands and knees but uses one foot predominantly in a "near step" pattern. The foot which exhibits this pattern is the same one which later appears to be dominant in kicking and stepping tests.

Under the theory that children start with the preferred foot in the walking board experiment, a careful record was kept of the foot which was first placed on the board by children of 4, 5, and 6 years of age. The results (see Table II) show that there were no noteworthy changes in footedness with age within the age range represented by these children, but that there was throughout a tendency to use the right foot more frequently than the left. The two largest groups consisted of those children who used the right foot on at least two-thirds of the trials and those who used the right foot on all trials.

Relationship between handedness, eyedness, and footedness. Parson believes that there is a definite relationship between handedness and eyedness. Castner (16) reports that studies of nursery and public school children by Parson, Selzer, and Updegraff indicate an incidence of hand-eye types varying from 63 per cent to 69 per cent for dextrals, and from 30 per cent to 36 per cent for partial and total sinistrals.

TABLE II

FOOT PLACED FIRST ON WALKING BOARD

Age, yrs.	Number of cases	Right always	Right on at least ⅔, but not on all trials	Left always	Left on at least ⅔, but not on all trials	Left or right on 4–5 trials	Total number of times each foot was used	
							Right	Left
4.......	24	7 29%	8 33%	1 4%	4 17%	4 17%	122	68
5.......	48	10 21%	16 33%	8 17%	9 19%	5 10%	227	188
6.......	14	3 21%	4 29%	2 14%	1 7%	4 29%	71	47
Total...	86	20	28	11	14	13	420	303

Discrepancies in the figures are due to the fact that some of the children failed to complete the series of nine trials.

Castner (16) studied handedness, eyedness, and footedness in a group of children first at 3 years, and then at 7 years of age. Handedness was determined in terms of the frequency of use of each hand in the series of prehensory situations commonly used at the Clinic, in which the choice of hand was not forced. If one hand was used more than two-thirds of the total number of times, it was considered the dominant hand; otherwise the child was designated as ambilateral. Eyedness was tested in ten trials of the Miles V-scope and by means of orientation cards; and footedness was determined by having the child kick a ball placed on the floor about nine inches in front of him, midway between his two feet. Although the number of children tested is small, the results are at least indicative. Altogether seventeen children were studied for handedness and sixteen also for eyedness and footedness.

As Table III shows, those children who were right-handed or ambilateral at 3 years were right-handed at 7 years; and the child who was left-handed at 3 years was left-handed at 7 years. Seven of the eight children who were right-eyed at 3 years were also right-eyed at 7 years; while one showed signs of ambilaterality. Five of the seven children who were left-eyed and one who was ambilateral at 3 years were left-eyed at 7 years; whereas two children who were left-eyed at 3 years were right-eyed at 7 years. All of the children who were right-footed and one who was ambilateral in the use of his feet at 3 years were right-footed at 7 years. The child who was left-footed at 3 years was also left-footed at 7 years. It was noted that ambilaterality occurred most frequently in the use of the hands.

TABLE III

HANDEDNESS, EYEDNESS, AND FOOTEDNESS IN SEVENTEEN
CHILDREN AT 3 AND AT 7 YEARS

	Ages	
	3 years	7 years
Number of children who were right-handed......	10	15
Number of children who were left-handed.......	1	1
Number of children who were ambilateral.......	6	1
Number of children who were right-eyed........	8	9
Number of children who were left-eyed..........	7	6
Number of children who were ambilateral.......	1	1
Number of children who were right-footed.......	14	15
Number of children who were left-footed........	1	1
Number of children who were ambilateral.......	1	0

Fifteen children completed all the tests for handedness, eyedness, and footedness at both age levels. Table IV shows that of the nine purely dextral types at 7 years, five were of this type at 3 years, whereas the remaining four were dextral in two of the three organs. One child proved to be purely sinistral at both age levels. The remaining five children who showed admixtures of laterality and ambilaterality at 7 years were of mixed or ambilateral types at 3 years. In general, dextrality prevailed over sinistrality or ambilaterality at both age levels, but was more marked at 7 years. A more detailed analysis of these results may be found in Table V.

Summary. The greatest changes in laterality from 3 to 7 years occurred in the instance of the hand. There was a marked increase in the number of right-handed children and a corresponding decrease in ambilaterality. There was also a marked increase in the number of right-handed, right-eyed children; in the number of right-handed, right-footed children; and in the number of right-handed, right-eyed, and right-footed children. There were only slight changes in eyedness, footedness, and in the relationship between these two.

Finally, the results of this and other studies point to a higher relationship between handedness and footedness than between eyedness and handedness, or eyedness and footedness.

TABLE IV

FREQUENCY OF OCCURRENCE OF DIFFERENT HAND-EYE-FOOT TYPES AT 7 YEARS, AND
THE RELATIONSHIP TO THEIR ANTECEDENT TYPES

(The letters R, L, and A stand for Right, Left, and Ambilateral)

3 years				7 years			
Frequency	Hand	Eye	Foot	Frequency	Hand	Eye	Foot
5	R	R	R	9	R	R	R
2	R	L	R				
2	A	R	R				
1	L	L	L	1	L	L	L
1	A	A	A				
1	A	L	R	3	R	L	R
1	R	L	R				
1	A	R	R	1	R	A	R
1	A	L	R	1	A	L	R

TABLE V

A COMPARISON OF HANDEDNESS AND EYEDNESS, HANDEDNESS AND FOOTEDNESS, AND
EYEDNESS AND FOOTEDNESS IN FIFTEEN CHILDREN AT 3–7 YEARS

	Age	
	3 years	7 years
Number of children who were both right-handed and right-eyed....	5	9
Number of children who were both left-handed and left-eyed.......	1	1
Number of children who were right-handed but left-eyed..........	4	3
Number of children who were ambilateral of hand, eye, or both....	5	2
Number of children who were both right-handed and right-footed...	9	13
Number of children who were both left-handed and left-footed......	1	1
Number of children who were ambilateral of hand, foot, or both....	5	1
Number of children who were both right-eyed and right-footed.....	8	9
Number of children who were both left-eyed and left-footed........	1	1
Number of children who were left-eyed but right-footed...........	5	4
Number of children who were ambilateral of eye, foot, or both.....	1	1

Directionality. Handedness frequently raises the question of directionality. Are there preferred directions in arm movements? Is the young child so physiologically constituted that certain movements are naturally preferred? Does the early predominance of flexion and adduction over extension and abduction determine the course of these movements, and are early directional tendencies reflected in the ease or difficulty of making drawing and writing movements?

At the Clinic, children of 4 and 5 years were required to copy from a model a circle, cross, square, triangle, and diamond. A careful record was kept of the direction in which each line was drawn. (The directions for giving these tests are found in Chapter VII.) The results of the tests are tabulated in Table VI. The inability of many children of 4 years to make the required drawings accounts for the paucity of cases at this age. This fact must be kept in mind in interpreting the results.

At 4 years a large majority of the children drew the circle in the clockwise direction, whereas at 5 years the counter-clockwise direction was used as frequently as the clockwise. We are uncertain as to just what these results signify, but it may be that in making continuous circular lines, the typical directional tendency for children who have had little or no experience in drawing is clockwise, whereas greater experience with writing tools makes for greater versatility of arm movements.

In the instance of the cross the preferred direction in drawing the vertical line at both years was downward, and this tendency was stronger at 5 than at 4 years. The horizontal line in the majority of cases was drawn from left to right. However, at both ages some children drew the right half of the horizontal line to the right, and the left half to the left. This tendency was less marked at 5 years than at 4 years.

In drawing the vertical lines of the square, 60 per cent of the 4-year-old children drew one line upward and the other one downward, while only half of this number drew both lines downward. At 5 years, this situation was almost entirely reversed: 65 per cent of the children drew both lines downward while 35 per cent drew one upward and one downward. Only one child, 4 years old, drew both lines upward. No age differences appear in the manner of drawing the horizontal lines. About half of the children drew one of the lines toward the right and the other one toward the left, while an almost equal number of children drew both lines toward the right. Altogether only seven of the fifty-nine children drew both lines toward the left.

Only two children at 4 years were able to draw a triangle. In both cases the sides of the triangle were drawn downward while the base was drawn toward the right by one child and toward the left by the other. Of the thirty-seven children at 5 years who drew the triangle, the large majority drew both sides downward. The base was drawn toward the right by 60 per cent of the children and toward the left by 40 per cent.

Only four 4-year-old children were able to copy a diamond with any success. Their drawings and the direction of the lines are indicated in the table. The nearest approach to a diamond was the drawing shown in the last column, where both lines are drawn toward the right. Only eight out of fifty-eight 5-year-old children drew a diamond. Four others, however, made figures which resembled a diamond. These twelve exhibited five different methods of drawing the figure. The two most common

TABLE VI

DIRECTIONS OF LINES IN COPYING OF FORMS BY CHILDREN OF 4 AND 5 YEARS

1. Copying Circle

Age	No. cases	Direction of movement	
		Clockwise	Counter-clockwise
4 years.....................	22	82%	18%
5 years.....................	58	48%	52%

2. Copying Cross

Age	No. cases	Direction of vertical line			Direction of horizontal line		
		Up	Down	Up and down from $\updownarrow$ horizontal	Right	Left	Left and right from $\leftarrow\!\mid\!\rightarrow$ vertical line
4 years....	19	16%	84%	—	68%	—	32%
5 years....	58	—	98%	2%	71%	12%	17%

3. Copying Square

Age	No. cases	Direction of vertical lines			Direction of horizontal lines		
		Both up	Both down	One up, one down	Both right	Both left	One right, one left
4 years....	10*	10%	30%	60%	40%	10%	50%
5 years....	49	—	65%	35%	43%	12%	45%

* 21 infants of 4 years attempted to copy the figure but only 10 completed a recognizable square. One child drew a circle counter-clockwise and another drew a base line toward the right and the two sides upward.

4. *Copying Triangle*

Age	No. cases	Direction of					Draws rectangle instead of triangle, counter-clockwise	Draws circle instead of triangle, counter-clockwise
		Sides			Base			
		Up	Down	One up, one down	Right	Left		
4 years....	5	—	40%	—	20%	20%	40%	20%
5 years....	37	5%	87%	8%	60%	41%	—	—

5. *Copying Diamond*

Age	No. cases	Manner of drawing								
4 years....	4	—	—	—	—	—	25%	25%	25%	25%
5 years....	12	8%	33%	17%	25%	17%				

methods were (1) drawing the four sides, counter-clockwise, without raising the pencil, and (2) drawing the two right sides clockwise and the two left sides counter-clockwise.

In reviewing the results we find that the general tendency is to draw vertical lines downward, and this tendency is stronger at 5 years than at 4 years. Horizontal lines are more frequently drawn from left to right than from right to left. Whether these directional tendencies are due to innate disposition or to cultural influences remains an open question.

§ F. MOTOR TEST PROCEDURES

As suggested in Chapter XI, many of the motor tests can easily be improvised at the end of the formal test situation. Many other motor items can be obtained by report. Following is a list of the more important items which may be observed incidentally or which can be reported upon by the mother or attendant.

M-1: Walking and running
M-2: Stair behavior
M-3: Hopping and skipping
M-4: Jumping

M-5: Seating self in chair
M-6: Riding tricycle
M-7: Articulation

A few of the motor tests should be given more formally. The procedures for these tests follow.

M-8: Throwing ball (18–30 months). After the child has had an opportunity to name the ball (*Test Objects* situation), hand it to him saying, *"What do you do with it?"* Move the table away from in front of the child, invite him to stand up, and say, *"Throw it to me."* The examiner then catches or retrieves the ball, rolls it toward the child, saying, *"You get it—catch it."* After a few trials proceed with *Directions with ball.*

(3–5 years.) Roll the (small) ball across the room on the floor. Ask the child to get the ball, adding, *"Hurry up. Run."* Or, *"Catch it. Get it."* After he picks it up, say, *"Now throw it to me."* Then throw it back to the child, adapting your throwing to his ability to catch it. This enables observation of the way he catches, as well as of the way he throws.

Suggested procedure for more detailed observation (2½–6 years). The child stands behind a chalk line with his arms extended at his sides. The examiner says, *"When you hear the signal* THROW, *raise your arm and throw the ball as hard as you can."* The child is permitted three throws.

M-9: Walking into or kicking ball (18 months–5 years). Replace the small ball with the large ball, putting it on the floor immediately in front of the child's feet, the child having first been led to the center of the room away from available supports. Say, *"Kick the ball, give it a big kick,"* or if necessary, *"Kick it with your foot,"* even touching his shoes (both) if he does not understand the instructions. If necessary, demonstrate. At 4–5 years the ball may be handed to the child to elicit drop-kicking.

M-10: Stands on one foot (30 months–5 years). The examiner stands facing the child, who has been led to the center of the room away from available supports, and says, *"Look, see if you can stand on one foot like this."* The examiner demonstrates, holding the position. As soon as the child tries, say, *"Fine, keep it up,"* and count slowly, a count to a second. Repeat once or twice so that the child has a fair trial. If the child seems timid about trying, take his hand and try; then have him try again without support.

M-11: Walking boards (3–6 years). All of the boards are 10 cm. high from the floor, and 2.5 meters long. A square platform at each end of the board makes it possible for the child to start flush with the walking surface of the board and to finish with both feet at this level. As the child stands on the small platform ready to start, the examiner says, *"See this board? I want you to walk on top of it, 'way to the end. If you step off, step right back on again at the same place and keep on going until you get to the end. Do you understand? Ready, go."* Time is taken from the moment the child's first foot touches the board until both feet are placed on the platform at the other end. The boards are presented in order from the widest to the narrowest. The child always starts at the same end of the board and is given three trials at each board. Children use the shoes in which they come to the Clinic.

For clinical purposes it is best to use the 6 cm. board at 3 and 4 years; the 4 cm. board at 4 and 5 years; and the 2 cm. board at 5 and 6 years.

M-12: Pellets and bottle. The child is asked to sit straight in the chair with arms down at the sides. The single pellet is placed on the table six to eight inches from the table edge in the median plane of the child. The examiner says, *"Will you pick that up, please?"*

Situation 1. If the child has used the right hand for picking up the pellet, the pellets are presented on the left, the bottle on the right. If the child has picked up the pellet with the left hand, the pellets are put on the right side of the bottle. The objects are, as before, six to eight inches from the table edge. The pellets are arranged on the table with the flat side up and separated so that the distance between their centers is approximately one-half inch. The distance between the center of the cluster of pellets and the center of the bottle is between four and five inches. The child is then asked to put the pellets into the bottle.

Situation 2. When he has finished, the pellets and bottle are again arranged on the table in the manner just described, with the pellets at the right. The examiner says, *"Now pick up the pellets one by one and put them in the bottle and use only this hand,"* touching the child's right hand.

Situation 3. The pellets are then placed at the left and the child is requested to *"Pick up the pellets one by one and put them in the bottle, but this time use only this hand,"* touching the left.

Records are kept of the time required to put all ten pellets into the bottle. Time is counted from the instant the child touches the first pellet to the instant the last pellet is released. Records are also kept of the number of pellets picked up and released by each hand, the number accidentally dropped, and the method of prehension. (All three situations are presented to children 3, 4, 5, and 6 years of age.)

M-13: Tracing diamond and cross. Fold the paper so that only the diamond is exposed. Then say to the child, *"Now take your pencil and draw a line right around here, but don't go outside of the lines. Start right here and go around this way,"* pointing in a counter-clockwise direction, and adding again the warning, *"But be careful, don't go outside the lines."* When he has finished, the cross is presented in the same way. This test, described and developed by Porteus (106), is useful in revealing motor coordination and incidentally it also discloses related emotional characteristics.

M-14: Laterality and directional tendencies. Many examiners will wish to include in their clinical study of the child such observations as may conveniently be made as to laterality, but without the addition of time-consuming situations to the regular examination. Many of the standard situations offer an opportunity for observing hand preference or directional tendency and the notation of this aspect of the response can readily become a simple routine matter. It is understood, of course, that conclusions based upon such superficial observations are of limited value. Findings are to be taken as merely suggestive and for filling in the clinical picture—not as a basis for sweeping generalizations or recommendations, except in the light of special familiarity with the complex and inadequately understood subject of laterality.

Observation of the responses listed below, in the course of the examination, will give an indication of the child's tendencies in the matter of handedness and other aspects of laterality. Two special situations are suggested—the V-scope and Orientation cards—for those who may wish to include consideration of ocular dominance and the direction of preferential eye movements.

Handedness. Note hand used for

> drawing
> throwing
> pointing (to pictures, etc.)
> cube manipulation
> placing forms in formboard
> counting a row of pennies
> placing ball according to directions
> creasing folded paper

Ask the mother if the child has ever seemed to be left-handed (ignore such reported sinistrality below one year). Ask also whether any members of the immediate family are left-handed or ambilateral. In estimating the handedness tendencies shown in the above responses, consider the effect of the position of the child with respect to the object to which he is responding.

Footedness. Note foot used for

> kicking
> standing on one foot
> "stepping off" on walking boards

Eyedness. Note ·eye selection in looking at objects through V-scope (see M-15).

Direction tendency. Note spontaneous dextrad or sinistrad emphasis in

> drawing horizontal lines
> counting a row of pennies
> naming pictures on Orientation cards (see M-16)

M-15: V-scope (89). Two V-scopes of the conical type, referred to on page 359, are. used, with ten individual pictures. Have the child stand with his back to the wall, and produce the first V-scope, saying, *"This is a thing to look through. You look through it this way,"* demonstrating briefly, holding in both hands and looking through the large end. *"You hold it in both hands"* (extending it, large end toward the child, and pressing it open) *"and look through it. See, look at my finger."* (As he adjusts it to his eyes, step back several feet, holding up one finger directly in front of him. Adapt directions as necessary, until he has the idea.) Produce the second V-scope, saying, *"Now, take this one, and look through it,"* exchanging it for the first, and stepping back to a point between six and ten feet from the child, directly facing him. *"See how quickly you can tell me what the picture is that I am going to show you."* Show the picture briefly, but long enough for the child to name it. Repeat with the other cards, changing V-scopes each time. In all this be careful not to force a choice of eye; point the V-scope with its large end toward the child, place his hands correctly on it if necessary, but do this well below his eye-level and let him lift it himself.

When the child looks at an object through the V-scope, holding the large end to his eyes, he is unaware that he is seeing the object with only one eye, and selection of the preferred eye is automatic. The eye selected for looking at the card is readily noted by the examiner. If it is the left eye, the small end of the cone will be held a little to the right of center from the examiner's point of view; if the right eye, the end will be a little to the left. Make at least ten observations if possible, and record the preferred eye for each one. Naming of the pictures is irrelevant; an incorrect response is accepted and approved as heartily as a correct one.

Some 5-year-old children are sufficiently mature to be allowed to use the standard procedure for older subjects, placing both V-scopes on a table and allowing the child to interchange them himself between observations. Some 3-year-olds, on the other hand, cannot be tested satisfactorily, or cannot sustain attention for the full series. Fewer than five observations do not give satisfactory results, as variations from the usually preferred eye are particularly likely to come on the first two or three trials.

A substitute for the V-scope procedure, which may be used on occasion, is to have the child look at pictures through a small hole in a card or a piece of paper. The relationship between this method and the one described is not, however, clearly established, and the two methods may not consistently yield equivalent results.

M-16: Orientation cards (3–7 years). An unstandardized method for observing directional tendencies in following eye movements consists of a group of three cards, 5 x 8 inches in size, each having a row of seven pictures (see Plate XIXi). The center picture in each case is drawn larger and with heavier lines than the others in the row. The other pictures represent common objects of relatively neutral interest value. All the pictures are of symmetrical form.

Secure the child's attention. Place one card flat on the table, directly in front of the child, simultaneously pointing to the center picture and saying, *"What is this?"* When the child responds, say, *"That's right; now tell me what all the other pictures are."* This must be managed fairly quickly, but smoothly, so as not to allow the child time to glance over the rest of the pictures before he gets his instructions. Repeat with the other two cards. Record the order in which the smaller pictures are named, following the system indicated below.

The principal systematic ways of naming the pictures are as follows:

a.	1 2 3	4 5 6			
b.	4 5 6	1 2 3			
c.	6 5 4	3 2 1			
d.	6 5 4	1 2 3			
e.	3 2 1	6 5 4			
f.	3 2 1	4 5 6			

Variants of these orders though occasionally met with are rare.

In the absence of experimental results with these cards, the significance of the results may not be pushed too far; but they have been found helpful in connection with other observations in indicating a pronounced sinistrad tendency in following movements of the eyes, which may have a bearing upon the question of reading readiness. Clinical use suggests that the occurrence of types *a* and *b*, the left-to-right responses, increases with age through 6 and 7 years.

Procedures for a few of the motor tests are given in the chapter on adaptive behavior, since these tests have a double significance, but are primarily tests of adaptive behavior. One motor test is described in the language chapter. They are as follows:

M-17 Cube behavior (See A-2)
M-18 Pellet and bottle (See A-8)
M-19 Paper folding (See A-11)
M-20 Paper and crayon (See A-16)
M-21 Drawing of forms (See A-20)
M-22 Picture book (See L-1)

CHAPTER VII

ADAPTIVE BEHAVIOR

ADAPTIVE behavior has been described as "a convenient category for those varied adjustments, perceptual, orientational, manual, and verbal which reflect the child's capacity to initiate new experiences and to profit by past experiences." This description is quite consistent with the usual psychological definition of adaptive behavior as either an instinctive or an intelligent response. Instinct and intellect are so inextricably interwoven in the behavior of young children that it is not practicable to measure one without the other. To speak of intelligence tests for the preschool child is to ignore the true character of behavior at these ages. Furthermore, we wish to appraise both traits because a young child's potential intellectual ability is as dependent on the timely development of instinct, or in other words on maturation, as it is on the utilization of mature behaviors.

It will be clear when we discuss cube behavior, for instance, that a child normally, without training, puts one cube on another, building a tower. The timely development of this trait is as necessary for and as indicative of future development as building a bridge from the model. We have sound reasons for considering the first behavior more "instinctive" and the second behavior more "intellectual," but both are adaptive and both indicate a child's developmental progress. The first behavior, even though largely instinctive, is delayed in defective children. There may be a question whether the delay is real or whether it is occasioned by the child's lack of appreciation and pleasure in exercising the instinct, but there is no question about the significance of the delay, especially if it is marked. The term adaptive behavior is therefore a very pertinent one to describe that category of behavior in young children which most closely correlates with what in older children and adults is designated intelligence.

Adaptivity is reflected in all modes of behavior whether motor, language, or personal-social. But a child may have a motor deficiency, a language defect, or inadequate social adjustment and yet perform with relatively superior adaptivity in situations which minimize the influence of the handicap. It is the more essentially adaptive behavior with which the situations described in this section are concerned. The normal associated motor, verbal, and personal-social responses are also given their due consideration, since it is necessary to recognize the part they play in any child's response and since it is this total behavior which the psychologist in studying the child must control and interpret.

The examiner's attitude when presenting the tests, observing the elicited behavior, and evaluating it, is particularly important. With the exception of very few tests, such as judging the relative weights of blocks, there are no right or wrong responses. The child's behavior, whatever he does, is significant in appraising his particular way of responding. Failure to conform to the usual pattern of adaptation does not necessarily signify inability. After the standard procedures have been followed, modification of procedure is not only permissible but advisable. The modification should be in the nature of a psychological experiment in which the controlled factors are varied to favor the analysis of behavior.

The situations have been grouped roughly according to the functions which they emphasize. The grouping is more for convenience of exposition than it is logical or psychological. Obviously a long treatise could be written on any one of the topics presented. The wealth of references on drawing alone prohibits a comprehensive discussion. But it is hoped that by acquainting the examiner with the complications of behavior interpretation, some of the erroneous mechanical and uncritical applications of psychometric procedures may be avoided.

§ A. BLOCK BUILDING

Block play is one of the most common interests of the preschool child. As early as 36 weeks the infant combines two cubes. When 56 weeks old he places one cube over another, and when about 15 months old he actually builds a tower of two. With further advancing age, block building becomes more engrossing and elaborate. Even the 10-year-old does not scorn blocks. It is highly significant from the point of view of human development that the child's own initiative, his own behavior drive, produces this block building behavior. Blocks or cubes may be classed with rattles and dolls as being universal in their appeal to children's activity interest. It is the exceptional child who does not respond to them.

The test situations employ ten cubes and begin with an observation of the child's spontaneous play. Following this, the child is induced to imitate and copy model structures which the examiner demonstrates.

(A-1) SPONTANEOUS CUBE PLAY

This situation may be the first formal one presented. The child should not be hurried into activity but rather he should be given ample opportunity to make his own adjustment. When the picture book is used as the starting point of the examination, as recommended in Chapter XI, it is assumed that the child is seated in his chair for the cube situations.

Procedure. The cubes are in formation on the table, nine forming a square with the tenth cube on the middle one. If the child spontaneously seats himself and begins playing with the cubes, no direction is necessary. If he stands by his mother's side, as he may do, particularly if he is under 2 years of age, invite him to sit down. If he does not accept the invitation, pick up a cube and proffer it to him. As he takes it, quickly proffer a second, then a third, and so on until he can hold no more. Repeated proffering of the successive cubes eventually will exhaust his capacity to retain them; frequently at this point the child will come to the table to store his cubes. The situation may be continued with the child standing, if he obviously so prefers. If the examiner considers that standing may have hindered his performance, the situation may, as a check, be repeated later in the examination. Observation of spontaneous behavior should not be prolonged if the child throws or scatters the cubes.

If a child waits to be told what to do, say, *"Build something for me, anything you wish."* If the child hands or carries the cubes to his parent, simply ask the parent to replace them on the table.

Behavior trends. The *15-month-old* child has a strong locomotor drive. He may insist on standing. If he sits he will need help in getting seated. He accepts three blocks but tends to give them to his parent rather than store them. He will, however, accept four if they are presented with sufficient rapidity. His attention to the cubes is fleeting. Usually he indulges in no building activity but merely transposes the cubes or carries them to his parent. If he does place one block over another, he gives real evidence of pleasure when a tower results.

The *18-month-old child* still has a strong locomotor drive, but it is less dominant than at 15 months. He may insist on standing but he may, on the other hand, accept the chair. He may seat himself but he will need to have the chair pushed up to the table. When rapidly presented with the cubes, one by one, he stores them by holding them against himself with his hand. At the table his attention to the cubes is more prolonged than at 15 months. However, only about one-third of the children build. Instead, they merely pick up the cubes, hold them in each hand, replace them on the table, or scatter them.

The *2-year-old* child is less motor driven than the 18-month-old child. He seats himself and remains seated at the table. His constructive activity is spontaneous. The child either builds a tower or puts the blocks in a row. There are, however, a large number of children who indulge in no spontaneous block building. Instead, they simply hold the blocks or transpose them on the table.

The *3-year-old* child remains seated. He arranges the blocks horizontally, usually in a row. Only occasionally does a child of this age spontaneously build a tower. The vertical arrangement is superseded by horizontal alignment.

The *4-year-old* has made great strides over his year-younger self. He now builds a complicated structure and names it. Out of the thirty cases of the normative group,[1] seven built a complicated structure, extending vertically and laterally; six built a double tower of five blocks each; two built a double-decker train; and two built a bridge. Thus, more than half the children built in two directions, vertically and laterally. Four children arranged the blocks in a flat mass; two built an angle; and one child placed the blocks in a round triangular shape, calling it a man. Thus 25 per cent built in the horizontal and lateral planes. Only four children built in one dimension: two children built a single tower and two built a train without a chimney. No child built in three dimensions. One child showed no spontaneous interest in the cubes and one child's response was indefinite.

Twenty of the thirty children named their construction. Eight called it a house; two called it a building; one called it a church; one, a tent; and one, a garage. In other words, thirteen considered their structure a building. Two children who built two towers of five blocks each said they had made a chimney. Other interpretations were: a table, a man, a train, steps, and a bridge.

The *5-year-old* builds a complicated, three-dimensional structure; he usually names it a house, but he may call it anything from a bug to an elephant cage. Some children build several separate units, such as small towers, two or three bridges, or rows. Only a few children do not name their construction. They all build promptly and are then ready for the next task.

The *6-year-old* reverts to building in two dimensions, usually in the lateral and vertical planes. He appears to have less ambitious notions than a year ago and he now suits his construction to his material. He names his structure as at 5 years.

Sex differences. At 18 months the boys tend to give greater attention to vertical placement than horizontal alignment while at 2 years they align more blocks than they pile. The reverse is true for girls. At 18 months boys build a tower of four blocks, girls one of three blocks; at 2 years boys build a tower of only four blocks while girls build one of eight. At 18 months boys align two blocks, girls four; at 2 years boys align seven blocks, girls only five. This sex difference is rather well defined. One explanation may be that boys are more advanced in block

[1] For further details describing the normative group of subjects, see §1, page 319.

building activity since they make the transition from the vertical to horizontal arrangement at an earlier age than the girls.

Significance of the behavior. Since motivation for block building in this situation is left largely to the child, his construction is an expression of the dynamics of his activity, his resourcefulness, and his imagination. Because the situation is presented promptly in the test series, differences in quickness of adjustment will be a complicating factor. Children who adjust slowly will be shy and restrained; this inhibition will be reflected in their response. It is also true that a child who lacks initiative will not be as responsive to this situation as to one in which the task is more definitely prescribed. Whether any one instance of meager behavior is to be interpreted as inadequate adjustment or as dynamic poverty is a matter of clinical judgment.

The scattered unit type of building seen sometimes at 4, 5, and 6 years may or may not have personality significance. However, it does not have the abnormal connotation that it might signify in adult behavior. Perhaps the greatest value of this spontaneous play is that it serves as a warming-up period to the more directed cube situations which follow.

The developmental changes from vertical building at 2 years, to horizontal alignment at 3 years, to vertical and lateral construction of the 4-year-old child, to three-dimensional building at 5 years, and back to a simpler two-dimensional structure of the child at 6 years, are noteworthy and reasonable. They are consistent with the child's motor skills and his intellectual appreciation of form. The fact that the blocks are ten practically identical red cubes rather than an assortment of shapes and colors undoubtedly accounts for any discrepancy with the findings of other investigators of block play. For instance, Bühler and Hetzer (12) find that children build a two-dimensional structure at 3 years. Their blocks are varied in shape, and the blocks therefore suggest a varied arrangement. It is to be expected that they would elicit a two-dimensional building at an earlier age than ten cubes all alike.

SPONTANEOUS BLOCK PLAY
PERCENTAGE OF CASES DISPLAYING BEHAVIOR

Age in years	1½	2	3	4	5	6
Number of cases	39	32	35	30	49	16
Behavior:						
Leaves table or shows no interest	18	6	4	7	10	6
No constructive spontaneous play	69	47	?	6	10	0
Builds a tower	26	25	25	13	12	12
Puts blocks in row	5	23	75	10	6	0
Names construction			@50	70	82	94
Builds two-dimensional structure			0	80	27	81
Builds three-dimensional structure				6	55	12

(A-2) Tower Building

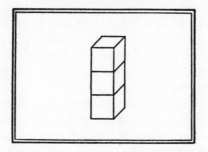

Tower building, as we have just seen, begins its spontaneous manifestation soon after the first year and continues to be the first response of one out of four children from 18 months through 3 years of age. After a child is a year-and-a-half old it is rare for him to make no attempt to imitate building the tower. Naturally if the child spontaneously builds a tower the examiner, after having observed the limit of his spontaneity, need only urge him to continue until the tower falls. If the tower is not a spontaneous response, the following procedure is used.

Procedure. Remove all cubes, except those which the child is holding, to the far side of the table. Attract the child's attention by saying, "*See,*" or "*Look,*" and build a tower of three blocks. Then push the blocks toward the child's right and say with appropriate gesture, "*You make one.*" If necessary, separate one block from the rest and point to it saying, "*Put it here,*" and at the same time give the child a block, if he does not already hold one. As a final resort, build a tower of two for the child and encourage him to place his cube on it. This may be repeated. After he starts building, urge him to continue building until the tower topples. Give him at least two trials to demonstrate his skill.

Behavior trends. The *15-month-old* child usually releases one block over the other with marked and rather abrupt extension of all fingers so that a tower may not be built on the first attempt. As the child repeats his performance a tower usually results. He will attempt to place the third block but as a rule he is unsuccessful, and in his attempt he is quite likely to destroy his tower of two. The child may be interested in repeating his successful performance but his interest is short-lived. He may hand the block to the examiner or to his mother, or he may simply push the blocks away or brush them to the floor.

The *18-month-old* child may attempt to add to the examiner's structure but when restrained he succeeds in building a tower of two blocks on his first attempt. The placement of the cube is more exact than at 15 months, although the release of the cube is still frequently exaggerated. The tower may fall with the third block but on repeated trials the child can usually build a tower of four cubes. The 18-month-old child persists longer than he did three months ago. He is still socially inclined and he may repeatedly hand the cubes to the examiner or take them to his parent who is asked to give them back to the examiner.

The *2-year-old* child still shows a tendency either to dismantle the examiner's model or to use it as a basis for his own construction. But he does build completely a tower of seven on one of three trials. It should be noted that although one child out of four of this age spontaneously builds a train, they all build a tower after demonstration.

The *3-year-old* responds to the verbal direction accompanied by gesture. For him the model is no longer necessary. On his best performance he can build a tower of ten cubes.

Sex differences. Although spontaneously 2-year-old girls are likely to build a taller tower than boys, the boys build as high as the girls when the task is set for them and they are urged. The difference in spontaneous activity is not one of skill but of motivation.

Significance of the behavior. There is a definite adaptive component to placing one cube on another and releasing it there. The behavior is a very natural one; it develops slowly but surely, so surely that children whose environment has lacked objects like cubes which could be piled, nevertheless display the ability at the appointed stage of their development. The appearance of the behavior cannot be hastened markedly by training.

It should be noted that a child can be induced to build a tower before he is likely to do so spontaneously. But this does not mean that his performance is purely imitative and that he learns to build a tower by following an example. The example merely elicits behavior for which the child is functionally mature. The period of spontaneous observation is brief. If it were lengthened, tower building would be observed more frequently.

After a child has learned to build a tower of two, erecting towers of greater height depends on motor skill; that is, on a cautious placing of the cumulative cubes and on aligning the cubes so precisely that a maximum of stability is secured. Below 3 years the height of the tower also depends to some extent on the child's attention span. However, the examiner's urging can usually keep the child sufficiently motivated so that attention span is here a relatively unimportant aspect of the behavior.

TOWER BUILDING

PERCENTAGE OF CASES SHOWING BEHAVIOR

Age in years	1	1½	2	3
Number of cases	25	41	34	34
Behavior:				
Dismantles examiner's structure	33	20	18	0
Adds to examiner's structure	5	27	38	0
No attempt to imitate	43	17	3	0
Approaches cube with cube in hand	76			
Places cube on cube	40			
Builds tower of 2 cubes	16	100		
Builds tower of 3 cubes	0	92	100	
Builds tower of 4 cubes		77	97	100
Builds tower of 5 cubes		44	85	97
Builds tower of 6 cubes		27	76	97
Builds tower of 7 cubes		20	56	94
Builds tower of 8 cubes		7	27	79
Builds tower of 9 cubes		7	15	73
Builds tower of 10 cubes		0	9	58

(A-3) TRAIN

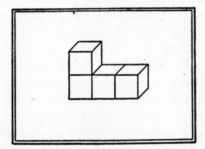

Putting blocks in a row, train-fashion, occurs in the spontaneous play of children as young as 2 years of age, and it is the preferred activity of the 3-year-old. The train which is demonstrated has a chimney added and is pushed as the examiner says *"Choo-choo."*

Procedure. If the child has built a three-cube tower, attract his attention by saying, *"Look," "See,"* or *"Watch"* and place three blocks slowly and with emphasis in line, saying *"One car, two cars, three cars,"* as the blocks are placed. Build well out of the child's reach, otherwise, he may disarrange the train before it is completed. Put the fourth block on the third and say, *"See, the train goes choo-choo-choo."* Leave the model standing and push four blocks toward the child saying, *"You make one."* If the child reaches for the model train, shield it with your hand and say, *"This is mine, you make one."*

Behavior trends. It is usually not profitable to give this test to the average *15-month-old child.* If it is given, the behavior will result either in continued block building or in roughly pushing the blocks.

The *18-month-old* child usually makes no attempt to construct the train, but if he does build, he makes a tower instead of placing the blocks in a row. Some children will either try to dismantle the model or add to it. However, if the child is a boy he will usually push the blocks. A few 18-month-old children can be expected to say "Choo-choo" or "Toot-toot" as they push the blocks along.

The *2-year-old* puts the four blocks in a row; he does not add the chimney. A minority, more girls than boys, make no attempt to build a train; instead they build a tower. A majority of the boys, but only a minority of the girls, push the blocks train-fashion. Less than one-fifth of the children of this age add the chimney to the train.

The *3-year-old* child builds the train with its chimney. He may even use the third car for a second chimney, but given a second trial he copies the examiner's model.

Sex differences. Some sex differences in behavior have been noted. At 2 years almost half the girls, but only about a quarter of the boys, make no attempt to imitate the train. Pushing the train is more of a masculine trait than a feminine one. Percentages at 1½ years for 19 boys and 21 girls are 53 and 33 respectively; at 2 years, for 15 boys and 19 girls, they were 60 and 37 per cent.

Significance of the behavior. The train combines a vertical and lateral alignment of the blocks. As in the tower situation, the demonstrated model elicits behavior before the same behavior occurs in spontaneous cube play. The sequence of response with age is unchanged. Even when the child has the model before him, the genetic seriation of his behavior is: piling the cubes one on the other, then aligning them on the table, and finally building in two dimensions.

Sometimes this situation is responded to later in the examination when the child has failed to respond at the time the situation was presented. The notion of train is a dramatic one, especially for the boys.

TRAIN BEHAVIOR
PERCENTAGE OF CASES SHOWING BEHAVIOR

	1½	2	3
Age in years	1½	2	3
Number of cases	40	34	25
Behavior:			
Scatters or throws cubes	23	12	0
Builds tower	25	29	4
No attempt to imitate train	48	38	4
Puts cubes in row	23	62	96
Pushes train	49	47	96
Adds chimney	0	15	96

(A-4) Bridge

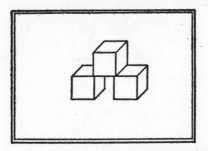

The bridge is a simple structure of three blocks, one block resting on the top edges of two separated blocks. The bridge is more difficult for the child to build than the tower or the train, but less difficult than the gate. The structure is called a bridge not for the purpose of naming it to the child, but merely to identify it on the record. To some children the structure represents a bridge, to others a tunnel, a building, or steps. To name the model may therefore merely confuse the child and had best be avoided.

Procedure. If the child built a tower but not the train, build a simple bridge of three blocks as follows: Attract the child's attention by saying, *"Look, see what I am doing."* Place two cubes on the table separated less than an inch, then place a third cube resting on the upper edges of the two buttress blocks. Leave the model in view. Give the child three blocks and motion him to build one like the model. If the child does not leave a space between the two buttress blocks, say, *"See"* and put your finger or pencil in the space of the model. If his design is unlike the model, ask him, *"Is it just like this one?"* If the child has built both the tower and the train, build the bridge behind a cardboard screen, remove the screen, and ask him to build one like it.

Behavior trends. The 2-year-old child makes no attempt to duplicate the bridge, instead he may build a tower or he may put the cubes in a row. A very few children at this age scatter or throw the cubes.

The *3-year-old* child cannot build a bridge from the model but he can build it when its construction is demonstrated.

The *4-year-old* child can almost invariably build the bridge, merely given the model.

Sex differences. No consistent differences were noted.

Significance of the behavior. The development of bridge building ability between 2 and 3 years is very rapid. Errors of construction are interesting. The first difficulty which a child encounters is in separating the blocks and the second is in placing the top block so that it spans the two base cubes. Occasionally a child is able to correct his error when the discrepancy with the model is indicated to him, but usually if given a second trial he repeats his mistake.

BRIDGE

PERCENTAGE OF CASES SHOWING BEHAVIOR

Age in years	2	3	4
Number of cases	33	34	30
Behavior:			
Builds tower	21	0	0
Puts cubes in row	21	0	0
No attempt to imitate	73	3	0
Imitates or copies	9	80	100
Copies	0	35	100

(A-5) THE GATE

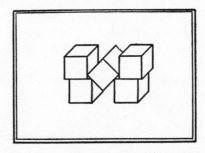

The gate is a more elaborate and delicately balanced structure than the bridge. It is usually not observed in spontaneous behavior but it resembles structures which the normal child from 3½ to 4 years of age is likely to build. The 3-year-old child may reject the situation, but after that age children appear to put forth their best efforts in duplicating the model.

Procedure. Say to the child, *"Shut your eyes and I'll make something for you."* Use a cardboard screen and build the gate as illustrated. When finished say, *"Look now."* Give the child five cubes, saying, *"You make one for me just like this."* Urge the child if necessary but let him work as he chooses unless he says that he is going to make something different. If his structure differs from the model, a sketch on the record will help in describing his error. If he is unsuccessful in duplicating the model, remake the gate as he watches and then give him a second trial. In building the gate use only one hand so that the child can see clearly how the blocks are placed.

Behavior trends. The *3-year-old* may reject the situation, but usually he will make some attempt to imitate building the gate. He is quite unsuccessful in duplicating the model.

The *4-year-old* builds the gate when its construction is demonstrated, but he cannot yet build it from the model.

The *5-year-old* easily builds the gate presented only with the model.

Sex differences. At 4 years the boys are more skillful than the girls. Only 42 per cent of the girls, as opposed to 75 per cent of the boys, gave a successful performance. At 5 years, however, 93 per cent of the girls, but only 60 per cent of the boys, built the gate from the model.

Significance of the behavior. To build the gate requires attentiveness, perception of form, and manual skill. Errors of construction are: placing the diagonal block as in the bridge, or resting the diagonal block on two separated towers of two blocks each.

Usually when the child refuses to cooperate it is because the performance is in advance of his ability. There are a few children, however, who on urging will be successful even though they doubt their ability.

THE GATE

PERCENTAGE OF CASES DISPLAYING BEHAVIOR

Age in years	3	4	5	6
Number of cases	34	30	59	16
Behavior:				
Attempts to build	53	100	—	—
Imitates building	6	60	93	
Copies	3	23	75	94

(A-6) STEPS

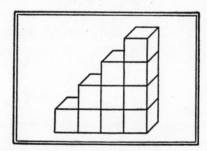

It is difficult for the adult to appreciate how much harder it is for the child to reconstruct the steps than to copy the gate. Although the 5-year-old easily builds the gate from a model, even the 6-year-old usually cannot complete the steps. To the adult the steps would probably have more meaning and thus be easier to reconstruct. Unlike the gate which children are sometimes reluctant to try because they anticipate failure, the steps appear to be easy to the child. He starts building with great confidence saying yes, he can do it, even though he promptly becomes confused as he builds.

Procedure. If the child succeeds in building the gate, say to him, *"Shut your eyes while I make something for you again."* Behind a cardboard screen arrange the cubes four on the first row, three on the second row, two on the third row, and one on top—as in the diagram above. Remove the cardboard and tell the child to look. Say, *"See the steps, one, two, three, four!"* touching the steps in turn. Ask the child, *"Can you make this for me?"* If he says no, urge him to try.

Behavior trends. The *5-year-old* child begins confidently to construct the steps but he is quite unable to do so. Instead he usually arranges the blocks in a solid wall. Probably more by chance than by design, two steps result. Occasionally a child will attempt to place one cube on top of another but out of alignment so that a steplike structure results. Since these blocks are only partly supported, they topple and the child either tries to hold them up with his hand or to erect some type of brace for them. He finally gives up the task without discovering the solution.

The *6-year-old* child is more successful than when he was a year younger. His finished product now has three steps but he cannot yet reconstruct the model. He may even reach the point where one block correctly placed would bring success but instead he uses the block to fill the space where a step should be. It is not until after 6 years that he correctly duplicates the model.

Sex differences. No differences have been noted.

Significance of the behavior. There is an important difference between the steps situation and other cube situations. In the other cube situations the model is left standing while the child builds; in the steps situation the model is destroyed. To build the steps a child must keep in mind a picture or a concept of what he is constructing. The construction which he views as he builds confuses him and he loses sight of his objective. His own natural building play is another diverting factor.

STEPS

PERCENTAGE OF CASES SHOWING BEHAVIOR

	5	6
Age in years	5	6
Number of cases	59	18
Behavior:		
Reconstructs two steps	61	83
Reconstructs three steps	36	67
Reconstructs model	5	39

§ B. FORM ADAPTATION

For convenience the following situations are grouped for discussion: cubes in (and out of) cup; pellet in (and out of) bottle; pellets in bottle; rod, block and ball into and ball out of performance box; and paper folding. These situations have genetic and behavior factors in common. The first four involve the fundamental relationships of container and contained; of "putting in" and "taking out." They involve perception and exploitation of relationships of shape, dimension and depth. In this sense they all demand form adaptation at a manipulatory level, although each situation calls for a different complex of abilities. Cup and cubes, and pellets and bottle behavior evoke spontaneous play activities; while pellets and bottle and the performance box with rod, square block and ball present problems to be solved. Paper folding, while it lacks the relationship of container and contained, nevertheless requires manipulation of the paper in an imitative adaptive manner in much the same way that these functions are necessary for the insertion of the square block into the performance box. To fold the paper correctly, the child must observe the examiner's movements and translate them into his own. He must keep in mind the sequences of maneuvers and, finally, he must differentiate between longitudinal, vertical, and diagonal folding. He must also keep in mind the form which results from the series of maneuvers.

Other situations which require adaptations to form are the cube situations of the previous section and the formboards of the following section. It must be recognized too that in a broad sense much adaptive behavior is combining activity, which entails orientation and adaptation to visual form cues.

Limiting our discussion to the first four situations which follow, it is interesting to note how complex simple "putting in" and "taking out" is for the unsophisticated child. He must learn to release the cube into the wide-mouthed cup, the pellet into the narrow-necked bottle, the rod into the small hole, and the square into its vertical slot. For each in turn a higher degree of maturity is required. The child can open his whole hand in the cup but only the tips of his finger and thumb can be inserted into the bottle. The rod must be held horizontal and perpendicular to the performance box surface, while the square must in addition be vertically oriented. To perceive these requirements, even in a partial, empirical way, is to respond adaptively.

(A-7) CUP AND CUBES

The cup and cubes situation is one which elicits significant and discriminating behavior even in infants as young as 32 weeks. Then the child begins to alternate his attention between the cup and cubes, rather than to manipulate one to the exclusion of the other. From this stage he develops to the point where he combines the cup and cubes in his play and he finally reaches the age of 1 year when he actually puts a cube in the cup. This putting of cubes in the cup becomes a more and more engrossing activity, reaching a peak at about 18 months. The situation elicits typical and spontaneous behavior in the child from 1 to 3 years.

Occasionally some parent who has restrained his child from playing with the cup will raise the eyebrows quizzically when it is presented as a test toy, but the examiner can easily explain that the cup is not like the child's cup. Children rarely show any inhibition in the situation because of their training and only very rarely do they reject the situation. The transition from cubes to cup and cubes is a natural and easy one.

Procedure. When the block building situations are terminated, either because they have been completed or because the child's interest has flagged, push the cubes toward the child and introduce the cup, placing it at the left of the cubes or at the right, if the child is left-handed. Usually no directions are necessary, particularly at the younger age levels. However, if the child does not spontaneously put the cubes in the cup, say, *"Put the blocks in the cup."* If this verbal suggestion does not release activity, point to the cup, saying, *"Put it here,"* or finally, even drop one cube into the cup as a nest egg.

Behavior trends. The *1-year-old* child releases one or more cubes in the cup. He may remove the cube or cubes from the cup, or he may transpose the cup with its contents to lap or chair. He also engages in activity merely with the cubes, throwing them, holding them, or otherwise manipulating them.

The *15-month-old child* puts several cubes in the cup, removes all but one, and then replaces the removed cubes in the cup. He works intently, referring occasionally to his parent. He rarely engages in play with the cubes alone.

The *18-month-old* child fills the cup, takes out five or six cubes, and then refills the cup. He repeats this behavior for long periods and is so preoccupied with his task that he rarely refers to his parent.

The *2-year-old* child fills the cup with cubes but instead of removing them he is likely to hand the full cup to the examiner. The few children who do take the cubes out of the cup, remove eight or ten cubes as contrasted with the four or six cubes which the 18-month-old child removes.

Sex differences. Boys and girls show similar tendencies to fill the cup, but girls are more likely than boys to repeatedly remove and replace the cubes. At 18 months, 71 per cent of the girls, and only 53 per cent of the boys, removed the cubes; at 2 years, the percentages were 36 and 18 for girls and boys respectively.

CUP AND CUBES

Percentage of Cases Showing Behavior

Age in years	1	1½	2
Number of cases	39	37	22
Behavior:			
Scatters or throws	69	14	9
Places cubes in cup	51	62	91
Number placed in cup	1	10	10
Removes cubes from cup	41	65	27
Number removed from cup		6	9

Significance of the behavior. Putting the cubes in the cup is playful adaptive activity, the counterpart of which is seen from early infancy to maturity. The infant puts his toe in his mouth and the adult putts the golf ball into the hole on the green, while the preschooler puts the cubes into the cup. But the adaptive significance of the cubes and cup play is not so much in the mere, fact of putting the cubes in the cup, as it is in the child's attention span when engaged in this activity. At 1 year he is satisfied with one cube in the cup. Other interests probably distract him. As he grows older he attends to the situation longer and he not only fills the cup with cubes, but removes them to repeat the activity. This repetitive behavior, quite normal at 18 months, may suggest abnormality when at a later age it is not superseded by more intricate or more constructive activity.

(A-8) Pellet and Bottle

Another "putting in" behavior is that associated with the pellet and bottle. It is astonishing how automatic the response of dropping the pellet into the bottle becomes at the toddling age. Direction is frequently unnecessary. The performance has great intrinsic interest. Even a child who rejects the cubes is finally won over when he sees the small pellet and the bottle. Extracting the pellet after it is dropped within furnishes a real problem which the child solves according to his maturity.

Procedure. Place the pellet and bottle on the table, the pellet at the right of the bottle as the child faces them. (At the left if the child is left-handed.) If he does not spontaneously put the pellet within, say to him, *"Put it in the bottle."* If the child is unsuccessful, drop the pellet within the bottle for him. If he starts to eat the pellet, gently restrain him, saying, *"No, put it in here,"* pointing to the bottle. As soon as the pellet is within the bottle most children will try to extract it. If a child makes no such attempt say, *"Get it out."* If he fails after making a reasonably persisting attempt, dump the pellet out and re-present the situation. In any event give the child at least two trials in extracting the pellet.

Behavior trends. The *15-month-old* child drops the pellet in the bottle.

10

He then tries to extract the pellet by shaking the bottle. This method may be successful. He may, however, insert his finger in the bottle, attempting to hook the pellet, or he may finally turn the bottle over so that the pellet drops out.

The *18-month-old* child very promptly drops the pellet within and then shakes the bottle, inserts his finger pulling at the pellet, and finally dumps the pellet out by turning over the bottle.

The *2-year-old* drops the pellet within and then almost as promptly turns the bottle on its side, and pours the pellet out.

Sex differences. No sex differences have been noted.

PELLET AND BOTTLE

PERCENTAGE OF CASES DISPLAYING BEHAVIOR

	1	1½	2
Age in years	1	1½	2
Number of cases	37	37	33
Behavior:			
Drops pellet in bottle	25	92	100
Shakes bottle or pokes within	78	68	39
Inserts finger in bottle	25	57	39
Finally dumps pellet out	33	65	97
Promptly pours pellet out	0	33	61

Significance of the behavior. The child only gradually learns the physical laws of his environment, and only gradually acquires an appreciation of relative size and shape. The various methods which he uses to extract the pellet from the bottle reveal his acquired knowledge. The alertness with which he perceives a solution to the extraction of the pellet is a good example of his adaptivity.

The motor skill involved in putting the pellet in the bottle has been discussed in Chapter VI. It must also be recognized that turning the bottle over to pour the pellet out requires a certain motor maturity and skill as well as insight.

(A-9) PELLETS AND BOTTLE

The pellets and bottle furnish for the child of 2 years and under a situation which is similar to the cup and cubes with respect to "putting-in" behavior. The occasional child to whom the cup and cubes situation does not appeal can usually be induced to respond when pellets and bottle are introduced.

For the older child the situation may be used as a test of manual dexterity by timing the performance. If the determination of handedness is important, the procedure described in Chapter VI, § F, is appropriate. Otherwise use the simple procedure which follows.

Procedure. Place the ten pellets, resting on their convex surface, and separated slightly for convenient prehension, at the right of the bottle (or at the left if the child is left-handed). Ask the child to put them in the bottle. Start the stop watch at the moment when he touches the first pellet and stop it as he releases the last pellet into the bottle. Give the child two trials.

Behavior trends. No time scores are available for 18 months and 2 years. At *3 years* the average time taken by seven children was about 30 seconds; at *4 years*, the average time of twenty-eight children was 25 seconds; at *5 years*, fifty-seven children, 20 seconds; and at *6 years*, eleven children, 18 seconds.

Sex differences. Slight differences of about 2 seconds were found in favor of the boys.

Significance of the behavior. There are great individual differences in speed of performance among children. On the average, the children showed no handedness differences in speed when they were first allowed to use either hand, then only the preferred hand, and then the less preferred hand—the preferred hand being determined initially by the prehension of a single pellet. Probably the increase in skill through practice was sufficient to offset any right-handed tendency of the average child.

(A-10) PERFORMANCE BOX

The performance box combines the features of the pellet and bottle and the formboard; its appeal to children is great. The fact that the box also serves as a container for other test materials, as well as a receptacle into which the child may toss the ball, makes the box triply useful. Occasionally at the end of the examination, children trudge the box about and thereby display informally gross motor skills which supplement the behavior observed in the routine tests. Furthermore, there are other tests of orientation for which the box may be adapted (Meyer, 88).

Procedure. Place the box on the table with the holes in the vertical plane and with the open end of the box at the child's right. The box should be at a convenient working distance from the table edge. Hand the child the round rod and say, *"Put it in here,"* pointing to the middle hole. If the child does not insert and release the rod after reasonable urging and pointing, slowly demonstrate the insertion while he watches. Then quickly turn the performance box, open end toward the child, and let the rod roll out. Reorient the box for the second trial or let him get it by reaching. Unless the response is prompt and well defined, give three trials.

In a similar manner present the square block. When demonstrating the insertion of the square, first tip it, introducing the lower corner into the hole, then turn the block up and push it within.

Behavior trends. The *15-month-old* child places the rod in the hole and releases it. He briefly tries to insert the square and then gives it to the examiner, puts it on the top of the box, or otherwise disposes of it.

The *18-month-old* child not only inserts the rod in the round hole, but he also explores the possibilities of insertion in other holes, frequently inserting the rod without release. He attempts to insert the square but he is unsuccessful. He may insert a corner in either the aperture on the right or that on the left of the box, but he cannot adjust the square for full insertion in its proper hole.

The *2-year-old* after demonstration inserts and releases the square into the box.

Significance of the behavior. Putting the rod or square into the performance box involves perception of form relationships and relative sizes, as well as adaptive, manual coordination. Rod insertion requires that the rod be directed so that it will not hit the edge of the hole. The square must be both turned and tilted properly for insertion.

The performance box emphasizes release ability. The fact that the block drops completely within may inhibit release even for those children for whom voluntary release is otherwise possible. Children of this age are loath to relinquish a treasured object, particularly if by doing so it appears lost to them. This may account in part for the fact that the child at 15 months is more likely to release the rod than when he is three months older. Also it has been pointed out in Chapter VI that release is facilitated by pressure against another object; the very act of dropping the rod or block within the box prohibits this facilitation.

The personal-social adjustment of the child is likewise a factor in his performance box response. The generous, uninhibited child will naturally be more likely to enter into the cooperative play that the situation demands than will a child of the opposite disposition.

We may say in summary that success on this test involves to a large extent adaptive, manual coordination and social adjustment and, to a lesser extent, form perception ability and traits of adaptive perseveration.

(A-10) Supplementary. Performance Box and Ball

The use of the performance box as a receptacle into which the ball may be thrown and from which it may be retrieved has been suggested. Throwing the ball into the box has only a very minor adaptive component; it is mainly a motor response. But since even the 2-year-old prefers to drop rather than throw the ball into the box, the test does not reveal genetic changes in throwing ability. However, retrieving the ball from the box presents a problem somewhat comparable to extracting the pellet from the bottle or securing the ball from the table. The test is useful only at the 18 to 21 months behavior age span when the child is steady on his feet and his reach is yet inadequate for obtaining the ball directly.

Procedure. After the *Following-directions-with-the-ball* test, give the child the ball and present the open end of the performance box at his elbow level and about four inches beyond his reach, tipping the box to an angle of about 45 degrees. Say, *"Throw the ball in the box."* If he walks toward the box, gently restrain him with your free hand. Urge him to try. If he fails, allow him to drop the ball within, or drop it within for him. Then place the box upright on the floor and say, *"Get the ball— get it out."* He may be urged with, *"I see the ball. You get it."* Guard against his falling with the box when he leans too far over it, or tries to climb in.

Behavior trends. The *18-month-old* child reaches into the box but is unsuccessful in retrieving the ball. He abandons his attempts to get the ball fairly promptly and he may instead push or carry the box about or exploit the box holes.

The *21-month-old* child reaches into the box, and not reaching the ball, he then tips or overturns the box, securing the ball.

The *2-year-old* can reach the ball directly.

PERFORMANCE BOX AND BALL

PERCENTAGE OF CASES RESPONDING AS INDICATED*

Age in months	18	21	24
Behavior:			
Reaches into box	93	95	100
Tips or overturns	32	61	28
Abandons task promptly	54	27	34
Secures ball by reaching	4	4	52
Secures ball by any method	21	56	72

* Based on clinical observations (see §1)

Significance of the behavior. Securing the ball from the box offers an interesting contrast to extracting the pellet from the bottle. The fact that the pellet is always visible while the ball may be lost to view is probably the reason why the pellet is pursued longer than the ball. Direct reaching is resorted to in both instances but with the pellet that method is less efficient and hence dumping is the mature response for securing the pellet, while reaching within is the mature response in the case of the ball in the box.

The situation not only reveals a child's ability to solve the problem but it also shows his response to a problem situation similar to those described in § H. In the face of failure the child may abandon his efforts good-naturedly persist, become temperish and somewhat violent, appeal for help, or ingeniously try various methods such as standing on a chair, apparently to lengthen his arms, or climbing into the box head or feet foremost.

Observations on handedness in difficult reaching are another by-product of this situation.

(A-11) PAPER FOLDING

The test is a very simple one which requires merely two sheets of paper. The size of the square sheet may be slightly varied from the convenient 8.5-inch specification. The examiner should fold the paper in the same direction which the child will use. The near corners should be aligned with the far corners.

The child's folded paper may be dated and filed away as part of the case record.

Procedure. Take a square sheet of paper, say to the child, *"Now watch me."* I. Fold the paper over once and crease it, as shown below I. Hand an uncreased square sheet of paper to the child and say, *"You do it."* II. If the child imitates, fold the paper two times and again hand over an uncreased sheet. III. Repeat II and add a diagonal crease, and hand over an uncreased sheet as before. The dotted lines in the figures indicate where each fold in its turn is to be made. Do not rotate the paper as it is folded.

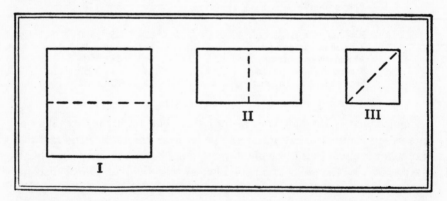

Behavior trends. The *18-month-old* child may turn the edge of the paper over or he may merely imitate the creasing motion without first folding the paper.

The *2-year-old* child definitely turns the edge of the paper over but he does not necessarily crease it.

The *3-year-old* folds the paper twice, creases, and may attempt the third fold.

The *4-year-old* folds the paper three times and creases.
Discriminative behavior.

Age	Behavior
21 months........	Folds over, not necessarily evenly
30 months........	Folds twice and creases
48 months.........	Folds three times, last diagonally, three creases

Significance of the test. The first attempts of the child to fold the paper are in terms of the maturity of his manual coordination. He may crumple it in his zeal to imitate; he may be impressed by the creasing and forget that the paper should be first folded over, just as he echoes the last of a sentence which is too long for him to remember.

The last diagonal fold is more difficult to execute than the two previous folds. Kuhlmann in his new scale (76) places diagonal folding at 4 years 7 months, and longitudinal or lateral folding at 1 year 11 months.

PAPER FOLDING*

PERCENTAGE OF CASES DISPLAYING BEHAVIOR

	1½	2	3
Age in years......................	1½	2	3
Number of cases...................	25	21	25
Behavior:			
Folds and creases once.............	0	19	96
Folds over......................	32	62	96
Creasing motion..................	32	29	96
Excessive folding.......:.........	24	33	0
Folds II.........................		?	84
Folds III........................	0		36

* Four-year norms are not available but clinical experience indicates that at least half of the four-year-olds fold the paper three times.

§ C. FORM DISCRIMINATION

A prompt errorless solution of the tests which are described in this section involves principally form discriminative ability. The forms are all simple, geometric ones and the test is either to put blocks of varying shape in their appropriate holes or to identify, from among an array of forms, the one which matches the form presented. At low levels of maturity, other abilities enter into the solution of the problem to such an extent that the form discrimination aspect of the test is almost completely overshadowed. Nevertheless, it is both convenient and appropriate to consider as a whole the developmental process by which the child's abilities mature and integrate until finally his form discrimination powers are permitted their more complete expression.

Manual and practical-minded children are more likely to do well on these tests than are the verbally minded and imaginative children. It will be interesting to compare the formboard situations with the performance box situation of the previous section. Both involve "putting in" behavior but the formboard involves relatively greater form perception ability and adaptation to success or failure, while the performance box emphasizes adaptive manual coordination.

(A-12) THREE-HOLE FORMBOARD

The three-hole formboard affords an excellent means of testing the young child's form discrimination ability, his attention span, and his general adaptivity. The behavior required, putting the blocks into their corresponding holes, is normally such spontaneous activity that verbal directions may be reduced to a minimum. The majority of children are promptly attracted by the board and blocks. They will frequently work long and persistently at the task of insertion. Even those few children who initially reject the test usually apply themselves well when it is re-presented later in the examination.

The test situation is one in which the child's performance can be very easily affected favorably or adversely by the procedure. It is essential that the child's attention be secured for demonstration of insertion and of rotation of the board. The child should be allowed his freedom, to sit or stand, as he prefers; he should be allowed to divert his attention to the room but he should be re-interested in his task at an appropriate moment. The board should be turned slowly so that he can see its motion, but not so slowly that his attention wanders. Urging at the proper moment, showing approval when a successful insertion is made, and being generally encouraging and responsive help the child to do his best. Actual aid by glance or gesture should of course be avoided. The specific procedure follows.

Procedure. Place the formboard on the table so that the round hole is at the child's right, the apex of the triangle is directed away from him, and the board is at a convenient working distance from the table edge. Allow the child to handle the board and otherwise inspect it if he wishes, replacing it before presenting the block or blocks.

Up to the age of 2 years, proceed as follows: Hand the child the round block and say, *"Put it in the hole."* If after a brief period of exploration he does not successfully insert the block, point to the round hole and say, *"Put it in here."* If the child either does not bring the block to the round hole or merely releases it over the hole without inserting it, secure his attention and slowly with deliberation place the round block in its hole, then lift the board, re-present the block, and replace the board in its original position on the table for the second trial. If the child prefers, he himself may be allowed to remove the block from the hole after the demonstration.

If the child is successful in inserting the round block, lift the board and rotate it 180°, keeping the plane of the board horizontal to the table. Be sure that the child perceives the turning of the board. Replace the board on the table with the round hole now at the child's left, and re-present the block as before. Give the child at least three trials to test his adaptivity.

If the child successfully adapts the round block to the board, proceed with the three-block test prescribed for 2-year-old children.

At 18 months, the examiner may prefer to begin the situation by presenting all three blocks at once, using the procedure for the 2-year level and then revert to the procedure used for younger children by testing for adaptation of the round block alone to the turning of the board. If the child is successful with the round block, the three-block situation may again be presented. If this order is used, there will be the corresponding modification in the child's response indicated in the section discussing behavior trends.

With 2-year-old children and older, begin as follows: Place the board on the table, round hole at the child's right and triangular apex pointing away from him. Then place the three blocks in front of their respective holes at the table edge near the child and say, *"Put the blocks where they belong."* If the child merely piles the blocks or otherwise does not conform to the expected response, point to the holes saying, *"Put them here."* If he does not fully insert the blocks say, *"Way in."* If necessary complete or demonstrate full insertion.

When all of the blocks are finally in their holes, lift the board and replace it on the table, pushing the blocks to the table edge for a second trial. Allow at least three trials. During any trial, replace on the table in its original position any block misplaced by the child.

If the child is successful in placing the blocks correctly in their holes, rotate the board 180°, keeping its plane horizontal to the table, and replace it on the table with the square hole near the round block and the round hole near the square block. As before, replace on the table in its original position any block which has been misplaced and which would hinder the placement of the correct block. When the child has completed the first trial, reorient the board by lifting and turning it as before; then replace it for the second trial. Give the child at least three trials. The time limit for successful scoring is one minute, but it is frequently desirable to permit the child to continue his efforts beyond this time.

Behavior trends. The *15-month-old* child promptly places the round block in its hole in response to pointing. He may adapt, by chance or otherwise, to the turning of the board by inserting the round block, or he is likely to attempt to insert the round block in the other holes in what appears to be an experimental manner. It is suggested that at this age he may know in which hole the block has recently fitted and yet not know that it will not fit in the other holes. He therefore explores all possibilities. At this age the child soon rejects the situation by leaving the table, by pushing the board away, by throwing the blocks to the floor, or by disregarding the blocks and manipulating the board itself.

The *18-month-old* child easily adapts the round block to the board when it is turned. Presented with all three blocks, he inserts the circle and either the square or the triangle, but he does not leave them in place and he tries them in holes other than the ones in which they belong, pressing them hard against the board as if to force the forms into place. The insertion of the blocks is accomplished by pushing them about rather than by adaptive turning. Frequently the blocks are merely placed over the holes rather than inserted. When the board is rotated, the child does not adapt to the turning.

If at 18 months of age the formboard is presented initially with all three blocks before their respective holes, the child usually merely piles the blocks in his spontaneous play. But if the round block adaptation precedes the presentation of board and three blocks, the child rarely piles but instead behaves as described above.

The *2-year-old* child easily inserts the blocks when they are in front of their respective holes and he also adapts to the turned board after a few errors. His best trial takes less than one minute. Frequently blocks inserted in their proper holes will be removed and tried in other holes. As at 18 months, pressure is frequently used rather than adaptive turning of the blocks for insertion. A child will sometimes press the block down in the wrong hole, first with one hand and then with the other.

The *3-year-old* solves the formboard and adapts to the rotated board in less than 30 seconds.

Sex differences in performance were not found.

Significance of the test. The influence of the procedure techniques on behavior is clearly illustrated in the formboard behavior at 18 months. If the three blocks are immediately presented to the child, he piles them one on another. If, on the other hand, the test for adapting the circular block is first presented, the piling reaction is rarely seen; instead, blocks are related to the formboard holes. This test is in some instances more indicative of personality traits than of potential adaptivity. Success on the test is more significant than failure. Attentiveness is necessary for success; frequently the young child is distractible. The inattentiveness may be due to competing interest drives which may signify desirable qualities of self-motivation and alertness.

Success also depends upon adjustment to an erroneous trial. Some children persist in their attempts to insert a block in the wrong hole. This persistence may be a good sign. If the famous spider had given up before the seventh trial, we might have said he was wise because he considered the task impossible! The adult knows that the dissimilar form will not fit, but the child has not had the benefit of wide experience. Persistence in a feat which is to him not impossible may be the very trait which brings success in other tasks. Naturally there comes a time and age when the child may be expected to appreciate the incompatibility of the square block in the round hole. At that age persistence is an unfavorable trait. Since it is impossible to define that age for any particular child, the interpretation of a child's success or failure must be left to the psychological insight of the examiner.

Discriminative items, as formulated in the developmental schedules:

Age 15 months—Places round block; adapts round block
  18 months—Piles three blocks spontaneously
  21 months—Places two or three blocks
  24 months—Places on board spontaneously; adapts in four trials
  30 months—Places three blocks on presentation; adapts with repeated error
  36 months—Adapts in less than thirty seconds

THREE-HOLE FORMBOARD
PERCENTAGE OF CASES SHOWING BEHAVIOR

Age in years	1	1½	2	3
Behavior:				
Round block alone				
Inserts	18	75		
Inserts only after demonstration	54	10		
Adapts to turning of board	19	68		
Three blocks				
Inserts circular block		80	100	
Inserts square block		45	90	
Inserts triangular block		48	97	
Inserts at least two blocks		55	100	
Inserts all three blocks		30	87	
Board rotated				
Solves		8	62	92
Time average, seconds			44	25

(A-13) THE GODDARD FORMBOARD

The Goddard formboard is an appropriate test for children even before they have completely mastered the three-hole formboard. The method of presentation is essentially that specified by Sylvester (120). The characteristic response of young children in solving this board and the Seguin formboard, which is essentially the same, have been discussed by other authors (Stutsman [118] and Baldwin and Stecher [4]). The discussion presented here will therefore be brief.

Procedure. The child may sit or stand as he prefers. Place the formboard on the table before the child and put the blocks in three piles at the child's right (at the left if he is left-handed), no block in the same row with its proper recess, the star at the bottom of a pile and the lozenge and elongated hexagon in different piles. Say to the child, *"Put the blocks in their places."* Unobtrusively replace in its pile any block which the child may leave on the board incorrectly placed. If the child works slowly, or if he slows down as he works, say, *"Do it as nicely and as quickly as you can,"* but do not otherwise urge the child to hurry. When all of the blocks have been correctly placed, quickly replace them in their respective piles for the second trial. Give three trials. Record for each trial the manner in which the child works, as well as his time and errors.

Behavior trends. The *3-year-old* uses a trial and error method of insertion. Sometimes he even removes a block fully and correctly inserted and tries it in an experimental fashion in other holes. After full insertion of a block, he may pat it two or three times in place.

The *4-year-old* picks up a block and surveys the board before placing it. He is likely to take a block in each hand and place first one and then the other.

The *5-year-old* works quickly and smoothly. His search for the correct hole is less obvious than at 4 years.

Significance of the test. Not only the child's score but the manner in which he works, his tempo, and his learning ability are valuable items of observation. The test is one on which "manually minded" children have an opportunity to show their more practical form-perception skill. It is of course an excellent test for deaf children since language is not essential either for presentation or response.

GODDARD FORMBOARD

	3	4	5	6
Age in years	3	4	5	6
Number of cases	7	29	57	18
Best trial, time in sec.				
Aver. time, boys and girls	96	55	34	28
Aver. time, boys	86	58	34	27
Aver. time, girls	107	52	34	28
Number of errors	18–10	12–5	2	none

(A-14) COLOR FORMS

Five bright red color forms (a disk, a half-disk, a square, a triangle, and a cross) are pasted on a white background as pictured in Plate XIX.

Five cut-out color forms identical with those on the card are presented one by one to the child to see if he identifies the forms. The test is obviously easier for the child than the Kuhlmann forms test or the Terman modification. The bright color appeals to the young child and the larger and fewer forms simplify the test. On the other hand, the test is harder for the child than the three-hole formboard. Thus it bridges the gap between the ages when the child fits forms into a formboard more or less by a trial and error method and when he is able to identify line-drawing forms. However, the test is applicable to only a narrow age range, namely 2 through 3 years. The test is quickly administered and, like most of the tests of this age, significant when the response is positive but less so when the child fails to respond correctly.

Procedure. Place the card of color forms on the table before the child so that the half-circle is in the lower right-hand corner as he faces it, and say, *"Oh, look,"* pointing to each form on the card. Then place cut-out circle on card of color forms above the cross and say, *"Where is the other one?" "Show me the other one just like this,"* or, *"Where does this one go?"* If the child does not respond correctly, point first to the circle, then to the cut-out, saying *"See, they are just alike."* Bring the cut-out circle close to the circle on the card.

Present the other cut-out forms (triangle, semicircle, square, and cross) in the order given and wait for the child's response. Do not indicate, as with the circle, the correct form until all forms have been presented.

Comment. Some children will attempt to pick the color forms from the card. They will need to be gently restrained. Some children will insist on placing the cut-out form over its corresponding form on the card. This is permissible and such responses when correct are considered a substitute for pointing.

The examiner should of course avoid giving the child a clue by looking toward the correct form, but frequently the child's own eye movements indicate his ability to identify the forms correctly, when pointing cannot be elicited.

Behavior trends. Although the test was not consistently given to the normative cases, it has received sufficient clinical application to define tentative age norms.

The *2-year-old* child identifies none of the forms; but the *30-month-old* places at least one form. The *disk*, the *semi-disk*, and the *cross* appear to be easier for the child to identify than the *square* or *triangle*. The *3-year-old* child identifies at least three of the forms.

(A-15) The Kuhlmann-Terman Geometric Form Recognition Test

This test was originally devised by Kuhlmann and was first presented in his 1912 revision of the Binet-Simon Scale. Terman reduced slightly the size of the forms and included the test in his 1916 Scale. The test has been found by several investigators—Kuhlmann, Terman, Holbrook, and Goodenough—to be highly reliable. It may be profitably used for the ages 3 through 5 years.

The test material consists of a white card on which are printed ten geometric forms in outline. The ten forms are in three rows, four in the first two rows and one on each end of the third row. In the middle of the third row there is an $\times$ where duplicate cut-out forms may be placed. The ten forms are pictured below. Each form has been numbered for convenience of reference.

Kuhlmann-Terman Geometric Form Recognition Test

Procedure. Use procedure indicated for color forms except omit any demonstration.

Behavior trends. The *3-year-old* child identifies four of the forms; the *4-year-old* child, eight of the forms; and the *5-year-old* child, all ten forms.

Significance of the behavior. The circle, No. 7, is the easiest one to identify; and forms 1, 3, and 6 are the hardest, according to the percentages for 4 years. An analysis of the errors made by normal children suggests that the 3-year-old regards the form as a whole, while the 4- and 5-year-old child gives greater attention to details. The *3-year-old* child errs in selecting a shape generally like the one presented, while older children err in selecting a shape which has a certain detail like the detail of the one presented.

The test is more specifically related to visual perception than other tests for these ages, but comprehension of what is expected and ability for concentrated attention influence the child's behavior, particularly at the age of 3 years.

Sex differences in performance do not appear to be significant at the critical ages, and differences that do appear in the percentages are not consistent.

THE KUHLMANN-TERMAN GEOMETRIC FORM RECOGNITION TEST

PERCENTAGE OF CHILDREN WHO IDENTIFY THE VARIOUS FORMS, AND TYPICAL ERRORS MADE AT DIFFERENT AGES

Form No.	Percentage identifying forms at			Form confused with		
	3 yrs.	4 yrs.	5 yrs.	3 yrs.	4 yrs.	5 yrs.
7........	81	100	100	4		
10........	69	96	100	6		
2........	69	92	98	4	4	8
5........	69	92	96	7	7	7
9........	69·	82	98	?	8, 10	6
4........	65	85	94	6, 7, 10	1, 10	1, 10
8........	65	81	98	6, 9, 10	2	2, 1
6........	69	75	96	2	2, 3, 4, 10	
3........	65	67	94	9	9, 2, 6, 8, 10	6, 10
1........	57	66	72	2, 6	2, 6, 3, 8, 10	6, 3, 8, 10, 5

Number of forms matched	Ages		
	3 yrs.	4 yrs.	5 yrs.
10.................	8	18	61
9.................	15	36	88
8.................	23	57	93
7.................	31	68	98
6.................	38	82	98
5.................	46	89	98
4.................	54	93	100·
3.................	66	97	100
2.................	77	97	100
1.................	89	100	100
No. of cases........	26	28	57

§ D. DRAWING

Both racially and ontogenetically, the ability to draw and write is second only to oral language in importance for the advancement of the race and the individual. While language is essentially a social trait, drawing is less so. The very act of drawing or writing is asocial at the point of execution. Although the ultimate goal of drawing may be social, the individual who engages in such an occupation is quite different from the one who prefers conversation to letter writing, and oratory to painting.

The preschool child is usually an enthusiastic artist. Given a pencil or crayon he will occupy himself for relatively long periods. If not restrained he would cover his surroundings—walls, lampshades, books, clothing, and any other available article—with his marks. In fact, it is the very exceptional child's room whose walls are not, in some unguarded moment, marked or marred to the child's taste and to the parents' or landlord's despair. As the child advances in age the character of his marks changes. Particularly in the preschool years, these changes appear to be more dependent on neuro-motor maturation and on general development in observation and eye-hand coordination than on special experience in drawing. Tests of drawing, although they involve a complex of abilities, furnish an excellent means of appraising a child's developmental progress, his learning ability, and his individuality. The series of tests which are presented in this section are appropriate tasks for the whole gamut of preschool years. Even the year-old child frequently makes a mark and the 6-year-old has by no means attained maturity in drawing and copying.

The early markings of the child lead in time to two adult activities: creative drawing and graphic arts. In the preschool period there is some evidence that creative drawing ability may be unrelated or even inversely related to eye-hand coordination skills. Imagination, or as Lowenfeld (81) so aptly explains it, haptic perception, is an essential for all creative activity. It may be that the inaccuracies of the child with poor eye-hand coordination stimulate fanciful ideas of what has been drawn and thus lead the child into the field of art; it may be that failure to produce an intended design is sufficiently challenging to arouse greater interest and effort in drawing as a pastime; or it may be that creative imagination is incompatible with faithful reproduction of what someone else has done. Undoubtedly there are many forces motivating drawing, especially in its formative stages, and the forces vary in individual instances.

Drawing and writing in adult life are undoubtedly more dependent on neuro-muscular coordination than on eye-hand coordination. The blind can learn to model, and to sculpture, and with proper guides, to write (Lowenfeld, 81). These abilities may evolve on the basis of the kinesthetic senses alone. But in the early childhood of the normal child, eye-hand coordination plays a very important role. Eye-hand coordination develops slowly. It is not until 6 years that the usual child is ready for printing and writing, the second of the three classical essentials of elementary education. To trace the evolution of this essential ability is of great interest even though the typewriter may to some extent displace writing in modern education.

The series of test situations which follows is designed to reveal different aspects of drawing. The child is given an opportunity to draw what he wishes, to draw a man, to finish a drawing of a man, and to imitate and copy geometric forms. Thus different degrees of restriction are placed on the child's performance; and by studying his record as a whole, the component aspects of his behavior may be analyzed.

But as Krötzsch (77) has pointed out, drawing has psychological value only if we are in a position to reconstruct the causal activity to which it owes its origin. It is not sufficient merely to examine the finished record. A record should be kept of the order and direction in which the child draws, of his spontaneous remarks, and of his interpretation of what he has drawn or copied. It is also important to permit only the prescribed degree of freedom in the different situations so that the performance will reveal the influence of the various motivating factors. Any unavoidable deviations from the formulated procedures should be as carefully recorded as the child's behavior. Properly administered and fully interpreted, the drawing situations are highly significant tests for the preschool ages.

(A-16) Spontaneous Drawing

A child is usually more cooperative if he is allowed to show the examiner what he can do before his activity is directed. Spontaneous drawing, therefore, makes an excellent introduction to the drawing test series. Moreover, spontaneous drawing when administered first in the drawing series, elicits a marking or drawing unaffected by the suggestions inherent in other drawing situations. The test also furnishes children of limited experience with paper and crayon or pencil an opportunity for adaptation, and thus renders their subsequent performance more reliable. However, when the pressure of time does not permit a full examination, this situation should be omitted in preference to the subsequent one, "Draw a Man."

The situation permits of distinction between the child who immediately draws and the child who when given a wide margin of freedom is confused or undecided. The younger child of limited repertoire draws what he can and names it according to the impression made by the finished product. It may have more than one association for him and he may offer alternate suggestions. When he nears the age of deciding in advance what he will draw, he not infrequently changes his mind as he draws. Either his limited skill produces an object different from that which he initially intended or the *Gestalt* of the unfinished product suggests an alternate possibility. The directions for the situation do not encourage a child to tell in advance what he proposes to draw, but they may elicit a name for an otherwise nameless form. We know from other studies (Hetzer, 55), however, that the 3-year-old ordinarily does not predict what he draws, that even the 4-year-old changes his designation to fit the product, and that it is not until the child is 5 that he names his drawing in advance of producing it. It is at this age that the child may hesitate to choose what he will draw. The subject of a child's drawing is influenced to a large extent by his environment and by recent happenings; a pumpkin or a pilgrim in the fall, a Christmas tree or a fireplace in December and January, an elephant at circus time, and a boat, a merry-go-round, or a flag in the summertime. However, the execution of the drawing is largely an expression of the child's own individuality rather than of training. The situation is important because it is one of the few tests which affords a child wide latitude in demonstrating his originality and imagination.

Procedure. Place a sheet of green paper, 8.5 x 11 inches, on the table before the child so that the narrow edge of the paper is at the table edge in front of him. At the same time place a red lumber crayon (or pencil at 3 years and after) in the center of the paper with the point of the crayon directed away from the child. If he does not promptly pick up the crayon, offer it to him. If he puts it in his mouth or bangs it on the table, point to the paper. Below the age of 2 years no verbal directions are necessary. Occasionally the paper slips as the child marks. If he is not able to steady it, it is permissible to hold one corner of the paper while he completes his markings. At 2 years and thereafter say, *"Draw something for me."* "Make" may be substituted for "draw" but no other word should be used which might suggest in any way the character of the child's marks or drawing. If necessary, add, *"Anything you like."* When the child has finished, say in an interested but not puzzled manner, *"What is it?"* and also inquire the details, but guard against suggesting an interpretation. After 3 years, the pencil sans eraser is used in place of the crayon. If the child does not spontaneously write or print his name, the examiner may suggest that he do so. Naturally at ages younger than 3 years, the suggestion is inappropriate, but occasionally even the 3-year-old will pretend to write.

Behavior trends. The *1-year-old* child usually brings the crayon to the paper but he does not necessarily leave his mark. However, four weeks later, when he is 13 months old, he may be expected definitely to mark on the paper. If the year-old child does mark, his mark is more likely to result from hitting rather than marking. But at 13 months, the reverse is true. Then twice as many infants mark on the paper as hit the crayon against the paper, making dots. It must be remembered though that a little less than one-half of the year-old children do not spontaneously combine the paper and crayon; and rarely do infants of this age scribble spontaneously.

The average *18-month-old* child not only marks on the page but he also scribbles. Only one-third of the children at this age still bang the crayon on the paper. Half of the children who scribble make their scribbling lines go off the page. The direction of the marks or scribbles made by these children is varied. One-third make them in the horizontal direction or vertical direction, a third make them circular or at an angle, and a third make their marks go in all directions. The marks are usually neither very heavy nor very faint, showing that the 18-month-old child exerts moderate pressure.

The *2-year-old* child's spontaneous drawings show very little advance over those made by the children six months younger. Although the 2-year-old rarely bangs the crayon on the paper, he still scribbles. His scribbling is better defined than it was six months ago, and his line now very rarely goes off the page. He does make an effort to hold the crayon in an adult manner and his marks tend to be heavier than those of the 18-month-old child. At 2 years the marks tend to be circular or at an angle, rather than vertical, horizontal, or in all directions. In fact, at this age we begin to see evidences of incipient representative drawing. Two of the thirty-four children even named their efforts: one called her marks a kitty and one said that she was drawing nines.

The *3-year-old* child is in his own estimation an artist. Over three-fourths of this group named their drawings, even though to an adult's eyes their product was more of an enigma than is an ink blot. Nevertheless, the imagination of the 3-year-old appears not to be taxed when asked to tell what he has drawn. In fact, he usually volunteers a designation and even names alternate possibilities. One girl versatilely called her drawing a "big ball," a "man's head," a "telephone pole like"! A boy said his was "tree," "boy," "carrots," and "that's April fool." About a third of the 3-year-old children scribble but even these usually name what they have drawn. We may consider this mercurial form of graphic expression a developmental sort of "doodling."

The *4-year-old* child rarely scribbles; instead his product really deserves to be called a drawing, because even to the adult's eyes it takes on form and meaning. The 4-year-old is an individualist in that in only two instances was there a duplication of object drawn. One boy and one girl said their drawing was a house; and one boy and one girl named theirs a horse. With the exception of one child who had six details in his drawing, the drawings were not differentiated into details, although the drawings were in a few instances merely a detail. For example, one child drew eight eyes, and another said his was a "bird nose." Three children attempted to print letters. This stage may be called one of dogmatic representation.

The drawing of the *5-year-old* is clearly recognizable for what the child names it to be, due probably to the differentiation of parts, as well as to lifelike representation. The 4-year-old does not differentiate parts, whereas the 5-year-old discriminates three or more parts: the flag has a pole, stars, and stripes; the house has windows, chimney, and steps; the tree has trunk, branches, and berries. The 5-year-old is still so individualistic that it is not feasible to present a complete statistical analysis of what he draws. It is noteworthy, however, that a fifth of the children print letters, a quarter of them draw a person, and another quarter draw a building. The remainder draw such things as a boat, an apple, a

Christmas tree, a fireplace, a flag, a merry-go-round, a bird's nest, a milk bottle, and a pumpkin. The child has reached, at 5 years, the realistic outline stage of art.

The *6-year-old* child's drawing shows improvement over the 5-year-old's in precision and detail. Six draws twice as many details as Five, and is quite realistic in what he draws. There is little change in his subject matter. He is more likely, however, to sign his drawing with his printed name, probably because he has learned to do this in school.

Sex differences. There are no clear-cut sex differences in performance until the age of 5. Then we find that a girl will usually draw a house, a lady, a pumpkin, a doll, a cat, or a girl; while the boy will draw a boat, a flag, a lighthouse, a merry-go-round, a bird's nest, or an elephant, reflecting probably a wider range of experience in the case of the boys. The 5-year-old girls, however, include many more details than do the boys at that age.

NUMBER OF DETAILS IN SPONTANEOUS DRAWINGS OF 5-YEAR-OLDS

PERCENTAGE OF 5-YEAR-OLDS DRAWING INDICATED DETAILS

	Boys	Girls
More than 3 details	26	70
More than 6 details	15	40
12 or more details	0	17

GENETIC SERIATION OF BEHAVIOR STAGES IN SPONTANEOUS DRAWING

Age 12 months—Marks by banging or brushing
15 months—Marks rather than bangs
18 months—Scribbles but marks go off page
2 years —Scribbles confined to page
2+ years—Holds crayon in fingers making small marks
3 years —Draws undifferentiated but named form
4 years —Draws differentiated form crudely
5 years —Draws simple but easily recognizable form

Interpretation of drawing. The value of this test lies not so much in its maturity significance as in its personality implications. The genetic stage of the drawing is indicative only to a very general degree. Beyond the stage of drawing a recognizable form, maturational or developmental factors play a relatively minor role. Below this stage maturity is, however, a more important role. For instance, if a 5-year-old child draws an unrecognizable form it usually signifies slow development. Although the average number of details drawn by Six is greater than the average number drawn by Five, increase in elaboration with age may not occur in the drawings of any particular child.

But what is it that the child does express in his drawings? He may express freedom or constraint in the size of what he draws, he expresses his present interest in the subject of his drawing. He expresses imagination or lack of it in what he draws, he expresses absorption with details in the elaborateness of his representation, he expresses neatness and efficiency in the manner in which he draws; and in all the foregoing traits he expresses his age propensities and limitations.

On page 144 the annual spontaneous drawings of three children from 3 through 6 years have been reproduced. Brief descriptions of these three children and of their spontaneous drawings previous to 3 years, as well as the running account of their behavior as they made the drawings follow.

B-34. BC is a well-composed child whose home environment is happy but impoverished. He is poised, has a sense of humor, and is imaginative. His movements are effective, controlled, and without waste motion. They tend to be restricted rather than expansive. The following records were taken as the child drew.

56 weeks. Picks up crayon with left hand, transfers to right, brings onto paper definitely. Mouths crayon, picks up paper, releases paper, draws it to left and puts crayon on paper again. Attention shifts from crayon to paper and vice versa but recurrently crayon is brought into relation with paper.

80 weeks. Picks up crayon in right hand and brings into contact with the paper, making a mark.

2 years. Picks up crayon in right fist. Applies it to paper, making very small, faint marks. Explores the crayon and then transfers to left hand and starts to pick up the paper.

3 years. "*Draw something for me.*" Takes pencil in right fingers and makes a small mark on the paper. When asked, "*What is it?*" replies something which sounds like "a gog."

4 years. "*Do you like to draw?*" Shakes head "yes" but does not approach the pencil. Looks at the examiner prolongedly. "*Would you like the pencil?*" Shakes head "yes." "*Pick it up.*" Picks it up and draws, on request. "*What is it?*" "A ball." Examiner points to marks under ball and asks what they are. "My name."

5 years. "*Will you draw something for me?*" Draws. "*What is it?*" "A car."

6 years. Requested to write name at top of paper. Takes pencil in right hand. Draws *C* first counter-clockwise; then *B*, making the downward stroke first. "That how the teacher tells me." Continues drawing spontaneously. "*What is it?*" "That's a bird. Birds what fly. Them are the ears. This here's a bird too. Have to make the legs," and adds to the drawing. "This here's a bird house."

G-43. BE is a thin, wiry, fastidious child who scatters her energy but who is occupied with details. She is at times a little apprehensive about adult approval. She is not very imaginative and lacks initiative, but is busy in a routine way. Her behavior was described in the records as follows:

60 weeks. Picks up crayon in right hand, turns it over, dangles wrong end

Child B 34

Child G 43

Child B 36

3 YEARS   4 YEARS   5 YEARS   6 YEARS

Age ⟶

Spontaneous Drawing at 3, 4, 5, 6 Years of Age

of crayon on paper. Finally reaches toward paper, picks it up. Then again holding crayon in right fist, she dangles the point against the paper and definite marks are made.

80 weeks. Picks up crayon in right hand and brushes it across the paper and then starts to pull up the paper to mark on the next sheet.

2 years. Spontaneous scribble.

3 years. "*Draw something for me.*" She takes crayon and draws. "*What is it?*" Turns to mother and shows her drawing, asking, "What is it?" "*You tell me.*" She replies, "A big ball."

4 years. "*Will you draw something for me?*" "I don't know anything to draw. My grandfather knows how to write some numbers." "*You draw something.*" "What would I draw? Cause I'll have to draw, my brother draws and he brought home a pretty picture, and Ma," turning to mother, "what was it on?" Then says something about, "cat and dog." "I don't know how to draw." Makes a small mark on paper at top edge. Immediately afterward when asked to draw a man, draws elaborately with many details.

5 years. "*Draw something that you like to draw.*" She observes the watermark on the paper and also the number at the top of the page. Says, "Black pencil. That looks like black crayon." After marking on the paper, making girl's hair, says, "This looks like I'm writing a name." She draws. "Ma, look at the nose. Gotta make de mouth. I made a little mouth instead of a big mouth. I don't think this is going to be a big girl. I would make her big if she were up here, but I don't want her big. It looks like a mouse." Chuckles. "What a shoe! I have to make the arms. If I hadn't got any arms she can't eat. Now the dress. It's a crooked girl. Look at the smoke. Smoke coming out of the girl's hat," turning to mother. "The buttons on the girl's dress." "*Is she all finished now?*" Shakes head, "yes."

6 years. Writes name. "*Draw something for me . . . What is it?*" "Some kind of a hand." Examiner asks parts. "Finger, part of the arm."

B-36. MB is a sober child who suffers from asthma. He works a little carelessly, quickly, absorbedly, and with imagination. He has shown some left-hand tendency from early infancy. A description of his behavior with the comment which he made as he drew follows:

56 weeks. Picks up crayon in right hand, transfers to left, and holding it between index finger and thumb of left hand, dangles it against paper. Then again holds in right hand, drops it against paper, transfers to left and brings end against paper. A few, very faint marks are made on paper.

80 weeks. Picks up crayon in right hand, transfers to left, and holds with point to paper. Crayon is brought against paper and marks made there but does not regard marks after made. Finally releases crayon on paper, then turns to right and drops crayon on right side.

2 years. Holds crayon in right hand in adult manner and marks on paper. Later held crayon in fist, and then in adult manner between thumb and first two fingers.

3 years. Takes pencil in left and then in right hand. "I have a pen home. It have an eraser on it." Makes the faint marks with his left hand and the line down the page with his right.

4 years. Picks up pencil in right hand. Draws (1). "Did you ever see a pistol off a boogy man taking a little boy away? Another boogy man. This one going to be a pistol (2). This going to be a little boy (3). This a little boy yeg. This is his other yeg. I have no place to make his other hand (4)."

(1) Draws circular spiral starting from center, adds legs and arms. Then mark for hair. (2) Adds mark at right side of man. (3) Draws smaller spiral in upper right, then one leg, then other leg. (4) Adds small line for hand at paper's edge.

5 years. "*Draw something for me.*" Takes crayon in right hand. Turns paper slightly. Draws a cross. Makes vertical line by drawing downward; makes cross line from left to right and then extends cross leftward. (Schooling: None.) "*What is that?*" "A cross."

6 years. "*Draw something for me.*" "I can draw an envelope." "*What is this?*" "You put that down and paste it," pointing to the flap. "*Write your name.*" "I don't know how." "*Can you make any letters?*" "I can too; I can make lots of letters. A, H, K, don't know what that one is, R."

(The first two drawings for child B-34 were actually very tiny and were placed in the lower left-hand corner of the page. The second drawing for G-43 was also very tiny and was placed in the upper left-hand corner of the page Drawings reproduced for child B-36 are symmetrically reduced and show exact placement of the figures on the original drawing sheets. Reading from left to right, the drawings are reproduced in the following scale:

B-34: x1, x1, x1, x⅜
G-43: x¼, x2, x⅜, x¼
B-36: x¼, x¼, x¼, x¼)

Our records show that, except in cases where a child deviates markedly and repeatedly, it is neither helpful nor appropriate to analyze the drawing in Freudian terms. For instance, B-36's drawing of a man with a pistol taking a little boy away was a passing interest stimulated by a recent kidnaping episode which had been discussed by the family. True, the fact that he drew it showed that it made an impression on him, but it was more of an intellectual interest than an emotional one. We have no particular reason for assuming that the child in any way identified himself with the little boy in the drawing. The drawing does, however, express the child's age by its immature representation of the man and the boy. The drawing also reflects lack of care in its hurried execution, lack of constraint by the expansive figures, and a certain originality and imagination in the general concept pictured. This interpretation is fully justified by the child's behavior in other situations, by his parents' report, and by his previous and subsequent development. Although a drawing does reveal many traits it must be evaluated as part of the total examination.

Compare B-36's drawings with those of B-34, whose 4-year drawing shows constraint, imagination, less interest in details, originality of concept, and efficiency and greater neatness of execution. The outstanding difference between the two children, particularly at 4 years, was difference in constraint and this difference is outstandingly revealed in their drawings. Even at 3 years, and at 2 years this constraint is apparent in their marks. At 2 years they made similarly small marks, but B-36's were scattered over the paper, whereas B-34's were confined to the lower right-hand corner. At 3 years B-36's extend at least two-thirds the length of the paper, whereas B-34's are again confined to a tiny area.

In contrast to the drawings of B-36 and B-34 (two boys), the annual spontaneous drawings of G-43 (a girl) have been presented. Her hesitation and her small mark indicate a poverty of ideas rather than constraint. At 4 years she had to be urged to draw spontaneously, although when asked to draw a man, she drew an elaborate form with meticulous care for details. This girl shows a characteristic feminine concern for details except at 6 years when she gives a rather surprising performance which may be influenced by school experience.

It should be emphasized again that the drawing should not be analyzed by itself, but should be considered as supplementary and corroborative evidence of the total personality revealed by the whole examination. The more we know about the total child, the better position we are in to interpret any one segment of behavior.

SPONTANEOUS DRAWING

PERCENTAGE OF CASES DISPLAYING VARIOUS BEHAVIORS

Age	52 wks.	56 wks.	80 wks.	2 yrs.	3 yrs.	4 yrs.	5 yrs.	6 yrs.
Number of cases	48	28	37	34	31	22	57	16
No combination of paper and crayon	46	26	5	6	3			
Bangs crayon on paper	31	32	35	3	3			
Linear marks	10	74	65					
Scribbles	0	0	57	62	39	9	16	7
Horizontal marks			16 ⎫	6 ⎫				
Vertical marks			16 ⎬ 32	18 ⎬ 24				
Marks at an angle			24 ⎫	35 ⎫				
Circular marks			3 ⎬ 27	15 ⎬ 50				
Marks in all directions			38	21				
Lines go off page			41	9	13			
Faint marks			3	18	23			
Medium marks			60	35	52			
Heavy marks			30	41	23			
Names drawing			0	6	77	64	95	100
Number details (median)						9	3	6
Draws a person					26	14	23	36
Draws a building					7	23	25	14

(A-17) "Draw a Man"

As soon as the young child becomes interested in graphic representation he sees in his markings resemblances to the human form. One-third of the 3-year-old children named their spontaneous drawings "a man," "a boy," "you," "a man's head," "a lady," or some other personage.

Although the usual child does not predict the end product of his drawing until he is older than 4 years, it is not because he cannot modify his markings to conform to some goal. Even the 3-year-old may adapt his spontaneous drawing to the task, "draw a man."

Goodenough (44) and others have shown the test to be very helpful in judging a child's intellectuality. It is therefore quite appropriate to incorporate the drawing of a man in a test series for defining individual dispositions and capacities. While the child's finished product has certain significance, it is very important, particularly at the preschool ages, to watch the child as he draws and when he has finished to ask him to interpret his art. Otherwise much of the meaning which the child puts into his crude attempts will be lost.

If the child has spontaneously drawn a man, this situation is omitted. If, however, the child has drawn a girl, a boy, a baby, a lady, or any person other than a man, the situation may be presented with profit.

Procedure. When the spontaneous drawing is completed and the child has told what he has drawn, say, *"That's very fine,"* then turn the paper over and say, *"Now draw a man."* If the child says, "I can draw a little girl," or some object other than a man say, *"Well, try to draw a man this time."* If the child protests, say in an encouraging tone, *"Oh, I am sure you can."* If necessary, add, *"Just try."* It is the very exceptional child who does not comply. Adaptability is, in itself, significant. Permit the child full freedom to turn the paper, but if necessary steady the paper as he draws. When the child has finished, ask him to name the various parts unless there is no possible ambiguity.

Behavior trends. The *3-year-old*, when caught at a favorable moment, unhesitatingly responds to the request, *"Draw a man."* The child quickly completes his sketch which may or may not have the intent attributed to it by an adult. Certainly the drawing must be titled to be interpreted. Sometimes the child merely draws one or more vertical lines or perhaps one or more circles; sometimes he draws a circle with appendages, or he draws a crude representation of a face; or what is more usual he may just scribble, saying that that's a man. As a rule there is no differentiation of parts at this age. The ratio of the length of the drawing to its width is very variable and extreme, depending on whether the representation is linear or circular. The size of the drawing is likewise variable and extreme. The marks may extend practically the length and breadth of the paper or they may be tiny.

At *4 years* the drawing of a man is beginning to take on definite form. The head is represented and the eyes are usually differentiated. Other facial features frequently are included. More than half of the children draw either legs or feet for their man, usually legs. The man may be represented upside down or across the paper, but usually normal orientation is pictured. The drawing still needs to be titled and even interpreted. When this is done, it is clear that the child is organizing his graphic representation to conform to his idea of a man, however crude his attempts may be. Mere scribbling is rarely encountered. As Gridley (51) and others have shown, this age is a very formative one with respect to graphic representation; the 4-year-old has no fixed formula, but on repetition modifies his drawing so that he cannot be relied upon to produce tomorrow the drawing which he makes today. Nevertheless, the man which the child does draw characteristically reveals his ability and personality. The 4-year-old's drawings are almost as variable in size as those made by the 3-year-old. The length of the 4-year-old's man is on the average two-and-a-half times the width.

The *5-year-old* child draws an unmistakable man. Mouth and nose are indicated, as well as eyes; the man is also drawn with a body, arms, legs, and feet. Upside-down or sidewise orientation is rare. Occasionally a child of this age will draw two-dimensional legs. Articles of clothing, such as hat, pants, and buttons, are sometimes added, although they are not usual. The 5-year-old man is definitely smaller than Four's. In width it is half as long and three-quarters as wide, but the ratio of the length to the width remains like Four's. Thus the 5-year-old, in spite of the direction to draw a man, draws a childlike figure.

The *6-year-old's* drawing of a man shows signs of growing up. The man now has a neck, hands on the ends of his arms, and he is dressed with hat and pants. His legs are now more substantial since they are two-dimensional legs rather than just sticks. Also, the man is now drawn four times as long as he is broad. The man grows up with the child.

Sex differences. There is a tendency, apparent at all ages studied, for the girls to include more details than the boys. Items which the girls more frequently include are the items which are just coming into prominence. The girls also more frequently include extraneous articles, such as ground, toys, a blanket, a pencil, a ball, and even ice skates.

Significance of the test. A high degree of complex abilities is involved in the test. At the mature level of performance, outstanding are: the selection of the representative features to be pictured, the integration and differentiation of these parts, the proper proportionality of the parts, and the orientation of the parts to each other and of the figure on the paper. Obviously these are factors requiring a high degree of observation, skill, and judgment. In the immature child each factor enters to the degree that it has developed. In addition the child's own personality is reflected in both what he draws and his manner of drawing. Particularly noteworthy are his adjustment to the task, the care and absorption with which he works, his tenseness as shown by the pressure of his crayon, and his autocritical ability evinced by various expressions of satisfaction with his work. His performance is thus psychologically highly revealing.

The child represents in his drawing both his concept of a man and what he has learned to draw that, to him, looks like a man or some part of a man. Whether a 3-year-old draws a head or legs may depend on whether he is at that time drawing lines or circles. A child does not draw circles and say they are legs; it is length that is to the child an outstanding leg trait. Likewise he does not draw a line for a head; it is roundness that is the outstanding head trait. Thus limitations of drawing ability determine to some extent the concept which the child expresses.

Marking over or shading the drawing is usually the child's effort to color or to eradicate the drawing because of dissatisfaction with it. When the shading is very black it may express tension or an escape desire; it does not necessarily imply reference to any one person.

When any characteristic of a normal stage of development persists beyond that stage, explanation is to be sought for in terms of either individuality of growth or specific disability. When a child after he is 6 years old persists in drawing an upside-down man it is evident that he has not assimilated the normal conventions. This failure, until it is overcome, will complicate and be expressed in associated aspects of behavior. It is because of this very individuality of growth that it is difficult to generalize concerning the interpretation of atypical behavior. To say, for example, that great detail represents a verbalistic type of child is to oversimplify the problem. It should be emphasized again that the significance of a child's drawing can only be validly determined by reference to his total behavior complex.

On Plate XV three characteristic drawings of a man have been reproduced for each of the four age levels, 3, 4, 5, and 6 years. The drawings of Row One with the exception of G-23's man are a little less mature than those of Row Two. Row Two represents a typically normal performance. All four drawings in this row were made by the same child and show clearly the genetic sequences in this one child's behavior. Her upside-down man at 4 years is interesting when compared with G-23's man, just above it. The drawings of Row Three are all more elaborate representations than we usually encounter. The 4-year-old man in this row was drawn horizontally since the child turned the paper after making the body. The shading of the 5-year-old man was explained by the child as coloring. It should also be noted that G-43, the artist of 6 years, is the child whose spontaneous drawings were illustrated on page 144.

The following records describe the child's order of drawing and his comments.

First Row. B-3, 3 years. When asked if he could draw a man, replied that he could not and then drew lines in the vertical direction along the right-hand edge of the paper. When asked what he had drawn, he replied, "A big, big man."

G-23,[2] 4 years. *Draw a man:* Draws without comment. On request names "mouth, eye, nose, eye, leg, leg, a man."

B-12, 5 years. *Draw a man.* "I know how to draw numbers." *Draw a man.* "I don't know how to." *Try.* "I know how to draw a table." *Draw a man.* "Dis way?"

Draws 1 and says, "Dat's his leg." Draws 2 and says, "Here's his other one." Draws 3, "Dis his head." Draws 4, "His eyes. He looks right through there." Breaks pencil. Says that he still has some. Examiner says she will give him another if it has no point. "If it does I'll have to have an ink one, huh?" "He's not gonna have nothin' else. That's all he's gonna have. It's all finished except his feets. One's his feet and one's his toes. And this part's his toe. That's all he needs."

G-34, 6 years. *Draw a man.* Draws. *"What is this?"* "Nose-mouth-pants-legs-legs-feet-feet-eye-head." "I can make a little cat, too."

Second Row. G-48, 3 years. *Draw a man.* Examiner points to marks and asks, *"What is that?"* "A man." *"What part of the man is this?"* "Depts" (steps). "Those is feet."

G-48, 4 years. *Draw a man.* Draws. Examiner asks parts. "An eye, an eye, a nose, a mouth, feet, his legs." Examiner: *"Isn't the man upside down?"* Shakes head, no. (Probably does not understand "upside down.")

G-48, 5 years. Spontaneous. *Draw a man.* Breaks point of pencil as she draws. "That's all right 'cause there's some there," pointing to the end of the pencil. Ex.: *"What is it?"* "A man, eyes, nose, mouth, his face, his feet (pointing to leg), his feet (pointing to another leg)."

G-48, 6 years. Starts to print name at examiner's request, at top of page. After U says has forgotten the rest. Continues F E T I. Draws man spontaneously. Examiner asks parts. "His hat—the other part of his hat—his face—his eye—his eye—his nose—his coat and body—that's his hands—that's the rest of his hands—his leg—his feet—his leg—his feet."

Third Row. G-44, 3 years. Spontaneously draws man. Examiner asks parts. "Face—head—head too—arm, arm—leg, leg."

B-23, 4 years. *Second trial on man.* Draws body, 1-4. Turns sheet to left 90°

[2] This drawing and that of B-23 at 4 years are also reproduced and discussed in a monograph by Gridley (51).

so that top of page is as indicated. Draws, saying "hea de eyes." Stops. Examiner points to 4 and asks what it is. This acts as a stimulus for further drawing. He says, "Dea de leg," and draws it, 7. Says, "Leg," draws 8. 9. Says, "Nodda leg." Then says, "Arms—gonna make." On request names side of body, 1 and 2, saying "Dot a man—a big man."

G-9, 5 years. Examiner: "Will you draw a man for me?" Draws. Is very absorbed in her drawing. Occasionally sticks out her tongue. Has not once referred to her mother, although twice the mother has made remarks. Examiner asks: "Is he finished?" Child: "Color him." Pencil has worn but she adjusts it so that it marks. Examiner points to different parts and asks, "What is this?" "His hair, his eyebrows, his eyes, nose, mouth. See this is his two sides—his lips, the buttons to his shirt, the coloring. That's the coloring beside the buttons—his pants—his feet. I can make a lady."

G-43, 6 years. Draw a man. Examiner asks parts. "His hair, fingers, his collar, his tie, hat, top of hat, the jacket, button, his pants, his leg, his knee, his ice skates." Examiner: "Do you skate?" "No. I got other kind of skates." Then goes on to say something about "When I was in school—write name—like I got me name now. I wrote that under the man. If I saw the man's name I could write it."

"DRAW A MAN"

PERCENTAGE OF CASES SHOWING THE BEHAVIOR INDICATED

Age in years	3	4	5	6
Number of cases	17	31	57	18
Behavior:				
Attempts to draw man	94	97	84	100
No differentiation of parts	82	55	16	0
Partially recognizable, has head, legs	12	39	37	11
Recognizable man, has features and body	0	3	47	88
Man drawn horizontal or upside down	?	35	11	11
Draws two-dimensional legs	0	0	26	67
Parts drawn:				
Head	24	79	95	100
Eyes	12	52	88	83
Legs	12	42	86	100
Mouth	12	32	82	83
Body	6	35	67	89
Feet	6	32	63	95
Nose	0	23	79	83
Arms	6	13	54	78
Hands	0	10	16	56
Hair	6	6	32	28
Fingers	0	3	25	33
Ears	0	3	11	22
Neck	0	0	9	56
Clothes man in:				
Pants	0	3	12	67
Hat	0	3	16	50
Shirt	0	3	4	44
Buttons	0	0	18	22

(A-18) THE INCOMPLETE MAN

The Incomplete Man was introduced as a preschool test by Gesell in 1925 (30). He noted, "This test has proved highly suitable for the 4-year level; and should be carried down to the 3-year and up to the 5-year levels to note qualitative and maturity differences." Accordingly, in the normative study we routinely included the test at 4, 5, and 6 years and presented it when feasible at 3 years. At 3 years the test was found to have brief interest value. The child of that age becomes restless if the examination is unduly prolonged and he may even become resistant if held too long at a boring task. The test is therefore not recommended as essential at 3 years, but when the 3-year-old is working well it may be briefly presented, or when the child has temporarily digressed from the examining table it may be used as something new to interest him in returning.

Procedure. NEVER PRESENT THE TEST BEFORE OR IMMEDIATELY AFTER THE DRAWING OF A MAN. It may be introduced conveniently after the imitation and copying of forms.

Place the incomplete drawing of a man on the table and say, *"What is this?"* Allow the child ample opportunity to respond, but if he does not, tell him it is a man and continue, saying, *"The person who made this man didn't draw all of him, did he? You finish him."* If the child does not attempt to add to the drawing, after he has been appropriately urged, say, *"See, he has only one ear. Draw his other ear."* Make no additional specific suggestions but urge the child to finish the man as completely as possible, respecting, of course, the child's endurance.

Behavior trends. The *3-year-old* child names the drawing a "man," a "boy," or a "girl" and may add an eye, or more rarely a leg. Usually, however, he just marks and then turns to another activity.

The *4-year-old* child is less likely than the 3-year-old to name the sketch a man, probably because Four is more critical and factual. The majority do name it a "snow man," a "baby," a "boy," a "girl," or a "man." More than half of the 4-year-olds add an arm, and more than half add a leg; but only about a third add both an arm and a leg. The majority do, however, add two details. They may be an arm and hand, a leg and foot, an arm and a leg, an arm and eyes, or eyes and a foot. The part added is usually correctly oriented; the arm may be displaced since the tie already drawn is frequently considered an arm. The added part is noticeably larger than the given part.

The *5-year-old* names the incomplete man a "man," a "boy," or a "girl" and he completes or adds seven parts: a leg, an arm, fingers, eyes, feet, ears, and perhaps hair.

The *6-year-old* child adds nine parts to the man. In addition to completing the parts supplied at 5 years, Six finishes the neckline and closes the part of the body at the tie. Some of the 6-year-olds clothe the man.

Sex differences. Girls add more details to the incomplete man than boys. The precentage differences are marked and occur especially at the ages when the particular parts are being included by the average child. A few examples will serve to illustrate the trend.

SEX DIFFERENCES IN RESPONSE TO THE INCOMPLETE MAN

	4	5	6
Age in years	4	5	6
Behavior:			
Completes leg:			
Boys	44	100	100
Girls	86	93	100
Completes hair:			
Boys	6	37	43
Girls	23	67	100
Completes ear:			
Boys	6	52	86
Girls	14	70	91
Completes body at tie:			
Boys	0	41	43
Girls	0	67	91

THE INCOMPLETE MAN

PERCENTAGE OF CASES RESPONDING AS INDICATED

	3*	4	5	6
Age in years	3*	4	5	6
Number of cases	13	31	57	18
Behavior:				
Names drawing a "man"	54	13	36	33
Names drawing a person, man, girl, etc.	69	32	56	73
Names drawing an animal	15	10	4	0
Gives no name	15	29	30	0
Completes:				
Leg	8	61	95	100
Arm	0	55	86	100
Eyes	31	42	65	78
Fingers	0	10	84	100
Foot (shoes)	8	35	97	100
Hair	0	13	53	78
Ear	0	10	61	89
Body at tie	0	0	54	72
Neckline	0	0	19	53
Added leg longer than original leg		40	23	5
Adds:				
Appendages, arms, legs, hands, feet	15	83	98	100
Features, including hair and ears	31	47	86	94
Clothing	0	0	21	27
Any three parts	0	53	100	100
Any seven parts	0	10	54	78
Any nine parts	0	3	19	50

* At 3 years 46 per cent of the cases do not respond to the test and 15 per cent merely scribble over the drawing.

Interpretation of behavior. It is interesting to compare the *Draw a Man* behavior with that elicited by the *Incomplete Man* situation. Naturally the *Incomplete Man* suggests certain features to the child which he would not draw spontaneously until he was older. There is a greater tendency to shade the incomplete man than the man. At 3 years this marking or shading is sometimes an attempt to complete the missing parts; in other instances it probably expresses impatience with the test; and in still other children it represents merely an attempt to satisfy the examiner in a test which is beyond their capacity. At older ages children have explained their shading as, "Make a dress on him," "All covered in his stomach," "Need color inside," "Pants," "Suit," "Color him," "That's his coat."

The child's manual skill and appreciation of symmetry is expressed in the relation of the size of the added part to the given part. By 6 years the added part is rarely out of proportion.

(A-19) MISSING PARTS

A test which may be considered an extension of the *Incomplete Man* is the *Missing Parts* test in which an essential of some picture has been omitted. The test described here is an original Binet-Simon test, restandardized by Terman (121) and revised by Kuhlmann (75). Binet placed it at 8 years, but he did not demonstrate the first picture when the child failed it. Terman and Kuhlmann who demonstrate the first picture, but who with Binet and Simon require three correct responses out of four, place the test at 6 years. Using the procedure to be described which is essentially like that prescribed by Terman and Binet and Simon, we find the test applicable as young as 4 years, although it is not until after 6 years that a child can normally be expected to respond correctly to all four pictures.

In the late 1920's and '30's, the fourth picture, that of a woman with a long gown, was considered such an unfamiliar sight that failure to recognize the missing arms was expected, but now with the variety in fashion, the picture is no longer out of date and the test can no longer be considered inappropriate.

Procedure. Take the card on which are printed the original Binet-Simon test pictures for *Lacunes de Figures* test and, using a plain white card, cover all but the picture of the face with the missing eye. Show the child the picture and say, "*See this face. There is something left out of the face; the face is not all drawn. Look carefully and tell me what is left out.*" If the child fails to note the missing eye, or if he gives an irrelevant answer, say, "*See, there is no eye, the eye has been left out,*" and point to where the eye should be, differentiating between eye and eyebrow.

12

Slide the card down exposing the face with the missing mouth and say, *"What has been left out of this face?"* If the child fails, do not explain but proceed to the next face and then the full-length figure, asking in turn, *"What has been left out of this face?"*, and *"What has been left out of this picture?"*

Scoring. Correct pointing without naming the part is considered correct if the child's response is clear and decisive. It is also considered correct if he names two parts, including the correct missing part. For the full-length picture, the designation of hands or fingers instead of arms is accepted. Any of these deviations are, of course, noted in the record.

Behavior trends. The *4-year-old* child usually must have the missing part of the first picture pointed out, but he does identify the missing part for at least one of the pictures, either by pointing to or naming it. His errors consist of the response, "nothing," or perseverative replies such as "eye," "eye," "eye," "ear," "ear," "ear," or some similar response.

The *5-year-old* also must usually have the missing part of the first picture demonstrated but when this is done he responds correctly to three of the four pictures. However, he is likely to name another part not missing, such as "eye, mouth," or "ear, nose," or "feet, arms."

The *6-year-old* may need to have the first picture demonstrated but he usually responds correctly to more than one picture. His advance in maturity over 5 years is particularly evident in naming only the correct missing part.

Significance of the test. The ability to identify the missing part essential to a picture requires that the child has sufficiently differentiated this part from the whole and from other parts to recognize its absence from the whole, when seen from the particular point of view from which the picture is presented.

In the first picture the eyebrow is confusing to the child. He has little need or occasion for distinguishing between eye and eyebrow. He early recognizes eyes, but eyebrows are of minor importance. It is noteworthy that there is but little difference between the percentage of children passing this test at 4 years and 5 years, and that it is not until 5½ years that the average child notes that an eye is missing. Some of the 4-year-old children undoubtedly give a spuriously correct answer, meaning by their response, that only one eye is pictured. They have not yet learned to picture the profile face.

It is difficult to find a simple adequate means of checking their notion. This first picture is the most frequently failed of the four pictures.

The second picture with the missing mouth is the easiest. The third picture is only slightly more difficult. Again in this third picture it is the profile representation which confuses the relatively immature child. He pictures a face with two eyes, yet he sees only one. An eye, therefore, is missing. Even though he may note the missing nose, he also answers, "eye."

The last picture is confusing because the child may have such a vivid picture of legs as essential to the human form that he is overimpressed by not seeing them pictured, consequently a wrong or a double answer may be given. A few relatively mature children consider that the lady has her arms behind her and thus answer, "Nothing."

In spite of the ambiguities in appraising the child's responses, the test is a very valuable one, since it is a test failed by older feeble-minded children. The test therefore depends more upon cortical maturation than it does upon mere specific training. It is of interest to compare responses to this test with those to the *Man Completion*.

MISSING PARTS TEST

PERCENTAGE OF CASES IDENTIFYING INDICATED PARTS

	4	5	6
Age in years	4	5	6
Number of cases	21	56	18
Demonstration necessary	57	52	39
After demonstration, response correct:			
1 picture	52	91	100
2 pictures	24	75	95
3 pictures	0	45	72
Identifies missing part, 4 pictures	0	20	39
Identifies missing:			
Eye	43	48	61
Mouth	27	75	95
Nose	32	59	95
Arms	14	77	72

IMITATED MARKINGS AND THE COPY OF FORMS

The drawing situations of this section test abilities antecedent to printing, writing, and copying. The child is shown a circle, cross, square, or other geometric form and asked to draw one like it. After his ability to copy the model has been tested, the examiner demonstrates the drawing of the form and asks the child to imitate it. Naturally at the age levels below 3 years the child is unable to copy, so the examiner begins by demonstrating the marking. Drawing after watching someone else draw is an easier task and develops earlier than drawing when given only the finished product as a model; and the ability to copy a model is requisite for printing and writing.

Genetically these performances may be traced back to the chance marks which an infant makes as he combines the crayon and paper. The marks stimulate an interest in and a continuance of the activity. The character of the marks is at first conditioned by the child's neuro-motor control; then, as he watches the motions of others in drawing, he learns to modify his movements and to imitate their markings.

Prior to 3 years, the situations about to be described are presented after the spontaneous drawing situation. They reveal maturity of visual perception and of neuro-muscular and eye-hand coordination, as well as general mental adaptability. These situations, therefore, are an integral part of the preschool psychological examination.

(A-20) IMITATED MARKINGS

Although the ability to copy the circle, cross, and square from the model should always be tested before the examiner demonstrates these drawings, *the order of discussion is reversed here* because genetically the child can imitate a mark before he can reproduce it from the model.

To imitate the examiner's mark, the child must have the ability spontaneously to make the necessary movements, then he must observe the examiner's motions, they must suggest similar movements to him, and he must be "set" to imitate rather than to "free lance." If the child has reached the stage of development when he can copy these drawings, the above factors are no longer important. Then he reproduces the finished product, using higher level abilities.

Vertical stroke. Procedure. When the drawing of a man is completed, place a fresh sheet of paper before the child, secure his regard, and, using the red lumber crayon (a pencil, beginning at 3 years) draw a straight vertical line at the side of the paper at the child's left. Then hand the crayon to the child, point to the right side of the paper and say, *"You make one here."* If the child's first response is not a well-defined imitation, repeat the demonstration with a fresh sheet of paper. If on the first trial, the child marks over the examiner's mark, on the second trial point with a little more emphasis to the right. If necessary give the child three trials.

Label the drawings with numbers and arrows on each line to indicate the order and direction of drawing. Any line not deviating from the vertical more than 70° is considered a vertical line.

Behavior trends. The *18-month-old* child is on the verge of being able to draw a vertical line; it is just a pace beyond him but he is more likely to draw a vertical line than to make any other one mark. Otherwise he may draw a line at any angle, he may make a horizontal line, or he may just scribble.

The *2-year-old* child imitates the vertical line, usually on the first trial, almost surely if given two chances. The most frequent erroneous response is an oblique line.

The *3-year-old* invariably imitates the vertical line.

Sex differences. No sex differences were noted.

THE VERTICAL LINE (IMITATED)

PERCENTAGE OF CASES WHO MARK AS INDICATED

Age in years	1½	2	3
Number of cases	38	34	22
Behavior:			
Lines predominantly vertical	47	79	100
Lines predominantly horizontal	32	12	0
Lines predominantly oblique	37	35	0
Lines predominantly circular	3	18	0
Lines predominantly scribble	32	24	0

Comment. The child's first marks are likely to be oblique and slightly curved. They are segments of the back and forth scribbling noted in his spontaneous activity. After the oblique stroke, the vertical stroke is the easiest direction for the child to draw. It is definitely easier than the horizontal stroke next demonstrated.

Horizontal Stroke. Procedure. Use the procedure described for the vertical stroke, only in this instance draw a horizontal line from left to right at the top of the paper as viewed by the child. If necessary give the child three trials. Any line deviating from the horizontal less than 20° is considered horizontal.

Behavior trends. The child of *18 months* makes a single mark. Usually the mark is not horizontal, although he is more likely to draw a horizontal line than to make any other single kind of mark, such as a vertical line, an oblique line, or a scribble—each of which is made on one of the three trials by a third of the children of this age.

The *2-year-old* makes either a vertical or a horizontal mark but he is a little more likely to make the vertical rather than the horizontal stroke.

The *3-year-old* makes a well-defined horizontal stroke.

Sex differences. None were noted.

THE HORIZONTAL STROKE (IMITATED)

PERCENTAGE OF CASES WHO MARK AS INDICATED

Age in years	1½	2	3
Number of cases	34	34	22
Behavior:			
Lines predominantly horizontal	47	41	95
Lines predominantly vertical	24	50	5
Lines predominantly oblique	24	21	0
Lines predominantly circular	9	12	0
Lines predominantly scribble	24	38	0

Comment. It should be noted that at *18 months* the child's imitation is more likely to be horizontal than vertical in response to the horizontal stroke, while at *2 years* the reverse is true. Perhaps the vertical marking at 18 months is a delayed response to the vertical stroke which was demonstrated in the immediately preceding situation. Similarly a child sometimes pushes the blocks, train-fashion, saying "choo-choo," long after he has seen the train demonstrated by the examiner. At these young age levels responses are sometimes delayed and what may be interpreted as a response to one situation, may in reality be the response to some previous situation.

For test purposes, the vertical mark test is better than the horizontal stroke, since the percentages for the vertical mark show a more consistent trend with age than the percentages for the horizontal mark. Clinically, however, it is of interest to test the child's adaptation on both tests.

The Circular Stroke. The circular scribble differs from the child's spontaneous marks and therefore when the demonstrated behavior is approximated, adaptation is obvious.

Procedure. Use the procedure described for the horizontal stroke, only this time draw a continuous concentric circular line, making three or four circuits. Indicate by pointing below the model the place where the child is expected to mark. Any continuous marking which leaves within its border a well-defined space even though oval in shape is considered circular marking.

Behavior trends. The *18-month-old* either scribbles or makes an oblique line. He may mark over the demonstration mark. As a rule, he has not yet learned to differentiate the circular mark from the single mark, or from his own characteristic scribbling—but it is significant that a few children of this age do adapt.

The *2-year-old* has just reached the age when he can imitate the circular stroke. He too may mark over the examiner's mark. However, a number of children at this age either just scribble or mark at an angle on one or more trials.

The *3-year-old* imitates the circular stroke.

Sex differences. At 18 months and 2 years, the girls excel the boys on this test: at 18 months, 45 per cent of the girls and only 17 per cent of the boys imitate; at 2 years, the percentages are 68 for the girls and 47 for the boys.

Comment. The circular movement required by this test is a skill required in winding thread on a spool, stirring with a spoon, and many other activities. The test yields, as a rule, a rather clear-cut, easily scored

THE CIRCULAR STROKE (IMITATED)

PERCENTAGE OF CASES WHO MARK AS INDICATED

	1½	2	3
Age in years	1½	2	3
Number of cases	38	34	22
Behavior:			
Lines predominantly circular	32	59	86
Lines predominantly horizontal	32	21	
Lines predominantly vertical	13	21	
Lines predominantly oblique	69	62	
Lines predominantly scribble	69	62	
Marks over or near demonstration	43	41	0

performance and the increase in percentage of correct responses with age shows a steady, well-defined trend.

The Cross. To imitate the cross requires more than being able to imitate the horizontal and vertical lines. The lines must be properly oriented one to the other, and the child must make a transition from vertical to horizontal, or horizontal to vertical marking. To do this requires that both vertical and horizontal drawing are mastered.

Procedure. Use the procedure described for the horizontal stroke only this time draw a cross, first making the vertical line by a downward stroke, then the horizontal crossline from left to right across the paper. Indicate by pointing below the model where the child is expected to mark.

Behavior trends. The *2-year-old* child makes a vertical line and then either makes another vertical line, an oblique line, or reverts to scribbling. He cannot, at this age, imitate the cross but he does modify his behavior in an attempt to do so. He shows a tendency to make marks over the examiner's cross.

The *3-year-old* child easily imitates drawing the cross. Errors occur principally when the child starts to make the horizontal line and is then unable to complete the pattern.

Sex differences. None have been noted.

THE CROSS (IMITATED)

PERCENTAGE OF CASES WHO MARK AS INDICATED

	2	3
Age in years	2	3
Number of cases	29	30
Behavior:		
Imitates model	3	77
Lines predominantly circular	31	32
Lines predominantly scribble	45	20
Imitates cross on first trial	0	50
Marks twice or imitates	23	87
Marks over or near demonstration	27	3

Comment. This is one of the best tests available for the 2-3 year period. Errors of marking are discussed in the section to follow, where the errors of marking for all of the imitated markings are evaluated.

Significance of behavior. The child himself through his errors gives us specific insight concerning the difficulties which he is experiencing. When imitating either the horizontal or vertical stroke, he may err by incorrect orientation of the marks. Perhaps he does not perceive directional distinctions, or perhaps he is unable to coordinate his movements to conform to the model performance, or perhaps it is his "idea" of a game in which the examiner does something and then he does something similar, such as tit-tat-toe where one makes a cross mark and the other a circular mark. There is evidence in certain instances that direction is perceived since, on repeated trials, the markings show a progressive approximation to the demonstration. Three trials are thus of considerable value in analyzing the child's abilities and difficulties. The satisfaction which a child may repeatedly show with his disoriented line is a clue to the maturity of his perception and his misunderstanding of what is required. Other less mature errors in response to the demonstrated vertical or horizontal strokes are merely scribbling, drawing a circular line, or making repeated strokes. In the first instance, the child gives evidence that he has either misunderstood the imitative aspect of the situation, or that he is playing a game, or that he has limited control of his movements. The latter interpretation is usually the correct one. A circular line response usually indicates immature coordination; making repeated strokes may be both an evidence of immaturity and of personality. To know when to stop and to effect the necessary inhibition is a necessary adaptation of growth, but it is also an individual characteristic.

Marking over the examiner's mark or marking along the edge of the paper is probably motivated by both a tendency to duplicate exactly the examiner's demonstration and a subconscious use of the examiner's mark or the paper edge as a guide. It is for this reason that the examiner should make an effort to have the child mark in the middle of the paper, since tracing the demonstrated mark on the paper edge is a simpler task.

The most common error in imitating the circular scribble is to brush rather than to circle. It is not unusual to see progressive adaptation on repeated demonstration.

In imitating the cross, further difficulties are encountered. Since there are two movements to perform, one after the other, the child's memory is taxed. Also, after the child has drawn one line, the *Gestalt* presented by that line is confusing and perhaps diverting. The child's product as he draws appears to him unlike the demonstration and if he is self-critical he may lose confidence and err by making just another mark. The concept of making two marks is easier than the concept of making a vertical and a horizontal mark, or even of making two similar marks. Thus errors in imitating the cross include both making two marks side by side, and making one straight line and one circular line.

Frequently the child could be credited with making a cross if he stopped at the proper moment. Instead, after making the cross, he continues the final mark, making a returning loop; or he may make an indefinite number of vertical or horizontal cross marks; or he may even revert to scribbling. In some of these instances the child is dissatisfied with what he has done; in others he does not recognize his success when it occurs but keeps on trying; and in still others, he merely continues his own activity after he has tried to satisfy the examiner. There is danger in overinterpreting a child's behavior, but close attention to the child's facial expression, manner, and subsequent behavior is helpful and instructive. If a record of spontaneous remarks is kept, it will be found that the child himself hints at or even verbalizes his attitudes and difficulties.

(A-21) THE COPY OF FORMS

It was pointed out in the preceding discussion that it is decidedly easier to imitate drawing a geometric form than it is to copy that same form from a model. To copy a form when only the model is shown requires that the child perceive it, that he recognize it in terms of his past experience, that he be "set" to copy, that he possess the necessary eye-hand control to draw the lines in the proper direction, and that he not be distracted by the change in pattern as he draws.

The forms which the child is asked to copy are pictured on Plate XIX, *c:* a circle, a cross, a square, a triangle, a rectangle with diagonals, and a horizontal diamond. These are presented in the order named. The procedure will be described but once, since presentation is the same for each form.

Procedure. This test must precede *Imitative Drawing* since clues received in that test invalidate this one. If for some unavoidable reason, imitation of forms has been given first, delay the copy of forms as long as possible so that the intervening tests will lessen the effect of demonstration.

Supply the child with a pencil and a sheet of green paper, then present the card to be reproduced and say, *"Make one just like this."* If there is any hesitation, encourage the child by saying, *"I am sure you can. Just try."* Be careful not to draw around the figure in pantomime nor to give the child any indication by gesture of the movements made in drawing. Such procedures alter considerably the psychological import of the test.

If the child asks what the figure is, do not give him its geometric name; merely say, *"It's just something to draw."*

Hold the model flat on the table, just above the paper, while the child draws. When necessary, prevent him from marking on the model by withdrawing it from his reach, saying, *"You mark here,"* pointing to the paper. Allow three trials.

Use the above procedure for each form, saying, *"Now make one like this."* If the child begins to lose interest, he can be held to the task with, *"We're almost through now," "Just a few more,"* or some similar encouraging remark.

Behavior trends. The Circle. At *3 years*, the child draws a circle, arc, or spiral; at *4 years*, he joins ends of circle but draws a misshapen or elongated circle; at *5 years*, he draws circle flattened on one side; at *6 years*, he draws a well-rounded copy.

The Cross. At *3 years* the child does not copy the model. Rather, he draws circular lines or scribbles. At *4 years* he copies, but errs on one trial. The lines may be broken or at an angle. At *5 years* he copies, but the length is greater than the breadth, or the breadth greater than the length. The lines are rarely broken or at an angle. At *6 years* he draws a good copy, correctly proportioned.

The Square. The *3-year-old* makes circular marks which may or may not close. At *4 years* the child draws a circle or draws one side straight and completes with a circle like a capital *D*. Usually one corner is inadequately drawn. Children who do succeed draw four lines, meeting at corners. At *5 years* the child draws three corners adequately. Corners may not be sharp but defined and rounded. The *6-year-old* draws a square with sharp corners.

The Triangle. The *4-year-old* indicates the apex by a scribble, a crossline, an indentation or a circular point. At *5 years* the child draws a triangular-shaped figure with apex. At *6 years* the child copies the triangle, all angles correctly drawn.

The Rectangle with diagonals.[3] At *5 years plus* the child copies.

The Diamond. At *5 years* the child draws an elongated shape, cannot make the points but indicates them by crosslines, by indentations, or by circular bulges. At *6 years* he copies the form.

Significance of behavior. As usual, it is the child's errors which are significant in analyzing his limitations. Errors, primarily of perception, are illustrated when a small diagonal line is added to the center of the

---

[3] Unfortunately this form was not included routinely in the normative examinations. It was, however, a test standardized as part of the Gesell scale (30). At *5 years*, 48 per cent of the children made a satisfactory reproduction. The drawing is reproduced with two diagonals; the vertical line may or may not be included.

COPY OF FORMS

Percentage of Cases Copying Form as Indicated

	3	4	5	6
Age in years	3	4	5	6
Number of cases	22	31	57	18

Predominant shape[4] on three trials:

Circle:

I. Well-rounded	9	8	21	72
II. Compressed	17	43	63	28
III. Misshapen	65*	48	14	0

Cross:

I. Well-balanced	0	0	21	60
II. Vertically or horizontally elongated	14	55	53	40
III. Imperfect	86	45	46	0

Square:

I. Four well-defined corners	0	10	38	83
II. One or more poorly defined corners	5	30	53	11
III. Cornerless, potato-shaped	95	60	18	5

Triangle:

I. Tricornered		0	40	95
II. One or more defective corners		0	23	0
III. Misshapen or quadrilateral form		100	37	0

Diamond:

I. Adequate		0	9	61
II. One or more corners inadequate		0	4	17
III. Misshapen		100	88	22

* Includes spirals, 22 per cent, and scribbling, 9 per cent.

cross, when several lines are drawn crossing at a common center, or when the horizontal line of the cross is made shorter than the vertical line. In the first two examples, the center of the cross may have been overperceived. In addition, perseveration of activity may be a causal factor. With respect to the last example, it is clear that some children perceive their cross to be inadequate in width, since they correct it by extending the crossline laterally first on one side and then on the other.

The copy of the rectangle with diagonals likewise reflects a child's perceptive processes. A child may focus his attention on the converging lines at the center so as to confuse his impression of the outer form, or he may "see" the outer form to the exclusion of the focus within. His drawing when erroneous will reflect the emphasis.

It is significant that no child *imitates* the cross by drawing lines radiating from a common center, even though this is a common method of *copying* the cross. In imitating a cross, the child imitates the motion which the examiner makes; while in copying the cross, the model does not necessarily suggest to the child one horizontal line and one vertical line; it

[4] On page 166 samples of the designated behavior are pictured. In evaluating any individual child's behavior, the examiner must use his own judgment. There are many borderline examples which will necessitate an arbitrary decision.

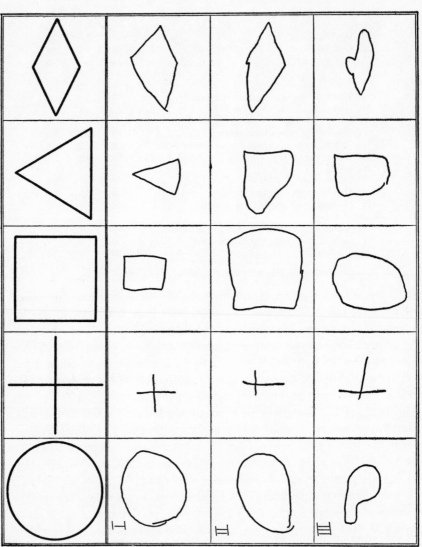

Samples of Responses to Copy of Forms

may suggest four radiating lines. This is one reason why a child may fail to copy the cross when he easily imitates its drawing, or why he fails to copy the circle but imitates the examiner's demonstration.

As an example of the difference between imitating and copying a form, the drawings of B-38 are reproduced in miniature. The numbers on the lines indicate the order of drawing and the arrows show the direction of the lines. The drawings tell their own story. B-3's drawings tell a similar story. He copies the circle, fails to copy the cross, but imitates it. Furthermore, his two successive trials to imitate the square are classic examples of learning and of the way in which a 3-year-old duplicates the square.

Occasionally a child will not be able to copy a form, usually the square, until he is given a name for it. Then he quickly draws an acceptable "copy." In such a case the verbal designation rather than the form has been associated with the kinesthesia of drawing and the model may not be an aid. Original procedure should therefore abstain from naming the model.

Eye-hand control is a prime factor in duplicating a form, when given the model. We may be uncertain whether the child who repeatedly draws a circle for a square notices the corners of the square, or whether he is making no attempt to duplicate them; but when a child copies the triangle by making a circle with three lines drawn across its circumference, we know that he sees the points but is inadequate in representing them. Also when a child draws a corner as a bulge or an arc or an inverted loop, we know that his eye-hand coordination is incapable of reproducing the right-angled turn, another indication that the child perceives the shape but is unable to duplicate it in the modifications in his drawing on repeated trials. B-14 more closely approximates the model of the square on each successive attempt. B-25, likewise, varies his performance in such a way that his goal to reproduce the triangle apex is clear. Some children, however, duplicate their errors so that interpretation of the difficulty which they are experiencing is obscure.

It should be noted that the children who copy the square at an age earlier than usual do so by drawing four lines. (See B-3's copies of the square.) It is easier to start anew to draw a line in a required direction than it is to change the direction in which one is drawing. At the age when the child is able to copy the square, it is not appreciably easier for the child to draw in one direction than another, and yet it is decidedly more difficult a problem for the child to draw a triangle than to draw a square, and it is more difficult to draw a diamond than a triangle. It is the complexity of the figures that makes the tasks of graded difficulty.

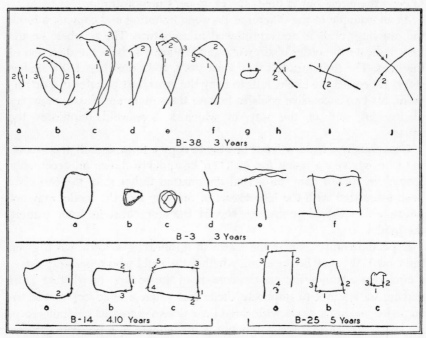

Examples of the Differences between Imitating and Copying

B-38. 3 years.
a. Copies circle, first trial.
b. Copies circle, second trial.
c. Copies circle, third trial.
d. Copies cross, first trial.
e. Copies cross, second trial.
f. Copies cross, third trial.
g. Imitates circle.
h. Imitates cross, first trial.
i. Imitates cross, second trial.
j. Imitates cross, third trial.
B-3. 3 years.
a. Copies circle.

b. Copies cross, first trial.
c. Copies cross, second trial.
d. Imitates cross.
e. Imitates square, first trial.
f. Imitates square, second trial.
B-14. 4.10 years.
a. Copies square, first trial.
b. Copies square, second trial.
c. Copies square, third trial.
B-25. 5 years.
a. Copies triangle, first trial.
b. Copies triangle, second trial.
c. Copies triangle, third trial.

Undoubtedly the *Gestalt* of the total drawing model, compared with the *Gestalt* of the unfinished product, is disconcerting. Also as in mirror drawing, a change of direction in the lines of drawing is obviously confusing.

GENETIC SUMMARY OF ABILITY TO IMITATE OR TO COPY FORMS[5]
Age 15 months—Spontaneous scribble
  18 months—Imitates vertical stroke
  24 months—Imitates circle
  30 months—Imitates vertical and horizontal strokes; marks twice for cross
  36 months—Copies circle, imitates cross
  42 months—Traces diamond[*]
  48 months—Copies cross
  54 months—Traces cross[*]
  60 months—Copies triangle
  66 months—Can print a few letters
  72 months—Copies diamond

§ E. NUMBER CONCEPTS

The basis of counting is similarity. We add like objects. Primitive number concepts are from this point of view traceable to beginning language. Concrete evidence of enumeration begins when, for example, a child points to all the cars that he sees, one after the other, saying "Car? car?" or "More car?" as though discovering the genus "car." Gradually and very soon after 2 years he uses the plural form to designate more than one, and the notion of one, as opposed to many, is built up.

The notion "two" likewise usually develops in relation to two objects, but "three" may first have either a collective or an ordinal connotation. The child may be taught to say the numbers 1, 2, 3—or he may learn to identify them with the visual pattern formed by three objects. However, a child may be able to match objects with a similar number of objects without having either an ordinal or cardinal number notion. Some children readily form the association between the ordinal or cardinal concepts while other children fail to relate them. For example, some children easily point successively to four objects, naming them "one, two, three, four," but are quite baffled when asked, "How many are there?" and if asked to "Give me four," are unable to do so. One child of 5 years repeatedly failed to count four objects, but when asked to "give me just

[5] The copy of the square has not been included in the above tabulation because of marked individual differences in performance, depending on the method of duplication which the child uses.
[*] See Chapter VI, pp. 100, 101.

four," readily did so. This is, of course, unusual. It has also been noted that a child might be able to differentiate two objects, such as apples, but not two objects such as fingers or legs. Counting is, therefore, a very specific ability.

It is well known that a child is able to say numbers in their correct order before he can say them while pointing to objects. This discrepancy of behavior is easily understood. In the initial stages of learning the number series, it takes real concentration to remember which number comes next. When enumeration is complicated by moving the finger from one object to the next, errors either of counting or of finger placement are likely to occur. Successful counting of objects is accomplished only when the recitation of numbers is learned well above the limen of recall.

When the number series is finally thoroughly learned, specific examples of addition and subtraction within the limits of visualization are easy steps forward. Beyond this stage, the abstract notions involved in calculating may be a stumbling block. Rote memory becomes of prime importance for further arithmetical progress.

It is easy to minimize the concentration demanded of the preschool child in solving what are to the adult the simplest of problems. One boy of 5 years who repeatedly and easily counted thirteen pennies, and who without pointing counted to thirty, was asked such questions as, "If you have two pennies and I give you two more, how many will you have?" His answers, quickly given, were so frequently wrong that the examiner attempted to make him try harder by saying, laughingly, "You're guessing—try hard." To which he replied with emphasis and feeling, "I'm thinking!" A review of his answers proved him right. Great patience and an appreciation of the child's difficulties are required of those who would help him learn.

The tests which follow are designed to reveal the child's stage of learning in its various aspects. They are the tests which we have found to be particularly adapted to the routine clinical examination. Other tests of number concepts will be found in the references cited in § 10.

(A-22) Placing Cubes in Cup

The 18-month-old child characteristically occupies himself with filling, emptying, and refilling the cup with cubes. As he grows older this repetitive activity gives way to more mature and considered behaviors so that he will put a requested number of cubes in the cup, according to the maturity of his number concepts. The test is appropriate for children between 2½ and 4 years old.

Procedure. At the end of the cube situations, place the cup beside the cubes and after the child has explored the situation in his own manner, empty the cup and say, *"Put just one in the cup."* If he succeeds, empty the cup and say, *"Put two blocks in the cup,"* and then in the same way, *"Put three blocks in the cup."* Repeat the test, varying the number to be put in until it is clear that the child either lacks or possesses the number sense and the control that the test requires. Be careful not to give the child a cue to the correct response by facial expression or glance. One way to avoid so doing is to look out of the window.

A variation of this test is to omit the cup and request the child to *"Give me two blocks,"* then *"Give me just one block,"* and *"Give me three blocks."* Another variation is to use pennies in place of cubes, asking the child to give the examiner *"just one,"* etc.

Behavior trends. The *2-year-old* child places or gives the examiner one cube after the other. Only rarely does he differentiate between one and many. At *2½ years* the child successfully places or gives "just one"; at *3 years* he places or gives both "one" and "two"; and at *4½ years* he adaptively places or gives three blocks.

Significance of the test. For practical purposes the three variations of the test are equivalent. If the response is questionable on one version, another version may be used as a check. This test furnishes fairly conclusive evidence of the child's appreciation of the cardinal significance of one, two, and three; but it does not necessarily mean that he can or cannot count. Counting should be tested separately.

All percentages for this section are given at the end of the section.

(A-23) COUNTING

The 2-year-old child distinguishes between one and many, but he usually does not count objects. As a rule he learns to enumerate numbers before he can count objects. Frequently children will be able to count objects but they do not necessarily associate the terminal number with the totality of objects. This test is devised to tap all three abilities.

Procedure. Place four pennies two inches apart in a row on the table and say, *"Count them and tell me how many there are."* If the child hesitates, say, *"See, like this: one—"* If the child counts without pointing, demonstrate and say, *"No, count them with your finger like this: one—"* When he finishes ask him, *"How many are there?"* If he correctly counts four, place thirteen pennies in a row and repeat the procedure. At the 5-year level, start with thirteen pennies and resort to four pennies only in case he fails to count thirteen. Give the child at least two trials and use the best trial as his score.

13

When counting pennies is finished, ask the child how far he can count, then say, "*Let me hear you.*"

Behavior trends. The *3-year-old* is just learning to count. He can usually only count two objects although he is reported to count up to five. When counting objects he may not start with one but with some other number and then proceed correctly.

The *4-year-old* is reported to count up to ten, but he counts with correct pointing to only three objects. He too may start with a number higher than one, even when he is specially directed.

The *5-year-old* rarely fails to start with one and he counts, with correct pointing, ten objects. As a rule, he fails to count thirteen objects, but he recites numbers up to thirteen. If he does correctly count thirteen pennies on one trial, he frequently errs on another trial.

The *6-year-old* child rarely errs in counting thirteen objects and he correctly recites numbers up to the thirties.

Sex differences. Girls count higher and err less in counting than boys.

Significance of the test. The test may reflect experience or native ability. Numbers up to five are such an integral part of our daily life that failure to count four objects at 5 years of age is significant.

(A-24) NUMBER OF FINGERS

The specificity of number concepts has been mentioned. This test presupposes that a child has had sufficient interest in numbers to have counted his fingers and to have remembered the number, or that he has a visual picture of five and ten which enables him to give an immediate answer to the question. The test is quickly given and is reliable in the sense that it differentiates age levels rather sharply.

Procedure. The test is conveniently given after the child has been asked to differentiate his right and left hand, eye, and ear. Then say, "*How many fingers have you on your right hand?*" Follow this with, "*How many on your left hand?*", then, "*How many on both hands?*" If the child starts to count them, put your hand gently on his and say, "*No, tell me without counting.*"

Scoring. A child may correctly consider that he has four or five fingers on a hand, but he must be consistent in his replies.

Characteristic behavior. The *5-year-old* gives the correct number of fingers for the separate hands but he can rarely give the total number of fingers. The *6-year-old* child rarely fails to give the correct number of fingers on a single hand, but he usually cannot give the number on both hands. It is not usually until a child is *6½ years* old that he can tell the total number of fingers without first counting them.

Significance of the test. Although the test is a reliable one, it is not as significant as some other tests of number concepts. It was probably for this reason that Binet omitted it in his 1911 revision. Considering the fact that it takes a very short time to administer, the test is, nevertheless, a useful one. Superior children do not usually pass the test until they are near the normative age, but dull children are likely to fail it when it is consistent with their general mental level to do so.

(A-25) DRAWING BUBBLES

This test was introduced by Gesell (30) as a "further evidence on the existence and intensity of any number sense which the child has acquired." Children are interested in the picture and readily respond.

Procedure. Place the picture of a boy blowing bubbles in front of the child with the remark, *"What is the boy doing? He is blowing bubbles, isn't he?"* Point to the bubble and if necessary draw around it to be sure that the child knows what the bubble is. Then say, *"Now you draw one bubble under the chair; just one bubble under the chair."* Follow this with, *"Now make two bubbles above the boy's head."* Then say, *"Make three bubbles behind the boy—three bubbles behind him."* Then, *"Make four bubbles in front of him—four bubbles in front of him."* If the child refuses because he does not understand where to place the bubbles, urge him just to put them where he thinks they should go.

Scoring. Since the main object of the test is to reveal the maturity of number concepts, minor misplacements of the bubbles are disregarded. For instance, the 4-year-old may consider "above" in the three-dimensional sense and put the bubbles on the boy's head. This would not be considered an error.

Behavior trends. The *4-year-old* draws one bubble correctly placed. He draws two bubbles but is confused as to their placement. He is rarely able to draw three or four bubbles although he responds correctly to the direction "in back of."

The *5-year-old* follows correctly the four directions. He finds no difficulty in correctly placing the bubbles although he may err in drawing four bubbles.

The *6-year-old* very rarely fails to make a perfect score.

Sex differences. No sex differences in performance were evident.

Significance of the test. The test response obviously involves more than the child's number concepts. He must have such a clear concept of the numbers that he is not confused by the additional directions of placement. He must not become so engrossed with drawing the bubbles that he forgets the number which he must draw. Because the test calls for an integration of performance, it reveals the completeness and the effectiveness of the child's number knowledge—a very important consideration as a basis for appraisal and guidance.

(A-26) Number Problems

Simple addition and subtraction are first mastered in the form of very concrete examples. In fact it is hardly necessary to point out that man himself is not very far removed from dependency on such calculating devices as stones or the abacus. This test was included by Gesell (30) as appropriate for the preschool years. The suggestion of possessing pennies is appealing to the child. The test is quickly administered and it reveals the child's readiness to deal with numbers.

Procedure. Ask the child the following questions: *"If you have two pennies and I give you another penny, how many pennies will you have?" "If you have one penny and I give you another penny, how many pennies will you have?" "If you have two pennies and I give you two more pennies, how many pennies will you have?"* and so on with similar problems, test the child's ability to add within five. Using similar questions, test his ability to subtract within five.

Behavior trends. The *5-year-old* only occasionally is able to add within five. The *6-year-old* both adds and subtracts within five.

Significance of the test. Success in solving the problems depends on experience as well as command of number concepts. However, it is the exceptional child of 5 years who has not had sufficient experience with objects to answer the questions, if he has the required number concept ability. Whether or not arithmetical ability is a special talent has never been established. Certainly there is a great variation among children which tends to persist during their student days. Children who fail completely at a level inconsistent with their general maturity level should receive special help early in their careers so that they will not dread and dislike arithmetic.

Summary of Genetic Sequences in Number Concepts

Age 2½ years—Gives "just one"
  3 years—Gives "just two." Counts up to 5, without pointing (reported)
  4 years—Counts, with pointing, three objects. Draws two bubbles
  4½ years—Gives "just three." Counts, with pointing, four objects. Draws three bubbles
  5 years—Counts, with pointing, ten objects. Draws four bubbles. Tells number fingers on one hand
  5½ years—Counts, with pointing, thirteen objects
  6 years—Adds within 5
  6½ years—Tells number of fingers on both hands

NUMBER CONCEPTS

PERCENTAGE OF CASES PASSING TEST AT EACH AGE

Age in years	4	5	6
Behavior:			
Counts objects:			
"Unable to count"	25	4	
Four	30	96	
Six	22	87	
Ten	5	72	100
Thirteen	0	42	88
Gives number of fingers on:			
One hand		66	80
Total		17	45
Adds within five	12	33	54
Draws bubbles:			
One	67	95	100
Two	52	89	94
Three	11	75	100
Four	7	61	94
Under	61	100	100
Above	30	89	100
Back	56	95	100
Front	41	95	100

§ F. IMMEDIATE MEMORY

During the last quarter of the first year the infant gives well-defined evidence of his immediate memory ability through the following activities. After demonstration, he rattles the spoon in the cup, rings the bell, squeaks a doll, pat-a-cakes, waves bye-bye, and imitates making sounds and saying words. All of these behaviors show an ability to retain an impression long enough to reproduce behavior. In contrast to imitating, the infant also tends to explore and exploit his own activity. It is only when the demonstrated behavior carries some meaning to the child in terms of his own repertoire that imitation occurs, and then it occurs only if it can compete successfully with current activity drives. Failure and success on tests of imitation must be carefully interpreted, since failure may mean merely that the child's own activity drives are relatively strong, while success may be due to fortuitous spontaneous activity.

Between the ages of 1 and 2 years, a child is so busily engaged with his own exploitations that it is difficult in the limited time of the examination to obtain evidence of immediate memory except as it functions in the more generalized situations, such as block building and drawing. At 2 years and thereafter the more specific immediate memory tests are appropriate and become increasingly important for differential diagnosis. At all ages the tests are significant both in their specific and general adaptive behavior connotations.

The tests which follow, *Digit* and *Sentence Repetition,* are classic and have the advantage of being applicable to practically the whole life span.

(A-27) DIGIT REPETITION

It is our experience that below 3½ years the digit repetition test does not have sufficient significance to be included in the series, unless a child is unusually cooperative or unless he is mentally advanced for his age. At 4 years, however, number concepts are beginning to develop and digit repetition begins to take on meaning. Then cooperation can usually be obtained. From that time on the test is traditionally and actually valuable. The digit series used are those listed by Terman (121).

Procedure. Secure the child's attention and tell him, "*Listen, say, 4–2.*" After he responds, say, "*Listen again, 6–4–1.*" When necessary add, "*You say it.*" Allow a little less than a second for each number. Some children do not delay their response until all three numbers are given. On the first occasion when that happens, say, "*No, wait until I finish,*" and repeat the series.

The directions for children 4 years old and older should explain the task more fully. Then the examiner should say, "*I am going to say some numbers and when I am through, I want you to say them. Listen carefully.*" Continue with series of increasing length until the child's full ability has been tapped. If the child appears discouraged when he senses failure, encourage him with, "*Well, that was a hard one,*" and intersperse a shorter series, saying, "*I know you can do this one. Listen carefully.*" The numbers should be enunciated in a monotone with equal emphasis. It is permissible to lower the voice for the last number. This, together with a nod of the head, will indicate to the child that it is his turn to respond.

Behavior trends. The *4-year-old* child can repeat three digits on two of three trials. He fails to repeat four digits, usually not giving even the correct number, but adds or omits one. However, three of the four digits are remembered, although not necessarily correctly ordered.

At *5 years* four digits are correctly repeated on one of three trials. The child now usually gives the correct number of digits, three of which are the digits given. There is little tendency to add a digit but a digit may be omitted. Thus the 5-year-old is on the verge of being able correctly and consistently to repeat four digits. Only rarely, however, can the 5-year-old repeat five digits and he usually does not even give the correct number of digits, but he omits rather than adds to them. A frequent type of error is to invert the digits.

The *6-year-old* almost invariably correctly repeats four digits on two of three trials. He may repeat five digits once in three trials, but rarely on two of three trials. The child may omit a number or he may add a number. He remembers correctly only four of the five digits.

Sex differences. No well-defined sex differences were found.

GENETIC SUMMARY

Age 2½ years—Repeats two   digits, one of three trials
3   years—Repeats three digits, one of three trials
3½ years—Repeats three digits, two of three trials
4½ years—Repeats four   digits, one of three trials
5½ years—Repeats four   digits, two of three trials
6½ years—Repeats five   digits, one of three trials

Significance of test. Failure to repeat the digits correctly may be due to several factors, the most important of which are hearing deficiency, lack of number concept, faulty attention, and inadequate auditory imagery. Undoubtedly certain children, familiar with numbers, translate their auditory experience into visual images. It is even common for a child to repeat the numbers under his breath as the examiner gives them, thus reinforcing the auditory impression with speech mechanisms. Failures and successes which are not in line with other expressions of adaptive behavior are frequently difficult to interpret. Some children give a parrot-like response which may be so evaluated; others show a real ability to retain and reproduce auditory impressions. In spite of the sometimes vague significance of the test, it taps an ability which is important for successful learning and is therefore of considerable clinical importance.

DIGIT REPETITION
PERCENTAGE OF CASES BEHAVING AS INDICATED

Age in years	2	3	4	5	6
Number of cases			24	53	17
Behavior:					
Repeats two digits	25*	85*	100		
Repeats three digits:					
One of three trials		59*	92	98	
Two of three trials			75	87	
Fails once			33	17	
Repeats four digits:					
One of three trials			22	58	89
Two of three trials			0	43	67
Fails once			83	58	39
Repeats five digits:					
One of three trials			0	17	44
Two of three trials				4	28
Fails once			100	98	83

* Goodenough (45).

(A-28) Sentence Repetition

The 2- and 3-year-old child is more cooperative in repeating a short sentence than in repeating digits. In fact some children of this age are veritable echoes. Failure to respond verbally is as frequently due to inability as it is to lack of cooperation. At 4 years and after, cooperation is rarely a problem. In addition to testing immediate memory, the test affords an opportunity for detecting immature and faulty articulation.

Procedure. Do not give this test immediately before or after digit repetition, nor near the beginning of the examination. In the first instance the child's powers of attention for this type of test may be fatigued; in the last instance, rapport may not be sufficiently established for verbal response.

Attract the child's attention by saying, *"Listen,"* using an appropriate gesture, then while he is looking directly at you say, *"Say—nice kitty."* If the child hesitates say, *"You say it."* Encourage him with, *"That's good,"* when he responds, then continue with *"Now say—see the cat."* Enunciate each word clearly, slowly, and with equal emphasis. Continue with the other sentences in order. If the child is uncooperative, do not persist with the test but return to it later in the course of the examination.

TEST SENTENCES

Introductory: *Nice kitty*

Group   I. (Three-four syllables):
    a. *See the cat.* (kitty)
    b. *I have a doll.* (dolly)
    c. *Where is mama?* (or daddy)
Group   II. (Six-seven syllables):
    a. *I have a little dog.*
    b. *In summer the sun is hot.*
    c. *The dog runs after the cat.*
Group III. (Twelve-thirteen syllables):
    a. *The boy's name is John. He is a very good boy.*
    b. *When the train passes, you will hear the whistle blow.*
    c. *We are going to have a good time in the country.*
Group IV. (Sixteen-eighteen syllables):
    a. *We are having a fine time. We found a little mouse in the trap.*
    b. *Walter had a fine time on his vacation. He went fishing every day.*
    c. *We will go out for a long walk. Please give me my pretty straw hat.*

Behavior trends. The *2-year-old* usually repeats a sentence of from three to four syllables, but cannot repeat the sentences of from six to seven syllables. Errors at this age consist of omitting the article or of repeating only the last word. Occasionally a child will misunderstand the directions completely and look for the cat or doll, or point to his parent.

The *3-year-old* easily repeats a sentence of from six to seven syllables, but he cannot yet repeat a sentence of from twelve to thirteen syllables. Errors are primarily repeating only the last part of the sentence.

The *4-year-old* repeats correctly one of the three sentences of from twelve to thirteen syllables. However, he usually omits words, adds words, or substitutes words on one of his three trials with sentences of twelve syllables or more. Also his articulation will probably be infantile in some respect.

The *5-year-old* is more proficient than Four in repeating a sentence of from twelve to thirteen syllables and he usually no longer gives any evidence of infantile articulation.

The *6-year-old* easily repeats a sentence of from twelve to thirteen syllables, but he cannot yet repeat without error one of from sixteen to eighteen syllables. His most frequent mistakes are errors of omission or substitution, such as omitting "very" in III a, and substituting "goes past" for "passes" in III b. Thus the child retains the meaning of the sentence but uses his own words.

Scoring. Faulty articulation and contraction of words do not constitute errors, but any omission, transposition, insertion, or other change is counted an error.

Significance of the behavior. This test differs from the digit repetition in content. We may reasonably expect children who show a discrepancy in number concept and language ability to show a similar difference on these two tests. Although both tests involve accurate auditory perception,

SENTENCE REPETITION

PERCENTAGE OF CASES RESPONDING AS INDICATED

Age in years	2	3	4	5	6
Number of cases	50*	50†	27	54	15
Behavior:					
Repeats correctly:					
Group I: 3-4 syllables:					
One of three	50				
All three	40				
Group II: 6-7 syllables:					
Sentence a			87	98	100
Sentence b			36		
Sentence c			63	100	
One of three	9	61	96	100	100
Group III: 12-13 syllables:					
Sentence a			17	16	47
Sentence b			17	38	80
Sentence c			50	67	100
One of three			50	67	100
Group IV: 16-18 syllables:					
Sentence a			13	3	39
Sentence b			9	18	17
Sentence c			9	3	11
One of three			29	13	14
Articulation infantile	?	?	56	39	13

* Data from Muntz (91); † Data from Holbrook (59).

hearing difficulties sufficiently severe to affect responses will manifest themselves in other ways.

Binet, in his discussion of the test, points out that echoing is the child's method of learning language and that his ability to repeat is in advance of his expression. This is true, of course, only in the initial stages of language development. At later ages the child's expression is far beyond his power to repeat exactly what someone else has said. For this reason, the test is probably closely related to language facility at the younger ages, and to more general adaptive behavior at the older ages.

GENETIC SUMMARY

Age norm 24 months—Repeats sentence of 3-4 syllables
*30 months—Repeats sentence of 6-7 syllables
*48 months—Repeats sentence of 12-13 syllables
78 months—Repeats sentence of 16-18 syllables
60 months—Articulation non-infantile

* One of three trials.

(A-29) OTHER TESTS OF IMMEDIATE MEMORY

The two tests of Immediate Memory which we have used as part of our normative series are auditory. Two other tests of visual recall should be mentioned as being of great value when examining a child with an auditory defect. They are the Knox Cube Test (74) and the Picture Memory Test (4).

The red cubes used in block building will serve also for the Knox Cube Test. For the procedure and behavior norms for this test, reference may be made to Pintner and Paterson's monograph (104). When examining a deaf child, the Picture Memory Test must be preceded with a demonstration of what is required. When this is done, the test can easily be administered without recourse to verbal directions or replies.

§ G. COMPARATIVE JUDGMENT

Obviously, comparative judgments are made by the child prior to verbalization. Whenever a child manipulates a toy in a distinctive and appropriate manner he may be credited with using a form of comparative judgment. But just when a sensori-motor type of discrimination, such as seeking the nipple, becomes a behavior controlled by cortical functioning is difficult to determine. The transition is accomplished gradually. Furthermore, when verbalization occurs, the child uses adjectives having a relative connotation, in an absolute sense. A dress or a flower is "pretty," hands are "dirty," food or radiators are "hot," a ball or a doll may be "big." Even the dichotomy of pretty-ugly, dirty-clean, hot-cold, and big-little is at first not appreciated. Instead the designations are used, usually for extreme conditions, to classify quality in much the same way that nouns are used for classification. Progress in development is made when a child says, for instance, "This is a big one and this is the little one," or, "This is the pretty one and this is the funny one." Further progress is evident when the child realizes, "Daddy is bigger than I am, but I am bigger than Susan," and still another advance is made when he says, "I am smaller than Daddy, but I am bigger than Susan."

The transitions from one stage of comparative judgment to another are made so gradually that frequently they pass unnoticed. Occasionally a child will be surprised by his own discovery and announce, for instance, "Tomorrow, today will be yesterday." Thus notions of relativity are slowly formulated.

The test situations which follow merely tap a few of the stages in the developmental process of making relative judgments. The child is asked to show the examiner the bigger of two lines, the prettier of two faces, and the heavier of two weights; and finally, when he is more mature, to seriate blocks according to their weight.

(A-30) COMPARISON OF LENGTH OF LINES

The following test is quickly administered since the directions are brief. Children readily respond to it, and it may be discontinued after two failures. The test material is that specified by Binet and Simon. The directions are simpler than those stated by either Terman or Kuhlmann.

Procedure. Present the card with the two lines drawn on it and say, *"See these lines. Which is the biggest (or big) one? Show me the biggest (or big) one."* If necessary add, *"Put your finger on it."* After the child has responded, quickly turn the card about several times and re-present it reoriented and say, *"Now which is the biggest (or big) one?"* Give the child three to six trials, according to the conclusiveness of his responses.

Scoring. Discrimination is shown by success on three of three or five of six trials.

Behavior trends. The *2-year-old* child is not able to identify the "big line"; he points indiscriminately. The *3-year-old* child distinguishes the "big line," showing some evidence of discrimination. The majority of *4-year-old* children make no errors in their choice whatever the orientation of the card.

Sex differences are negligible.

Significance of the test. The directions for the test are brief and in the child's own vernacular. Thus simplified, the test is more truly a measure of comparative judgment than of language comprehension. Children 2½ years old are familiar with the word *big* but, as noted above, they use it in extreme cases. There is little doubt that if one line extended across the page and the other line were less than an inch long, all children of this age could easily pass the test. But to a 2½-year-old there may be little difference in the bigness of the two lines, even though he may be able to choose a comparably bigger piece of candy. A big piece of cake or candy and a big line are distinct to the child. He has a specific notion of bigness for different objects, depending on his experience with them. A child may show his indecision by pointing between the lines, or he may guess, looking up to the examiner for confirmation, or he may simply point indiscriminately.

(A-31) AESTHETIC COMPARISON

This test is similar to *Comparison of Lines*. It is of interest that although "pretty" is one of the child's first words, it is not until he is between 4 and 5 years old that he is able to pick out the "pretty one" of two faces. Pretty is a more abstract concept than big and has a correspondingly later development. This test, like the preceding one, is quickly administered and generally pleasing to children.

Procedure. Using a plain white card, cover up all but the two top pictures of the card picturing the pretty and ugly pairs of faces. Present the exposed pictures to the child and say, *"Which is the pretty one? Show me the pretty one!"* Make no comment on the child's choice. Move the card down exposing a second pair of pictures and say, *"Which is the pretty one of these two? Show me the pretty one."* Then move the card up, exposing the third pair of faces and repeat the question.

If, as occasionally happens, the child appears to be purposefully pointing to all the ugly faces in a teasing spirit, soberly without comment, re-present the series.

Scoring. All three responses must be correct.

Behavior trends. The *4-year-old* does not differentiate the pretty and ugly face, but the *5-year-old* does so easily. By *4½ years* the average child can make the three choices correctly.

Sex differences. Boys develop aesthetic discriminative ability a little later than girls.

Significance of the test. The child frequently gives evidence that he is responding to "pretty" in the absolute sense by saying, "This is the pretty one and that's the funny one." The less pretty one is not less pretty or even ugly, but is instead, funny. Sometimes a child even laughs at the unaesthetic faces.

In spite of the fact that aesthetic preferences are frequently unrelated to intelligence, this test is definitely related to mental maturity. For a child to pass this test, he must have an abstract notion of what is pretty and apply that notion to the human physiognomy. To do this is an intelligent act, but it does not follow that there is an innate aesthetic sense which is an aspect of intelligence.

Conversely, however, failure on the test may result from lack of aesthetic experience. The fact that boys are a little later than girls in developing aesthetic discrimination is undoubtedly due to unintentional differential training.

COMPARATIVE JUDGMENTS

PERCENTAGE OF CASES RESPONDING AS INDICATED

	2	3	4	5	6
Age in years..........................	2	3	4	5	6
Number of cases.....................	50	50	27	54	18
Behavior:					
Length of line:					
Responses correct five of six trials...	14		70	96	
Responses correct invariably........			52	96	
Aesthetic comparison:					
Invariably correct................		32	36	75	95
Boys.........................			31	67	
Girls.........................			45	83	

(A-32) COMPARISON OF WEIGHTS

Tests involving the comparison of weights have long been considered tests of intelligence. Binet and Simon, Kuhlmann, and Gesell all included such tests in their scales. The two-weight test involves comparative judgment similar to that required for comparison of length, and for aesthetic comparison. The difference in weight between the two blocks is sufficient to enable the child to distinguish them if he is mature enough to compare. The five-weight test involves the more advanced response of seriating the weights. After a child has reached the age when he is able to hold the problem in mind long enough to attempt seriation of the weights, the test does become more especially one of sensory weight discrimination than of comparative judgment. However, up through 6 years the adaptive aspect of the test predominates. It is, therefore, properly grouped here with other tests of judgment.

Two-Block Test. Procedure. Place the 3- and 15-gram weights two or three inches apart before the child. Say, *"See these blocks? They look just alike but they are not, one of them is heavy and one of them is light. Try them and give me the heavy one."* If the child chooses a block without testing them say, *"No, like this,"* and demonstrate lifting the blocks pincer-wise. Then repeat, *"You try them and give me the heavy one."*

Trial II: Pick up the two blocks and shake them in your cupped hands, or juggle the blocks behind your back. Replace them on the table as before, except that if Trial I was passed, reverse the position of the blocks. If Trial I was failed, do not reverse them.

Trial III: Repeat as for Trial II, reversing the order of placement only in case Trial II was passed.

If the examiner has any reason to suspect that chance rather than judgment has brought about success, additional trials should be given. Make no comment on the quality of the response until the entire test has been given.

Behavior trends. The average *3-year-old* is not able to comply with the directions and respond correctly, but the *3½-year-old* responds correctly in two of three trials. It is necessary for the examiner to demonstrate and insist that the child try each block. The majority of *4-year-olds* invariably select the heavier block, but it may still be necessary to insist that they follow directions. At *5 years* the test is rarely failed.

The Five-Block Test. Procedure. Dump the five blocks on the table and say, *"These blocks all look alike, don't they? But they are not. Each one is heavier or lighter than another. Now I want you to try them all, find the very heaviest one and put it here; then find the next heaviest one and put it here; the next heaviest here; the next heaviest here; and the lightest one here."* Indicate successive points in a row on the far side of the table as you give the directions. Do not demonstrate the method of testing the blocks, but allow the child to use his own scheme. When the child has finished and the order of placement has been recorded, say, *"That's fine,"* then put your hands over the blocks. Mix them up and re-present them to the child with an appropriate comment, such as, *"Do it again."* When necessary repeat the directions in full. Using the same procedure, re-present the blocks for a third trial.

Scoring. An error constitutes the selection of a lighter block when there remains a heavier one not chosen.

Behavior trends. The *4-year-old* makes not more than two errors on his best trial, but it may be necessary for the examiner to repeat the directions, emphasizing *"Try them all."* The *5-year-old* makes not more than one error on his best trial and on two of three trials chooses the 12- or 15-gram weight first. The *6-year-old* makes no errors on his best trial. However, he does not correctly place the blocks in two of three trials.

Sex differences. At the critical age of being able to discriminate weights and carry out the directions, boys are consistently more skillful than girls.

Significance of the test. Baldwin and Stecher's study (4) would indicate that at 4 years, the difference between a 3-gram and a 15-gram weight is sufficiently great that the test is really one of being able to compare the two weights, rather than just a test of weight discrimination, although sensory inability to discriminate may be the cause of failure for a few children. To achieve a successful performance a child must understand what heavy means and keep the problem in mind. His performance may be affected by several factors. A child may, with a twinkle in his eye, give the wrong block; he may be careless in his testing of the blocks; and he may, in spite of the directions, use an individual and less sensitive method of testing the weights, such as tossing them in the air or putting them on his palm.

Baldwin and Stecher concluded that the difference between a 3-gram and a 15-gram weight is so great that the test can be used at the 4-year level to elicit a true comparative judgment, as opposed to a mere discrimination. Even so, a sensori-motor inability to discriminate may be a cause of failure in a few children.

Handedness tendencies are frequently noticed. A child may use one hand exclusively, both hands simultaneously, or first one hand and then the other.

The test is quickly administered, and is enjoyed by most children. It is a valuable part of the preschool scale.

COMPARISON OF WEIGHTS
Percentage of Cases Showing Indicated Behavior
Two Block Test

	3	4	5	6
Age in years	3	4	5	6
Number of cases	50	29	54	18
Behavior:				
Correct in two of three trials	44	73	90	100
Correct in three of three trials		55	82	95
Examiner insists try each block		31		

Five Block Test

	4	5	6
Age in years	4	5	6
Number of cases	29	54	18
Behavior:			
Best trial:			
No errors	0	40	56
Not more than one error	15	55	94
Not more than two errors	53	61	100
Two of three trials:			
No error	0	13	53
Chose 15- or 12-gram wt. first	43	61	100
Distinguished between heavy and light group	38	56	100

SEX DIFFERENCES
Two Block Test

Correct in two of three trials:			
Boys	81	90	100
Girls	62	90	100
Correct in three of three trials:			
Boys	62	86	
Girls	46	79	

Five Block Test

Correct in one of three trials:			
Boys	0	48	43
Girls	0	31	27

§ H. PROBLEM SOLVING

Any situation presents a problem when it arouses a goal to which there is an obstacle. The problem may be solved either by adaptive manipulation, actual or mental, or by insight concerning the nature of the obstacle. The more indirect or complex the solution the more puzzling the problem.

Whether or not a situation is a problem for any individual depends also on the mental maturity of the individual. A pellet within a small bottle usually presents a problem for the 18-month-old child but is no problem for the 3-year-old. He has full appreciation that the pellet may easily be removed by turning the bottle over. Putting the square block in the performance box is a problem for the 21-month-old child but to the 30-month-old child the solution is obvious.

When the solution is not obvious and the obstacle real, a baffling situation is encountered which brings out individually typical behavior. Because adjustments to life constantly involve being baffled or frustrated, it is important to appraise the child's individual response to such situations so that when necessary, education for more adequate and effective modes of adjustment may be planned. It is from this point of view that problem solving or puzzles are used as tests in the complete psychological examination of the young child.

This section presents three test problems suitable for different maturity levels: the ball on the table for the normal 18-month- and 2-year-old child; the puzzle box for the 3-year-old and the Garden maze for the 4- and 5-year-old.

(A-33) BALL ON THE TABLE

Securing an object out of reach is a common objective of the young child. The method which he uses in reaching the goal varies with his maturity. The situation presented here occurs frequently in the home: the desired object is out of reach, and may be secured by indirect climbing, or by using some object as a tool for reaching. The situation is suitable for the child from 18 months through 2 years.

Procedure. Place the large ball on a table (about 30 inches high), well beyond a child's reach. Along the table edge place a square stick 15 inches long. At the end of the table arrange a Windsor chair, convenient for use in climbing up to the table. Lead the child to the table edge near the stick, point to the ball and say, *"Get the ball."* Any large toy may be used in place of the ball if the ball is not sufficiently enticing.

Behavior trends. The *18-month-old* child does not as a rule spontaneously secure the ball. He may reach directly toward the ball or he may ask for help. He usually does handle the stick, which he uses ineffectually, pushing the ball further away. Those children who do succeed in securing the ball climb onto the chair.

The *2-year-old* uses the stick spontaneously and with it secures the ball. He does not need the chair.

Significance of the behavior. The use of a stick as a tool depends on motor skill as well as on an adaptive appreciation of the use of tools. Insight into the use of tools develops gradually. The 18-month-old child fumbles around in a trial and error manner, displays no insight into the use of the stick and solves the problem if at all by the motor skill which he does possess, that is, climbing. The 2-year-old on the other hand has had more experience in handling sticklike objects, he therefore has insight. The stick has for him meaning in terms of getting the ball. He uses the stick, since that method is easiest for him.

BALL ON THE TABLE
PERCENTAGE OF CASES DISPLAYING BEHAVIOR

	1½	2
Age in years...............................	1½	2
Number of cases...........................	32	21
Behavior:		
Spontaneously secures ball....................	31	71
Uses stick spontaneously.....................	50	71
Uses stick, but not as a tool...................	28	9
Asks for help or reaches directly...............	34	25
Succeeds using stick (of those who succeed)......	33	75
Succeeds using chair (of those who succeed)......	66	25

(A-34) PUZZLE BOX

The puzzle box is partially open on one side. Through the opening a ball is exposed. To secure the ball the box must be turned over and a stick which secures a string looped around the box, removed. The box can then be opened and the ball removed. (See Plate XVIII, m.) The 2-year-old child may become very much disturbed when he cannot secure the ball, but the 3-year-old is so intrigued with the problem that he not only solves it but, having solved it, he reinstates the situation so that he can re-solve it.

Procedure. Give the small ball to the child and ask him to place it in the puzzle box. Then close and fasten the box in full view of the child. Hand it to him with the ball showing through the top of the box and say, *"You may play with the ball if you can get it without breaking the string."*

Behavior. Seventy-two percent of the *3-year-old* children succeeded in opening the box. No sex differences were apparent. The test has not been standardized for other ages.

Significance of the behavior. The most frequent error is to attempt to pull the ball through the small opening in the box. Success involves an

14

understanding of the spatial and physical relationships of the rod, string, box and ball. Form adaptation is involved to a high degree.

(A-35) THE GARDEN MAZE

The Garden maze is very similar to the Porteus maze. Compared with the Porteus mazes, the Garden maze is more realistic in design, and the problem is to reach the center of the garden rather than to go from the center of the maze out. The test is suitable for children of 4 and 5 years. Like the Porteus maze, the Garden maze elicits interesting individuality traits in attacking the problem.

Procedure. Say to the child, "*Suppose this is a garden, and these are the paths. The lines are fences which you cannot get over. I want you to go in here and find your way to the center here, as quickly as you can, without going down any blocked paths. Take this pencil and draw a line to show me where you would go.*" The child is allowed to correct his errors. Score may be in terms of time and errors.

Behavior trends. Seventy-four per cent of the *5-year-old* children reached the center of the maze in less than 110 seconds. The test has not been standardized for other age levels.

Significance of the behavior. In addition to testing the child's adaptivity, the Garden maze distinguishes between the impulsive and the playful child; the child who after one error is cautious and the child who does not learn; the child who becomes confused as he works and the child who keeps his goal clearly in mind, as well as between other contrasting personalities.

GENETIC SEQUENCES IN PROBLEM SOLVING BEHAVIOR:

Age 1½ years—Does not use tool; instead climbs to secure objects
2   years—Uses stick to secure ball
3   years—Solves puzzle box
5   years—Solves Garden maze

CHAPTER VIII

LANGUAGE DEVELOPMENT

§ A. THE CHANGING ROLE OF LANGUAGE IN PRESCHOOL DEVELOPMENT

THE field of language behavior is one of major importance in the clinical study of the preschool child, but its relationship to the total behavior organization of the individual differs considerably from that which it takes on with increasing age. Despite the wide use of performance tests in the study of school children and adults, these are commonly used as supplementary tests, or as tests of special abilities, while scales for testing general mental abilities depend largely upon the use of situations presented verbally.

It is easy to understand why the verbal type of test is the most commonly used at those ages and in those cases for which it is appropriate. Aside from such matters as convenience, the avoidance of cumbersome sets of materials, and the establishment of closer rapport between subject and examiner, there is the advantage that the range of situations that can be presented is virtually unlimited. Language eventually becomes so thoroughly integrated with the individual's total behavior that almost any kind of situation, dealing with practical problems of real life, or with the most abstract type of concept, can be presented and attacked in verbal terms. Although such ability is not always accompanied by the ability to deal efficiently with similar practical situations as encountered in daily life, tests of this sort have shown relatively high correlation with success in making real-life adjustments. The most widely used psychometric examination, the Stanford Revision of the Binet-Simon scale, depends almost wholly upon verbal presentation and solution of tests; and Terman has approved, with reservations, the use of its vocabulary test alone as yielding a score approximating closely that of the entire scale, when time does not permit a more complete study, and when there are no specific language complications.

The integration of language with other fields of behavior which eventually permits most conscious activity to be verbalized does not, however, exist from the start. It is a gradual process, taking place at an accelerating rate toward the end of the preschool period, but even then incomplete and showing wide individual variations.

Spoken language appears first as a relatively independent activity, engaged in as play for its own sake, as an accompaniment to other types of behavior, or as a social response without a specific communicative aspect. The first single words and short phrases occur as simple responses to familiar objects or situations; the verbalizing of wants follows toward the end of the second year; the narration of simple experiences develops between 2 and 3 years. The answering of even simple questions dealing with non-present situations presents difficulty as late as from 2½ to 3 years. A language accompaniment to the presentation of tests is used throughout this whole early period; but, even as late as 2½ years, it is doubtful how much part it plays in producing most responses, beyond making the situation a more normal one for the child, and helping to maintain continuity of attention.

During these early stages, the development of speech may show retardation of greater or less degree without a necessary corresponding retardation in other fields of behavior. This becomes less true with increasing age; and the examination of a child of 4 years or more who is seriously deficient in speech presents many difficulties.

Specific acceleration in language is less common, and not as troublesome from the standpoint of the clinical examination, since the likelihood of a spurious impression of superiority based upon it is relatively remote. The child whose language is actually superior to the rest of his performance in terms of the stage of development represented—as contrasted with the mere proliferation of language in an earlier developmental stage— usually lives up to the promise shown by this early specific advancement.

§ B. DEVELOPMENTAL STAGES

THE JARGON STAGE (12-18 MONTHS)

The development of language after the appearance of the first word. which usually occurs within a month or two of the end of the first year. does not immediately show itself through a rapid increase in vocabulary. Appearing first as a simple conditioned response to an object or situation, the spoken word only gradually assumes its utilitarian and communicative function. Even as late as 18 months "talking" continues to be largely a form of play, or an accompaniment to action, rather than a surrogate for it. Communication needs are met by the more facile language of gesture and expressive vocalization. Within the limited environment of the age, most needs are readily interpreted by the child's associates, and this type of language serves efficiently to aid the necessary understanding.

Meanwhile, however, development in the preliminary stages of spoken language is far from being dormant. A few words are acquired between

12 and 15 months, and these may tend to increase in number toward the 18th month, although there seems to be some tendency for a temporary drop in the rate of acquisition between 15 and 18 months, with a rapid acceleration thereafter. Vocalization increases in the variety of sounds used, and in inflection, until it takes on a conversational character so strongly marked that the child almost seems to be carrying on long meaningful conversations in some foreign language. For the most part, this jargon takes place as a running accompaniment to play, or as a form of play in itself.when he is otherwise quiet, but it is often directed conversationally at others. The use of jargon reaches its peak between 15 and 18 months, dropping out rapidly thereafter, and having been practically given up in favor of verbal expression by 2 years.

As in the case of other language items, wide differences are encountered among normal children in the individual characteristics of their jargon. Some children seem never to pass through this stage at all, but to communicate in words from the time these first appear, falling back on gesture when words will not suffice. Such children are likely to prove exceptionally bright, though the tendency is by no means found in all superior children. Personality differences may lead to variability in the development of enriched vocalization as may such environmental influences as the extent to which vocalization is encouraged or suppressed, the opportunity to hear adult conversation or to associate with older children, or inhibition based upon severe emotional experiences.

Language at 18 Months

Vocabulary. There seems to be a tendency for vocabulary to increase relatively more rapidly during the two or three months following the appearance of the first word, than in the period immediately preceding 18 months. The most extensive study of this aspect of development is that of Smith (113), who obtained data from lists compiled by the mothers, which were checked by questioning and by observation of the children. Her figures for extent of vocabulary up to 2 years, as given in Table VII, are higher than those which are obtained clinically, but illustrate the trend as far as rate of acquisition is concerned. Her subjects as will be seen, added an average of sixteen words between 12 and 15 months, and only three words between 15 and 18 months. The figures show rapid acceleration thereafter, with an average increase of 96 words between 18 and 21 months, and 154 during the last three months of the second year. It would appear that the child first learns a small group of words which have some especial significance in relation to the earliest stage of development, and then adds only a very few to these before the communicative aspect of language becomes important, shortly after 18 months.

TABLE VII
VOCABULARIES OF CHILDREN UP TO 2 YEARS OF AGE
(Adapted from Smith, M. E., [113])

Age (months)	Number of children	Number of words	Gain
8....................	13	0	
10....................	17	1	1
12....................	52	3	2
15....................	19	19	16
18....................	14	22	3
21....................	14	118	96
24....................	25	272	154

TABLE VIII
REPORTED VOCABULARIES OF FORTY CHILDREN OF THE NORMATIVE GROUP AT 18 MONTHS

	Number of children		
	Boys	Girls	Group
Number of Cases:	20	20	40

Number of words	Percentage of children		
1– 5......................	20	25	22
6–10......................	35	25	30
11–15......................	30	25	27
16–20......................	15	5	10
21–25......................			
26–30......................		5	3
"Innumerable"..............		15	8

Smith's figures, as has been pointed out, were compiled on the basis of lists which the mother was asked to keep, and were carefully checked by questioning and observation directed solely toward the obtaining of language data. This method cannot ordinarily be followed to the same extent in clinical practice, because of the length of time required. If a record is kept by the mother over a period of months, words will be recorded that have been used only once or twice, and then dropped out; and the directing of specific attention to what words are used will result in some being heard that would otherwise have been overlooked. Moreover, Smith's subjects were a little above average in general endowment, if the intelligence quotients given for older children used in the same study are to be taken as an indication.

Vocabulary figures obtained clinically for average children will correspond more closely with those for our Normative Group (Table VIII) which were obtained by asking the mother what words the child used, and then asking for specific common words which were not spontaneously reported. Forty children were studied, as opposed to Smith's fourteen at the same age. The smallest number of words reported was four, while three mothers reported that there were too many to enumerate. The median number of words for the group was between ten and eleven. Proper names were included in the count.

The sex differences are not striking, but it may be observed that the four largest vocabularies were reported for girls. While extensive data on sex differences in language development have not been reported at the 18-month level, most investigators have agreed that girls are relatively accelerated over boys in language development during the first two or three years of life. Responses to the picture cards at this age show the girls identifying a greater number of pictures correctly than the boys, but the boys were much more likely to name at least one picture.

Retarded language development. The individual variations in extent of vocabulary during these early stages are very great. Cases in which only one or two words, or even none at all, have been heard by 18 months are not rare among normal children, while others have been encountered in which as many as 150 to 200 words have been heard by the age of 15 months. These latter children have usually proved later to be of superior intelligence; but a mere absence of words in itself is far from indicating dullness, or even from ruling out potential superiority.[1]

When a child has not begun to use words by the age of 18 to 24 months, and even a little above the latter age, caution must be used in estimating the significance of this fact. If the child gives other evidence of normal potentialities, and is not hampered by deafness, the outlook is favorable, and it may be stated with confidence that the child will eventually talk. It is necessary to inquire into circumstances in the home and past history, to determine whether there is likelihood of suppression on an emotional basis, a history of severe illness at about the usual age of starting to talk, or a home situation which fails to supply normal encouragement of talking. Institution children are especially likely to show delay in this field, and to show spontaneous improvement following foster home place-

[1] A discussion of the problem of retarded speech development in early childhood, with a detailed account of two cases, will be found in *Biographies of Child Development* (40), pp. 127-169.

ment. Clinical experience has borne out the suggestion of Nice (96) that children who are late in developing a definite preference for the use of one hand are likely to be retarded in their early language development. There are also cases of lapse of speech in children who have already begun to talk. This is often found to have followed severe illness or emotional shock.

Deafness is difficult to rule out in this age range. The extent to which the child shows comprehension of spoken words should be investigated, not only in the test situations and others that may be improvised, but carefully and concretely in the interview. The response to softly played music, to a bell tinkled lightly out of the child's sight, and to a speaking voice behind his back, may be enlightening. Absence of response to the examiner's voice alone is not sufficient; the mother should be asked to speak his name softly, and gradually louder if necessary, to see whether he turns to her or gives other indications of hearing. The tonal quality of his vocalizations is likewise significant. The child who has a varied, well-inflected, conversational jargon is unlikely to be significantly handicapped in hearing. It should be stated here that, while the possibility of deafness should be given the fullest consideration, clinical experience with many cases of retarded speech has revealed that it only rarely proves to be the cause of the retardation.

When deafness can be ruled out or seems improbable, and when development in other respects appears to be normal, the strongest reassurance should be given the parents. This is necessary, because delay in talking is one of the most disturbing deviations which are noticed by parents during the first years of the child's life.

Word combinations. While some children begin to combine words meaningfully and spontaneously as early as 14 or 15 months, this is still not the rule at the end of the third half-year. Such learned combinations as "all gone" and "so big" are equivalent, from the point of view of maturity, to two-syllabled words.[2] Toward 18 months, spontaneous combination is increasingly met with, and by 21 months is encountered in nearly all normal children. Toward the end of the second year, the length and variety of the child's phrases and sentences increase rapidly. At 18 months, it seems probable that frequent use of spontaneous combinations, and the use of phrases made up of several words, are even more suggestive of superior endowment than a vocabulary above the average.

Comprehension of language. At the age of 18 months, this is a factor that must ordinarily be determined more on the basis of report than upon the child's responses in the clinical examination; although, if there is

[2] A group of characteristic 18-months combinations, as compared with a similar group for 24 months, will be found on page 197.

opportunity for extensive observation of the child under conditions of varied activity, much information may be gained directly. While a number of the tests at 18 months provide for verbal instructions to be tried initially, it is usually necessary to fall back upon gesture and demonstration. Good results are seldom obtained by persisting with the verbal directions alone, in the hope of ultimately getting a response.

The most successful language-comprehension tests at 18 months are those involving identification of pictures and of parts of the body. The chief difficulty encountered with such tests at this level lies in the difficulty of interpreting failure. On the one hand, this may be due to inability to understand the instructions as given. On the other hand, it may be the result of inattention, distraction by some more attractive stimulus-element in the situation, or even unfamiliarity with the specific wording used in giving the instruction. The daily life situation of the 18-month-old child is not one which ordinarily calls for much adjustment to situations presented only orally. When outstandingly good responses are obtained to such situations, a relatively high level of personal-social maturity is indicated.

Summary. Of the language status of the 18-month-old child, then, it may be said (a) that he is beginning to use spoken words instead of jargon in his language-play and in his social responses, but that his verbal behavior is usually accompanied by gesture or concurrent activity; (b) that his vocabulary may consist of from three or four to a hundred or more single words, with ten to twelve as the most common number verifiable clinically; (c) that he is just beginning to form occasional spontaneous two-word phrases; (d) that he understands and responds to simple directions calling for familiar responses, although reinforcement by gesture is often necessary; (e) that even a complete absence of spoken words is not seriously disturbing, provided that development is otherwise normal and that the child shows normal comprehension of the speech of others.

Language from 24-30 Months

The age of 24 months, as far as the field of language is concerned, is outstandingly a period of transition. The one-word sentence and the short and stereotyped combinations which have been characteristic of earlier stages of development are still common; but longer and more varied combinations are on the increase. Jargon has almost universally dropped out. Compound and complex sentences, and even sentences with brief subordinate phrases, are rare until along toward 3 years, but are occasionally heard at 2 years. Pronouns are beginning to be used prominently and often correctly. The speaking vocabulary has shown a sharp increase in rate of gain during the months immediately preceding the second birth-day, and may at this time consist of 200 to 300 words. Although talking is still used to a great extent as a running accompaniment to action, and as a play activity in itself—listen to the 2-year-old left by himself to go to sleep!—it is beginning to be used extensively as a means of communica-tion not only of wants, such as toilet needs and food, but of ideas and information. Simple experiences begin to be verbalized and the child can often tell things he has seen, or things that have happened to him.

Vocabulary. As in any outstandingly transitional period of develop-ment, particularly when the changes are as rapid as in the case of language at this time, wide variability may be expected among normal children. In twenty-eight cases of our Normative Group at 24 months, the mothers reported vocabularies so extensive that they could not estimate them, while in the remaining five cases, we had reports of 5, 6, 9, 10, and 17 words, respectively. Nice (97) in her tabulation of forty-seven published vocabularies of 2-year-old children found the average of these to be 328 words, with the tremendously wide range of from 5 to 1212 words. At 30 months, the range was still enormous, the eleven vocabularies varying from 30 to 1509 words, with an average of 690. Smith (Table VII) does not give the range of variation, but reports an average of 272 words for twenty-five cases at 24 months, representing a gain of 154 words over 21 months.

It is impracticable, in the ordinary clinical study, to attempt to list these enlarged vocabularies, although a sampling should be obtained to gauge the range and types of words which comprise them. While an unusually small speaking vocabulary is an important part of the clinical picture of the child who shows such a limitation, the maturity level is more clearly indicated by the flexibility of its use, and the extent to which it is appropriately adapted to varying situations.

Cases of otherwise normal children who do not talk at all are rare at 2 years and older, but are not unheard of. They are to be interpreted in general in the way that has been indicated in the discussion of language retardation at 18 months. With other development proceeding normally, speech may still be expected to come in spontaneously during the ensuing year in the majority of cases, although study of the nature and causes of retardation and of the possibilities for encouraging the use of language is not to be neglected.

Word combinations. Smith (113) considered that "the most significant trend in the development of the sentence with age was an increasing tendency toward the use of longer and more complete sentences." She found that between 2 and 5 years complex and compound sentences be-came more frequent with advancing age, questions increased in relative frequency, and exclamatory sentences became relatively less frequent. McCarthy (83) reports that compound and complex sentences occur late, and continue in very small proportions throughout the upper preschool levels. Our own observations indicate that compound sentences are rare at 2 years, but are occasionally encountered there, while sentences with simple phrases are not uncommon.

The following samples of phrases and sentences reported for our Normative Group at 18 and at 24 months have been selected to give an idea of the range from the simplest to the most complex combinations. They were obtained from the mothers by asking for examples of the longest combinations heard.

18 months

See that.	Pretty dress.
Bad girl.	Who is that?
Drink of water.	I see . . . (one-word completion)
Come over.	Open door.
I do it.	Bye-bye in the car.
Daddy going bye-bye.	Gimme cracker.

24 months

Papa gone.	Where's the ball, Mamma?
Come kitty.	I see Daddy go bye-bye car.
I see Daddy.	I put it on the chair.
Cup all gone.	I don't want to go to bed.
Where's Daddy gone?	Take 'em and put 'em in there.
Get the . . . (one-word completion)	Mother, why me left in bed?
I want my cup.	Don't forget the 'nanas.
You get it for me.	Harold's out in the yard.
Shut that door.	Baby sat in my lap.
I want some more.	

It will be observed that a number of the 2-year-olds used sentences with phrases, while complex and compound sentences are also encountered at this age. A rather striking fact also is the structural and grammatical correctness of a large proportion of even the longer sentences, although the structures are of a relatively simple order.

McCarthy (83) recorded fifty language responses of twenty children at each of seven age levels during the preschool period, while Smith (113) recorded the spontaneous conversations of eighty-eight children during the same age range. Their findings, recorded in Table IX, reflect the tendency for such responses to increase in length most rapidly during the period from 24 to 42 months, with some increase thereafter, though at a slower rate.

TABLE IX

MEAN NUMBER OF WORDS PER RESPONSE BY CHRONOLOGICAL AGE FOR CHILDREN OF PRESCHOOL AGE, AS REPORTED BY SMITH AND McCARTHY

(Table adapted from McCarthy, [83], p. 54)

Age in months	(Smith)	(McCarthy)	S. D. (McCarthy)
18....................	–	1.2	.64
24....................	1.7	1.8	1.40
30....................	2.4	3.1	1.99
36....................	3.3	3.4	2.06
42....................	4.0	4.3	2.83
48....................	4.3	4.4	2.86
54....................	4.7	4.6	2.95
60....................	4.6	—	—

While these figures are significant as showing the trend of development, they are of little practical value from the clinical point of view as a basis for estimating the developmental status of the individual child at a given age level. For 24 months the occasional use of three- to four-word sentences may be considered the norm, individual differences in maturity being indicated by the relative frequency of their use, their flexibility in expressing ideas, and the variety of situations to which they are adapted.

Parts of speech. The infant's first words are preponderantly the names of objects, simple verbs of action taking second place. In their use, however, these names of objects function in a much more variable fashion than as the nouns which they become later, as the use of language develops. The word *"milk"* as used by the 16-month-old child, for example, may be simply a conditioned response to the appearance of the object, or the equivalent of, "Give me a drink of milk," the interpretation being based upon the tone of voice and the other overt behavior of the infant, in the light of the total situation of which the spoken word is a part.

The earliest combinations tend to be of the verb-noun type—*Daddy go, bye-bye car* (*bye-bye* being the verb), etc. Adjective-noun combinations —*good girl, pretty dress,* and the like, though not uncommon, are probably for the most part learned phrases. Modifiers are rare, even by 24 months, as will be seen from the representative examples of sentences previously given.

The most conspicuous development in the matter of parts of speech at 2 years is the common use of pronouns, especially in the first and second persons. *I, me,* and *you* are differentiated, though *I* and *me* are frequently confused.[3] *My* and *mine* come before other possessives. Many children of this age still use the proper name instead of the personal pronoun in referring to themselves and others.

The reciprocal relationship existing among the three pronouns *I, you, me*, requires that their correct use must come in at practically the same time. That this is the case is indicated by the figures of Muntz (91), who gathered data on fifty children at the age of 2 years. Forty-eight per cent of these children used all three pronouns correctly, while 38 per cent used none of them. Only 6 per cent and 8 per cent, respectively, used one or two of the pronouns, but not the others. These figures suggest that the criterion is a little high for 24 months, but it is probably more appropriately placed there than at 30 months, where it is too low. In any case, it appears to be an all-or-none test; complete success or complete failure is the rule.

The use of plurals and of the past tense, though coming into use by many children at 2 years, is still not found in the majority of children. Muntz, in the same group of children mentioned above, found only about 36 per cent using both of these constructions correctly. As in the case of the pronouns discussed, the two seem to come in together; 54 per cent of the children used neither construction, while only 10 per cent used just one of them. Correct use of both should probably be expected by 30 months.

Variations in special groups. The general finding that girls are superior to boys in language development has been reported by a number of investigators. Such differences as have been reported are often small, but seem to tend in favor of the girls in most aspects of language that have been studied. This may be related to the general finding that, at older ages, the two great clinical problems associated with language, namely stuttering and specific reading disability, are met with far more frequently in boys than in girls. In view of the small and extremely irregular amount of difference between the sexes found at 2 years, it is scarcely necessary to make allowance for it in the individual clinical case.

More important, from the clinical point of view, is the difference between children from widely varying cultural backgrounds. Descoeudres (21), Gesell and Lord (34), McCarthy (83) and others, have reported findings indicating that the advantages of high economic and social status are reflected in the language performances of young children. Children with long institutional experience are known to be handicapped

---

[3] A superior 5-year-old boy was recently observed who consistently used *me* for *I*. In this case, the usage had been encouraged by the family through mimicking and a show of amused interest, as well as through the general encouragement of infantile behavior.

in language development. The child from a bilingual home, while apparently not permanently handicapped in the acquisition of English, is often at a definite disadvantage during the early years, partly because of the fact that it is so often the mother in the family who clings the most to the foreign language. In the case of foreign families, it is always necessary to find out which language is commonly used in the home, particularly in talking to the child who is being studied.

Language in the developmental examination. At the age of 24 months it is still necessary to get most of the information as to language development through reports of home behavior, and, where possible, through Guidance Nursery observation. In the test situations themselves, while more provision is made for administering directions orally, it is usually necessary to supplement these directions by gesture and demonstration. This necessity decreases rapidly, however, from 30 months on, although it is possible to fall back upon such supplementary action in the case of most tests up through 3 years.

At 24 months, the tests dependent upon language comprehension alone are identifying pictures and carrying out directions in placing a ball. The majority of 2-year-olds meet these situations satisfactorily. By 30 months one or more answers are expected to the question, *"What do we do with it?"* in the object naming test; naming is required instead of pointing in the response to the picture cards; and the child is expected to give his full name.

Articulation. Some children pronounce all their words sharply and clearly from the time they first begin to talk; others remain almost incomprehensible to outsiders until a relatively advanced age. At 2 years, the individual variations in this respect are very great, and it is often necessary to call in the mother as an interpreter in estimating the response to a test. Such differences seem to depend, to a large extent, upon constitutional differences in the children themselves, but may be considerably influenced by the kind and amount of speech the child hears.

It should scarcely be necessary to point out that defective articulation is seldom to be considered a serious problem at the age of 2 years, and guidance relative to it is rarely necessary, beyond reassurance that it will improve as the child grows older. In some cases it may be desirable to advise that the parents take pains to talk clearly and simply to the child, using single words and short phrases; that they take pains to secure his active attention before addressing him; and that, particularly, his incorrect pronunciations are not to be mimicked. Any sort of systematic pronunciation drill is, of course, not to be considered at this age.

LANGUAGE AT 3 YEARS

Up to the age of 2 years, the development of language has taken place, in great part, as a relatively independent type of behavior, related only incidentally to other fields such as those of adaptive and personal-social reactions. The communicative function is not lacking, to be sure, even before 24 months, but when speech is used for communication of wants, ideas, and experiences, it is accompanied by expressive action, which it points or supplements, rather than serving as a substitute for such action. The fundamentals of speech are being acquired, but they are new, their management is still awkward, and in time of need it is easier to fall back on the more primitive methods of communication which fulfill quite satisfactorily most requirements at this early age. Measurement of language development during this first period can be satisfactorily made, for the most part, in simple quantitative, objectively determinable, terms. How many words does the child use? How long are his spontaneous combinations? How often does he combine words? What pronouns does he use correctly? Does he use plurals or the past tense? The answers to all these questions give an indication of the child's relative language development in terms of the mechanics of speech. Even tests involving the use and comprehension of language, such as picture-naming and carrying out simple instructions, are, at 2 years, not far from the elementary conditioned-response stage.

Toward 3 years, the outstanding change in language behavior, aside from the quantitative development of vocabulary and complexity of sentences, is the progress toward functional integration with the total behavior of the child. Although language is still a new and imperfect instrument, the fundamentals upon which the imposing structure of later years is to be reared are mostly present. Vocabulary is extensive; long sentences including compound and complex structures are common; tense, moods, and parts of speech are distinguished, however imperfectly. Generalization is common, and both in talking and in comprehension of the speech of others, non-present situations are dealt with verbally.

From 3 years on, as a result of these changes, language maturity must be estimated on the basis of its relationship to the total behavior patterns of the child, and in terms of the relative complexity or difficulty of the situations which can be dealt with verbally. Extent of vocabulary, where it is tested for at all, is estimated in terms of the number of words which can be defined satisfactorily by the use of other words. Comprehension of increasingly complex directions, and the ability to deal verbally with hypothetical situations, make up the greater part of the language tests used hereafter, and indeed, the majority of the more satisfactory tests of abilities in general.

Vocabulary. From the age at which vocabulary passes beyond the stage where the child's words can be counted, or roughly estimated—usually around 2 years or a little earlier—there is no satisfactory clinical test for extent of vocabulary until the age of 6 years, when the Stanford vocabulary test first appears. Smith's (113) technique is admirable, but is too cumbersome and time-consuming for ordinary clinical use. The Action-Agent test is properly considered as a comprehension test, and gives no measure of the total number of words the child understands.

According to Smith, the average vocabulary of 3-year-olds is 896 words, with an average of 1222 words at 42 months. The 3-year figures represent a gain of 100 per cent over 30 months, the most rapid rate of increase between any two test ages, after the first great influx of new words between 18 and 24 months.

Comprehension. The simplest test of language at 36 months is the picture-naming test, which at this age calls for practically complete success. This represents the completion of the stage at which the ability to respond with the appropriate name to the simple visual stimulus of a familiar object, presented directly or pictured, is of significance with respect to language development alone.

The Action-Agent test, appearing for the first time at 36 months, is the first calling for comprehension on the child's part of a non-present situation presented verbally, and requiring him to formulate a simple—usually a one-word—verbal response. This test, based upon one of the Woodworth-Wells association tests, and standardized by Stutsman (117) has proved valuable between the ages of 36 and 60 months. The results for the Normative Group at 36 and at 48 months are in substantial agreement with Stutsman's figures. The principal difficulties with the test at 3 years arise from the frequent refusal of the child to respond verbally to tests at that age, and from the fact that it requires a rather longer period of attention than many 3-year-old children can sustain.

The Binet picture test, used here in the Stanford adaptation, adds to the simple picture-naming situation the requirement of analysis. The requirement that the child spontaneously name three elements in the picture seems to be appropriate for 3 years. Occasionally a descriptive phrase or two is encountered, or even an early evidence of dynamic comprehension of the picture by means of an action-phrase, but these are not to be expected of the average 3-year-old.

The question, *"What must you do when you are sleepy (hungry, cold)?"* brings a satisfactory answer on one of three trials at 3 years, and on two trials at 42 months. Giving the child's own sex correctly is fairly easy at 3 years, but is hard to elicit at 30 months.

Individual differences in language responses at 3 years. Although the language situations described as representative of the 3-year stage of maturity will bring satisfactory responses from the majority of children of that age, there are many and wide individual differences, even among those whose later history shows them to be of normal endowment. The child who does not talk at all is rare at this age, but there are many whose language is still representative of the more immature stage of 24 to 30 months, particularly in answering questions. The great activity, and the concern with their own objectives, which are characteristic of so many 3-year-olds, play a considerable part in producing these differences, by making it difficult to secure attention for even the short period of time necessary to present the test questions. This may lead to no response at all to the question, or to a response based upon some fragment of it which has been caught by the child. When the situation, as in the Action-Agent test, calls for a series of questions, attention is apt to flag very quickly, and perseverative or random answers are likely to be encountered, with eventually a complete "going out of the field." It is rarely possible to give the complete Action-Agent series at this age and maintain adequate rapport throughout the entire list of questions.[4] Interpretation of failure on these language tests, in terms of attention or personal-social immaturity, is somewhat easier than at earlier ages, but must be based upon familiarity with actual use of the tests in many clinical examinations.

Questioning of the examiner by the child is a much more prominent part of the examination at 3 years than it has been at any earlier age, though it does not reach its peak until toward 4 years. At 3, it is often automatic or rhetorical in nature, with no reply expected, and no disturbance of rapport when the question is ignored.

Articulation. Although a high proportion of 3-year-old children still exhibit traces of infantile pronunciation in varying degrees, their speech is as a rule comprehensible to those outside the family, and there is seldom much difficulty in the examination situations, where a known type of answer is expected. The infantilisms, moreover, tend at this age to fall into familiar patterns—the substitution for example of the *w* for the *r* sound in such words as *run* and *ride*; *d* for *th* in *that* or *then*; and the common *t* for sounds which the child finds hard to make as in *tee, to', ti', tik,* for *three, four, five, six.* Frequently he will give evidence of ability to

---

[4] Responses to the Action-Agent and the Comprehension tests which are characteristic of 3-year-old children, as compared with the 4- and 5-year-olds, will be found in the sections describing these tests (L-9 and L-11).

make all the essential speech sounds when he tries, but drops back into the more slipshod pronunciations in his ordinary conversation.

Since this type of infantile articulation is commonly found in children who talk quite normally by the age of 5 or 6 years, or even earlier, it is not to be regarded, at 3 years, as a problem requiring special treatment. Attempts at "correction" indeed, except in the most expert hands, may easily disturb the functioning of the complex, delicate, still imperfectly integrated, response system involved in the production of speech, create self-consciousness and insecurity with respect to talking, and lead to more serious and persistent language problems.

LANGUAGE AT 4 YEARS

As compared with other stages of preschool development, the age of 4 years may be described as the flowering period of language. The 3-year-old, though talkative enough, has not as yet discovered the transcendent power of words and the excitement of using them to control or to enrich all types of situation. The more mature 5-year-old—a young adult by the side of Three and Four—handles his language equipment with relative deliberation and self-control. But the 4-year-old talks—talks about everything, plays with words, questions persistently, elaborates simple responses into long narratives, comments with approval on his own behavior and criticizes that of others, balances comparisons. The examination of a bright, active child of 4 years often resembles nothing so much as a headlong free-association experiment.

Some of this extensive conversation is of a rambling turn, related to the immediate examination situation only through the often obscure association which has set it off. There will be anecdotes and reminiscences suggested by minor details of a test situation, which must be heard out before the goal can be reset, as in the case of the 4-year-old girl who, on being asked, "What swims?" replied, "Oh, I'll tell you. I was playing with Barbara and a big dog came in and he bit me right on the arm. Which arm was it, Ma?" She was obviously giving a delayed response to the preceding question, "What bites?" which she had answered correctly; but the connection is not always as clear as this, and many apparent "flights of ideas" occurring in the examinations are actually (from the point of view of 4-year maturity!) quite logically related to the point in hand.

But most of the 4-year-old talkativeness is in terms of the examination itself. All the situations are likely to be verbalized, even such as block construction, or form-matching: "Well, now, let's see . . . it must be that one there." The child, asked to point to the longer of two lines, to the prettier of two pictures, cannot simply point to one, but must characterize both, "This is the big one and this is the little one"; "That's the nice one and that's the funny one."

Drawing is extensively verbalized, as suggested in the preceding chapter. A typical example of a 4-year-old's monologue while drawing a man is as follows: "This is going to be a little boy. This a little boy's yeg (leg). This is his other yeg. I have no place to make his other hand—I'll make it up here. See, that's going to be a man. See, hah, see? That's the man's face; that's his hands; that's his curl. That's his mouth and that's his nose. Here's his arm. That's his five hands." Nearly all drawings are named in advance, although they often undergo one or more changes of name as they develop.

The matter of naming a drawing in advance is, in fact, a highly important matter at 4 and 5 years in many cases. We find at these ages a good many children who in drawing, say a house, will make a perfectly satisfactory approximation to a square, but who have great difficulty in the test calling for copying the square. Some of these children, verbalizing their difficulty, engage in persistent questioning as to what the model represents, "What is it?" "Is it a box (or a house, or a window)?" In some cases it is impossible to get any attempt at the test until they have arrived at an answer to such questions. Sometimes the child will answer for himself, "It's a box," or something of the sort, and go ahead with assurance to draw his usual picture of the object named, with little or no reference to the model.

Such a response is, of course, in an entirely different category from the simple copying response; but a differential interpretation is often impossible. This furnishes a relatively simple and clear-cut example of the way in which language is becoming functionally integrated with the total behavior pattern during this period; a process which from this stage of life makes it increasingly difficult to consider tests as measuring specifically language development, or motor, adaptive, or personal-social development, and leads to the stage at which we may speak of what we are trying to measure as "general mental development" or "general intelligence."

Other tests than drawing also elicit questioning from the child, questioning that occasionally represents intelligent analysis of the problem, but that more often is simply verbal overflow, or stalling while the situation is being sized up. The 4-year-old, unable to see through a test, may evade by "going out of the field" verbally, or by turning the question back on the examiner—often so persistently that, in order to avoid answering, the examiner must go out of the field himself by shifting to another test for the time being.

The child of 4 comments appraisingly on his own performance, particularly to seek reassurance if he is none too sure of its quality—"I made it good, huh?" "I'm smart, huh?" Praise is always accepted, no matter how obvious the failure. Excuses are also offered—"That's hard." "I never did it," or, more subtly, "My mother doesn't want me to do that one." Criticism of others offers another "out" to the child who is not quite sure of his own response—"Jimmy (a younger brother) can't do that, but I can." This tendency to be critical of others is by no means confined to the clinical situation, as many an embarrassed mother could testify.

The manner in which the child's language is spreading out beyond the egocentric or the immediate situation is reflected in the change in the type of comprehension questions which can be used at this age. The group of questions borrowed from the old Stanford scale, asking the child to verbalize habitual behavior related to physical needs ("What must you do when you are sleepy?" etc.) has been found somewhat too easy for 4 years. More appropriate for the 4-to-5 stage have been found questions dealing with learned social behavior, or more generalized situations, represented in the scale by "What must you do before you cross the street?" and "What must you do when you have lost something?"

In the sections describing the Action-Agent and Comprehension tests are illustrative examples of 4-year-old responses as compared with those encountered at adjoining ages. The tendency to over-respond comes out clearly in many of these examples, as do the other tendencies described here. The other test at this level in which language figures most prominently is that calling for a response to the Stanford pictures. Here the characteristic 4-year language behavior does not show itself so clearly. About one-fourth of children at this age get beyond simple enumeration of objects in the picture by inserting one or more descriptive phrases, and a few furnish some sort of interpretation; these are likely to be the more superior children.

While the loquacity that has been described is characteristic of the age of 4 years in general, it is the superior child of that age who exhibits it in all its glory and richness. Potential superiority, in fact, is often suggested more by the range and complexity of the child's language at this age than by his actual successes and failures. The alertness, the response to tiny details, the eager interest which leads him away from the immediate problem, may be in themselves aspects of a superior level of intelligence; yet they may be the very factors that lead to a scattered or spuriously reduced performance in terms of plus-and-minus scoring. While this problem persists up through the age of school entrance in some children, the majority of them pass through it during the 4- to 5-year period, and by the latter age have developed sufficient social maturity and self-control to meet examination requirements with fewer complications.

LANGUAGE AT 5 YEARS

The 5-year-old, then, has not only acquired the ability to use language efficiently, but has begun to have a sense of the social standards and limitations with respect to its use. To some extent this is the result of increased maturity and poise, and of better insight into what is appropriate to a given situation; but in many cases, the effects of suppression, and the lack of self-confidence are also evident in the briefer language responses. Inhibition of language in the clinical examination is far more common at 5 years than at 4, the child is more critical and more uncertain of his own performance, and tactful commendation and encouragement by the examiner are more often required to carry through the examination, and to secure the best responses of which the child is capable.

In comparing the 5-year-old with the child a year his junior, the quality and stability of his greater maturity is likely to be overestimated. It is still a relatively new acquisition, reinforced to some extent by recent widening of social experience, including frequently the beginning of kindergarten attendance. The responsibilities called for by these environmental changes require many adjustments of values and habits; the child is often under considerable strain as the result of conflicts thus set up, and, under pressure, may easily drop back into earlier modes of behavior.

New language tests appropriate to this age differ somewhat from those of the earlier preschool situations, resembling rather those commonly used for school children. Concept of number—up through ten—is expected to be pretty well established, the more familiar color names are to be correctly used, names of familiar objects are to be verbally defined in terms of use, the child's own age is to be remembered. Response to the Stanford pictures gets beyond the merely enumerative stage, and usually includes some description. Comparative selection (as in the weights and aesthetic discrimination) between two objects on the basis of verbal direction should be prompt and sure. The beginnings of economic understanding are seen in the ability to name two or three coins correctly. As many as three simple commissions, given together, are kept in mind and carried out consecutively. Comprehension questions require verbal adaptation to hypothetical or socially significant situations. While most of these tests deal with abilities that have started to come in by 4 years or thereabouts, they are not as a rule securely established until around the age of 5.

Another distinguishing character of this group of tests, taken as a whole, is the fact that the "language," "adaptive," "personal-social," and even the "motor" components no longer stand out as significant individual aspects of response. The process earlier described as the integration of these fields, with language serving to unify the behavior related to all of them, has begun to reach a culminating stage. From now on, in the absence of specific complicating factors, tests dependent upon the presentation and solution in verbal terms of problems of all types have particularly wide application in the estimation of intellectual maturity.

The problem of reading readiness. At the age of 5 years, a new form of language behavior, fully as important to the individual's later development and adjustment as speech was in the early years, is looming on the horizon. Within the next year or so, he will enter the first grade and be exposed formally to the problem of learning to read. Although the question of reading is one which lies, for the most part, outside the scope of the present work, it has very definite relevance to consideration of the status of the child of 5 to 6 years.

The persistence of old tradition dictates that reading should be begun by the age of 6 years, despite the skepticism and even downright disagreement expressed by numerous recent investigators. The great majority of first-grade curricula are built upon this assumption, and few schools today make anything like adequate provision for those children, of normal intelligence, of whom it is not true. The attempt to force reading in such cases frequently leads to temporary or permanent maladjustment and more or less serious disturbance of the course of normal school achievement. The resulting problems are common among the cases of school children referred to a guidance clinic after the damage has been done; the psychologist whose practice takes in the preschool field may prevent many of them, by familiarizing himself with their early stages, and by alertness to detect such advance indications as may be identified before the child enters school.

Most children, presumably, can begin to learn to read between the ages of 6 and 7 years. The question as to whether or not this means that formal training should usually be begun at this time does not concern us here. But it should be recognized that there are many who, despite normal intelligence and normal capacity for eventual achievement in reading, should defer such training until a more advanced stage of maturity. This is of particular importance in relation to those children who, because of apparent intellectual advancement, are considered for possible admittance to first grade at an age lower than is usually required. Guidance with respect to this question is often requested of the clinical psychologist, and the responsibility attached to such advice may not always be fully recognized.

Too often admission of an under-age child to the first grade is made on the basis of a high psychometric rating alone, in the absence of any gross indicators of incompetence. But a superior intelligence test score is far from being the only factor of importance that should be considered. While complete understanding of the problem of reading readiness awaits more clearly defined studies than have yet been reported, the child who is to be subjected to the usual first-grade training should show all or most of the following traits, in a degree equal to that of the average child of 6 to 6½ years:

1. Normal (or corrected) vision
2. Normal hearing
3. General mental level of 6 to 6½ years
4. Good motor coordination, particularly manual control, as evidenced in drawing
5. Relatively mature personality
6. Normal use and comprehension of language
7. Articulation not more than slightly immature
8. Relatively even development in the various fields of behavior
9. Interest in, and ability to follow, stories of moderate length
10. Ability to control attention on set tasks
11. Ability to adjust to the requirements of schoolroom routine

Information as to most of these points may be gained in the course of the ordinary clinical examination, through observation of the child's responses, supplemented by interview. Where it is desired to do so, one of the standard "Reading Readiness" tests may be used.

If a child shows a satisfactorily high degree of maturity on the items listed, there can be no objection to giving him first-grade opportunity in most cases. If he appears less mature on them than is expected for first-grade children in general, such advancement should not be approved except under very unusual circumstances.[5]

§ C. BEHAVIOR SITUATIONS

(L-1) PICTURE BOOK
(15 months—4 years)

This situation, originally designed for transitional and warming-up purposes, has been found to have real value in developmental appraisal, particularly of language behavior and motor control. As a test it is unstandardized, and should probably remain so, since the great flexibility allowed in the manner of its presentation makes it particularly useful as a means of initiating interest and building up rapport, as well as

[5] Two cases illustrating the problem of early first-grade entrance are presented on pages 299, 300. *Biographies of Child Development* (40) contains a section (included in the references given for the present chapter) devoted to the problem of predicting reading disability, which complements the discussion of reading readiness as given above.

allowing scope for the examiner's ingenuity and insight in getting responses from the less responsive children of those ages (15-30 months) at which it is not always easy to elicit language behavior.

The procedure here outlined is intended as a general guide and will be varied by the experienced examiner according to the interest and responsiveness of the individual child. The book may be followed through in detail, page by page, skimmed over with close attention to only the more interesting pages, or quickly skipped through. There is no persistence in questioning the child; questions to which he does not respond are answered by the examiner, after giving an appropriate—usually very brief—opportunity for the child himself to answer.

Procedure. The book is in position on the table as the child enters the room, and his attention is immediately called to it. The examiner begins to demonstrate it almost before the child is in position, beginning with the

Cover (15-24 months). Point to one of the children on the cover, saying, "*See the baby; she's riding on a chicken.*" Turn the page by the upper corner, hesitating briefly after the page is lifted to give the child an opportunity to complete the turning if he wishes. (30-36 months) Point as above, saying, "*What's she doing? What's she riding on? Turn the page?*"

Pussy in the Well (18-30 months). "*See the baby,*" pointing to child in the foreground. "*Where are her shoes? Has she got shoes on? Where's her hat?*" etc. (30-36 months) "*What's the girl doing?*"

Tommy Tucker (15-18 months). "*Where's the doggie (bow-wow)?*" indicating the left-hand page. If the name of the family dog is known, it sometimes helps to substitute this. (24-30 months) Point to the dog saying, "*What's this?*" If no response, say, "*Where is the doggie (bow-wow)?*" (36-42 months) "*How many girls are peeking in the window?*"

Bo-Peep (36-42 months). "*Do you know 'Little Bo-Peep'? Has lost her ———?*" Give the child an opportunity to finish the line, doing it for him if he does not respond.

Miss Muffet (18-24 months). "*See this little girl?*" (pointing); "*has she got a spoon? Where is the spoon?*" (30-36 months) "*See this little girl? What happened to her dinner?*" (36-42 months) "*Do you know 'Little Miss Muffet'? Sat on a ———?*"

Simple Simon. This can be used at 18-24 months, particularly if the child is just beginning to respond to questions. Ask for the boy's shoes, hat, eyes, etc.

Rock-a-bye Baby (18-24 months). If the dog was identified in the Tommy Tucker picture, or if the child has since begun to point to the pictures, he may be asked to name the dog this time. (30-36 months) *"What's the baby doing?"*

Pease Porridge (18-24 months). *"Where are the flowers?"* (30-36 months) *"What are the little girls doing?"* *"How many little girls eating their supper?"*

Daffy-Down-Dilly (18-30 months). *"What's that?"* pointing to the parasol.

Variations and extensions of this procedure are to be used as the situation suggests them, the aim being to keep the child interested and to get as many indications as possible of his use and comprehension of spoken language. If little interest is shown in the book at the beginning of the examination, or if language appears inhibited, the situation may be dropped and reinstated at an opportune moment later on.

Behavior trends. The child of a year or younger treats the book as a manipulative object, dragging it off the table, putting it on his head, or perhaps simply pushing it away. As early as *15 months*, however (although his mother reports that he only tears up books and magazines), he will allow the book to remain on the table, and even assist the examiner in turning its pages. The brightly colored pictures are patted with evident interest.

At *18 months*, he turns the pages without help, although the examiner may need to steady the book to keep it from sliding off the table. The turning is done awkwardly, however, and usually more than one page at a time. The child pauses to look at the pictures selectively as they are pointed out to him, or he may name or point responsively to a picture, usually the dog or baby.

The *2-year-old* turns the pages singly and deftly, and names or points to the dog, baby, shoes, spoon, etc. At *3 years* there are answers to the action questions: *"What is the girl doing?"* etc., and sometimes completion of one or more of the lines begun by the examiner. Most children of this age are too self-conscious to recite the verses unaided, even when they know them, especially this early in the examination. By *42 months* they will sometimes do so, and even give the number (two or three) of children in some of the pictures, or comment spontaneously on them.

The book appeals to most children, but is not so irresistibly interesting that they refuse to relinquish it for other test materials. It has the great advantage that there are no pictures of automobiles in it, so fascinating to modern motor-minded moppets.

Significance of the test. The types of question asked, and the responses called for, are in a number of cases similar to those used in such standard tests as the picture cards, object naming, etc.; and the situation may therefore be very enlightening in cases where the more fixed procedures used in those tests fail to overcome inhibition or inattention sufficiently to produce a clear-cut success or failure. While success in naming or identifying pictures in the book cannot be considered as fully equivalent to success with the picture cards, there is probably little difference in the ages at which these are found; and in case the card test is refused and the book accepted, success on the latter will influence strongly the examiner's impression of the maturity level for this type of behavior.

GENETIC SEQUENCES

Age 15 months—Inhibits grasping and manipulating of book. Assists in turning pages. Pats pictures.

18 months—Shows active interest in book. Turns pages, two or three at a time. Looks at pictures selectively. Names or points to dog or baby.

21 months—Names or points to shoes.

24 months—Turns pages singly. Names or points to many details of pictures (the child with better than average vocabulary names the parasol as "umbrella").

36 months—Gives action when asked, "What is he doing?" etc. May supply last word of line begun by examiner.

42 months—Supplies last word of line or recites verse. May tell how many (up to two or three) children in picture.

(L-2) EARLY LANGUAGE, REPORTED
(12-30 months)

The information called for in this section is to be obtained from the parent, although it is expected that such words and phrases as are heard by the examiner will be recorded, with notes as to the quality of articulation and appropriateness of use.

Procedure. a. Vocabulary (12-24 months). Ask how many words the child uses, and if there are no more than fifteen or twenty, what they are. If an extensive list is not reported, ask specifically for *no, yes, hello, bye-bye, car, go,* and other common early words. Ask further whether or not the child has names for persons, toys, animals, food, clothes, and common articles of furniture. This sort of questioning will sometimes extend considerably the list of words remembered by the mother. Ask further, whether the child indicates wants, such as food, playthings, or toilet, and find out how he does so.

b. Jargon (12-24 months). If this is not heard extensively in the examination, ask if it is heard at home. Does it sound like real conversation in a language of his own? Does he talk to himself? or does he direct his jargon toward others? How long are these "conversations"? Do they consist mostly of repetitions of a few sounds, or are they varied in character? Does he "talk" to himself when alone, when put to bed, etc.?

c. *Length of word combinations* (15-24 months). Ask, *"Does he put words together of his own accord?"* Get as many examples as possible, and ask particularly for the longest combination that has been heard. Ask specifically if he says "daddy go," "daddy bye-bye," "go car," or similar common combinations. Such learned phrases as "all gone," "so big," and other common nursery combinations are the equivalent of single words.

d. *Parts of speech* (24-30 months). Inquire concerning the use of pronouns, *I, me, you,* and the use of past tense and plural forms. Invariably correct use of the pronouns called for is not expected at 24 months, but there should be some discrimination shown.

Significance of the behavior. The development of vocabulary during the first two years has been discussed at length in the general section of the present chapter, and attention has been called there to the wide variability encountered among normal children within this age range. The norms represent only the central tendency, and frequent deviation from them is to be expected in clinical application. When vocabulary lists have been carefully kept by the mother, more reported words can be expected than when she is depending solely on her memory. The significance of marked deviations can be interpreted only in the light of the complete clinical study of the child and his environment, as indicated in the general discussion.

Vocabulary and jargon may to some extent influence each other. Some children who show a rapid increase of vocabulary during the period from 12 to 18 months, may use very little jargon, or none at all. On the other hand, the child with a highly expressive, richly varied, conversational jargon, may find this so satisfactory a means of expression that he does not begin to extend his vocabulary significantly until the second half of the year. Either an advanced vocabulary or an unusually well-developed jargon is suggestive of superiority, but not a clear indication in the absence of confirmation from other fields. In general the expectation is: more jargon than words below 18 months, and more words than jargon above that age.

Spontaneous combination of words is infrequent below 18 months, and increases rapidly thereafter. The first combinations usually involve a single noun and verb. Toward 2 years, the length of the combinations increases, and the sentence form begins to come into use, although pronouns and modifiers are not common until a little later.

Among forty children of the Normative Group examined at the age of 18 months, combinations were reported in only 25 per cent of cases, these being about equally divided between two- and three-word phrases.

At 2 years the norm falls between three and four words, three or more being reported in 76 per cent of cases, and four in 43 per cent. In only 9 per cent of cases were no combinations at all reported.

For examples of word combinations at 18 and 24 months, the reader is referred to the general discussion of language at 24 months, where there will also be found discussion of the use of pronouns, past tense, and plural forms.

GENETIC SEQUENCES

Age 15 months—Four to six words, including names. Uses varied jargon. Combines vocalization with gesture in indicating wants.

18 months—Ten words, including names.

21 months—Twenty words, including names. Spontaneous combination of two words. Vocalization consists more of words than of jargon.

24 months—Spontaneous combination of three to four words. Uses pronouns *I, me, you,* with partial discrimination.

30 months—Uses past tense and plural forms.

(L-3) INDICATING PARTS OF BODY
(18-24 months)

Procedure. Say, "*Show me your hair; where is your hair?*" A smile usually helps. Ask similarly for eyes, nose, and mouth. If necessary, use "*Open your mouth,*" "*Shut your eyes,*" or similar forms. A doll or a large picture may be used for indicating the responses if they are more easily secured in this way, but we have seldom found this necessary.

Significance of behavior. Binet (9) and Terman (121) both located this test at 3 years, requiring three successes; but it is actually much too easy for that age, or even for 2 years. Of nineteen children of the Normative Group at 18 months, only eight failed to respond correctly to one part of the test, while 48 of Muntz's fifty 2-year-olds passed all four. This ability to respond to all four at 24 months represents a jump from 5 per cent at 18 months.

At *18 months*, the hair and eyes are correctly identified with about equal frequency; nose and mouth are less often known. Boys do a little better on the test than girls.

The chief value of the test is that it is one of the few at this early age which calls for response to a language stimulus alone, without accompanying gesture or demonstration. It is thus of especial value in those cases in which the child's own speech is not up to standard, and it is desired to determine whether or not his comprehension of spoken language is also retarded. The situation involves an almost universal nursery trick which is part of the adult play with the baby in most homes. Institution children may fail it because of lack of this experience.

GENETIC SEQUENCES

Age 18 months—Knows one part.
24 months—Knows four parts.

NUMBER OF CHILDREN IDENTIFYING HAIR, EYES, NOSE, AND MOUTH AT 18 AND 24 MONTHS

	18 months (19 cases of Normative Group) %	24 months (50 cases of special research group—Muntz) %
Identifies no part............	42	
Identifies 1 part.............	21	
Identifies 2 parts............	16	2
Identifies 3 parts............	16	2
Identifies 4 parts............	5	96

PARTS IDENTIFIED BY 18-MONTH GROUP

Hair	correctly identified by 42% of children
Eyes	correctly identified by 47% of children
Nose	correctly identified by 26% of children
Mouth	correctly identified by 16% of children

(L-4) NAMES OBJECTS
(18-30 months)

Procedure (18-21 months). The test is here used as an introduction to the situation which calls for throwing a ball. The ball is produced and held toward the child, but out of his reach. Say, *"What's this?"* (variants: *"Tell me what it is"; "Tell mother what it is."*) Repeat as necessary, but do not prolong the situation to the point of producing emotional disturbance in the child who is concerned only with getting possession of the ball. Instead, hand it to him and proceed with the ball-throwing situation.

(24-30 months). Show, in order, the penny, key, shoe (the examiner points to her own shoe), pencil, knife, and ball. As each is shown, ask, *"What's this?" "And what is this?"* Repeat as necessary, but note the caution above as to persisting too long. Whether or not the object is named correctly, ask in each case, *"And what do we do with it?"* Note whether this question is answered by language or gesture (such as mimicking the turning of a key). The ball, the last object presented, is handed to the child, and the throwing situation is immediately begun.

Behavior trends. This is a still unstandardized test which represents the clinical residuum of two tests tried out earlier and discarded in their original forms. It has served very well to reinforce the general insight into the child's language development within the age range indicated.

Analysis of the responses obtained from groups of children to whom the test was presented as part of a clinical examination indicates that few children under 2 years give a satisfactory response to any of the objects except the ball. At *18 months*, about half the children name the ball and respond to *"What do we do with it?"* by throwing.

At *2 years* it is usually possible to get a response to several of the items. In case of a very poor response, or lack of attention, it may be desirable to skip some of these, going directly to the ball, which always arouses interest. The key and knife are the least likely objects to be named at this age.

The child of *30 months* gives more sustained attention to the series, and may be expected to name at least three of the objects.

Results for the question, *"What do you do with it?"* cannot at present be stated in terms of even approximate norms. Few 2-year-old children give verbal replies to it, but a correct response is given in at least one instance by probably about half of the children at 30 months. (Examples: *Key:* "In the door." *Penny:* "Pocketbook"; "Put it in pocket"; "In the bank"; "Candy." *Pencil:* "Write"; "On paper." *Shoe:* "Put it on.") As included in the present form of the test, it merely gives the child another opportunity to answer a standard form of question, and reinforces the examiner's general impression of his language maturity. The question should not be asked in the form *"What is it for?"* since most children at these ages will reply, "For me," or the equivalent.

Genetic Sequences

Age 18 months—Names ball.
　　24 months—Names two objects.
　　30 months—Names three objects. Answers at least one "What do you do with it?"

(L-5) Following Directions with Ball
(18-24 months)

Procedure. Place the child's chair against the wall, not too near the examining table or the mother. Hand him the ball, saying, *"Take the ball to mother"*; *"Put the ball on the chair"*; *"Bring it to me"*; *"Put it on the table."* Give him a reasonable time to comply after each part, and repeat directions if necessary without change. Look directly at the child while speaking, and be careful to avoid any glance or gesture that will suggest the goal. Maintain an even tone of voice, emphasizing "to mother," "on the chair," "me," "on the table." Give a second chance with increased emphasis if he does the wrong thing, but allow him to complete his response before doing so. Be careful not to interrupt, or to indicate a "no-no" suggestion by the tone of voice.

Significance of behavior. A satisfactory response to this test requires evidence of comprehension of the full direction, "*Put the ball on the chair,*" etc. In most cases this calls for following out the instruction completely. An occasional child will clearly start to comply by walking to the chair and starting to place the ball, but without actually relinquishing it; or he may extend it toward the examiner but refuse to give it up. Such responses are satisfactory. A mere glance or gesture toward the goal, however, is not sufficient, as it is very likely to be merely a response to the word "chair," "mother," etc., alone. Throwing the ball toward the chair or goal can usually be considered a positive response.

As in the case of some other tests within this age range, the present one cannot always be either given or scored on a straight plus-and-minus basis. The difficulty of controlling attention is increased by the fact that the child is up and moving about during the presentation, and the interest in ball play may effectively nullify the instruction, particularly in the case of boys. In such cases, differential interpretation of failure, as due to inattention or lack of ability to pass the test, is often impossible, and neither should be assumed without clear evidence. Going through the entire group of four tasks, also puts a too prolonged strain on the attention of many children of 18 months, and it is often wise to stop before giving all of them. These considerations have less force at 2 years, although the factor of attention is still an important one in many children of that age.

Behavior trends. At *18 months* in those cases where cooperation is given, more than half the children hand the ball to the mother, and place it discriminatively on either chair or table. Girls are somewhat more responsive to the test than boys, many of whom engage in active ball play instead of giving attention to directions. At *24 months* all four instructions are carried out correctly by half of the children, when cooperation permits all four to be given. There is no significant difference between boys and girls at this age.

GENETIC SEQUENCES

Age 18 months—Carries out two instructions, if cooperative.
21 months—Carries out three instructions.
24 months—Carries out all four instructions.

(L-6) PICTURE CARDS
(18-36 months)

It is not until about the middle of the third half-year that an interest in looking at pictures begins to manifest itself, or that an association is made between the picture and the object which it represents. Even up to 2 years, such interest is apt to be brief and superficial, except to the accompaniment of a story told while looking at the pictures, and in this there is very great individual variation. The presentation of the picture cards meets the requirements of this stage of development by calling for only short periods of attention, with repeated reinforcement from the examiner when needed. The test covers the period of development from the age at which the child first makes his association between the picture and the object, up to the stage at which pictures of all familiar objects are recognized without difficulty. It is not in any important sense a test of vocabulary, since practically all the objects pictured are represented in the spoken or comprehension vocabulary of the 2-year-old child, whereas the maximum performance on the test is not encountered until a year later.

Procedure. Take up Card A, saying, *"We're going to look at some pictures."* Hold the card, appropriately oriented, toward the child, and let him take it if he reaches for it. Point to the picture of the dog, and say, *"What's this?"* In case of failure to obtain a response, do not persist too long, but repeat the question for the other pictures. If comprehension of what is wanted suddenly appears on one of the pictures later presented, the test may be repeated for the ones previously failed. If one or more pictures on Card A are named correctly, proceed similarly with Card B. If all on Card A are failed, the "clock" on Card B may be tried; or if a satisfactory response seems unlikely, the second part of the test, described below, may be begun.

If eight or more pictures are correctly named, this suffices for the test at the highest level where it appears—36 months.

If fewer than eight pictures are named, begin with Card A (or with Card B if all on the first card were correctly named), and say, *"Where is the ———?"* (Alternatives: *"Show me the ———"; "Put your finger on the ———"*) "Doggie" is preferred for dog with the youngest children, and "bow-wow" and "tick-tock" may be substituted for their adult synonyms if the latter are not understood. "Flower" is more likely to bring a correct response than "leaf."

Timing is important in sustaining interest; there should be no long pauses between questions, and abbreviations should be freely used in recording responses.

The order of questioning, for both naming and pointing, is as follows:
Card A: Dog, shoe, cup, house
Card B: Clock, basket, book, leaf, flag, star

Behavior trends. Responses are recorded verbatim, and phonetically as far as possible. Any appropriate word is scored as a success. An apparently irrelevant response for the dog may be the name of a dog or cat known to the child. "Bow-wow" (or other imitation of a dog) and "tick-tock" are perfectly acceptable. "Kitty" or any other familiar animal may be accepted for the dog, but such responses are of an immature type, more characteristic of the lower age ranges of the test. "Milk," "coffee," or other food or drink taken from a cup or bowl, is an immature but acceptable response for *cup*. "Flower" or "tree" for *leaf* are more common than the correct word, even at 36 months, and should be counted as successes.

At *15 months*, some children will identify the dog. Others when asked to find the shoe will indicate their own. One or the other of these responses is found in more than half of the cases at this stage. Of those who fail, a large proportion show no evidence of comprehending the task at all.

A common response at *18-21 months* is to accept the card, glance quickly at it, turn it over to look at the other side, and hand it back to the examiner. Repetition of the question in many cases brings an appropriate response after this, but too much persistence is not advised. At *24 months*, many children still turn the card over to see what is on the other side, but they are less likely to return the card immediately after having done so.

The principal causes for failure, aside from simple inability to identify any of the pictures, are failure to comprehend the task and inability to sustain attention throughout the test.

There is a definite sex difference in the type of response encountered at 18 months; the girls as a group were able to identify a larger number of pictures than the boys, but the boys were rather more likely to name at least one picture. This difference is diminished by 24 months, and is not found at 36 months. If the test is given at 42 months the child shows his greater maturity by reading off the objects in order, without individual direction from the examiner.

GENETIC SEQUENCES

Age 15 months—If cooperative, points to one picture (usually *dog*) or to own shoe.

    18 months—Identifies one or more pictures (usually *dog*) by naming or pointing.

    21 months—Identifies two or more by naming or pointing.

    24 months—(a) Names three or more.

            (b) Identifies five or more by naming or pointing.

    30 months—(a) Names five or more.

            (b) Identifies seven or more by naming or pointing.

    36 months—Names eight or more.

    42 months—Goes through card spontaneously, naming ten.

NUMBER OF ITEMS ON PICTURE CARDS *IDENTIFIED BY NAMING OR POINTING*, BY CHILDREN OF NORMATIVE GROUP AT 18 AND 24 MONTHS

No. of pictures identified	18 months			24 months		
	Boys %	Girls %	Group %	Boys %	Girls %	Group %
0..................	37	32	34	7		3
1..................	47	26	37	14		6
2..................	16	26	21	0		0
3..................		5	3	21	26	24
4..................		5	3	7	16	12
5..................		0	0	0	11	6
6..................		5	3	21	26	24
7..................				14	11	12
8..................				7	5	6
9..................				7	5	6
10.................						

NUMBER OF ITEMS ON PICTURE CARDS *NAMED* BY CHILDREN OF NORMATIVE GROUP AT 18, 24, AND 36 MONTHS

No. of pictures named	18 months			24 months			36 months		
	Boys %	Girls %	Group %	Boys %	Girls %	Group %	Boys %	Girls %	Group %
0.............	53	79	66	7	16	12			
1.............	42	11	26	29	11	18			
2.............	5	5	6	0	21	12			
3.............		5	2	21	16	18		6	3
4.............				21	16	18		0	0
5.............				21	16	18		6	3
6.............				0	0	0	13	12	12
7.............					2	3	27	23	25
8.............							20	23	22
9.............							20	18	19
10............							20	12	16

(L-7) GIVES FULL NAME

Procedure. Ask *"What's your name?"* If only the first name (or nickname) is given, such as David or Buddy, say, *"David what?"* *"What's the rest of it?"* *"What's your other name?"* If necessary, ask, *"Is your name David Smith?"* using, of course, an incorrect surname. A nickname is perfectly acceptable for the first name.

If a response cannot be obtained by the examiner, the mother may be requested to ask the question, using the prescribed forms.

Significance of behavior. The test is easy for 3 years where it was passed by 85 per cent of the Normative Group, and success may be appropriately credited at 30 months. Very poor attention may cause failure, but the brevity of the situation makes it possible to meet this difficulty in most cases. Failure may result from negativism, perhaps because of too much asking of the same question at home. Responses will occasionally be incomprehensible because of defective articulation.

There is relatively little variation in the types of response encountered. The most common failure at 30 and 36 months is simply giving the first name or nickname. Individual responses—e.g., giving the wrong name, replying, "I'm a little girl" (if the test involving telling the sex has preceded)—are rare at 3 years. There is a little more variation when the test is used at 4 years, where it is, to be sure, not ordinarily tried. This variation is found almost altogether among the boys, among whom, "Don't know," and a failure to respond, are more common than at 3 years, usually because of inhibition; and comic responses, such as giving the names of other children, are sometimes met with at this age.

Norm: 30 months: Gives full name.

(L-8) ANALYZES PICTURES

Procedure. Say, *"Here's a picture I'd like to show you."* Present the Dutch Home picture, wait a few seconds to give the child an opportunity to take it in and perhaps comment spontaneously on it, and say, *"Tell me what the picture is about."* Give a little encouragement if necessary, but if no response is forthcoming, say, *"Tell me everything you see in the picture."* If there is still no response, say, *"Show me the kitty; where is the kitty? . . . That's right; now, what else do you see?"* Repeat *"What else?"* as necessary.

Repeat with the Canoe picture, the Post-office picture, and, if desired, the Colonial picture. If there is a good deal of inhibition, the test may be cut off after one of the first two pictures, if spontaneous enumeration of three or more objections in one picture has been obtained.

Behavior trends. Terman has differentiated (in the old form of the Stanford scale) three types of response—principally enumeration, principally description, and interpretation. These were assigned to the maturity levels of 3, 7, and 12 years, respectively In the 1937 Stanford, the test is omitted at the two upper levels, but retained at 3 years.

Within the preschool range, the most common type of response is simple enumeration of objects in the picture, with occasional descriptive phrases, increasing in proportion as the children grow older. At *3 years,* description is rare, beyond an occasional "Cat's lying down," and the learned phrase "Little girl." Some description is encountered in about a fourth of the cases at *4 years*, and in nearly three-fourths at *5 years*, where a predominantly descriptive response is given in about 40 per cent of cases. A few—usually superior—children furnish a satisfactory interpretation of one or more of the pictures at 4, 5, or 6 years, but such a response is very rare at 3 years and is likely to be far-fetched. It is interesting to note that a number of children who give interpretation at 4 years confine themselves to description at 5, possibly as a result of the more detached and critical attitude which is characteristic of that age.

Failure to respond, sometimes because of lack of comprehension and sometimes because of inhibition, is rather frequent at *3 years*, though not at the higher ages. If a little encouragement does not bring a response, further persistence seldom proves worth while. The 3-year-old will sometimes name one object in the picture, under pressure, and then return the card with a positive "That's all."

Bright 4- and 5-year-old children will sometimes associate the picture with some familiar story, and tell, for example, the tale of Little Red Riding Hood in response to the Dutch scene. This tendency at 5 years, and possibly even the tendency to interpret more logically, are often found in the superior children who are also somewhat immature, over-active and overtalkative. One very bright, but extremely immature, child of this age recently gave three different interpretations of the Dutch scene, any one of which would have been acceptable at the 12-year level in the old Stanford-Binet scale. The more stable, socially mature, child of 5, even when of equally superior intelligence, usually confines himself to a studied deliberate description of the picture, frequently with an appended enumeration of objects which have not been covered in the descriptive part of his answer.

At 4 and 5 years, girls show a little more tendency to confine themselves to enumeration than do the boys. At 6 years this tendency is reversed. At 6 also, the girls do a little more interpreting than the boys.

The Canoe and Post-office pictures are more likely to elicit description than is the Dutch scene, possibly because of improved adjustment to the test, since they are the second and third pictures presented.

GENETIC SEQUENCES

Age 3 years—The almost universal positive response is enumeration of a few objects in the picture, with occasionally, one or two descriptive words.

Inhibition, or failure to comprehend the task, occasionally leads to a failure to respond.

4 years—Enumeration is still the standard type of response, but some descriptive comment is found in about one-fourth of the cases.

Failure to respond is rare.

A few children give interpretation of one or more pictures.

5 years—About three-fourths of the children furnish some description of the pictures, and about 40 per cent confine their responses to description.

Failure to respond is rare. It is practically never due to lack of comprehension of the task, but primarily to inhibition based upon lack of confidence, a trait encountered more frequently at 5 years than at earlier ages.

Interpretation, though representing less than 5 per cent of the total number of responses, is a little more frequent than at 4 years.

6 years—Nearly half the children confine their responses to description, and more than three-fourths use some descriptive comment.

Complete failure to respond is seldom encountered.

Interpretation is found in more than 10 per cent of cases among girls, representing a sharp increase over 4 and 5 years. No such increase is found among the boys.

(L-9) ACTION-AGENT TEST
(3-5 years)

This test, the outstanding language situation within the upper half of the preschool range, is best given at a point in the examination when good personal rapport has been established between child and examiner, but well before interest has begun to flag, or fatigue to set in. It requires a relatively long period of attention, and, since much of the examiner's impression of the child's personality may be based upon his responses to it, he should be given the best possible opportunity to show up well. In addition to providing a measure of language comprehension, the test gives the opportunity to observe such matters as the ability to sustain attention and interest, tendencies toward perseveration or stereotypy, confusion by similarities of sound or associated ideas, critical consideration of responses, as opposed to random answering, tendencies to give up easily or to go out of the field in the face of an increasingly difficult task, and other details which throw light upon the child's personal-social stability and maturity. Because of the significance of these factors in estimating the total clinical impression, careful consideration must be given to the influence of all disturbing or unusual features in the situation in which the test is given.

Procedure. Secure the child's attention and say, *"What runs?" "Tell me something that runs."* It may be necessary to repeat the question, but do not persist too long. If no response, or an inappropriate one, is given, say,

"*A car runs, doesn't it? And horses run, too.*" (It is best to avoid an example, such as "Boys and girls," which is appropriate to two or three of the next few questions, to avoid setting up a perseverative response with doubtful comprehension.) Pause briefly. "*What cries?*" "*Tell me something that cries.*" Again, if the response is unsatisfactory, answer the question. Proceed with the test proper, without supplying any more answers. If a good response is obtained to the first sample question, it is often unnecessary to give the second.

Examples: What runs? What cries?

1. What scratches?	11. What sails?
2. What sleeps?	12. What boils?
3. What flies?	13. What floats?
4. What bites?	14. What growls?
5. What swims?	15. What stings?
6. What burns?	16. What gallops?
7. What cuts?	17. What aches?
8. What blows?	18. What explodes?
9. What shoots?	19. What roars?
10. What melts?	20. What mews?

Scoring. All responses are recorded verbatim. Many standard responses, such as "wind" for "What blows?" and "gun" for "What shoots?" can be recorded by their initial letters alone. Multiple answers, such as "babies and pussy-cats and birdies" for "What sleeps?" as well as added comments, relevant or irrelevant, are to be recorded complete.

Successful responses, according to Stutsman (118), are those which name:

1. Agent performing act
   a. Object (such as "knife cuts")
   b. Person manipulating object (such as "I cut"). In the case of such responses as this, however, it is best to ask, "*How do you cut? Show me how you do it?*" to make sure that the question has been understood
2. Direct object, when the direct object is usually associated with the act (such as "paper cuts")
3. Unusual responses with logical association
   a. When word begins with *s* as "What sails?" (child may interpret as "What's sales?" replying, "For boys' suits," or a similar response)
   b. Other unusual replies (as "Sail, baby, sail"; or "Sally," the name of a boat, to "What sails?" or "Tiger" to "What melts?" based upon *Little Black Sambo*)

Perseverative responses must be scored as successes if they are discriminatively used, otherwise they are usually failures, even though appropriate to some of the questions to which they are given. "Baby" may be reported as scratching, sleeping, biting, and if a more appropriate response is given to the intervening "What flies?" and other questions, all these are correct. If, however, the perseverative response is given to more than one inappropriate question as well, all should be counted as failures, although the examiner may get a rather clear impression of the amount of insight shown and weigh it in forming his total judgment of the child.

Characteristic forms of response.

Simple correct responses. The appropriate single word or brief phrase ("kitties," "the birds," "dogs bite") is the most frequent type of response at all ages, accounting for nearly half of the recorded responses even as early as 3 years, slightly more than half at 4, and from two-thirds to three-fourths at 5 years. Thus the difference between 4 and 5 years is more marked in terms of the proportion of these simple responses to the total number, than on the basis of the actual number of acceptable answers, in which 5 has an advantage of only a single word over 4.

Multiple responses. Although few in number at any age, these appear to be more characteristic of the bright, talkative 4-year-old than of either the 3- or 5-year-old.

Personal reference. The answer, "me," or "I do," as well as reference to persons and animals known to the child, appears to reflect a stage of immaturity which is rapidly passing by 4 years, and gone by 5.

Sound confusion. There is a little of this at all ages. *Stings* understood as *stinks*, *melts* as *milk*, *aches* as *eggs*, and *mews* as *music*, account for the majority of these errors. The interest in word-play found in many children at 5 years is reflected in rhyming responses, such as (What growls?) "Owls."

Perseveration. This diminishes steadily from 3 to 5 years. In its simplest form, with one or two responses repeated non-discriminatively, it is commonest at 3 years. At 4 and 5 it is most likely to take the form of the occasional repetition of a previously accepted response, when the correct one is not known, or when interest is beginning to lapse. A perseverated response may be quite acceptable when used with obvious discrimination. A dog sleeps, scratches, bites, swims, growls, etc., and if the response is given to these questions and not to inappropriate ones, scoring credit is given. Such a response, however, taken in conjunction with other behavior, may suggest lack of imaginativeness or a limited background of experience.

Simple incorrect responses. Examples of this type are (What swims?)

"Houses"; (What explodes?) "Hoppy-toads." Sometimes there is an obvious association of ideas, but frequently no connection is clear. It is necessary to be on guard against dismissing as irrelevant a response based upon a definite experience. (What floats?) "Houses" might be a very good answer for a child who had seen flood pictures in the papers and been strongly impressed by them. A little questioning of the child or the mother will usually clear up doubtful answers.

Elaborated responses. Responses in the form of sentences, complete ("Boys swim when they go in the water"), or incomplete ("What floats?" "On your back when you put your head down and your feet up and float"), are more characteristic of certain individuals than of any particular age. The loquacious 4-year-old, or the deliberative Five who considers and qualifies his response ("Well, now, let me see: I guess dogs growl sometimes"), is likely to give one or more responses of this type, as is the child who is most completely adjusted and at home with the examiner.

No answer. This is indicated usually by "I don't know," or simply by remaining silent or by repeating the final verbs: ("What cuts?" "Cuts"). It may indicate (at the beginning of the test) lack of comprehension, as is found occasionally at 3 years; actual lack of knowledge of the word or the correct response (usually the case at 4); or inhibition based upon timidity or lack of certainty as to the correctness of the answer in mind, sometimes met with at 5 years. Ordinarily, when other responses have been given satisfactorily, such answers may be taken at their face value; in any case, over-persistence in questioning is best avoided, as tending rather to increase negativism than to overcome it. If some such comment as, *"Oh, I'm sure you know that one,"* does not produce a response, it is better to pass on, repeating the question later, if desired.

Between "I don't know" and a failure to respond at all, there seems to be a division between boys and girls at 5 years, the girls tending to remain silent rather than express a lack of knowledge. Two-thirds of the boys said "I don't know" at least once, while slightly fewer than one-half the girls gave this response. One or more refusals to answer were encountered in 36 per cent of the 5-year-old girls, and in only 25 per cent of the boys.

Other ways of turning aside an inability to answer correctly are occasionally encountered. The 3-year-old is likely to answer at random rather than refuse, as long as he is maintaining attention. A succession of puzzling questions, however, leads him to drop his attention, and he may give no heed to further questions, say, "I don't want to do that any more," ask for some specific substitute, or go out of the field completely by talking about irrelevant topics. A favorite escape is to get up and walk about the room, commenting on other things seen there. Similar responses may be encountered at 4 years, but the 4-year-old is inclined to be more positive in his demand that the questioning be dropped. The 5-year-old devises excuses, or tries to shift the blame—"My mother doesn't want me to say that one." Both 4 and 5, especially the superior children, may turn the question back on the examiner—"*You* tell *me* that!"

Miscellaneous responses. Occasional responses are encountered which are not readily classifiable in terms of the above categories, or are highly individual variations of them. The superior 4-year-old is likely to use one or more of the stimulus questions as the starting-point for an elaborate account of a personal experience. Home influences as well as personal idiosyncrasies are reflected in such answers as (What blows?) "God," or the list of eight successive kinds of food given by an obese 3-year-old, in answer to as many questions.

GENETIC SEQUENCES

Age 3 years—Six to seven correct responses.

Multiple responses are rare.

Attention is difficult to hold for the period of the entire test, with a marked tendency to "go out of the field" as the questions get harder.

Apparently random or inappropriate responses are given, or no response at all, rather than "I don't know."

Personal reference, to the child himself or to a person or animal of his acquaintance, is encountered in many cases.

Perseveration of response is slightly more frequent than at 4 and 5 years.

4 years—Thirteen correct responses.

About half the children give one or more multiple responses.

Attention can usually be maintained for the entire 20 questions, but this may require some management on the part of the examiner.

"I don't know" is given by more than half the children, while simple failure to respond is encountered among only a few.

More than half the girls, but only a third of the boys, say "I don't know."

Personal reference occurs occasionally, more often among the girls, but is less frequent than at 3 years.

Perseveration is less frequent, and less prolonged, than at 3 years.

5 years—Fifteen correct responses.

Fewer than one in four children give any multiple responses.

Attention seldom gives any difficulty; but deliberate escape attempts are occasionally met with.

Two-thirds of the boys and slightly fewer than half the girls say

"I don't know" at least once. 36 per cent of the girls and 25 per cent of the boys give no response to one or more questions. Personal reference is practically never encountered.
Perseveration is rare, as compared with 3 and 4 years.

ANALYSIS OF RECORDED RESPONSES TO ACTION-AGENT TEST BY 3-, 4-, AND 5-YEAR-OLD CHILDREN[6]

	3 years %	4 years %	5 years %
Simple correct responses............	33	56	73
Multiple responses.................	1	5	2
Personal reference..................	5	2	0
Sound confusion....................	4	2	3
Perseveration......................	3	4	2
Simple incorrect responses...........	8	10	9
Elaborated or qualified responses.....	2	2	2
"Don't know"......................	6	11	5
No response.......................	11	2	5
Miscellaneous.....................	3	5	less than 1%
Not given.........................	22	0	0

PERCENTAGE OF CORRECT RESPONSES TO ACTION-AGENT TEST MADE BY CHILDREN OF THE NORMATIVE GROUP AT 3, 4, AND 5 YEARS

Age in years	3	4	5
Number correct:			
0......................	5		
1– 3...................	15	12	
4– 6...................	30	0	2
7– 9...................	25	8	4
10–12..................	20	21	13
13–15..................	5	38	51
16–18..................		21	29
19.....................			2

(L-10) TELLS SEX

Procedure. This brief test may be introduced at any convenient point in the examination after a good rapport has been established. It may serve very well to hold the child's attention between tests while one set of material is being put away and another being brought out.

Be sure attention is secured, and ask casually (if a boy), *"Are you a little boy or a little girl?"*; (if a girl) *"Are you a little girl or a little boy?"* If there is no relevant response, ask (if a boy), *"Are you a little girl?"*; (if a girl) *"Are you a little boy?"* If the answer is "No," ask, *"Then what are you?"* The questioning should be carried on in a light and pleasant manner, but too smiling an approach will encourage a joking response, deliberately incorrect, in some children.

Behavior trends. The ability to pass this test seems to come in between

[6] Since decimals have been dropped in compiling these tabulations, all of the columns do not add up to exactly 100%.

30 and 36 months. Few children pass it at the earlier age, whereas from two-thirds to three-fourths of the 3-year-olds do so, as do practically all at 4 years. Failure is therefore more significant than success at 3 and 4 years, and may be the result of real inability to comprehend the question or make the distinction, or of inattention or negativism. At 3 years many children reply by giving their own names. A tendency to respond to only the last part of the question is an immature type of behavior, and makes it essential to follow the prescribed form. Such a response may take the form of repeating the second-named choice, or simply of answering, "No." The jokingly incorrect response mentioned is not common, but is some-times encountered in the brighter children. The discriminative type of answer, "I'm not a girl, I'm a boy," is more characteristic of 4 years (com-pare "This is the little one and this is the big one," to the lines, and "this is the pretty one and this is the funny one," to the aesthetic discrimination test). The indignant denial of the implication of the wording, "No, I'm a *big* boy!" is occasionally met with between 3½ and 4 years.

A strong negative response to the question may reflect the traditional teasing of small children enjoyed by relatives, of attributing to them the wrong sex. If there is a marked hint of this, the question had better not be pressed.

There is a slight sex difference in favor of the boys on this test, the girls being a little more likely to reply, "I'm a boy."

(L-11) COMPREHENSION QUESTIONS
(3-5 years)

Group A (3-4 years)

Procedure: "What must you do when you are hungry?"
"What must you do when you are sleepy?"
"What must you do when you are cold?"

Some small children do not understand "must." When this seems a possible cause of failure, the question may be repeated, using the form, "What do you do when . . . ?" Otherwise, the form should not be changed. When a response has been obtained, supplementary questions may be asked, if necessary, to clarify the answer.

Significance of behavior. Ability to understand and answer this simple type of question is rarely found below 3 years, and is still not present in many children of that age. It represents a degree of maturity slightly above that necessary to understand the action-agent type of question (L-9), to which successful responses are obtained from the majority of 3-year-old children. From the standpoint of comprehension, there is little difference between 4 years and 5 years on this test; two acceptable responses out of three represent the median performance at each age. From the point of view of objective scoring, therefore, the test is not closely discriminative above 4 years. There are, however, interesting qualitative differences in the characteristic responses at the two ages, which make it desirable to give the test in many cases at 5 years.

The third question in the series is one that lends itself to misinterpretation, "when you are cold" being often understood as "when you have a cold." This misunderstanding is not common at 5 years, but is nearly as common as the correct sense at 3 and 4 years.

The questions differ considerably in their tendency to elicit a simple, relatively uniform, type of response. The first question ("hungry") brings out the most uniformity in this respect, with the simple response "eat" leading all others, and increasing proportionately with advancing age. The second ("sleepy") brings out slightly less uniform answers, but "sleep," "Go to bed," "Go to sleep" are the most frequent responses at 4 and especially at 5 years. The third question ("cold") is not calculated to produce a standardized form of response, even when it is correctly understood, and brings out much more variety.

Genetic Sequences

Age 3 years. Responses are varied and specific, with frequent personal reference. Where the 4-year-old replies "eat" or "sleep," the 3-year-old says, "I eat" or "I sleep." "When you are cold" is almost always understood as "when you have a cold" at this age. Immediate reference is also often understood, bringing forth the response, "I'm not sleepy," "no," or "I didn't." Characteristic 3-year-old responses are as follows:

> *Hungry:* Eat my breakfast up.
> Candy.
> Eat cereal (or potatoes, or bread, etc.).
> I eat.
> Drink of milk.
> Get some supper.
> *Sleepy:* I sleep.
> Get up.
> Get off my bed.
> Beddie–night.
> Go to bed.
> Go to sleep on pillows.
> *Cold:* Go out.
> I got a cold.
> I sick.
> I blow my nose.

Freeze—it's wet out.
I sneeze every day.
Have a coat on.
Have a doctor.
Her cold will get better.
Have some medicine.
My coat's on.
I didn't.

Age 4 years. Responses are nearly as likely to be specific in nature as at 3 years, but they are longer and more detailed, and with rather less personal reference. At the same time, the simple standard responses ("Eat," etc.) are becoming more frequent. The "cold" question is more frequently understood than at 3, but "have a cold" is still a common interpretation of it. Some characteristic 4-year-old responses:

Hungry: Go to my grandmother's. (Questioned) I eat over there.
   Climb up on the shelf and get a knife and have a piece of bread.
   Eat dinner. (Breakfast, supper, etc. Compare "eat bread," etc., which
    is more characteristic of 3 years.)
   Get something to eat.
Sleepy: Go to bed (to sleep).
   Lay down.
   On the couch I go.
   You're tired.
   Get up.
   Just get up, and my mother is out in the kitchen doing her dishes,
    and she says, "Hey, Jimmy!"
   Lay in bed.
Cold: Get warm.
   Get a coat (sweater, etc.).
   Go in the house.
   Get a fire.
   Put on the covers.
   Get medicine and get better.
   Get sick.
   Put a hot water bottle to your feet.
   My mother puts ointment on my chest.
   . . . Go in the store and say, "How about kicking that bed over me?"
   (Part of a long, partially incomprehensible, story.)

Age 5 years. As in other fields, the 5-year-old shows much less tendency to over-respond in answering the questions; and the simple appropriate response, particularly to the first two questions, is the rule at this age. "Eat" is given in answer to the first question in more than half the cases, and "sleep," alone or as part of a short phrase, in nearly half the cases for the second question. When more elaborate responses are given they are adaptive and realistic. When personal reference is made, it is in terms of "you" and "your," instead of the "I" and "my" of 3 years. The "cold" question is seldom misunderstood. Some sample responses of 5-year-olds, illustrating the type of responses, other than the simple ones, given by children of this age:

> *Hungry:* Eat.
> Make food.
> Get your dinner.
> Go in and get a piece of bread and butter.
> *Sleepy:* Go to sleep (or to bed).
> Lay down.
> Snore.
> Cover yourself in bed.
> *Cold:* Go in the house.
> Start a fire.
> Cough.
> Put a blanket on.
> Get down in the covers and pull them up.
> Go in and get a coat and hat.

Norms: 3 years: Answers one question.

42 months: Answers two questions.

NUMBER OF QUESTIONS OF COMPREHENSION GROUP A CORRECTLY ANSWERED AT 4 AND 5 YEARS

No. answered	4 years %	5 years %
0	8	1
1	12	5
2	46	53
3	34	40

Group B (4-5 years)

Procedure. a. *"What must you do when you have lost something?"*
b. *"What must you do before you cross the street?"*

Correct responses to question *a* should refer to search: "Hunt for it," "Find it," "Ask my mommy to help me look for it," etc. "Get another" is less directly responsive to the main implication of the question and is counted as failure. Some children will answer, "Find a policeman," or something of the sort, indicating that the question has been understood as "What must you do when you are lost?" In such cases, say, *"Yes, that's right. And what must you do when you have lost something that belongs to you?"* Failures include such responses as "Cry," "Get a spanking," "I broke my dolly," "Nothing."

For question *b*, the answer should suggest caution or conformity with regulations in crossing the street: "Look out for the cars," "Wait for the light," "Take my mommy's hand," "Wait for my mother," "Look up and down." Failures are: "Run," "Hurry up," "Get a spanking," etc. Misunderstanding of the question is sometimes indicated by a child who has been conditioned against crossing the street while playing: "Don't cross the street," "Don't go in the street." In such cases, the question may be rephrased: *"If you're out for a walk with your mother and come to the corner, what must you do before you go across the street?"*

Significance of behavior. These questions while incompletely standardized at present, have been found clinically serviceable for filling in the gap between the questions of Group A and those for higher ages. The social implications of the second make it particularly significant in relation to the 4-5 years maturity level.

The test was given by Dr. E. E. Lord to forty-five children at the age of 4 years. The group was carefully selected from the standpoint of intelligence and parental occupation, showing a normal distribution on both points. Of these forty-five children, 53 per cent failed to answer either question correctly, 27 per cent answered just one, and 20 per cent answered both. The number of successes is high enough to make it desirable to give the test at 4 years, but it is a little hard for this age. Clinical experience suggests that one success should be expected at 4½ years, and two at 5 years.

(L-12) DISCRIMINATES PREPOSITIONS
(36-48 months)

Procedure A. Stand up, and have the child do so. Place the performance box on the floor, and draw the child's chair out a little way from the table. Be sure you have the child's attention, and say, *"Put the ball on the box,"* stressing the words *on* and *box,* and handing him the ball. If it is necessary to repeat the direction, do this before the ball is given. When he has responded, retrieve the ball, get his attention again, and say, *"Now put the ball in the box."* Repeat for *behind* (or *in back of*), *in front of,* and *under,* the *chair,* always stressing the preposition or phrase and the object. Make no comment on the performance until all items have been given.

Procedure B. Use the red cubes or the ball, and the chair alone, without the performance box. Require the cubes or ball to be placed *on, under, in back of* (or *behind*), *in front of,* and *beside* the chair. Some children will respond by placing the object on the chair seat in all cases, but making apparent distinction between *in front of, in back of,* etc. In such cases, rephrase the direction, *"Put the block on the floor in back of the chair,"* etc.

Significance of behavior. Form A of this test is that first used by Muntz (91) with his research group of fifty 2-year-old children, and later by Holbrook (59) with fifty 3-year-olds. The alternate methods described have tended to displace it in clinical use, because of the advantage of using only a single object to which the prepositional distinctions relate. As yet, however, there are no final norms for these alternate procedures.

Holbrook found that 76 per cent of her 3-year-olds responded correctly to three parts of the test, *on* and *in* being the most frequently known. Only 40 per cent passed four parts. The 2-year group showed practically no ability to discriminate among the instructions.

The types of procedure described under *B* omit *in* and add *beside.* This changes the difficulty of the task; but preliminary results indicate that, although the proportion of children passing three parts will be somewhat reduced from Holbrook's 76 per cent, the figure will be slightly over 50 per cent, which will leave the age requirement for 3 years unchanged. Four successes are expected at 4 years.

The use of the cubes has the advantage that they do not roll after being put in place. The ball is favored especially with the younger children, because of their spontaneous interest in it, and because it permits of the test being used as a transition situation, in conjunction with other tests using the ball.

NUMBER OF CORRECT RESPONSES GIVEN BY FIFTY 3-YEAR-OLD CHILDREN OF SPECIAL RESEARCH GROUP TO PREPOSITIONS TEST
(Holbrook)

2 correct responses	94%
3 correct responses	76%
4 correct responses	40%
5 correct responses	36%

SUPPLEMENTARY LANGUAGE TESTS
(54-72 months)

To gain additional information as to the language status of the child of 4 to 6 years, it has been customary in clinical practice to use selected tests from the (1916) Stanford and the (1922) Kuhlmann scales. These supplementary data not only broaden the clinical picture, but aid effectively in giving continuity to a series of examinations begun during the preschool age and carried on after the age of 6 years.

Tests of this group most closely associated with language development are as follows:

(L-13) *Definitions in terms of use* (Stanford V-4; Kuhlmann V-6)

(L-14) *Names Red, Yellow, Blue, Green* (Stanford V-2; Kuhlmann V-8)

(L-15) *Knows coins* (Stanford VI-5)

(L-16) *Executes three commissions* (Stanford V-6)

(L-17) *Knows age* (Stanford V-alt.)

(L-18) *Distinguishes morning and afternoon* (Stanford VI, alt. 2)

Our own findings have modified slightly the age-placement of some of these tests, as have later revisions of the original scales themselves. There is no intention here of going extensively into these modifications, but a few of the more significant observations are briefly indicated in the succeeding paragraphs. The procedure for the tests has been specified by the original authors.

Definitions in terms of use. The test may be given at 4 years, where two or more successes are to be expected. The 5-year-old passes five out of the six parts. When time is short, or attention hard to control, success on the first three, or three of the first four, may usually be taken as a 5-year performance, since practically all children of that age who get as many as three, get four or five in the entire test.

Knows colors. 74 per cent of the Normative Group at 4 years named one color—usually red—while only 42 per cent named two or more. At 5 years, all four colors were named correctly in 61 per cent of cases. This is in agreement with the Stanford-Kuhlmann placement.

SUCCESS IN GIVING DEFINITIONS IN TERMS OF USE
IN CHILDREN OF THE NORMATIVE GROUP
AT 4 AND 5 YEARS

	4 years %	5 years %
No success....................	37	10
Defined 1 or more..............	63	90
Defined 2 or more..............	52	88
Defined 3 or more..............	37	88
Defined 4 or more..............	30	81
Defined 5 or more..............	4	70
Defined 6 or more..............	0	39

SUCCESS IN NAMING RED, YELLOW, BLUE, AND GREEN
IN CHILDREN OF THE NORMATIVE GROUP
AT 4 AND 5 YEARS

	4 years %	5 years %
No success....................	26	11
Named 1 or more..............	74	90
Named 2 or more..............	41	83
Named 3 or more..............	22	72
Named 4 or more..............	19	61

Names coins. These are the nickel, penny, quarter, and dime, presented in that order. The Stanford 6-year requirement, three correct, was met by 61 per cent of our Normative Group at 5 years, and we have regarded it as a 5-year response.

Distinguishes morning and afternoon. This test is made more significant, in the case of 5- and 6-year-old children, by adding the question, *"And when does afternoon start?"* This provides a check against a purely for- tuitous success, or the occasional misinterpretation of the question by the child. It is failed at 5 years, but generally passed at 6. Any approxi- mately correct indication is acceptable, such as, "When we have our dinner," "After morning," "When we come home from school," "When we go to school" (for half-time kindergartners who attend the afternoon session), "twelve o'clock," "one o'clock," etc.

(L-19) INTERPRETATION OF HUMOR
(4-5 years)

Procedure. Present the picture (Plate XIX) of a man fishing up a shoe, and say (without smiling), *"You like funny pictures, don't you? Is that funny?"* Record any response. Then ask, *"Why is it funny?"* again record- ing the response.[7]

Significance of behavior. The child's sense of appreciation of the comic is one of the most difficult traits to measure by means of standardized procedures, and his response to such a test as the present one involves great difficulties in the matter of interpretation. The test has, in fact, rarely been used in clinical practice, because of this difficulty. It is practically impossible to word the question so that it is not leading, and the extent to which the answer is influenced by the examiner's facial expression, his general manner, and the total atmosphere of the examina- tion, is scarcely determinable for the individual case.

What does the child mean or understand by the word "funny?" Origi- nally, it seems to be applied to the unusual or disproportionate, or to any unfamiliar disposition of familiar things. One 2-year-old girl, in the nightly reading aloud of the Beatrix Potter "Peter Rabbit," regularly (and spontaneously) used the word when the picture appeared of Peter caught in the gooseberry net, upside down. When this picture appeared, she invariably pointed to it and uttered the single word, "funny," in a solemn voice and with no hint of amusement in her facial expression. Even as late as from 4 to 5 years, this is the generally accepted meaning of the word (note "This is the pretty one and this is the funny one," in response

---

[7] If, in special cases, it is desired to make further observations of the response to comic pictures, use may be made of the picture cards reproduced in Figs. 16A, B, and C, pp. 56-59, *Mental Growth of the Preschool Child* (30).

to the Aesthetic Comparison test), and one that is commonly retained even in adult speech, with no connotation of humor.

This significance of the word "funny" likewise begins, toward 5 years, to take on a defensive function. The 5- or 6-year-old, none too confident of his ability to draw a satisfactory man, will often forestall criticism by announcing that he will make a funny one. Occasionally he will refuse to draw at all until this suggestion appears. It has rarely been observed that the announced "funny man" has any special character that would distinguish it from the ordinary picture to be expected.

The test was given to a research group of forty-seven children of 5 years. Thirty-one (66 per cent) of these replied, "yes" to the question, "*Is that funny?*" but in only twenty cases was there any indication that any of the "funny" aspects of the picture made any impression on the child, and in a number of these, misinterpretation was involved. Several, for example, took the dock for a table or a chair—"His dog and him up in a chair"; "The dog's on the table"; "Boy has a dog on the table and a tree in his hand." Only nine laughed, while seven more smiled at the picture— or at the examiner! Two adopted the noncommittal reply, "Because they drew it funny," "It looks funny." Others note that the man is a Negro— "He's all black"; "He's got black hands and face." Only five comment on the fact that he is fishing up a shoe, and in only three of these is it clear, because of the exclamatory tone of voice, or accompanying laughter, that this has struck the child as unusual—"Fishing with a boot!" "He catches a boot" (laughing). The simple statement, "He's catching a shoe," or the equivalent, may, without accompanying evidence of appreciation, be taken for just that.

In selected cases, however, this type of test is effective for revealing conversational abilities and personality characteristics. It may do service in special studies of superior ability and the genesis of the "humor sense" in young children.

CHAPTER IX

PERSONAL—SOCIAL BEHAVIOR

THE term personal-social has proved to be a very useful one in describing not only the child's ways of responding in social situations but also his individual and characteristic manner of responding in all situations. Personal-social behavior includes not only primarily social behavior, but also the modes of behavior which characterize the child's own personality or individuality. Actually much personal-social behavior is essentially personal rather than social. Studies which have been concerned chiefly with social behavior as such have been somewhat barren so far as yielding us a better knowledge of the individual child, and it is the individual child and his responses in which we are primarily interested in the present volume.

The behavior which we term personal-social does not have to be isolated to be observed. It is in evidence wherever we have a child responding to any situation whatever. We see it in motor, language, and adaptive behavior; we see it in the home, in the nursery school, and on the street. Within its scope are items which have a much wider range of occurrence than in any other field.

In studying the personal-social behavior of the individual child we find first of all a need for generalized age norms. In spite of wide variations in behavior and multifarious influences at work, a basic developmental determination controls behavior. In general very specific age characteristics may be observed, and these age characteristics when arranged in genetic gradation outline developmental trends which are common to most children and which largely determine the course which behavior will follow with increasing maturity.

Such normal and usual patterns of development may be used as guideposts of comparison in studying the individual child, especially if the trends are formulated according to their developmental sequences rather than statically as isolated performances. It is the flow of a developing pattern which helps us to know a child dynamically. If we know him only at certain age levels and only in relation to certain norms, then we are indeed only approaching him statically. By following the flow of a pattern sequence we may judge whether its course swings from one extreme to the other, whether it dips into a subterranean course and then reappears in full force, or whether it moves predominantly forward with a few backward eddies.

Once we have familiarized ourselves with normatively typical modes of development, we are in a position to weigh fairly the individual child's deviations of behavior and to interpret the flow or trend of his individual developmental pattern. One child may consistently exhibit wide swings of behavior from one extreme to another. He may, for instance, attain an unusually early proficiency in a certain behavior only to lose it at a more advanced age. For example, he may lace his shoes at 2 years and yet ask for help at 4. Or he may lag far behind the usual norm and then suddenly perform in a manner fully up to or even above his age level. Thus he may refuse to lie on his stomach until 10 months of age and then begin to creep, and creep practically as well as a 10-month child who has been creeping for a month or more. He may have an extremely poor appetite up to 2 years and then suddenly develop a ravenous appetite. He may consistently wet his bed at night until 3½ years and then suddenly have a dry bed and never return to wetting.

A child who has these wide swings of behavior in one field will probably have wide swings of behavior in all fields. That is the way he develops, and what appears to be an inconsistency in development is actually consistent with his particular type of development. Such a seemingly erratic course is more clearly understood when it can be matched against some normative type of pattern around which it varies.

At certain ages these swings from one extreme to another may be very wide and yet remain normal. For instance at 2½ years, as Hattwick (54) has pointed out, it is quite normal for a child to vary between the two poles of aggression and withdrawal. Part of his behavior is marked by extremely aggressive tendencies such as grabbing and refusing to comply, while at other times he will be extremely withdrawn and will, for instance, yield much too easily. A child whose typical style of development is to swing from one extreme to another may be expected to exaggerate these normal 2½-year swings. The exaggeration may be so marked, and may lead to such inconsistencies of behavior, as to give the erroneous, impression that each specific environmental situation, and not his developmental status, is determining his behavior.

A clear understanding of the more basic modes of development and their modes of operation also makes possible a realization that what is deemed a failure at one age level may actually be a more advanced stage than an earlier "success." Training which was apparently successful at one age level may no longer be successful at a succeeding age level. Very often babies who have been trained to the toilet for their bowel movements up to one year of age suddenly resist the toilet and have their daily movements at irregular times. The mother may feel ineffectual, or she may force the child to comply with her wishes since he has complied so well before. Actually the child is acquiring a voluntary sphincter control, and his "failure" is due to sphincter contraction. Voluntary sphincter contraction precedes voluntary sphincter release and later becomes associated with the child's ability to verbalize his sensations so that he may reach the toilet before he relaxes the sphincter.

In no other field are the ups and downs, the progressions and "regressions" so clearly seen as in the personal-social. Since the requisite neurological structure is more complex it is therefore more subject to deterioration under stress. How often do we see regressions in elimination, eating or dressing when a new baby comes into a family, depending upon which ability is the most recently acquired. But this is not always true, for some children respond to this situation in just the opposite way, that is, by progression in these fields. They seem to be spurred on by this new social influence and take on a mother role rather than an infant role. The child's basic and underlying individuality or personality characteristics are at all times active, determining the way in which he will respond to any given situation, and the extent to which he will express the behaviors commonly characteristic of his age level.

However, the personal-social behavior of the preschool child does not depend on himself alone. It is sensitive to environmental influence. Like postural behavior, developing personal-social behavior follows a basic maturational sequence, but it does not cling to this sequence steadfastly and with precision. Rather it needs guidance. Since it is usually the child's mother who is his guide during the early years, it becomes extremely important for her to have a knowledge of the general route along which he is traveling. It is almost as if the child's nervous system were completed by his mother, her part being that she must think ahead for the child. If she has in mind a preview of the genetic sequence through which a behavior is likely to develop, she is in a position to foresee and to interpret the developing behavior in all of its variations. She will know why the child behaves as he does and she will know better what to expect next. She will not try to make him do too much by himself. Since she knows at what stage he is, she can herself supply the first and second steps of a given behavior and then let him supply the third step (which he could not do unless she had supplied the first two). For instance, he may not be ready to put toys away on command, but if his mother hands him a toy he can put it away. This kind of treatment contrasts to a static handling in terms of an isolated age. The by-products of tension felt by a mother who requires too much of the child because she does not know what to expect and cannot see a single bit of behavior in its true perspective, may actually cause the trend of total behavior to be deviated from its normal course.

For orientation purposes, therefore, it is desirable to stress the natural sequences of behavior patterning. One important principle which the mother should keep in mind, and which will be illustrated in the sequences which presently follow, is that the child, in much of his behavior, learns backward rather than forward. He undresses before he dresses, takes a morsel of food out of his mouth before he puts it in, has to understand puddles before he can stop making them, and empties wastebaskets before he fills them. (This is not surprising when we stop to think that the adult is actually learning backward when he learns by experience. He sees the end result and then changes his original action to get a better result.) It is only very gradually that the child's interest in the ends of things gives way to an interest in beginnings as well. As he gets older he responds to more and more of a situation until finally he is able to carry through a whole process unaided.

Some of the more characteristic age sequences in the patterning of personal-social behavior are here set forth. Separate sections are devoted to eating, sleeping, elimination, dressing, communication, play, aesthetic behavior, and developmental detachment. Communication is to a certain extent discussed in relation to each of the other fields, but it is also of interest to consider it by itself and to follow through such general sequences as "No," "I don't want to," and "I won't." Behavior expressive of developmental detachment likewise is included in the other fields, but there is a more general development which needs to be outlined in relation to the child's ability to become detached from his mother and to become emotionally as well as physically independent. The various categories cannot be, in the nature of things, mutually exclusive.

It is of course apparent that some personal-social behaviors evidenced in everyday situations depend to a large extent on home training. Even in such cases the developmental concept is important, inasmuch as the training could never have been successful unless the organism was ready to be trained. However, since the child may be taught many personal-social behavior "tricks" some little time before he would have exhibited them without coaching, the early appearance of any one of the listed behaviors is not in itself an indication of precocity or of superiority. On the other hand the items are placed late enough so that it is fair to say that a child who has not attained any one of them, with or without training, at the age indicated, is retarded so far as that item is concerned. However, all age placements are approximate. The genetic sequence tables are offered as orientational outlines of typical trends and of sequence order. For the reasons just explained, *liberal allowance must be made for normal individual variations.*

Each of the following sections is introduced with a tabular summary. Photographs, in Chapter V, which illustrate selected items are indicated in brackets. A brief general comment is added. Items which are statistically most representative and clinically serviceable reappear in the developmental schedules in Section 1, pages 319-343.

§ A. EATING
DEVELOPMENTAL SEQUENCES

SELF-FEEDING (CUP)

15 months—Holds cup with digital grasp.
  Apt to tip it too quickly with wrist rotation and thus spill most of contents.
  Close supervision is necessary.
18 months—Lifts cup to mouth and drinks well.
  Hands empty cup to mother; if she is not there to take it, is apt to drop it.
21 months—Handles cup well: lifting, drinking and replacing.
24 months—Holds small glass in one hand as drinks.
36 months—Pours well from a pitcher. (Plate VI, h)

SELF-FEEDING (SPOON)

15 months—Grasps spoon and inserts into dish.
  Poor filling of spoon.
  If brings spoon to mouth is apt to turn it upside down before it enters mouth.
18 months—Fills spoon.
  Difficulty in inserting spoon in mouth; apt to turn it in mouth.
  Considerable spilling.
24 months—Inserts spoon in mouth without turning.
  Moderate spilling.
36 months—Girls may have supinate grasp of spoon.
  Little spilling.

GENERAL RESPONSE TO MEALS

15 months—Inhibits grasping of dish.
  Interested in participating in eating.
18 months—Hands empty dishes to mother.
24 months—Continues to need help in feeding.
  Is apt to dawdle and play with food, especially stirring it.
  Refuses foods.
  Very little conversation with meals.

36 months–Rarely needs assistance to complete a meal.
    Interest in setting the table.
    Either talks or eats.
    Frequent getting up from the table.
48 months–Sets the table well.
    Desires to choose menus.
    Combines talking and eating, well.
    Rarely gets up from the table.
    Likes to serve self.
60 months–Eats rapidly.
    Very social and talkative during meal.

The preceding sequences of abilities do not give a complete picture of eating behavior but they do give a suggestion of the main trends. Individual differences stand out very clearly in relation to eating. Appetite, response to taste, sight, smell, consistency and color, and response to new foods all play a definite role. Appetite sometimes seems to follow a definite curve, with a lowest point between 15 and 18 months; while at 30 months appetite fluctuates from extreme hunger to none at all. Comparable swings may be noted in other fields of behavior at this latter age zone.

Feeding difficulties when chronic have usually been present from birth or soon after. Children suffering from such difficulties are peculiarly sensitive to the eating situation. They may refuse to eat when anyone other than the mother is in the room, they gag at the slightest lump even up to 4 years of age, or they vomit when they see others eating. Something more fundamental than management lies at the basis of such serious feeding problems. Fortunately, with proper handling they tend to ameliorate with age.

In ordinary cases, management has much to do with the success or failure of eating. Many difficulties arise between 15 and 24 months because insufficient participation in the meal is allowed. On the other hand, at 24 and even at 36 months difficulties may arise because too much is expected of the child. Feeding the child with no one else in the room, filling his spoon for him without feeding him, giving him his meals in courses, confining him to the high chair if he is difficult to keep at the table, allowing him to eat by himself and call out when he is finished, allowing him to have occasional meals with the family when he is ready, allowing him to choose his menus–these and many other factors may influence greatly the success or failure of eating. "Success" here means wholesomeness of management rather than mere success in getting the food into the child.

The child gives cues as to his capacities and idiosyncrasies all along the way. It is up to the adult to be alert to these cues and to respect the child's appetites and desires. With a foreknowledge of the way in which feeding behavior ordinarily matures, it is possible to strike a balance between the child's preparedness and the demands made upon him.

§ B. SLEEPING

DEVELOPMENTAL SEQUENCES

NAP

15 months—Usually has one nap a day, which has shifted from late A.M. to early P.M.

36 months—Nap is beginning to disappear though child rests or plays in bed without resistance.

If he goes to sleep, has at least an hour nap.

48 months—Nap is definitely going out, but 36-month patterns still persist. May begin to resist resting in bed.

60 months—Nap is rare.

GOING TO BED: EITHER NAP OR NIGHT SLEEP

15 months—Put to bed easily.

18 months—Difficulties may arise when leaving child. He may cry for mother to be with him.

Lying down beside child or sitting next to crib usually induces sleep.

21 months—Doesn't go to sleep at once.

Keeps demanding things such as a drink, food or the toilet before goes off to sleep. This is more common at night.

24 months—Demands to take toys, such as teddy or rubber car, to bed with him.

30 months—Prolongs process of going to bed by setting up a complicated ritual which must be rigidly adhered to.

36 months—Less dependent on taking toys to bed with him.

48 months—Tries to put off starting to go to bed.

Rarely takes things to bed with him.

DURING SLEEP

18 months—May awaken during the night crying. This is often associated with wetting the bed.

21 months—May awaken crying or may ask to go to the toilet.

24 months—Usually responds without fussing to being taken up to go to the toilet in the evening. Is half asleep when taken up.

36 months—Beginning to sleep through the night without wetting or having to be picked up.

48 months—Sleeps through the night without having to get up to urinate.

May awaken crying from a dream and can usually tell dreams.

60 months—Quieter during sleep.

Sleeping may be one of the easiest aspects of the child's life to manage; or it may be the most difficult. Many difficulties arise because the child is put to bed too early, or because he is expected to take a nap when he wishes only to rest. The child is usually the winner in any battles which occur, and it is unfortunate that he is not more frequently met halfway, for when he is so met, he is much less demanding.

The preceding sequences have touched upon the more common difficulties in going to bed, the occasion when most sleep difficulties occur. But there are many other forms of pre-sleep adjustment which show how difficult it often is for the child to release consciousness. Various methods to which he resorts to bring about this release are singing, talking, head rolling, head banging, and thumb-sucking. Each of these follows its own sequence until it is no longer needed.

It is the emotionally dependent child who presents the most difficulties in relation to sleep. As late as 4 years he may verbalize to himself during the day that he is a big boy, but at night he is only a little boy. He has difficulty in falling asleep unless his mother is in the room, and if he awakes during the night he wants to crawl into his mother's bed. No one can put him to bed but his mother and no one can care for him when he wakes up but his mother, not even his father. Drastic handling does not improve his sleeping behavior and only increases his dependence upon his mother. A slow separation can be planned for and executed as the child seems ready, but usually he cannot make the adjustment without adult help and planning.

§ C. ELIMINATION

DEVELOPMENTAL SEQUENCES

15 months–1. Cooperative toilet response especially for bowel movement.
     2. Indicates wet pants or puddles, usually by pointing.
     3. May awake dry from nap.
18 months–1. Toilet regulated for both bowel and bladder control.
     2. May awaken at night and cry to be changed.
21 months–1. Beginning to tell needs of toilet and usually uses same word for both functions.
     2. Increased frequency of urinating.
24 months–1. Verbally differentiates bowel and bladder functions but is not dependable.
     2. Has to be taken to toilet at special times.
     3. Rarely has bowel movement accident.
     4. Dry at night if taken up.
30 months–1. Longer periods between eliminations.
     2. May show resistance to toilet if taken too frequently.

36 months—1. Responds to routine times and usually does not have to go to the toilet between these.
2. Takes responsibility for toilet himself, but always tells that he is going.
3. Is apt to hold off too long, dances up and down and just begins to .wet pants before he reaches the toilet.
4. Is able to go by himself, but needs help on back buttons.
5. Attempts to wipe himself but is not very successful.
6. Verbalizes difference between boys and girls in that girls sit down and boys stand up to go to the toilet.
7. Girls may attempt to urinate standing up in imitation of boys (42 months).
8. Is dry at night without being taken up (42 months).

48 months—1. Goes by himself and can manage clothes without difficulty.
2. May still tell before he goes, but insists upon going by himself and often prefers to have the bathroom door shut.
3. Likes to go in bathroom when others are there.
4. Marked interest in bathrooms in other people's houses.
5. Shows excessive interest in bowel movements and asks many questions about humans and animals in relation to this function.

60 months—1. Takes complete charge of himself including wiping.
2. Does not mention to adult that he is going to the toilet.
3. Boys and girls are usually separated for toileting at kindergarten.
4. Becoming self-conscious about exposing himself.
5. Beginning to show a silly response about going to the toilet.

The former tendency to train a baby for elimination as early as 3 weeks of age is rapidly giving way to a new understanding of the manner in which a child achieves control. The "successes" of early training were often transient and superficial, and they overlooked the excessive amount of time spent at the toilet! Voluntary control is complex and gradually attained. From the child's overt behavior as outlined in the preceding sequences, we may deduce the physiological changes taking place in the bowel and bladder systems to produce such behavior. Take for example bowel control. There is often a successful response to training after meals at from 1 to 4 months of age. Previous to this time the bowel movement has usually occurred during the meal. But after 4 months this close relationship of eating and eliminating no longer holds and the time of elimination becomes very irregular. At 8 to 9 months a similar relationship is again set up after one or possibly two meals and the child appears to be definitely trained at 1 year of age, only to repeat his former lapses even to the extent of definitely resisting placement on the toilet. A very frequent incidence of the bowel movement at this time is during or just after a nap.

By 15 months a resistance to the toilet may have dropped out, but release of the bowel movement does not occur until just after the child has been taken from the toilet. Within a few weeks, however, when he is put on at the usual time that his bowel movement occurs, he will respond to the toilet and often expel his bowel movement explosively. This behavior may be interpreted as the child's method of developing sphincter control. At first he responds to the toilet by contracting the sphincter and then by relaxing it too sharply. He makes similar errors of exaggeration in other forms of motor control.

The course from 15 months to 2 years is not a steady one. The time of the movements shifts, the toilet may again be resisted, and occasional accidents occur up to 2 years of age. Accidents are rare after this age, but a new complication may arise at 27 to 30 months of age when the child withholds bowel movements for as long as two to three days and when they do occur they are constipated. The withholding is an exercise and expression of increasing bowel control.

In a similar way bladder control is attained. An added phase occurs at 21 months when there is a marked increase in frequency. This may be either due to the attempt to contract on small amounts or the incomplete evacuation of the bladder by a sphincter contraction. The 30-month stage of going for long periods without urinating and then having difficulty in relaxing the sphincter presents the same difficulties for the child as those just noted for bowel movements. By 36 months the child holds off so long that he just begins to wet his pants and has a rapid and easy release when he reaches the toilet. After this, voluntary control is markedly improved and routine times are accepted.

The verbal tie-up with elimination is very significant in that it expresses exactly what stage in development the child has reached. Here as in other behaviors he learns backward. At first he is able only to point out a puddle or wet pants. Later he is able to "tell" verbally during the act. Finally he tells before the act. A child who is just beginning to indicate wet or soiled pants at 2 years instead of at the usual 15 months has still a long way to go before he is "trained." The words adopted may have some bearing upon the effectiveness of training. The words "bathroom" or "toilet" may mean little or nothing to the child, but simple words concretely expressing the function of elimination are more effective for establishing control.

§ D. DRESSING

DEVELOPMENTAL SEQUENCES

15 months—1. Cooperates in dressing by extending arm or leg.
18 months—1. Can take off mittens, hat and socks.
      2. Can unzip zippers.
      3. Tries to put on shoes.
24 months—1. Can remove shoes if laces are untied.
      2. Helps in getting dressed—finds large armholes and thrusts his arms into them.
      3. Helps pull up or push down panties.
      4. Washes hands and dries them, but does neither very well. (Plate V, d, h)
36 months—1. Greater interest and ability in undressing. May need some assistance with shirts and sweaters.
      2. Is able to unbutton all front and side buttons by pushing buttons through buttonholes.
      3. In dressing does not know back from front. Apt to put pants on backwards, has difficulty in turning socks to get heels on in back. Puts shoes on but may put them on wrong feet.
      4. Intent on lacing shoes, but usually laces them incorrectly.
      5. Washes and dries hands.
      6. Brushes teeth with supervision.
48 months—1. Is able to undress and dress himself with little assistance.
      2. Distinguishes between front and back of clothes and puts them on correctly.
      3. Washes and dries hands and face.
      4. Brushes his teeth.
60 months—1. Undresses and dresses with care.
      2. May be able to tie shoe laces (usually at 6 years).

Children's clothes have indeed been simplified within the past years so that the child not only tries to cooperate in dressing but can actually do many things for himself long before he was able to do so with more complicated clothing. This fact tends to make us err on the side of expecting too much from the young child. Dressing is so intimately bound up with motor coordination that we should attempt to measure just how much the child can do for himself and not expect him to do more.

In dressing behavior we see a marked sex difference. Girls dress themselves much more efficiently and earlier than boys, due to a better fine motor coordination and especially a more flexible rotation at the wrist. Some girls at 2 and 3 years dress themselves so skillfully that they may dress and undress just for fun, while at the other extreme are boys of 5 and 6 years who still have difficulty in buttoning buttons and dressing in general. The poor wrist rotation of the boys may also be observed in hand-washing, when they are unable to get the customary rotary movement but instead rub the two palmar surfaces together; and also in their inability to turn a doorknob far enough to open a door.

The early dresser is difficult to manage because he (or she!) will not allow any help though he still needs it, while the late dresser needs help long after the mother wishes that he were dressing himself.

Surprisingly enough it is found that the emotionally dependent child is not as a rule dependent upon the mother in dressing, but is the opposite and at an early age shows marked independence in dressing. Dressing difficulties may extend into kindergarten and if too much is asked of the poorly coordinated child, it may disturb his entire adjustment to school.

§ E. COMMUNICATION

DEVELOPMENTAL SEQUENCES

15 months—1. Uses massive, total response gestures.
        2. Indicates refusal by bodily protest.
        3. Responds to a few key and catch words.
18 months—1. Communicates both by gestures and words but words are beginning to replace gestures.
        2. Responds to simple commands.
        3. Verbalizes ends of actions such as "bye-bye," "thank you," "all gone."
        4. Refusals may be expressed by "no" but more usually by bodily response.
21 months—1. Asks for food, toilet, drink.
        2. Repeats single words said to him, or last word or two of a phrase.
24 months—1. Speech accompaniment of activity.
        2. Asks questions such as "What's that?"
        3. Verbalizes immediate experiences.
        4. Much vocalization in a group, but little conversation.
        5. Refers to himself by his name.
        6. Refusals expressed by "no."
30 months—1. Demands to do things by himself though he may not be able to.
        2. May repeat everything said to him. (This type of child has difficulty in comprehending what is asked of him.)
        3. Gives his full name.
        4. Refers to himself by pronoun rather than by name.
        5. Elicits attention of adult. "Look at me."
        6. May say "no" when he means "yes."
36 months—1. Interest in conforming expressed by, "Is that right?" "Do it this way?"

2. Expresses desires verbally. "I can do it all by myself," or "I want to do so and so."

3. May ask for help especially from mother though he may be capable of doing what he is asking to be helped in.

4. Asks questions rhetorically.

5. Expresses limitations by "I can't," or "I don't know," or may quickly change the subject.

6. Expresses refusals by "I don't want to" more often than by "no."

48 months—1. Can carry on long involved conversations.

2. Reasoning more complicated—figuring things out for himself.

3. Can tell a story which may be a mixture of real and unreal.

4. Precedes sentences with interjections such as *oh, hey, ooh,* and *yes, sir.*

5. Demands detailed explanations, often asks "Why?" until adult is unable to answer.

6. Interest in things being funny. "Wouldn't it be funny to ride on a broken bus!"

7. Lavish use of the word *everything,* such as "I know everything." Apt to end a sentence with "and everything."

8. Tendency toward self-praise. "I'm smart." "I have good ideas, don't I?"

9. Bosses and criticizes others.

10. Calls people names. "You're a rat." "Hello, Mrs. So and So." "Naughty lady."

11. Elicits attention of adult to specific abilities with such remarks as, "Wanna see me?"

12. Does not like to admit inability and covers it up by saying, "I will do it a little different." May become angry at failure and say, "I'll sock you in the jaw," or, "I'm mad."

13. Refusals previously expressed by "No" and "I don't want to" may be superseded by "I won't."

60 months—1. Can tell a long story accurately.

2. May keep adding and adding to reality making it more and more fantastic.

3. Polite and tactful in speech. When asked to do something says, "Sure." If the task is too hard may say, "I don't know how to do hard ones."

4. Everything is "easy" even before he has attempted a task.

5. Asks many questions about how things work, what things are for, and the meaning of words.

Communicative behavior is an extremely significant category of personal-social behavior for without communication of some sort it would indeed be difficult for the child to manifest many forms of personal-social behavior. In spite of this significance, relatively little is known of one of the most important aspects of language behavior, namely, the verbal equipment of the child in the way of understanding.

The maturing expressive-language behavior of the child has been detailed above and, more particularly, in Chapter VIII. But we do not know as much as we should about what the child really understands. Long before many parents cease to talk about the child in his presence he is well aware of what is being said, in general purport, if not in detail. At older ages we find that the verbal approach to the child is by far the quickest and most effective, provided that he is contacted at the right maturity level. Often the right word or phrase can bring release from a difficult situation. "You *could* give it back to him," allows the 2½-year-old to return a plaything without loss of face. Greater efforts to utilize a verbal approach based upon the child's increasing powers of understanding will result in more harmonious personal-social relations. More precise insight into the purely maturational aspect of language comprehension would vastly improve our methods of child care. Here again the significance of the developmental point of view asserts itself.

§ F. PLAY ACTIVITIES

DEVELOPMENTAL SEQUENCES

15 months—1. Endless exercise of walking activities.
     2. Throws and picks up objects and throws again.
     3. Puts one object after another in and out of receptacles.
18 months—1. Very rapid shifts in attention especially expressed by gross motor shifts. Moves actively from place to place and "gets into" everything. (Plate IV)
     2. Pulls toy.
     3. Carries or hugs doll or teddy bear.
     4. Imitates many things such as reading newspaper, sweeping, dusting.
     5. Solitary or onlooker play.
24 months—1. Less rapid shifts in attention. Interest in dawdling and manipulating play material to feel, pat and pound. (Plate V)
     2. Interest in dolls and teddy bears (domestic mimicry) (Plate V, k); beads (strings them) (Plate V, b,g), or drops them in holes in tops of boxes or cans only to dump them out and repeat the process; blocks and wagon (transports blocks in wagon more than building with them).
     3. Does not imitate things which he remembers, but only those events which are present to his senses.
     4. Parallel play predominates when with other children, though he obviously enjoys being with other children. (Plate V, e)
     5. Little interest in what other children do or say, but may hug

them or push them out of the way as though they were physical objects.

6. Little social give-and-take but much physical snatch and grab accompanied by defending rights by kicking and pulling hair which may end in hilarious scuffle.

7. Does not ask for help; adult must be constantly watchful and ready to help him without waiting to be asked.

36 months—1. Dramatization and imagination beginning to enter into play.

2. Interest in combining playthings such as blocks and cars, making roads, garages and bridges. (Plate VII, b)

3. Increasing interest in playing with other children rather than playing alone (Plate VII). May play in groups of two or three, but these are constantly shifting in make-up and activity.

4. Cooperative activity taking the place of physical contacts. (Plate VII)

5. Is willing to wait his turn. (Plate VII, e)

6. Will put away his toys with some supervision.

48 months—1. Considerable increase in constructive use of materials and in manipulation and dramatization of play. (Plate VIII, f,h)

2. Has very complicated ideas but is unable to carry them out in detail, and has no carry-over from day to day.

3. Prefers to play in a group of two or three children (Plate VIII, f,h). Often chooses favorite companion of own sex.

4. Suggests turns but is often bossy in directing others and is often silly in his play and may do things wrong purposely.

5. Puts away toys by himself.

6. Marked rise in activity.

7. Likes to "dress up." (Plate VIII, c,d,e)

60 months—1. Very fond of cutting out and pasting and in working on a specific project such as a store or a boat (project is carried over from day to day), and in dressing up in adults' clothes.

2. Definite interest in finishing what he has started even though it takes several days.

3. Plays in groups of two to five. Friendships are becoming stronger.

4. Spurred on in activity by rivalry.

5. Interest in going on excursions.

The increasingly mature kinds of play behavior, from the gross motor activity of 18 months, through the simple individual manipulative or parallel onlooker play of Two, the increasingly social play of Three, the dramatization of Four, and the more restrained and creative play of Five are well illustrated in Plates IV through IX. These pictures for the most part illustrate naturalistic nursery school play but the behavior shown is as typical for other situations.

A more controlled normative method of observing play behavior has been in use at the Clinic during the past ten years (124, 125). At the end of the formal examination, the child is asked if he would like to play with some toys. "Yes" is the practically invariable answer. He is then taken to a room equipped with a few toys standardized in kind and arrangement. The examiner enters the room with the child saying, as they enter, *You may play with anything you wish. I shall be busy but you can play any way you like.* The examiner seats herself in a chair arranged for convenient unobtrusive observation and takes notes, keeping a marginal time record of what the child does and says. The play period lasts for fifteen minutes at which time the examiner rises and says, *Shall we go now?*

The toys in the room were chosen to appeal to a wide range of ages. They are: blocks, a hammer toy, steps, a wagon with rope handle, a doll with mattress and blanket, a child's chair and table, white sheets of paper and crayons, and two children's books.

The number of times a child changes his play interest from one toy to another, the constructiveness of his play, and choice of play toys change markedly from age to age. However, when any individual child's play behavior is studied in terms of the usual play activities of normal children at his age level, significant individual characteristics are revealed. To mention only a few examples: there is the child who scatters his energies, trying first one toy and then another; the child who concentrates his attention on whatever first comes to his notice; the child who works apparently just to please the adult; the child who demands the examiner's attention even though he has been warned that she is busy; and the child who taps gently on the hammer toy, looking up repeatedly to see if he is disturbing the observer.

Traits of individuality are concretely brought into relief when a child's play behavior is appraised with the aid of maturity norms. The child who lacks resources within himself can easily be spotted. The child who scatters his energies without productiveness can be discovered and his efforts directed more purposefully. The method has proved very valuable for observing both genetic trends and sex differences in play behavior, as well as basic traits of individuality.

§ G. AESTHETIC BEHAVIOR[1]
DEVELOPMENTAL SEQUENCES

18 months—*Painting*
1. Whole arm movements.
2. Very few strokes on a page, often in the form of an arc.
3. Shifting of brush from one hand to the other.
4. Satisfied with only one color.

Blocks
1. Carries blocks around the room, pounds them together, or dumps in a mass.
2. Only building may be a tower of 3 or 4.

Music
1. Spontaneous humming or singing of syllables.
2. Wide range in tone, pitch and intensity of voice.
3. Very much aware of sounds such as bells, whistles, clocks.
4. Rhythmic response to music with whole body activity.

Pictures, rhymes and stories
1. Attends to pictures of familiar objects in books.
2. Listens to short rhymes with interesting sounds, especially when they are accompanied by action, or pictures. Likes to have them sung.

24 months—*Painting*
1. More wrist action than at 18 months. (Plate V, e; Plate XIV, c)
2. Less shift in handedness, though often paints with a brush in each hand.
3. "Scrubbing" paper with little regard for color. Paints several colors over each other vigorously, with muddy effect. (Plate XIV, a)
4. Experimenting with vertical and horizontal lines, dots and circular movements. (Plate XIV, a,b)
5. Goes out of bounds: painting on table, easel, floor, own hands, other children.
6. Process, not end result, important to the child.
7. Easily distracted and does not always watch hand movements. (Plate V, e)
8. Social enjoyment of painting on same paper with another child.

Finger painting
1. Initial objection to feeling of paint and getting hands dirty; but enjoyment after a few trials.
2. Rhythmical movements with whole hands.

[1] The following sequences are descriptive of nursery school behavior, and were drawn up by Miss Janet Learned, M.A., guidance teacher in the Guidance Nursery of the Yale Clinic.

Clay

1. Initial objection to feeling of clay, and getting hands dirty, but enjoyment after a few trials.
2. Manipulates—pounding, squeezing and pulling off small pieces; often handing to adult.
3. Uses other materials in combination with clay, such as tongue depressors, blocks, cars and wooden animals.
4. Often experiments with the taste of clay.

Sand, stones, water

1. Fills pails and dishes with sand and stones, dumping and throwing. (Plate V, a)
2. High interest in water play—soap bubbles, "painting" with water, sailing boats, and extensive hand-washing. (Plate V, c,d,h)

Blocks

1. Used manipulatively filling wagons, dumping, and rolling.
2. Sometimes used imaginatively as coal, ashes, lumber, etc.
3. Some building of towers and lines, often combining various sizes of blocks in random order.

Music

1. Sings phrases of songs, generally not on pitch.
2. Recognition of a few melodies.
3. Enjoyment of rhythmical equipment such as rocking boat, swing, and rocking chair. These often stimulate spontaneous singing.
4. Rhythmical responses as bending knees in bouncing motion, swaying, swinging arms, nodding head, and tapping feet.

Pictures, rhymes and stories

1. Enjoyment of simple pictures with few details and clear color.
2. Interest in rhymes.
3. Language (of the child) often rhythmical and repetitive.
4. Attends to short simple stories with repetition and familiar subjects.

Miscellaneous

1. Strong tactile sense: liking to touch fur, silk, angora, etc.
2. Also tastes many objects and materials as clay, paint, crayon; puts tongue against glass, wood, etc.
3. Imitation strong at this age.

36 months—*Painting*

1. Strokes more varied and rhythmical.
2. Beginnings of design emerging. (Plate XIV, d)
3. Often covers whole page with one color, or blocks of various colors.
4. Sometimes names finished product, but seldom any recognizable resemblance.

5. Joy and pride in product; exclaims, "Look what I made!"
6. Works with more concentration and precision.
7. Dislikes to share paper with others.

Finger painting
1. Experimenting with finger movements as well as whole hands.
2. Some feeling for design.

Clay
1. Enjoyment of manipulating with hands, patting, making holes with fingers, and squeezing. (Plate XIV, f)
2. Beginning of form: making flat round "cakes," and balls. Rolls long narrow strips, etc. (Plate XIV, e)
3. Some naming of product with general approximation in shape.

Sand
1. Makes cakes, pies, etc. (Plate VII, g)

Blocks
1. Order and balance in building.
2. Combining with cars, trains, etc.
3. Often names what he is making.

Music
1. Many can reproduce whole songs though generally not on pitch.
2. Beginning to match simple tones.
3. Less inhibition in joining group singing.
4. Can recognize several melodies.
5. Experimenting with musical instruments.
6. Enjoyment of group participation in rhythms.
7. Gallop, jump, walk and run in fairly good time to music.
8. Enjoy dressing up in costumes for rhythms.

Stories
1. Much longer span of interest in listening to stories. (Plate VII, d)
2. Continued enjoyment of the familiar, with more details and less repetition.
3. Insists on stories being re-told and re-read word for word without changes.

48 months—*Painting*
1. Design and crude letters.
2. Active imagination with shifting of ideas as he paints.
3. Increase in verbal accompaniment explaining pictures.
4. Products have personal value to child—he wants to take them home.
5. Holds brush in adult manner.

Finger painting
1. Continued experimentation with fingers, hands and arms in rhythmical manner.
2. Some representation and naming.

Clay
1. Large masses of clay used.
2. Increase in representation and imagination. (Plate XV, h)

Blocks
1. Extensive complicated structures combining many shapes of blocks in symmetrical manner. (Plate VIII, f)
2. Little carry-over of interest to following day if structure is left standing.
3. Cooperation in building in small groups. (Plate VIII, f,h)

Music
1. Increase in voice control.
2. Can play simple singing games.
3. High interest in dramatizing songs.
4. Creates songs during play—often in teasing other children.

Stories
1. Delight in the humorous in stories and nonsense rhymes.
2. Creates stories with silly language and play on words.

Miscellaneous
1. High interest in dramatic play. (Plate VIII, d)
2. Great increase in sense of humor.

60 months—*Painting*
1. Begins with idea in mind.
2. Products usually recognizable. (Plate IX, c; Plate XIV, k,l)
3. Pictures usually simple with few details. (Plate XIV, k)
4. Details most important to child drawn largest—often flower larger than house.
5. Knows colors and uses their names accurately.
6. Subjects: people, houses, boats, trains, cars, animals and landscapes with sun. (Plate XIV, k)
7. Often begins to feel inadequate in ability to portray ideas.

Clay
1. Recognizable objects generally with purpose in mind—i.e., made as gifts, or to use in dramatic play in dollhouse, store, etc.
2. Often paints products.

Blocks
1. Large groups plan block structure before building, and carry out group enterprise in detail.
2. Large sturdy structures often combined with other materials, such as boxes, barrels, chairs, etc.
3. Extensive dramatic play centered around structure, with carry-over of interest for several days.

Music
1. Majority can reproduce simple tones accurately from middle C to second F above.
2. Many can sing short melodies on pitch.

3. Large repertoire of songs for recognition and appreciation.
4. Majority can synchronize hand or foot tapping with music.
5. Majority can skip, hop on one foot and "dance" rhythmically with music.

Stories
1. Spread of interest to function and origin of things.
2. Beginning of enjoyment of fanciful stories.

Appreciation of aesthetic experiences is established well before artistic expression. By the time the child is 18 months old he has been responding to music, pictures and rhymes for many months, but his creative experiences are still very limited, with the exception of rhythmic expression and sound play which may come in the first year of life. His first artistic attempts are simple and random as he experiments with the different media. At 2 years his experimentation is still largely motor and manipulative, but is becoming more vigorous, more defined, and more complicated. He is less individual in his artistic expression than he was earlier, being strongly imitative of his contemporaries. At 3 years, order begins to emerge along with more precision and control in the use of artistic media. Gradually imagination enters (about 4 years) and is combined with humor to form products which are a delight to the child and toward which he feels possessive. As he becomes more serious, at 5 years, with a higher level of aspiration which he has difficulty in attaining, he becomes self-conscious concerning his ability and concentrates his talents on more conventional subjects. When his artistic attempts become well organized, the child may lose some of the joys of expression but this joyousness is replaced by a deeper satisfaction in achievement.

Individual differences are perhaps more marked in aesthetic expression than in any other field of behavior. Greatest variation is shown in musical ability. A child of 21 months may sing songs accurately, while some adults never attain this ability. Lack of ability, unless dependent upon physical handicaps, may not show itself during the preschool years, but giftedness in artistic expression may be detected very early.

§ H. DEVELOPMENTAL DETACHMENT

DEVELOPMENTAL SEQUENCES

OUT-FOR-A-WALK BEHAVIOR

15 months—Walks only a very short distance and then demands carriage.
　　　　　Likes to walk holding on to carriage (rather than on to attendant).
18 months—Runs ahead of adult; interested in all byways.
　　　　　Can often be handled much more easily in a harness.
　　　　　Enjoys the harness. It often helps to break his falls.

21 months—More conscious of adult's presence.
       Less exploring.
       Often wants to hold adult's hand.
       Enjoys helping to push carriage.
24 months—Lingers over activities along the way—picks up sticks and stones.
       Adult has to wait, call to child or lure him on to some new interest.
       Under pressure child is more apt to go in opposite direction.
       May refuse to hold adult's hand except on curbs or walls, which
          are his delight.
30 months—Dawdling still persists, along the way.
       Responds to "good-by" as adult walks off and leaves him by run-
          ning to join her.
       Holds adult hand by choice and may not wish to leave adult.
       Beginning to have thought of a destination in his mind.
36 months—Definitely has thought of a destination in his mind.
       May refuse to hold adult's hand except at crossings.
48 months—Runs ahead of adult and waits at the crossing.
       Resents holding adult's hand to cross the street.
       Wants to go on short errands outside the house. Can manage if
          they are on same side of street.
60 months—Can go to kindergarten by himself.
       Can safely cross streets, if not too hazardous, and can even help a
          younger child to cross the street.

ADJUSTMENT TO SCHOOL

18 months—Adjusts well to a nursery group if doesn't see mother depart.
       May refuse to be taken to the toilet by anyone but mother.
24 months—May be able to say good-by to mother.
       May ask for her during stay, but responds to reassurance that
          she is coming back.
       Usually responds to being taken to toilet by the teacher.
       Very happy to see mother again.
30 months—Is able to say good-by, but may have more difficulty in leaving
          mother than at 2 years.
       Brings things from home to school and may cling to them at school.
       Shows more extremes of adjustment.
       Though happy to see mother again, often delays departure.
36 months—Good adjustment coming to school, during session, and in leaving.
48 months—Good adjustment on coming to kindergarten.
       Tendency to go out of bounds in school, such as running out into
          corridor.
       Wants to take school equipment home.
60 months—Comes to school by himself or with other children if school is
          within easy walking distance. Adjusts to leaving adult at home.
       Good adjustment—is eager to comply.
       Wants to take home and keep things he has made.

Individual differences with respect to developmental detachment are marked. Some children rarely show an attachment to any adult, whereas others show marked attachment from birth, and find it difficult to adjust outside the home as late as 4 or 5 years of age. In general, however, children go through a process of slowly gaining self-dependence, and of increasing detachment from the mother both at home and away from home. Growth takes care of much of this detachment, but careful handling can smooth out the rough spots and prevent in part too great extremes of attitude either toward or away from the parent.

Two sequences of development outside the home have been outlined above. Many aspects of the development of detachment in the home have already been discussed in relation to eating, sleeping, dressing and elimination. It is interesting to note that a strong attachment to the mother most often affects and disturbs sleeping behavior, for it is at bedtime that separation from the mother is most keenly felt.

As developmental detachment pursues its natural course, increasing self-dependence is reflected in the way a child manages his tasks and enterprises. At first he can only start or finish an undertaking, but does not carry through. Later he can initiate, carry through and terminate, all on his own resources. However, children usually behave in a way which is characteristic of them. Thus some children typically have trouble in beginning any activity: going to bed, going to the bathroom, coming to the table. Others have trouble during the activity; while others begin and carry out an activity successfully but exhibit difficulties in finishing the behavior and in making transitions.

Detachment is a relative concept. The degree of detachment inevitably depends upon the general psychomotor maturity of the individual. The course of increasing detachment is indicated by the following suggestive characterizations of the preschool age levels:

18 months—The child at this age shows an interest in and a need for completion as well as a great difficulty in making transitions from one situation to another. Transitions have to be largely physical. He may need to be bodily removed, or a substitute object must be offered to accomplish a diversion.

24 months—An interest in beginnings is coming in at this age and transitions are easier. They are accomplished largely through language. However Two still exhibits a hesitancy in seeking new experiences, largely due to a lack of physical control. (53)

30 months—This is a period when wide swings and marked extremes of behavior are characteristic. The child first clings more closely than ever, then goes farther afield. Thus he may be unable to separate from his mother at nursery school but runs away from home.

36 months—Three years is definitely a period of coming into focus. The child seems to be temporarily rather sure of himself and to be capable of making necessary adjustments. Three has been characterized as a level where the child can pause for a "breathing spell." (53)

48 months—Four years is above all an age of going out of bounds. This kind of behavior is observed in all fields: physical, language, personal-social.

60 months—Again the child comes into focus, but this time at a higher level. Out-of-bounds tendencies have been largely inhibited so that the child can comply readily with the requirements of fairly formal situations.

A key to the mental hygiene of early childhood lies in building up adequate self-dependence. Even in infancy this principle of self-dependence must be respected. Not only from the breast must the child be weaned. By slow gradations he must develop fortitudes which lie at the basis of detachment. He cannot always play in his mother's lap; he must in time begin to play in his pen. He cannot always play in the same room with his mother; he must learn to play in an adjoining one, first for a few minutes, later for an hour at a time. If his mother must leave the house, he must be content to watch her through the window, even though it costs him a struggle. In time he must learn to go to bed alone, and later, to school alone.

These are elementary lessons in self-reliance, but the detachment must not be hurried, and all along the path of preschool development our demands should be tempered to meet the child's immaturity.

PART THREE

CHAPTER X

THE PHILOSOPHY OF A DEVELOPMENTAL
EXAMINATION

THERE are many different ways of observing the behavior characteristics of a young child: formal and informal; casual and planned; experimental and opportunistic; naturalistic and normative; psychometric and biographic. We may place our child in a chair (if he is so minded); we may let him rove about a room; we may ask his mother to tell us a hundred and one details about his ordinary everyday life, and the extraordinary events in his past career. The possible lines of inquiry and of direct observation are so multitudinous that we are obliged to systematize and economize our efforts. The child may be at our disposal for a brief hour only. What is the most productive approach? What principles should guide us in our critical investigation and appraisal of his movements, his words, his adjustment to us?

To ask such questions is to raise a philosophical issue concerning the purpose and the theory of psychological examinations. Unfortunately the philosophical assumptions are often meager or overlooked. The amateur and the narrow technician (the expert mental tester) frequently apply their psychometrics in a stereotyped and myopic manner. They are "scientific" testers, for have they not been told that they must not vary the established procedure? They put the child through his paces. They derive a precise mental age and a mental quotient, sometimes even adorning the latter with decimal values. While the arithmetic computations are being made, the anxious and over-impressed parent waits without. And to cap the biometric climax, this parent may receive a bare I.Q. devoid of interpretation and qualification, but conveyed with a certain air of authority. The case is then dismissed. The child has been "psyched." Next!

If the foregoing paragraph is slightly overdrawn, it nevertheless will serve to emphasize the importance of a liberal and humane application of psychological methods in the study of young children. The preschool child has come upon the educational scene; he has attained vastly increased social status. It would be a misfortune if in an uncritical way we attempted to apply to him the same short-cut psychometric methods which have proven none too adequate for the educational classification and guidance of children of school age. Oversimplified methods of mental measurement rest too heavily on a concept of general intelligence. They cannot do justice to the rich variety of individualities and the diverse growth characteristics of children from 1 to 5 years of age.

Our task is to get a better appreciation of the individual ways in which individual preschool children mature. A developmental examination is not so much concerned with the general ability of the child as with the relationship of several specific maturing abilities and the pattern of his individuality as reflected in his past history and his present status. The *total child* ceases to be an academic abstraction as soon as we try to ascertain the grouping of his behavior traits and the trends of his growth career. The examiner who is truly imbued with a developmental point of view is keenly sensitive to the past history of the child, and looks upon the psychological examination, not as a series of proving tests, but as a device or a stage for evoking the ways in which this particular child characteristically meets life situations. The examination, indeed, is in itself a life situation so charged with stimulus values that the child is bound to reveal himself.

As soon as the developmental examination is regarded in this broader light, it is no longer confined to the sharp and narrow grooves of mental scoring. It becomes a many-sided expedient for observing the facets of the child's personality, the modes and manners of his responses, his general demeanor, and his adjustments to the social demands of the entire situation.

This philosophy of the examination does not imply careless use of methods, lack of skill, or neglect of precision and control where precision and control are desirable. The developmental approach taxes skill and encourages acumen. It also humanizes the whole procedure of psychological observation and banishes some of its false solemnities and pretensions.

To begin with, we take the parent (usually it is the mother) into our confidence and make her an ally. We doubt the advisability of a routine and sometimes difficult separation of mother and child. The "examination" starts as soon as the child comes within our view. How closely does he attach himself to his mother? What part does she assume in this initial adjustment? Much is learned in those first few moments, observing the natural, irrepressible manifestations of the parent-child relationship. Already we have some clue to the child's social maturity. More clues are forthcoming as we advance toward the formal part of the examination. Perhaps he is ready to leave his mother for that purpose. Perhaps she must sit near by, offering reassurances. The management of the examination must be tempered to the limitations of the child. Undeviating adherence to prescribed procedure in the administration of tests should be reserved for only certain aspects of the examination, when a high degree of external uniformity is desirable. But major reliance should be placed upon skillful management of the total sequence of events, so that the examination will give an optimum yield as a life situation. Maximum psychological data are secured by an effective combination of freedom and control. Therein lies the art of the developmental examination.

Accordingly we must leave some scope for the individuality of the examiner as well as the individuality of the child. But again each examiner will be obliged to strike a fair balance between uniformity and variation. The examiner will indeed wish to preserve rather jealously certain standardized procedures, because only by approximating standard reduplication can he (or she) make comparisons from child to child and from age to age. Whatever clinical insight the examiner develops from experience will be derived from observing more or less comparable children in comparable situations. He is very likely to have one or two favorite tests—favorite because in his ordered experience they have proved especially revealing.

In spite of the fact that every child (and therefore every examination) is unique, there remain basic laws and basic patterns which define and delimit the deviations. For this reason intelligent, practiced perception perfects the norms of experience. Some examiners are said to have a natural gift of observation. Such a gift usually rests upon favorable personality traits. That these examiners also have heaven-born intuition, we doubt. For on analysis, intuition proves to be facile, expert judgment born of previous, clear perceptions.

For all these reasons we favor a systematic type of developmental examination—one which is measurably standardized in its mechanics, but which is conducted in a spirit of free exploration. Even when the developmental examination is supplemented by extensive observation of the child's behavior at home, school, or nursery, it should still retain a central place in the whole scheme of study. If there are apparent contradictions between the behavior displayed in the examining room and that displayed elsewhere, the contradiction must be reconciled. More often, however, it will be found that the developmental examination indicates the very features of behavior which it is desired to investigate further. So revealing and systematic is a developmental examination that some examiners prefer to complete it before undertaking an interview. Perhaps we approach the child with least preconception if we observe him first under the impartial conditions of the systematic examination. In many instances it proves convenient to have a brief preliminary interview before the examination. A later interview may then take into account behavior characteristics observed during the test situations. In our experience at

19

the Yale Clinic it has been found that observation of the child in the nursery groups is more productive if it has been preceded by a clinical examination. And if the mother has observed the examination from behind a one-way-vision screen, a discussion of the child's responses to the examination may become a medium for interpreting his behavior to the mother

All the advantages of a systematic developmental examination are reinforced if we make a follow-up examination after a lapse of time, or after a course of educational treatment. The first examination then becomes a touchstone to the second. If we proceed systematically each of a series of examinations falls into sequence; and we are able to compare the child with his previous self. He is in a sense the most fundamental norm. In our quantifications we compare him with others as well as with himself; but our final appraisal should rest on his own demonstrated ability to solve the continuous problem of development.

This is the most fundamental ability, because it includes all the rest. It is the most pervasive factor in his whole make-up, because it lies at the basis of all his successes, difficulties, and failures. We cannot frame a just opinion of his "morals" without considering the dynamics of his development. Nor can we define his educational needs without taking into account the nature of development as a concrete morphogenetic process. This process determines the forms and trends of the child's reactions. Even growth and maturity become idle concepts if they are not translated into the actual realities of behavior patterning. A developmental examination, at its best, is not concerned with end products as such, but with the underlying mechanisms of psychological growth.

CHAPTER XI

THE CONDUCT OF THE DEVELOPMENTAL EXAMINATION

THE conduct of the developmental examination in the preschool years requires special techniques. In a previous chapter the 18-month-old child has been described as a non-conformist for whom sudden changes are precipices; the 2-year-old child as having a wholesome restraint with respect to strangers, not being easily led, and following his own devices; the 3-year-old as having a certain active adaptivity, being open to suggestion but not very dependable as his cooperations tend to be desultory, sketchy, and wayward; the 4-year-old as independent and sociable, talkative and assertive; the 5-year-old as being relatively dependable and obedient, and showing a positive form of amenability. These characterizations, without further elaboration, indicate not only that there is a gradually increasing adequacy in social situations with age, but also that it is necessary to vary the management of the examination to meet the social maturity or immaturity of the child. It goes without saying that at any age some children are much more difficult to examine than others, and conversely, some are so cooperative that they practically examine themselves.

§ A. MANAGEMENT AND MATURITY DIFFERENCES

When the child arrives at the Clinic he and his mother (or attendant) are conducted to the reception room where they are invited to take off their wraps and make themselves comfortable. The location of the bathroom is indicated so that the child may be taken to the toilet if necessary. Mother and child are then left alone with the assurance that the examiner will be in shortly. Inasmuch as many children have unpleasant associations with a physician's office, the use of the word "doctor" and wearing apparel or paraphernalia that might suggest "doctor" are best avoided.

The examiner's approach to the child is extremely cautious at the younger ages and becomes, as the child grows older, more and more simple and direct. It is therefore most conveniently described in terms of age levels. It will also be convenient to use the feminine pronoun to refer to the examiner, and the masculine to refer to the child.

15 Months

At the age of 15 months, the child must still be regarded and managed as an infant rather than as a "run-about." The preschool examination procedures appropriate to 18 months are used, but the 15-month age period presents special problems of management which will be briefly indicated.

The examiner waits until all is quiet before entering the reception room where she finds the child either in the playpen, crawling about on the floor, walking, or seated on the mother's lap. The examiner ignores the child, seats herself, and addresses herself to the mother. The interview is obtained rather expeditiously and then the mother is requested to carry the child to the examining room, even if he is able to walk unassisted.

He can be examined at a low table and chair but, because of the strong motor drive at this age, he is best handled in a high chair (Plate XVIII), if he is accustomed to using one at home. He usually accepts fairly prompt placement in the chair. The mother makes the placement and then seats herself near him. The picture book is on the elevated table in front of the chair. The book is immediately shown to him. If he protests and tries to climb out of the chair, he may sit on the mother's lap with the table before him.

At this age, the examination proceeds rapidly. As the child's activity is almost entirely spontaneous, very little altered by demonstration, and practically unaffected by verbal instructions, the examiner must take pains not to be insistent in asking for performance. If the child throws a toy to the floor, this gesture should be interpreted as a refusal and another situation should be substituted immediately in an attempt to prevent throwing from becoming the only response the child will make. He will often stop throwing cubes to the floor when the opportunity to put them in the cup is offered. In other respects the management does not differ greatly from that at 18 months which is given in more detail.

18 and 24 Months

The examiner delays her entrance a few moments, allowing time for the child to explore and adjust to the room. If the child is crying on his arrival it is particularly advisable to wait until he has been quieted. The examiner should take pains not to burst into the room unexpectedly, but should try to give some warning of her approach. If by chance the child has wandered away from his mother or into the hall alone, he is allowed plenty of time for a judicious retreat. If he stands his ground he is hardy enough to tolerate being shepherded into the reception room by the examiner as she enters. The examiner closes the door, smiles at the mother, and, choosing the chair most removed from the child, seats herself at once. A stranger seated is not nearly as formidable and unpredictable as a stranger standing.

The examiner then talks briefly with the mother, first on neutral topics, and then turns to questions which will be useful in orienting herself as to the child's abilities. Problems and difficulties that the mother has with the child are not discussed in his presence. No approach is made to the child, but the examiner responds casually and pleasantly to any overtures the child may make. The examiner discourages the mother from attempting to make the child perform in any way, as shaking hands, saying "hello," showing off his toys, or his nursery tricks. Anything of this sort which is spontaneous, however, is given a smiling acknowledgment. Usually the child busies himself during this time with a small chair or a book made available to him, or a toy he may have brought with him. If he clings to his mother or seems uneasy, it may be wise to suggest that she take him on her lap. If he becomes restless the interview is curtailed. The ideal moment to terminate the interview and to suggest moving on to greener pastures is when the child first begins to be just slightly bored.

At 18 and 24 months no attempt is made to separate the mother and child. At the conclusion of the interview, which should not be prolonged over ten to fifteen minutes, the examiner looks directly at the child, saying with a smile, "*Let's go play with some toys. Mother come too.*" With a nod to the mother, the examiner opens the door and all start for the examining room, the examiner leading the way. The mother can usually quite casually and without comment remove any toy the child has been playing with, or she may say, "*It will wait for us.*" If the child puts up a real protest, he may bring it with him to the examining room where it can be removed at a favorable moment after he has become more interested in something else.

The mother holds the child's hand as he goes to the examining room unless he prefers to be independent; or if he seems fearful of the expedition he may be carried. The examiner enters the examining room first, saying, "*This is where the toys are; this is where we play; isn't this nice?*" (a rhetorical question purely). The examiner walks well into the room and after the mother and child are in, doubles back and closes the door. At the same time she indicates the mother's chair, "*That is Mommie's chair, this is Bobbie's*" (pointing and indicating that he may get into it by walking around the table, pulling out the chair for him, and calling attention to the book in position on the table), "*and this is my chair,*" seating herself. The mother is expected to assist in this maneuver, which is smooth and easy, not hurried, but not at all prolonged. If all goes well, the child will by now be seated.

If he clings to his mother, the chair may be moved closer to her, and the examiner will say, "*Sit here by Mommie.*" At the same time the examiner begins to show the picture book. If he gets behind the table and begins to look at the book while standing, the book is shown as though he were seated, and very soon the child will spontaneously seat himself, or will accept the invitation to sit down. This invitation need not always be verbal but may consist only in moving the chair slightly. At this age some assistance or at least protection should be offered as he seats himself, particularly if he is interested in the book while he is doing so. A fall to the floor at this moment might terminate the session abruptly. The child who is independent enough to walk about the room away from his mother can usually be shepherded (never forced) back to the table and induced casually to take his position. Often the child who stands by his mother, not fearful but not making any move toward the chair, can be seated by his mother without protest. If real resistance is encountered, he is permitted to sit on his mother's lap and a high table is substituted. A concession from the examiner at the beginning leads surprisingly often to concessions from the child.

The examiner begins to demonstrate the book almost before the child is in position. This situation is used for transitional and warming-up purposes, though it has real value in developmental appraisal. Complete freedom is allowed by the examiner in its use: the book may be quite carefully conned or very hastily glanced through. If the child is unresponsive, the examiner covers this lack of response by giving the responses herself. E.g., "*What is this? It's a doggie,*" etc. To most children this attack is quite disarming.

At the beginning of the book demonstration, the mother will often try to help by urging, pointing, etc. This is an excellent time to indicate to the mother her proper role. "*It's all right. I'll talk to him now. He'll be all right.*" The mother is expected to lend moral support by her presence, but not to intrude in the examination unless requested to do so. The examiner should be quick to intervene if a mishap such as breaking a crayon or even wetting the floor should occur, lest the mother chide the child or indicate to him that he has misbehaved.

As interest in the book begins to wane, the examiner offers the cubes. Not until then does she remove the book. This control of the relationship between interest, offer, and surrender, is the key to the management of the examination at these ages. The child's attention span is very brief and the examination moves along with proportionate rapidity but the transitions from situation to situation are made with some care. The child is never expected to sit without interesting occupation, nor is he expected to be amenable to reason, nor to do anything just to please the examiner. He will only respond as he is moved to do so by his own inner urges and desires. He will not necessarily relinquish a toy because the examiner wants him to, but will usually drop it as soon as something new is offered. Taking a test object from the child is sometimes hazardous, but can usually be accomplished without difficulty if the examiner simply takes hold of it and waits until the child releases his hold before removing it. Sometimes he will give the article to his mother, who may then pass it to the examiner.

At 18 months, verbal instructions or commands to the child are put in short phrases, usually repeated; at 2 years, short single sentences may be used. He is always addressed by his nickname or name, rather than by the personal pronoun: *"Bobby do it."*

If he shows a disinclination to remain at the table once the examination is well under way, it is ordinarily either because he is losing interest or because he is losing his self-confidence. Dependency on the mother and a drive to motor activity are the most common complicating factors. The careful approach and consistently careful attitude of the examiner and the presence of the mother should obviate the first complication; the proper pacing of the examination ordinarily takes care of the latter. Verbal assurances are not in themselves particularly helpful, as the child's comprehension at these ages is distinctly limited. The tone of voice, however, often seems to convey something to the child, and he occasionally responds in a surprising manner to a happily chosen phrase as "all gone," "no more," "big boy." On one occasion, when a child was seated on the mother's lap and had turned away with his thumb in his mouth, his eyes closed, shutting out the examiner and the inducements to play that were being offered, the examiner in a flash of inspiration said, *"Time to wake up,"* with amazing and completely satisfactory results!

THREE YEARS

The induction of the 3-year-old child into the examination differs only slightly from that of the younger child. When the examiner enters, she may give the child a direct smile and *"hello,"* without requiring any response. The length of the preliminary interview is determined, as before, by the child's activity during that time. If he seems at ease, the examiner may then get up and say, *"Shall we go play with some toys?"* holding out her hand to him. He may or may not accept the hand, but if he accepts the verbal invitation, the examiner says, *"Mother will wait,"* and to the mother, *"We'll be back soon,"* and starts out of the door with the child. As they go toward the examining room the examiner says, *"This is where the toys are,"* etc., keeping the child's interest in the toys alive and attempting to forestall a retreat to the mother. If he hesitates about acceping the invitation, the examiner quickly adds, *"Mother come too,"* and the mother accompanies the child. About one-third or slightly less of the children of this age will leave their mothers with hardly a backward glance. As there is no great advantage in examining without the mother at this age, the matter is never pressed. The child's response to the suggestion is, however, revealing and the invitation is offered unless the child is obviously very dependent on the mother. If he starts out bravely and then thinks better of it, the examiner is always ready to say, *"Let's get mother too."* It is occasionally necessary to interrupt the examination to get the mother.

The examiner should note whether the child wishes to hold either the examiner's or the mother's hand as he enters the examining room, or whether he prefers to be independent, and should respect his wishes. Many children of this age walk into the examining room and seat themselves quite spontaneously. If the child seems uncertain of what is expected of him, the examiner may say, *"That's your chair, and this is my chair. Let's look at the book."* If the child does not seat himself but stands in position behind the table, the fact that he is not seated is ignored and the examination begins. As at the younger ages, as soon as he becomes interested, usually in the block building situations, he will seat himself spontaneously or on suggestion. It is seldom necessary at this age to enlist the mother's help and she is usually merely a passive onlooker. The examiner should not hesitate, however, to call on the mother if she is needed to aid in adjustment.

The 3-year-old child is ordinarily examined without any difficulty, providing the tempo of the examination is adapted to him, and the examiner is not insistent. One may expect at this age, even in the most amenable child, however, a refusal of one or more situations. This refusal should be respected, though the examiner may say, *"We'll do it later."* The situation may be offered again, later in the examination, *"Let's do this now."* A second refusal should be accepted by the examiner. The 3-year-old child can often be bargained with, *"Let's do this now and then we can ———"* (something appealing to the child).

One occasionally meets a highly overactive child at this age, who is more interested in climbing on the table and chairs or in moving furniture than in complying with the examination requirements. Very rapid progress from situation to situation with excited comments by the examiner and a profusion of praise will control some of these children. Others simply must be allowed to work off some of their energy at intervals throughout the examination. They are allowed to get up and run about and then, *"Now let's come back and see something else."* Some will work fairly well while climbing and tumbling. In some cases it is necessary to remove the child's chair from the room.

The dependent child can sometimes be reached through the mother who sits very close to him and participates in the examination, building towers, giving demonstrations, entering into the spirit of the examination, etc. One very inhibited and dependent 3-year-old was practically examined by a very unusual father. The father's insight and tact were remarkable and the examiner was able to indicate to him almost wordlessly how to apply each situation.

FOUR YEARS

The examiner's approach to the 4-year-old child is more direct than heretofore, though it is never precipitate. After the brief adjustment period and a few opening remarks, the examiner may say, *"Did you come to play with some toys?"* and invite him to accompany her, in a manner that assumes he will leave his mother. *"Shall we go and play? Mother will wait for us here."* And to the mother, *"We'll be back soon."* The examiner should use discretion in offering her hand to the 4-year-old, as some are not ready to accept the examiner so completely, while others may resent the implication that they cannot go independently. If the child seems to need assurance, he may take the examiner's hand gratefully. Most children of this age will go with the examiner unquestioningly if she seems to expect it, and though they may inquire frequently for the mother during the examination, they are readily reassured when told that she is waiting. Many are more at ease in the examination and talk more freely when they are alone with the examiner. It is desirable, therefore, to effect a separation if possible, but the child should never be coaxed, wheedled, shamed, or pleaded with. If any real difficulty is encountered in separating the child from his mother, she should be invited to accompany him. In the examining room she is instructed, once the examination begins, to be a passive onlooker, unless her failure to respond to the child seems to distress him unduly.

On entering the examining room the child's chair is indicated to him. At this age there is practically never any difficulty in getting the child to seat himself. As at the previous ages, the examination must proceed fairly rapidly; transitions are as a rule accomplished without difficulty. Many 4-year-olds will ask to go to the toilet in the course of the examination. Most children, however, will remain at the table throughout the examination but they often show tension or restlessness by shuffling the feet, squirming in the chair, etc. The examiner should be alert to these signs and should move along from one situation to another rapidly enough to keep the restlessness from getting the upper hand. If the child gets up, he will usually return to the table on request.

At this age more than any other, the examiner may find that the business of the hour is being successfully sidetracked by the child's questions and anecdotes. She may even find that it is the child who is doing the examining. Most questions should be answered as simply as possible, followed by a reminder of the task in hand. If the questions become too numerous and diverting, the examiner should say, *"I'll tell you about it after we have finished; let's do this now."* The 4-year-old responds well to praise and should be commended for his efforts as well as for his successes. The inhibited child, particularly, should be encouraged, and made to feel at ease. The exuberant, overproductive child may need to be kept in gentle check, and reminded at times that there is something he is supposed to do. If he is pressed too hard, however, he may indignantly "blow up" and refuse to comply further with the examination requirements. It is best to foresee this and pass to the next situation, or intersperse a few situations more interesting to the child.

FIVE YEARS

The 5-year-old child has lost much of the naïveté of his predecessors and the examination, as adapted to his maturity, is no longer a play situation. It has become a series of not unpleasant tasks imposed upon him by an adult in something of a teacher role. This child is, however, accustomed to meeting strangers and standing his ground; he is becoming accustomed to controlling his attention, his activity, and his loquacity, and when placed in an adult situation he tends to take his cues from the adult. All this within limits, of course. He can and should, therefore, be treated in an adult fashion—also within limits.

He has usually had some simple but satisfying explanation for his visit before he comes for examination and can be greeted quite promptly after he arrives by the examiner. *"I have some things to show you. Will you come with me?"* with a friendly smile, usually suffices and the child will willingly accompany the examiner to the examining room. Any hesitancy can be met with the remark, *"Mother will wait here,"* and to the mother, *"We'll be back pretty soon."* It is expected at this age that the child will be sufficiently self-reliant to leave his mother. He may inquire after her once or twice during the examination, but he rarely insists on seeing her. If real difficulty in separation is encountered, the mother is allowed to accompany the child into the room. She is seated at a distance from him and remains quiet during the examination though she may assist in bringing about acceptance of the chair and table. The presence of the mother, however, is less desirable at this age than formerly, for the 5-year-old child is more self-conscious than his juniors.

The 5-year-old is ordinarily capable of adjusting to almost any order of the examination situations, but it is usually wise unless he is immediately talkative, to defer tests requiring verbal answers until he is thoroughly at ease. Block building and drawing are both well liked as a rule, and either situation may be used to open the examination. He is also able to adjust to pauses in the examination, but even so they are undesirable, and the examination should proceed quickly enough to keep interest and attention from flagging. There should not be undue insistence on a response, nor too many repetitions of one test or of similar tests, in the face of refusal or failure. A refusal to respond should be met with, *"Well, we'll do that one later,"* if the cause of the failure seems to be an inhibition. If he seems afraid he will fail, the examiner may say, *"That's a hard one, isn't it? But you try it; do the best you can."* As the child is now more keenly aware of his inadequacies and failures in the test situations, they cannot always be glossed over with a *"That's fine,"* when it quite obviously isn't fine. If the failure is glaring, the examiner may say, *"That was a hard one. You did it very well,"* or some such remark indicating that she appreciates the child's difficulties and effort.

Under ordinary circumstances the examination of the 5-year-old child presents no difficulties. An occasional child becomes restless and may be allowed a brief recess, to get up and look out of the window, and *"Then we'll finish."* Some children need a little urging to complete the examination, but can usually be persuaded to stay by the remark, *"We're almost finished now. Just a little more."*

§ B. TEMPO AND ORDER

TEMPO

The ideal examination does not consist merely of a series of tests applied one after the other to a well-behaved and cooperative child. At 18 and 24 months particularly, the success of the examination depends much more upon the examiner than it does upon the child. (In speaking of the success of an examination, the eliciting of representative responses, with a minimum of refusals and no emotional upheavals, is referred to, rather than how well the child succeeds in responding at his age level.) The child is a dynamic little being, with a fairly strong locomotor drive, a relatively short attention span, and relatively limited abilities, and he is particularly disinclined to prolonged sedentary occupations. These factors make for difficulties, but not ordinarily for insuperable difficulties, in a situation requiring of him sustained attention while seated, to problems which test, strain, and in some cases exceed his abilities and interests. At these ages also the child is just beginning to realize and try out some of his own powers, independent of adults. The urge to do a thing himself often expands into the urge to do a thing in his own way, and may lead conversely to the impulse *not* to do it in the way the adult requests, or even not to do it at all. It is interesting that these particular factors must be reckoned with when our every move must also reassure the child that he is safe, that mother is with him, that we have no designs on his person, or on the *status quo*. Perhaps he may change the *status quo*, but we may not.

Different examiners meet these problems in different ways, but in general we may say that we try to disarm the child by keeping his mother with him, by making no direct approach, and by making no demands on him. This tends to eliminate the "No," so often described as characteristic of these ages; indeed, it is only the unwary examiner who accepts "no" unhesitatingly at its face value. We also try to step down from the level of the adult who is asking him to do things, to that of a friendly person who plays with him on his own level. This not only means that the examiner enters into the spirit of the game, for game it should be to the child, but that she may play the game too if that seems necessary, and that she will limit her interest and attention span to the child's ratio.

When the child is wary we are cautious and non-insistent. When he becomes interested we are pleased, and when he is "finished" we are also finished. Transitions are quickly made and interest is held up by substituting new material as soon as the old has been exploited to the child's satisfaction. This may even mean no exploitation at all. One child may run through the whole series of test objects in less than ten minutes. We may feel that we have not found out every possible thing that this child could do with each object, but if he has played with each one and abandoned it, we could not get more but actually less by trying to make the child repeat and expand his performance. Another child may be reluctant to relinquish a toy when we feel that further play will tell us nothing more. The thing to remember is that if we disrupt his trend of interest because our own is exhausted, he may show us nothing when the next toy is presented.

At all the preschool ages the interest in the examination should mount, be built up, as the examination proceeds; nothing should be quite exhausted. This means that the tempo of the examination is of prime importance. It differs for each child; it can only be determined empirically. It is usually rapid after a slow or a relatively slow start. The examiner who has to stop to make elaborate recordings of each response or to look up what comes next, etc., will find that tempo bogs down, interest wanes, the child gets up and runs around the room, and must be enticed back to the table, his interest must be roused again, and indeed resistance rather than interest may be roused. If, however, the shift from situation to situation acquires a smooth swing, one can even insert a situation or two that interests the child very little, and get a real effort from the sheer momentum the examination has acquired. The examiner is quick to come back to an appealing situation to recover the slight loss in motion this will bring.

ORDER

That order is the best which stimulates, builds up, and sustains interest throughout the examination. Just as children show individual differences in the rapidity with which they exhaust the possibilities of the various test situations, so they also differ in the amount of interest a given situation arouses. It is up to the examiner to sense these differences and act upon them, and for this reason the order of the situations is occasionally altered to meet the demands of the occasion. It is, however, better to deviate from a basic plan than to apply the tests at haphazard. The deviations, if made consciously and selectively, acquire meaning and assist us in interpreting the child's behavior in terms of his maturity and also of his personality.

In examining a child we wish to find out what he can do, and also what he cannot do; how he does the things he can do, and how he tries to do the things he cannot do. The first requisite is the child's cooperation, and to secure this we must have his trust and his interest. Tasks that are too difficult quickly exhaust interest and discourage effort. In general, therefore, the examinations are so constructed that within a given situation or group of situations we progress from simple to relatively difficult tasks, returning then to something within the range of the child's ability.

Because repetition of the same type of situation becomes boring to the child fairly rapidly, variation is frequently introduced. It may seem convenient and logical, for example, to give all the tests requiring simple verbal answers in a series (at 4-5 years); it may, however, be wiser to give only a few, and then intersperse a few performance tests, and later give the remainder of the verbal tests.

At the younger ages in particular (18-24-36 months) the question of transition from situation to situation is important. The child may have difficulty in relinquishing one toy for another unless a "bridge" is supplied, or he may tend to be so perseverative that the examiner must take care to provide situations at frequent intervals that tend to produce a change in the direction and flow of behavior. Situations that meet with resistance or refusal are postponed until cooperation is more complete.

As far as general principles go, we may summarize by saying that we give the easy tasks first, we vary the tasks, we provide easy transitions, we are alert to signs of waning interest and of resistance, and we try to sustain a feeling of success in the child.

The standard order for administering the test situations is outlined in § 2, page 347. The Situation Sequence was designed on the basis of clinical experience to impart organic unity to the examination and to maintain a maximum fluency of performance. The order is, however, only a means to an end, and the examiner may alter the order in behalf of any particular child, if the alterations will promote the two important objectives of unity and fluency.

CHAPTER XII

CLINICAL ADAPTATIONS TO ATYPICAL CONDITIONS

THE preceding chapter was concerned with the examination of the preschool child under ordinary examining conditions. The difficulties described with which the examiner must cope are within the normal range of individual variation or are more or less characteristic of the age levels under consideration. The recalcitrant or inhibited child, and the child with physical handicaps that interfere with the application of the tests will now be considered, for it is not proposed to leave the reader with the impression that the techniques described will meet all conditions encountered in a diversified clinical practice. It is even true that for various reasons some exceptional children are un-examinable in a formal sense at a given period in their careers, although the number of such cases is exceedingly small.

The usefulness of the developmental examination in estimating and predicting maturity is based on the assumption that development takes a certain consistent course, that events follow each other in natural sequence; that if a child has reached a given level of maturity at one age, at the next age, as day follows night, he will attain the next level of maturity. This assumption is true only under certain conditions: it is true for a child with a normal physical and mental endowment and with opportunities for normal experiences. When the mental endowment is mildly or moderately limited, other factors being equal, the course of development will not be greatly altered but the rate is proportionately affected. If the physical equipment is grossly faulty, opportunities for normal experience are limited and experience is often unusual in character; if the mental endowment is very seriously reduced, the child is unable to profit from experience in a normal manner; if experience itself is very abnormal, development cannot follow its usual course because it is so dependent on experience.

Normal experience eludes precise definition. It is determined by the endowment as well as by the environment. The best environment for normal social experience for the young child has been described as a single family home with a stable family situation, wholesome emotional relationships, and a consistent and kindly attitude of child management.

Opportunities for play, for companionship with other children, and for learning are implied. This broad description only hints at the multiple elements that make up normal experience. It is, however, obvious that the child who cannot hear, or who cannot see, who cannot walk or use his hands with normal control, cannot enjoy all the experiences open to the normal child; nor can the institution child, nor the child who is confined for months on end to a hospital bed, nor the child who is beset by fears, anxieties, or resentments, nor even the child who is regulated from morning till night and never allowed to do anything for himself. Many of these children may eventually attain a normal or relatively normal development, but the course through which that development goes may be atypical to a greater or lesser extent.

Great caution should therefore be used in appraising the development of any child whose equipment, either physical or experiential, deviates widely from the normal. Many an examiner has been taken aback when a child previously labeled grossly defective returns a few years later, a walking refutation of old predictions. One hates to think of some of the mistaken advice that must have been religiously followed on the basis of such unwary fortune-telling. Nor are mistakes in the other direction uncommon. False hopes of future normality are roused only too often, not so much on the basis of performance in examination, but by erroneous insights, inexperience, too great readiness to excuse failures on the grounds of handicaps. The wish is often father to the thought.

It cannot be emphasized too strongly that under atypical conditions, final judgments based on a single developmental examination are exceedingly hazardous. Repeated observations over an extended period during which the child is under the best possible conditions for development are necessary. These examinations should be supplemented by observations of the home behavior and by an evaluation of the child's response to a carefully planned training program carried on over a period of months or years.

EXAMINATION OF THE EMOTIONALLY DISTURBED CHILD

The appraisal of an emotionally disturbed child should be cautious. He must be very adroitly approached and handled or the examination may only intensify his difficulties. If the child is unusually fearful of strange persons or strange places, or excessively inhibited under those conditions, the presence of the mother and all the tact in the world on the part of the examiner may not be enough to put him at his ease. Such a child may cry bitterly and inconsolably, or he may scream and struggle and fight, or he may withdraw into himself and passively refuse all the inducements that can be offered.

When active resistance is offered, above the age of 18 months particularly, it is the writer's conviction and experience that only very rarely is anything gained by persisting in the attempt to secure an adjustment to the examination. If the trouble begins as soon as the child enters the clinic and the mother has been unable to quiet him before the examiner enters, the examiner as a rule only adds fuel to fire by her presence or by any maneuvers she may try. If the trouble begins with the examiner's entrance, or with the entrance to the examining room, the child can sometimes be appeased by the mother or by being permitted to keep on his coat and hat as a guarantee that he will be allowed to leave; in the meantime the examiner demonstrates her benevolent intentions by offering a toy, or by playing with a toy herself. The examiner should not show more than one or two toys in advance as she will otherwise completely dispel the novelty of the situations in the examination proper. Some children will respond to ball play, which may be offered as a last resort.

In the face of vigorous, persistent crying, evidences of real fear or anger, the examination should be abandoned fairly promptly. Significantly enough most of these children stop crying as soon as they are dressed to leave, and will even say "good-by" quite pleasantly. This is the examiner's opportunity to pave the way for a more successful second visit by saying, "*Good-by; next time we will play nicely with the toys. Next time we'll have fun with them.*" The mother should be instructed not to scold or shame the child, or take him to task in any way for his behavior at the clinic. Indeed, the mother may need considerable reassurance, for she may be very embarrassed and humiliated by her child's exhibition. The examiner's attitude is one of sympathetic understanding; neither the mother nor the child is led to think that anything very unusual or unexpected has occurred; certainly the examiner should never show annoyance or disappointment, nor should she ever feel called upon to discipline the child or exert pressure or authority over him. Nor should the mother be made to feel to blame; she may, however, be instructed to make some mention of the "nice lady" and the "nice toys" preparatory to the next visit. If a second visit is equally tempestuous, six months or more should elapse before another attempt is made, and during the interval the mother should have the benefit of guidance and advice.

An occasional child refuses the examination by indulging in what appears to be deliberately willful, perverse behavior: knocking the chair over, kicking the table, throwing the toys around, tearing his clothes, spitting, etc., while he seems to be enjoying himself hugely. If ball play does not direct his behavior into more acceptable channels fairly promptly, he should also be dismissed with the invitation to "play nicely" the next

20

time he comes. The examiner should never allow herself to be drawn into a contest of wills with the child.

The child who simply fails to respond, standing silently beside the mother and refusing to yield to any enticement should be ignored for a while. The examiner may chat with the mother or pretend to read the picture book. One of the little girls in the 3-year-old normative group resisted quite passively in this manner for over an hour and finally cooperated well. Ordinarily one would not persist for so long, and usually the child can outdo the examiner at this game. Occasionally if the examiner leaves the room for five or ten minutes, she will come back to find the child playing and willing to continue; he is just as likely, however, to resume his former attitude. A period of free play in another room well equipped with toys often releases such a child, and on returning to the examining room no further difficulty is encountered. In this case, the child should be warned that he is to go back to the examining room. Sometimes a different examining room, or even a different examiner will work wonders. It is true that women, while no more skillful than men, are often more successful in dealing with small children just because they are more readily accepted by the children. Once in a while, however, one meets a child who "does not like women."

There remains the occasional child who does not respond to any of these tactics but who is adamant in his refusal to speak or play, and the wise examiner, as already suggested, will concede the honors without any resentment, merely suggesting that *You can come again and next time we'll play with the toys.* If the examiner has pressed the child too far, a second visit will be no more successful than the first. If, however, the examiner has let the child off easily, has shown no annoyance, and has protected him from censure or criticism by his mother, she may have won his confidence.

PHYSICAL HANDICAPS

Many children present themselves for examination with physical disabilities and handicaps that make standard techniques inapplicable. Under such circumstances it is clearly unfair to the child to insist on controlled conditions and it is quite permissible to adapt the examination in almost any way that will enable him to show his abilities.

It is impractical to cite and describe all the abnormalities that may be encountered. The adaptations the examiner makes vary from case to case, depending on the type and degree of handicap the child presents, the compensations he has made, his age, etc. It may be quite impossible to determine the child's I.Q. or D.Q. in the conventional sense in one examination; but with tact, flexibility and insight the examiner should be able to learn a great deal about the child's maturity, his personality, and even much that is revealing about his potentialities.

MOTOR HANDICAPS

In the presence of a motor disability, failures and retardations in the motor field should not be "counted" as failures and retardations; they should not be "counted" at all. The child's development should not be appraised in terms of his motor accomplishments though of course his motor capacity should be estimated. The crippled child who does not walk at 3 years of age is undoubtedly retarded in the development of walking, but he is not necessarily a retarded child. While the level of his motor development should be estimated, his maturity should be determined on the basis of his responses in the other fields of behavior, and a failure to walk, and to stand on one foot, should not be reckoned adversely.

If this were the only adjustment to be made, there would be no great difficulty in examining the crippled child. It is rare, however, that a disability is so selective and can be so neatly subtracted from the examination. Although we separate the different fields of behavior for purposes of discussion, they are actually very closely interrelated. The examiner must be very sure in appraising a response in any field whether or not it is seriously influenced by the motor handicap. If the child's motor control, for example, is so poor that he must hold the table to maintain the sitting position, he is at an obvious disadvantage in manual manipulations. If the child's motor difficulties include numerous involuntary uncoordinated movements, prehensory and manipulative patterns will be distorted and even visual responses may be adversely affected by uncontrollable head and eye movements. Speech may also be affected. The examiner will have to rely as much as possible on those responses which are unaffected or least affected by the disability.

Success then becomes much more significant than failure. And even "success" cannot always be appraised in the conventional manner. We are accustomed to judge performance in large measure by its end product. If a child imitatively draws the cross, we are certain he can do it, and he is credited with a successful performance at the 3-year level. Theoretically and actually it is possible, however, to "pass" this test, not on a motor level, but on an adaptive level, without making a recognizable cross at all. The examiner with clinical judgment and experience is permitted considerable latitude in interpreting the *intent* of the child's behavior.

The actual techniques the examiner will use can only be determined when she is confronted by the child and his limitations. The examiner should then be willing to try almost anything that will enable the child to respond in some revealing way. She should follow any lead or cues the child gives. In examining a crippled child, the examiner must first of all adjust the equipment so that he is comfortable and secure in his chair. Maintaining the sitting position may require so much effort and attention from the child, and he may be so constantly on his guard against falling, even though he appears to be sitting very well, that he is unable to do himself justice in the examination. He may only need an armchair to be comfortable and at ease; he may need to be tied or supported in his chair, or he may need to be held at the examining table by his mother on her lap. He may also need occasional brief relief from the strain of the sitting position.

It should be remembered that success is as important to a handicapped child as to a normal child, if not more so. The examiner may give him any amount of assistance. She may place the cubes, crayon, etc., in his hand, and assist him in closing his fingers around them; she may steady his hand and his head; she may steady his tower and assist him in releasing and aligning the cubes, and in manipulating the crayon. After he has done his best, she may even guide his hand and give him, quite deliberately, a fictitious success. His response to this success may indicate insight into the task that is much more significant than his inability to perform the task unaided.

Judgment should always be qualified by the complicating factors: the actual disability, the halo of disability that may extend into other fields of behavior, fatigue due to working under a severe handicap, the limitations of experience imposed by the handicap, deviations in examination technique, assistance, interpretation, etc. It should also be recognized that in many conditions the child is under a greater disadvantage at some ages than others. The child with cerebral palsy, for example, who is old enough to have acquired speech may appear in a much more favorable light than his junior who cannot talk but whose manual adaptations are no less seriously affected. Repeated examinations are nearly always necessary for a full understanding of the handicapped child.

LANGUAGE HANDICAPS

If hearing is normal, the examination of a child who does not speak intelligibly, or who does not speak at all presents no great difficulty. At the younger ages particularly (18 months–3 years) there are relatively few situations where verbal responses are essential, and the child can easily show his abilities by adaptively meeting manual tasks, or by pointing or other gesture. At the older ages (3-4-5 years) the examination can be reinforced with additional performance tests. Many verbal tests can be given, however, since pantomime responses are perfectly acceptable in the absence of language. For example, it is possible to respond to a large number of the Action-Agent questions by gesture, though the response will be more *action* than *agent*. The comprehension questions are often similarly answered, as closing the eyes or snoring in response to "sleepy?"; pretending to eat in response to "hungry?" Even higher in the scale the definitions (What is a chair, fork? etc.) can be conveyed by gesture without the use of language. Satisfactory *comprehension* appropriate to his age, combined with normal performance in performance tests is all that is necessary to establish the intellectual normality of a hearing child who does not speak, and also to establish the potential normality of his language development.

Many such children are at a loss to respond to verbal tests or are inhibited due to consciousness of their handicap; they are at once relieved and responsive when assured they do not need to reply, but may *"show me."*

If the language defect is combined with a serious motor handicap, and the child cannot respond to either performance or language tests, he has no reliable medium through which he can demonstrate his abilities. In such a case the examiner is reduced to interpreting the normative indications of attention, interest and effort, an undertaking so hazardous that judgment is better deferred than pronounced.

AUDITORY HANDICAPS

It is the absence of comprehension of speech, rather than the lack of speech itself, that makes for difficulties in examining the deaf child. When a serious hearing defect is present the examiner as well as the examinee must use gestures and pantomime for communication. Since the child cannot speak, the examiner must use performance tests in evaluating maturity, and since the child cannot hear, performance tests that require verbal instructions (as drawing bubbles) cannot be used. Tests must be so selected that the child has no difficulty in understanding what is expected of him.

Many tests situations (block building, drawing, formboard, form-matching, ball play, etc.) practically explain themselves; the examiner simply demonstrates or points and then offers the child his opportunity to respond. Some purely verbal tests cannot be used at all, but many others can often be quite successfully adapted to the deaf child. The following paragraphs describe some of the adaptations that can easily be made. Other variations and applications of the tests will doubtless suggest themselves. They may even be necessary in the examination of a child who only speaks and understands a foreign language, if there is no interpreter. It should always be remembered that in many instances the tests become so altered that they are no longer the same tests, and cannot correctly be evaluated as equivalent to the regularly assigned age levels. The responses can, however, be used to build up a rough determination of the level of comprehension and insight, and to supplement the information furnished by the performance tests, including especially devised tests for the deaf.

Bridge (3-4 years). In presenting this situation to a hearing child, the structure is often called a "house," the opening between the two base cubes, a "door." To give the deaf child roughly the same cues, the door may be demonstrated by passing a pencil through the opening.

Pellet and Bottle (18 months–2 years). The young child either inserts the pellet into the bottle spontaneously or can easily be induced to do so by pointing from pellet to bottle. To elicit extraction of the pellet from the bottle, the deaf child is first shown a pellet in the palm of the examiner's hand; then the examiner's empty hand is held out and the pellet in the bottle indicated.

Incomplete Man (4-5 years). The instructions for completing the Incomplete Man cannot always be successfully conveyed to the deaf child. The examiner will usually find it necessary to indicate the man's ear, and the place for the man's other ear; she may pantomime drawing in the second ear or even actually draw it. If the child does not proceed with other parts, the drawing is returned to the child, the pencil is re-offered, and he is encouraged by gesture to continue.

Missing Parts (4-5 years). If the child successfully completes the Man, the Missing Parts may follow immediately, the missing parts being given by gesture by the child.

Picture Cards (18 months–3 years). With the ordinary examination setup and equipment the Picture Card situation cannot be used in its entirety, but the examiner can determine the deaf child's ability to recognize pictorial representations. The white enamel cup and the picture card are presented side by side, the examiner pointing from one to the other; the examiner can point to her own shoe and then look inquiringly at the child and present the card. The clock and the book can be similarly presented. It would obviously be quite possible to have other objects on hand to present in the same manner.

Stanford Picture Cards (3-4-5 years). The Stanford Picture Cards may be shown to the deaf child who may or may not respond to them. Success is, of course, much more significant than failure. Pointing, with real evidence of interest, may sometimes be interpreted as enumeration; gestures, as imitative crying in the Dutch Scene, may similarly be considered description.

Counting (4-5 years). This test is occasionally successfully responded to if the examiner demonstrates with two and then three cubes, pointing and then holding up the correct number of fingers. Four cubes are then placed in a row and the examiner looks expectantly at the child. The pennies may be used if the cube response is correct.

. . . .

In all these situations successful performance is the significant thing because only then can the examiner be sure that the requirements of the test were understood. It is amazing how quickly a bright, deaf child grasps small cues from the examiner. His desire, almost anxiety, to understand and to comply correctly is an interesting and significant trait, and his insight into success can be distinctly revealing.

In evaluating the results of the examination, it should be remembered that the deaf child is seriously handicapped in comprehension, expression, and experience, and therefore even with a potentially normal mental endowment he will, on the basis of ordinary tests, almost inevitably show some degree of retardation in comparison with a normal child. Mild degrees of retardation on examination are to be expected even if special training has been given over an extended period.

Visual Handicaps

The amount of difficulty a visually handicapped child experiences in meeting the requirements of a developmental examination depends largely on the severity of the visual defect. In a general way it may be stated that the child who sees well enough to walk about indoors unprotected can respond fairly adequately to the examination, even though vision is obviously poor. Demonstrations may have to be made closer to the child than is customary, made slowly and with considerable emphasis, and where possible enlarged, but it is surprising how seldom gross deviations in technique are necessary. Failures that are clearly due to inability to see should be disregarded; successful performance at the child's age level is highly significant.

These facts are perhaps best illustrated by brief accounts of actual examinations. One striking story relates to a 3-year-old boy whose pupils had been dilated in the erroneous belief that he was to visit the eye clinic. He succeeded in giving a superior performance at the 3½-year level and even made an excellent showing with the geometric forms and pictures in spite of the paralysis of accommodation. Re-examination a few days later, without atropin, did not show any significant improvement in performance.

We have followed with a great deal of interest the developmental career of a little girl with congenital cataracts and a high degree of myopia. Although she fails consistently on tests requiring real visual discrimination, she has never had any difficulty in demonstrating her normality. At 18 months she had a vocabulary of ten words; she succeeded in building a tower of three cubes, dumped the pellet out of the bottle, imitated the scribble, and placed the ball on the chair and table on request. The visual defect obviously interfered with her responses to drawing a stroke, to the formboard, and the performance box; she apparently did not see the holes in the box at all. She was very interested in the lights, and her vague social rapport with the examiner could be attributed to an inability to notice changes in facial expression. Actually, the working rapport was excellent.

At 2 years, six months after needling of the cataracts, she imitated the five-cube train and tried to imitate the bridge. She identified three pictures. She was using short sentences as, "Mother sitting in chair," and was able to give her full name and to recite one or two nursery rhymes with some prompting. She had difficulty with the drawing situations, the color forms, and the formboard because of her defective vision. Vision was so seriously affected that she even had a few blindisms.

At 3 years she is wearing glasses. Again she fails to imitate the bridge, and although she now imitates the stroke she does not discriminate the direction, nor does she imitate the cross. She places one enlarged geometric form correctly, and all the color forms. The formboard is solved with some difficulty, but it is solved. She answers two comprehension questions correctly, responding without difficulty to verbal tests. She shows for the first time a tendency to "cover" her deficiency in her response to pictures:

dog	"dog"
shoe	"car"
house	"That's a garage"
clock	"That's a bowl—looks like a bowl"
basket	"moon"
book	"That's a car"
leaf	"That's a dish"
flag	"That's a cat"

When given the Dutch Scene picture she said, "Dat's a boy. Put that back."

Undoubtedly this little girl's endowment is perfectly normal. By her ability to cope with the examination in spite of her handicaps she has shown herself from the earliest ages to be of entirely normal intellectual caliber.

Complete blindness is another matter. The examination of such a child by ordinary formal procedures would be almost impossible at 18 months and 2 years, though much could be learned by observation of his spontaneous play and from his adaptations to his daily routines. After 3 years of age verbal tests can be applied. Much of the blind child's ability to respond depends on the type of care and training he has received; considerably more would be expected of the child who had had special training in an institution for blind children than from one who had been overprotected at home. As in the case of the deaf child, the handicap is so serious that even under the best conditions some degree of retardation is to be expected in the preschool years. The response to training is the acid test, the response to an examination is merely an indicator.

THE SIGNIFICANCE OF DEVIATIONS IN EXAMINATION MANAGEMENT

With a thorough knowledge and understanding of normal development, the experienced examiner can go far beyond mere appraisal of maturity level. The developmental examination in seasoned hands is much more than a series of tests. It is also, among other things, a social situation which the child should be able to meet. The social requirements of the examination depend on the age level of the child, and the whole experience is so planned that the child should have no real difficulty in accepting the novel situation; he should even enjoy it. He is given time to make his own estimate of the examiner's intentions, he is given time to work out his own ideas, he is protected, he is praised, the toys are enticing, he is not hurried or harried or pressed or censured. As he grows older, he is expected to have profited sufficiently from cumulative experiences to become trustful and reasonably amenable in social situations. The developmental examination is indeed designed to make conformance easy and pleasant.

The assumption therefore is that a normal child whose life experiences have not been unusual will accept and enjoy the examination. That this is a valid and modest assumption is borne out by the fact that in a large clinical service taking preschool children of all kinds and from all sorts of backgrounds, at the very most only about two or three out of a hundred fail to adjust to the first examination, and at no age is this proportion significantly greater than at any other. If a given examiner has a very much higher percentage of children who fail to adjust, the presumption is that examination conditions are inadequate; this may mean that the physical arrangements and equipment are unsuitable, or that the methods are themselves at fault. If the conditions for examination are favorable, the child who fails to meet the examination situation is certainly a deviate. If the conditions must be greatly altered to accommodate him, he is also a deviate. The deviation may lie in his past experiences which have not prepared him for such a contingency, or it may lie much deeper.

The examination, so regarded, tests not only the child's ability to build towers and draw circles, but also his ability to meet strange persons, to conform to new situations, to confine his behavior to the task in hand; it shows his interests, the quality of his attention, the rapidity with which he exhausts his interest, his persistence in the face of difficulty, his insight into his own abilities, his willingness to "try," his reaction to praise, to success, to failure, his communicativeness, his meticulousness, or carelessness, his readiness to accept or ask for help—in innumerable ways he reveals himself. Unusual and bizarre responses have import and are immediately recognized as significant; the manner and mode of response is as meaningful as the responses themselves.

The examination situation can also be used to learn a good deal about the mother and parent-child relation, an added reason for permitting the mother to accompany the child to the examining room at the younger ages. If the mother is not advised of her role until after the examination begins, the examiner has an excellent opportunity to observe how intuitively the mother reacts and how much insight she has. It is amazing how many mothers immediately realize that they do not know what is expected of them, and how alert and responsive they are to the examiner's cues. They wait for a word or gesture, take their place and do not intrude into the examination uninvited. Other mothers show themselves to be overanxious, overofficious, too ready to help or to excuse, impatient, unsympathetic, antagonistic, or merely awkward. The child may ignore his mother, even exclude her, or he may wish to show her everything or receive a word of commendation from her for each performance; he may insist on sitting close to her, he may apply mutely for permission to touch the toys. Even when the mother does not accompany the child to the room, the way in which he leaves her and the frequency or absence of reference to the mother during the examination all tell their tale.

The developmental examination reveals, therefore, not only the child's maturity and his potentialities but also much of his personality, his emotional stability, his drives and interest, his fears and antagonisms. It is not offered as a device for the final analysis or diagnosis of his emotional disturbances, but it serves as an effective means for identifying many children who are in difficulties. It identifies them and to the guidance therapist it furnishes basic clues for planning re-educational measures.

. . . .

The following is an abbreviated account of an "unsuccessful" examination of an institution child for whom examination was requested because of behavior difficulties. He was reported to hit and bite the other children, to hit himself, pull his hair, to fight the ministrations of the attendants; he did not play but was content only when sitting alone rocking back and forth. He did not talk. The agency wished to know if this child were seriously retarded, or whether foster home treatment offered hopes of amelioration.

Examiner	*Dan—Age: 21 months*
	Walks into exam. room holding nurse's hand.
	Stands before chair—stolid expression, mouth open.
Ex. turns pp., talks about pictures. .	Regards for few moments, *turns away*, looks at book again.
Presents cubes.	Fingers top cube, *turns away.*
Builds tower 2, brushes top cube off.	
Retreats.	No response.
Moves cubes about.	*Reaches* toward cubes, *turns away.*
Builds tower 4, knocks down.	Watches.
Repeats tower.	Watches.
	Turns away.
Ignores (reads book).	Looks at chair.
	Squats, then sits on floor.
Puts cubes on floor before him.	Ignores, wagging a finger, *rocks* trunk.
(Nurse places him in chair).	No protest.
	Reaches for cubes on table.
	Drops one, then another to floor.
Cup added—request and gesture to	Regards cup, fingers it—rocks.
insert cubes.	*Grasps and releases a cube—rocks.*
Drops a cube in cup.	Approaches cube, and rocks.
	Grasps and releases cube.
	Grasps cup, releases, rocks.
	Reaches into cup, *withdraws* hand.
	Approaches cube, rocks.
Builds tower of three.	Grasps and releases cube—rocks.
Offers cube to child's hand.	Takes, releases, rocks.
Slowly inserts 6 cubes in cup, waits. .	*Brushes* cube to floor.
Inserts 2 more.	Grasps, releases cubes on table.
	Grasps, releases cubes to floor.
Pellet[1] and bottle presented.	Immediately grasps pellet[1].
Points to bottle.	Grasps bottle, brings p[1] toward mouth.
Points to bottle.	*Rocks, releases p[1] on table.*
Drops p[1] in bottle.	Takes bottle, peers in.
"Get it?".	Stares at Ex.
	Sits immobile—rocks.
	Sits holding bottle, peering in.
Ex. asks for bottle.	No response.
	Turns bottle about, watching p[1] roll.
	Rocks.
	Shakes bottle slightly.
Second pellet placed on table.	Grasps, brings toward mouth, holds, nodding head, *brings to mouth without inserting several times, looks at bottle.*
	Stares at Ex. blankly.
	Holds p[2] near mouth, turns bottle, p[1] falls out.
Re-inserts p[1].	P[2] toward mouth, rocks, p[2] to lips, rocks, rubs bottle on table.
Grasps bottle, "Thank you".	Releases after delay.
Picture book re-presented	*Still holding p[2] at mouth.*

Examiner	*Dan—Age: 21 months*
Points to pictures, talking.........	Stops rocking, regards p², rocks.
	Reaches tentatively toward book.
	Finally assists in turning page, dropping p².
Cubes re-presented	Reaches two hands, grasps and releases.
Tower of two...................	*Brings cube to tower,* releases, it falls.
	Casts cubes to floor.
Train.........................	*Vigorously brushes* them off table.
Cup is added, given one cube after another.	Immediately inserts, once starts to *try tower,* then *puts cube in cup.*
Cup and cubes removed..........	Looks at Ex., says *"meh-meh"* (*more?*)
Cup and cubes given again........	Inserts 6, stops.
"More"......................	Continues.
	After finished, rocks.
"Take them out?"...............	Removes 2 and replaces.
	Removes 2 and replaces.
Cup and cubes removed..........	"Meh-meh."
Paper and crayon given...........	Takes crayon, taps on paper.
Takes crayon, demonstrates scribble.	Tentative reaching crayon, twice *bangs crayon, breaking it.*
	"meh-meh."
Demonstrates scribble.............	Takes crayon, releases.
Demonstrates scribble.............	Delay, *crayon to floor.*
	"meh-meh."
Formboard.....................	Brushes to floor.
Inserts blocks and re-presents......	*Protests, turns away.*
Table removed, given ball........	Takes, sits and holds.
Invites to throw.................	No response.
	Passive during attempts at ball play
Cup and cubes re-offered..........	*Casts cube to floor, looks at Ex.*
	Casts all to floor. Cup to floor.
Re-offered.....................	Inserts all.
Offers her hand to go.............	Takes it willingly.

Dan's behavior is obviously full of abnormal, or, if you like, psychiatric implications. Here is a child who does not accept the examination situation, at least not wholeheartedly, but who also does not entirely refuse it. He can be interested but he cannot quite yield to his interest. He is repeatedly on the verge of catching the spirit of the occasion; each time he retreats again. The one feat he does perform he wishes to do again and again. When he finally tries to build a tower and fails, his behavior immediately deteriorates and, although he is really tempted, he cannot quite allow himself to try again. At the end he is apparently trying to see if he will be punished for throwing toys to the floor; when no punishment is forthcoming he immediately complies with the situation.

As far as developmental items go, Dan walks alone, fills a cup with cubes, inhibits eating the pellet, conveys to the examiner that he wants the cup and cubes and that he does not want the formboard. This is meager evidence on which to formulate an estimate of his status in terms of developmental quotient; one might call the examination a failure.

But was it actually a failure? Without analyzing his behavior in any detail, the fact remains that although he did not respond to the examination in the conventional manner, he did display behavior and very significant behavior under the stress of the examination situation. And although a developmental quotient cannot be assigned in terms of passing or failing test conditions, the examiner is at the very least justified in saying: first, Dan's endowment is probably *not* seriously deficient; secondly, his behavior difficulties are most probably *not* explainable in terms of serious mental retardation; and thirdly, foster home care can be strongly recommended as a therapeutic measure for his emotional difficulties.

The maneuvers the examiner used attempting to secure cooperation are not presented as ideal or as the only possible moves the examiner might have made. It is improbable, however, that any devices could have induced this child to comply with the requirements of the examination in a normal manner; it is extremely probable, on the other hand, that more strenuous measures would have produced a complete refusal, either passive or active, the very reaction that had been freely predicted by the nurse. In that event we would have been deprived of informative clues both to his developmental status and to his emotional organization.

In such instances the examination is viewed, not as a single and conclusive episode from which the child's future is determined, but as one link in a chain of events. It is but a part of the story, one of a series of observations designed to follow and evaluate the *course* of development. So regarded, the individual examination acquires new values, and unconventional behavior in the examination becomes fully as significant as the more usual adjustment and performance.

CHAPTER XIII

INDIVIDUALITY AND ITS CHARACTERIZATION

H OW does individuality manifest itself? In the physical make-up of the child, in biochemical and physiological characteristics, in patterns and dispositions of behavior, in distinctive methods of maturing and of learning.

Needless to say this chapter will not attempt any comprehensive survey of a topic so vast. However, if the psychological observation of a child is to result in something more than a bare psychometric rating, it becomes necessary to reckon with his distinctive demeanors and characteristics. A psychological examination should result at the least in a paragraph which epitomizes the observed manifestations of individuality.

A. Possibilities of Characterization

If there were a neat and accurate method for measuring or even classifying personalities, it might be possible to sum up a child's individuality in a neat phrase or label. But even such apparently decisive categories as *introvert, extrovert, aggressive, schizoid, unstable, alert, sociable,* etc., have their limitations. These limitations must be formulated in terms of concrete situations and qualifying circumstances. It is possible to draw up useful psychographic profiles which plot the appraised magnitude of selected traits. But such profiles likewise are always in need of interpretive elucidation. In the present state of psycho-technology there is no escape from descriptive formulation in recording behavior individuality. The formulation may cover pages; it may be couched in one or two paragraphs.

The length and the content of any characterization will naturally vary with the individual child; with the nature of the problem, if any; with the purpose and the perception of the observer. So far as characterization tools are concerned, they are no less numerous than the trait names and adjectives of the English language. Allport (1) listed some 18,000 trait terms. Among these there are a few hundred which can be conveniently used for delineating the observed individuality.

Since each characterization must be adapted to an individual child and may have to take into account the unique history of this unique child, it is difficult to set up universal rules of procedure. The method of characterization which relies on a vast store of trait terms is in a sense literary. It exploits the naturalistic by-product of the test situation and of the inter-view. It seizes upon telltale attitudes and reactions. It regards the examination as a whole, as well as the symptomatic details. It demands clinical insight. It becomes most fruitful in the examiner of wide and ordered experience.

This means, of course, that the method has its dangers and pitfalls. In an uncritical, overimaginative, or overintuitive observer, the literary characterization may rest too much on subjective impressions. A realistic approach, however, when combined with a skillful use of the resources of the English language can yield a form of portrayal which will be helpful in interpreting the child's nature and in defining his individual needs.

The best way to avoid subjective errors is to formulate the characterization in terms of the objective evidences of actually observed behavior. Evaluation of this behavior in terms of invisible and inferential emotional factors is another matter. Evaluation and characterization should not be carelessly confused. It is therefore advisable to rely primarily upon a summarizing reportorial statement of the behavior displayed in the four fundamental fields: motor, adaptive, language, and personal-social.

To each of these fields it is possible to assign a descriptive maturity level rating, based upon the normative values of the tests administered. If there is a wide scatter within any one field, this fact may be specifically noted. If, for example, there is a marked discrepancy between fine motor control and gross motor control, this may be indicated in a concrete way. If there are marked discrepancies in the maturity levels for the four fundamental fields, this fact is in itself an important characterization item.

Within each field it is possible to record selected behavior events or peculiarities of reaction which have symptomatic significance. In the *motor* field such items as output of energy, bodily activity and fatigability, postural demeanor are characterized, particularly if they are atypical or markedly above or below usual expectation. Postural demeanor is noted to determine whether it is tense, relaxed, poised, steady, variable.

Trained common sense and the psychological outlook of the observer will determine what items are chosen for special mention. But it is hazardous to look for traits as entities or to pigeonhole the observations on the basis of preconceived schema. It is sounder to record the salient, symptomatic features of the behavior and to let the record itself tell the story. And it does tell the story, if the recorded items are happily chosen and are considered as functional indicators of the individuality of the child.

In the field of *adaptive behavior*, one may take note of special evidences of insight, inquisitiveness, originality, decisiveness, initiative, etc. Without attempting to estimate the magnitude of such traits in the abstract, it may be illuminating to put a few concrete manifestations into the record.

It is often advantageous to make specific mention of the typical or optimal performance.

In the field of *language*, it is well to note the child's articulation, the flow of his speech, inflections, inhibitions, conversational rapport, his expressiveness by words or physiognomy.

The field of *personal-social behavior* invites attention to all reactions which reflect the emotional vitality and the motivations of the child; his reactions to success and failure and fatigue; his reactions to novelty and surprise; his sense of humor. Here, again, it is a good rule to succinctly describe selected bits of revealing behavior in preference to attempting a trait portrayal.

To the summary comments on the four fundamental behavior fields a brief statement may be added to epitomize the course of the child's reactions to the examination as a whole; for these reactions in their entirety may be highly revealing of individuality. They may be particularly suggestive as indicators of talents and general giftedness.

A characterization even within the cautious limits above outlined enriches the yield of psychological examination and takes us beyond the confines of psychometric scoring. It obliges us to regard the child as a unique individual who is displaying a behavior individuality in his every reaction to both the controlled and the incidental stimuli of a dynamic sequence of situations. Through such characterizations we may hope to extend the usefulness of developmental examinations, to detect individual differences in terms of the child's constitution and personality. This is a conservative effort to understand the child rather·than to classify or to quantify him.

The interview furnishes important data for the characterization of a child, particularly when he presents a behavior problem or a developmental handicap. In such cases the interview will be particularly directed toward an inquiry into the child's developmental history. How did he meet the demands of development, and the obstacles of learning? How did he acquire, modify, and shed habits of personal adjustment? Every child has a distinctive pattern and style of growing. In special instances it becomes important to arrange a series of developmental examinations, to ascertain the problems and peculiarities of behavior growth in an individual child.

In complicated cases the evaluation of growth characteristics and the interpretation of behavior individuality may require clinical judgment of an expert order. An adequate evaluation may then need special neurological and pediatric investigation; and also a careful exploration of the life history of the child.

To illustrate different kinds and degrees of characterization, several specimen summaries are appended. These summaries are not offered as models but rather as examples of various modes of statement. They chiefly concern children of normal mentality. A few examples of social problems and defective conditions are included.

B. Illustrative Characterizations

1. A School Beginner (*Tabular Descriptive Summary*)

Girl SH. Age: 5 years 1 month
General maturity level: Slightly advanced in all fields
Developmental outlook: High average. Should be ready for school entrance in a
  year
Descriptive characterization:

Motor. Average amount of activity. Remains quietly at the table. Drums heels while waiting for something else to happen but otherwise is quiet. Climbs up on the scales and jumps down repeatedly, however, and wants to climb the stairs in the dome. Handles materials well: builds well, draws well. Is not clumsy or awkward.

Adaptive. Many details in her drawing: garage, dollhouse, rabbit, and ball accompany her house. She puts wheels on the baby carriage which she draws spontaneously. Elaborates drawing of man: pants, buttons, hair. Doesn't think she can draw forms but does so correctly.

Language. Talkative. Information about what she likes to do: "I love to cut." Imaginative: "That's not scribbling; that's grass." Excuses failures: "I don't know how to tie a bowknot. Once I tried." Conversational rapport excellent. Observant: "The other one of these (tables) is out in the other room, but it's smaller."

Personal-social. Friendly. Talkative. Says, "I like it here." When leaving, responds to invitation to come back again with, "You come and see us. Any time."

Says, "I can't," "I don't know," but is usually successful. Is persistent: "Do you remember what I said I could do? I said I could write on the back." Does so.

Does not look for help. Goes about each task rather competently (except for verbal excuses). Changes subject if fails: Writes name incorrectly. Smiles and says, "I guess I'll write something else." When her bridge falls, she says, "Oh, I don't want to use these. I'll use these others."

Adjusts well. Is very conscious of appearance and does not wish to muss her dress. Accepts each new situation placidly.

2. A Candidate for First Grade (*Brief Discursive Summary*)

Boy KC. Age: 5 years 3 months
General maturity level: Approximately 5½ years. Range: 5 to 6 years
Developmental outlook: Average
Descriptive characterization:

General characterization. Cooperative, pleasant, well poised. Appeared to enjoy examination and smiled frequently. Comment was principally confined to that called for by the test situations but there was no suggestion of inhibition or blocking. Gave good attention to directions, and worked concentratedly on set tasks. Performance was not scattered; all 5-year tests were passed, with two successes at 6 years. Responses throughout were of a character consistent with the developmental level indicated.

Motor behavior. Drawing control was good, with lines perhaps a little straighter and surer than usual at this age. The square and triangle were done easily, and the diagonal was satisfactory after erasure of one false line. The diamond was failed, but he approached success on the second and third trials. He is right-handed, and according to his mother, has never shown any inclination to prefer the left hand.

Adaptive behavior. He counted four and ten pennies correctly and responded to "How many?" but could not continue beyond eleven. The gate was constructed from the model without difficulty, the blocks being surely and evenly placed. All ten forms were correctly matched.

Language behavior. Articulation is clear with no infantile residuals. There was little spontaneous conversation but he talked freely as called for by the test situations and the examiner's questions. He answered seventeen questions in the Action-Agent tests, with one-word responses throughout.

Personal-social behavior. Dresses himself without help, including buttons; laces his shoes, and tries to tie them, but cannot yet manage a bowknot. He can go to the store and remember one or two things to bring home, without having them written down. Has attended kindergarten for only about the last two months of the school year but made a good adjustment with children who had been all year in the group. His teacher feels he will be ready for first grade in the fall.

Comment. A child of good average intelligence, with a well-integrated, relatively mature personality. Although he will be a month or two below first grade age, this slight difference is balanced by the slight margin above the average in his level of abilities, and the total picture suggests that he should have no serious difficulty in meeting the grade requirements.

3. DELAY IN SCHOOL ENTRANCE RECOMMENDED (*Extended Discursive Summary*)

Boy NR. Age: 5 years 1 month
General maturity level: 5 years. Range: 3-7 years
Developmental outlook: Above average, but may be slow in early school progress
Descriptive characterization:

General characterization. An active and energetic boy but not too highly excitable and without suggestions of marked instability. Interested and cooperative in most tests but attention showed some fluctuation. There was a tendency toward over-precipitate response in several cases, without sufficient study of the situation; where the conditions of the test permitted (e.g., cube construction) he corrected for this after the initial failure. In at least one case where this could not be done (form-matching) he failed the test, but gave full evidence of sufficient insight to have enabled him to pass it. Showed a tendency to go off on irrelevant conversational topics, but could always be brought back without difficulty to the task in hand. Performance rather widely scattered, with failures at 4 and 4½ years, and successes at 6 and 7 years. The quality of his best responses suggested a basic level at least a little above his age. He has not attended kindergarten.

Motor behavior. Drawing was quite weak. He copied the cross but his production was not symmetrical and his lines wavered. On all three trials his attempt to copy the square resulted in a hurriedly drawn circular figure, and his triangle was indistinguishable from his square. His man was practically unrecognizable, but he identified feet, hands, head, eyes, and mouth in his drawing. He spontaneously produced another amorphous drawing which he said was an airplane. The pencil was gripped tightly and awkwardly in his right hand. He is said to prefer the right hand, but even as late as 3 years, his mother thought he might be left-handed.

Adaptive behavior. Number comprehension was inferior; he counted four pennies as three, combining the last two in a sweep of his finger. This was repeated, and he showed no comprehension of the question, "How many?" In constructing the gate he rushed into the task with only a brief glance at the model, achieving a result that was substantially correct, except that the center block was flat on the table between the two side ones. When asked to compare his structure with the model, he immediately made the necessary change. His form-matching performance, with only seven successes instead of eight, must be technically scored as failure at 4 years; but here an over-precipitate attack on the problem, with random pointing for the first three forms, was responsible. At this point, however, he suddenly showed full insight into the task and quickly identified all the remaining forms correctly, including those most commonly failed.

Language behavior. Articulation was infantile but it was usually possible to understand most of what he said. Improvement in this respect is reported to have become accelerated recently. Despite the faulty pronunciation his highest test successes involved the use and comprehension of language. He answered seventeen questions on the Action-Agent test, comprehension questions at 4, 4½, and 6 years, and gave definitions in terms of use. He gave superior descriptions of the Stanford pictures, introducing interpretation ("The girl went outside and got something in her eye.") in response to the first of these. He named five days of the week.

Personal-social behavior. He is reported as being able to dress himself, usually needing ordinary attention to correct his omissions and mistakes. He manages even small buttons, but somewhat awkwardly, and is usually helped with these. He can go to the store for two or three things without a list and seldom forgets any of them. Play with other children is reported as normal, although most of his playmates are a year or two older. He distinguishes morning and afternoon and explained that afternoon starts "after morning—when school gets out," although he does not attend school. Nickel, penny, quarter, and dime were identified correctly. He is usually a happy child but sometimes has fits of temper under conditions of strain, fatigue, or excitement. He eats well, with few marked food preferences, but does not like to sit long at the table. Sleep does not come until he has been in bed half or three-quarters of an hour, but he then sleeps soundly through the night.

Outlook. It is probable that, with increased maturity and stability, school attendance, and widened social contacts, the psychometric performance will even out, showing a high average, perhaps slightly superior, rating. He will be just under the minimum age for first-grade entrance when school opens in the fall, and there may be some temptation to start him in the first grade instead of kindergarten. This would be unwise for several reasons. In the first place, the speech defect is still sufficiently marked to be something of a social handicap, and it will be more readily overcome under the freer conditions of the kindergarten than in the first grade. In the second place, the combination of scattered performance, with motor, language, and number concept specifically retarded, and immature attention control, indicates a type of poorly integrated personality, not sufficiently mature to do satisfactory first-grade work. In cases of this type, it has been frequently found that the child is not yet ready to undertake reading; and serious school difficulty may be avoided by giving him the advantage of being a little above, rather than a little below, the average age when he enters the first grade.

4. A Dynamic Nursery School Child (*Functional Characterization*)

Girl SN. Age: 2 years
Performance: illustrative items

Motor. Walks, runs, walks up and down stairs holding banister.

Adaptive. Tower of four, four-cube train, imitates vertical and horizontal strokes, matches all color forms.

Language. Talks in phrases, articulation jargon-like, identifies ten pictures. Three commands with ball.

Personal-social. Toilet regulated during day, feeds self with help, imitative play with doll.

Characterization. The outstanding qualities of SN's performance are speed, decisiveness, and control. Although she is reported to be recently quite shy, she makes an immediate and easy adjustment to the examination. On entering the room she shows her shyness in only minimal ways, hesitating before going through the door, lifting her dress, and putting her little finger in the corner of her mouth. As soon as she sees the picture book all these signs disappear.

She walks quickly with the legs and knees close together, planting her heels down, the feet pigeon-toeing slightly. She seats herself easily, almost without looking. Her handling of toys is deft and quick. Her speed is seen, however, not so much in the speed of movement as in the immediacy and completeness of each response and then the very quick shift to the next situation. The decisiveness shows itself in the immediate competency of the performance and in the fact that she is then *finished* and cannot be induced to repeat herself. The decisiveness of her performances led the examiner to try for partial responses at a higher level. Almost without exception the situation is refused; when not refused it is failed. SN does not give many partial responses. She either does a thing very well or she does not do it at all.

Control is shown in many ways and pervades all fields of behavior. SN controls her shyness and does not cry or retreat to her mother. She controls her volubility. In contrast to the continuous flow of jargon she produced at her 18-month examination, she is now for the most part silent, though she does make a few spontaneous remarks. She answers questions but only those that interest her. She is too busy to pay much attention to adults; she refers to her mother only once during the examination and she occasionally invites the examiner to share her pleasure in an object. She does not allow her very rapid attention shifts to interfere with the completion of a response, nor does her behavior deteriorate. Play is robust but not boisterous and she does not over-respond. The motor drive is also under control. Although she is an active child and leaves the table several times, this is chiefly because of her interest drives and not because she is unable to sit still. Even at top speed the examination does not always move quite fast enough for her and the forthrightness of her make-up translates idea at once into action. She is easily controlled by the verbal suggestion, "Come and sit down and I will give it to you."

The conflict between impetuousness and control is perhaps best shown in her response to the formboard. After the first rotation she is too precipitous in her attack on the problem and fails to adapt; on the second trial she corrects her error immediately, and on the third trial she looks before she leaps.

5. A FOSTER INFANT. CANDIDATE FOR ADOPTION (*Clinical Memorandum*)

Girl LW. Age: 15 months
General maturity level: 15 + months
Developmental outlook: High average

Descriptive characterization. Petite blond child, soft abundant hair, little button face, looks fragile and doll-like. She walks well, began at 11 months, feet close together, slight stagger, stumbles over things. Has difficulty in release. Builds tower of two, fills cup, scribbles, makes near-placement of circle, and makes near-adaptation to rotation. Jargons and has over twenty-five words. Selects dog in picture, shows own shoe, looks toward materials-bag for cup. Some verbal rapport, responds to encouragement. As is common at 15 months, resents the examiner directing the examination (but not to point of casting toys). Insisted on sitting in foster mother's lap, not by crying but by urging and refusing to exploit toys until put there. This did not seem to be timidity but dominance. Not fearful, stands own ground. Difficulty with release is not only manual but also emotional; refused to give up toys, screamed threateningly at examiner when toys were removed. Demanded toys from material-bag, but no strenuous demands except to retain what she has. Is immediately appeased and can be diverted. Not persistent nor repetitious; exploits quickly, then wants more and also wants to keep what she has. No breakdown. Foster mother expects too much ideal behavior.

Her general maturity level is slightly above 15 months; language is definitely accelerated. Development is slightly above the average for her age, and we consider her a promising candidate for adoption in a home offering some advantages. She should have the usual year's probationary period and re-examination, and because of her positive personality traits, a home should be selected that will respect her personality and will not feel that a child with spirit needs strong discipline. Placement should not be delayed.

6. A DEFECTIVE PRESCHOOL CHILD. FOSTER HOME PLACEMENT
(*Brief clinical note*)

Boy LM. Age: 4 years

This boy was examined at 2, 3, and 4 years of age. The maturity level ratings to date are recapitulated below.

Age in years	2	3	4
Behavior field:			
Motor	44 wks.	18 mos.	24± mos.
Adaptive	1 yr.	17 mos.	24 mos.
Language	44 wks.	18— mos.	21+ mos.
Personal—social	1 yr.	18— mos.	24± mos.

Descriptive characterization. Chunky, tow-headed boy, small for age. Typical Mongolian facies and habitus. Very docile and obedient, a little merry. Responses immediate and complete and gives a 2-year performance that (superficially at least) does not seem very defective in quality; attention and drive are of really good quality. In the entire past year, however, he has only slightly improved his method of seating himself in a chair (it is still a very precarious undertaking) while in the normal child this ability is perfected in a matter of days. He is accepted without any difficulty in his foster home and is the family pet, creates no problems. Institutional care will be necessary later. Re-examination at yearly intervals.

7. MOTOR HANDICAP WITH NORMAL MENTALITY (*Letter to Social Agency*)

The _____ Crippled Aid Association

_____ _____, Director

Dear Sir:

We are writing to report in summary our findings in the case of C_____ P_____, age 6½ years, whom you referred to us for developmental examination.

We first examined this boy at the age of 4 years. He came with a history of difficult birth, having shown symptoms of brain injury three days after instrumental delivery. His motor disability at the time of the first examination was so great that it was almost impossible for him to adjust to the ordinary test situations. His behavior status was briefly as follows:

Motor characteristics. Severe double athetosis and spasticity. Cannot sit alone; has to be held in lap; head has to be supported. Prehensory movements aimless, but can seize cubes with examiner's help and drop them severally into a cup. Can roll from supine to prone and pivot when prone.

Adaptive behavior. Points to pictures; counts to five; gives age.

In spite of this meager performance, he gave many indications of potential normality of general intelligence, particularly in number sense and in comprehension. Emotionally he was friendly and cooperative, although reported to be occasionally "stubborn." Parents were urged to give muscle training a prolonged trial and to provide as much normal experience as possible, particularly play with other children.

Language. Voiceless enunciation of names (Don = John). Says *gone, car, more milk, no good, may gon kool* (Mary gone to school).

Personal-social. Feeds self with bread with great effort. Toilet trained since 11 months. Enjoys companions. Beats drum with feet. Keeps time to radio with feet.

C_____ P_____ was again examined at the age of 6½ years with findings as follows:

Motor characteristics. He now has a walker which he uses very well, propelling and steering by means of his feet. Tolerates being tied into the walker for over an hour, until back and neck begin to tire.

Cannot handle objects any better. Points only with great difficulty.

Adaptive behavior. Identifies coins. Knows name of president. Repeats three digits backward. Defines in terms of use.

Language. Speaks in whisper, exerting tremendous effort. But articulates responsively to questions. Likes to be read to (Black Sambo). Corrects errors and omissions in the reading.

Personal-social behavior. Still fed by hand. Always tells toilet needs. Dry at night. Dramatically projects self as a truck driver.

On the basis of these two examinations we are pleased to report that his mentality is developing quite normally and in a very satisfactory manner. From the standpoint of his emotional control, alertness, and general intelligence we consider him (in view of his disabilities) a remarkable young boy.

He is capable of acquiring an education. He should learn silent reading. This may become a very important resource for the proper development of his personality. At present he cannot go to school, but he should have the services of a visiting teacher. The possibility of some especially adapted or partial vocation in adult years should not be excluded in the general planning of a program.

Yours sincerely,

8. SUPERIOR PRE-KINDERGARTEN CHILD (*Informal Narrative Summary*)

Girl VS. Age: 3½ years

This child was previously examined at 2 years and at 3 years of age. The following is an informal summary of the impression made by the last examination.

VS was told she was to come upstairs today to play with the examiner. She was eager to come, was waiting at the door of the nursery and darted down the hall ahead of the examiner. She wanted to go up in the elevator and nodded "yes" when asked.

There was little or no overflow in conversation, no asking for the next situation, as she had done at her 3-year-examination. When the door slammed she did not even look up and in general she disregarded all extraneous sounds, so complete was her concentration. Her speed and executiveness were especially evident in her drawing. She held the pencil pronately, close to the tip, and showed remarkable maturity in her control.

As with all of her examinations, the difficult task is the one she enjoys most. Her response to the diamond was, "Well, we'll see what we can do about this one!" She did not master it, however. She passed the rectangle with diagonals on the first trial and mastered it completely in two trials. She responded immediately to situations that were too easy for her by answering in a silly voice. Her superiority is remarkably well rounded.

She became a bit restless during the language situations but released her tensions by doing motor gymnastics on her chair, readily answering questions at the same time. She gave her name, sex, and repeated digits, whereas on previous examinations she was self-consciously silent at these questions. After drawing what appeared to be an umbilicus on the Incomplete Man, she refused to name it and when asked if it was a belly button, seemed embarrassed. She referred to herself by the pronoun *I* five times in answering the Action-Agent questions and also referred to herself as *we.* "We don't cry any more." This is probably the self-consciousness and restraint of a much older child, but at the same time this trait is and has been a strong characteristic of VS.

Superior attentional organization was shown in her ability to delimit her responses as follows:

(1) Not disturbed by noises
(2) Only one multiple answer on Action-Agent test (there had been many at three years)
(3) Pointed to geometric forms (did not pick them up)
(4) Pointed only to pretty ladies (no reference to ugly ones)
(5) Pointed only to longer line (no reference to smaller one)
(6) No overflow of conversation.

Superior potentialities are shown not only in the maturity ratings but in vocabulary and choice of words, and in artistic expression (spontaneous drawing) and in her command of social situations.

9. INDIVIDUALITY IN INFANCY (*Comparative Sketch*)

For good measure we add a brief informal sketch of Boys B and D who have already been pictorially introduced to the reader in Chapter V. We saw these boys repeatedly throughout the first year of life and again in their fifth year. On the basis of their behavior during the first year, we appraised them comparatively with respect to fifteen behavior traits as follows:

1. *Energy output* (general amount and intensity of activity)
2. *Motor demeanor* (postural bearing, general muscular control and poise, motor coordination, and facility of motor adjustment)
3. *Self-dependence* (general self-reliance and self-sufficiency without appeal to the assistance of others)
4. *Social responsiveness* (positive reactivity to persons and to the attitudes of adults and of other children)
5. *Family attachment* (closeness of affection; degree of identification with the family group)
6. *Communicativeness* (expressive reference to others by means of gesture and vocalization)
7. *Adaptivity* (general capacity to adjust to new situations)
8. *Exploitation of environment* (utilization and elaboration of environment and circumstances in order to gain new experience)
9. *"Humor" sense* (sensitiveness and playful reactiveness to surprise, novelty and incongruity in social situations)
10. *Emotional maladjustment* (balance and stability of emotional response in provocative situations)
11. *Emotional expressiveness* (liveliness and subtlety of expressive behavior in emotional situations)
12. *Reaction to success* (expression of satisfaction in successful endeavor)
13. *Reaction to restriction* (expressiveness of behavior in reaction to failure, discomfort, disappointment, frustration)
14. *Readiness of smiling* (facility and frequency of smiling)
15. *Readiness of crying* (promptness and facility of frowning and tears)

Comparative estimates of the above traits as manifested in the first year of life proved to be highly predictive.

Boy B and Boy D presented contrastive individualities which we may now summarize, if the reader will kindly understand that we do not suggest that one set of traits is necessarily superior to another set. Each boy, like each of us, is in his psychological make-up a mixture of assets and some liabilities.

As early as the ages of 8 and 12 weeks the highly dynamic personality of Boy D made a strong impression even when observed only through the medium of the cinema. The following adjectives were used to characterize his individuality: quick, active, happy, friendly, well-adjusted, vigorous, forceful, alert, inquisitive. Although he was definitely extrovertive he showed at the early age of 24 weeks a surprising discriminativeness in reading the facial expressions of his mother. By the age of 28 weeks he had developed a moderate temper technique for influencing domestic situations which did not altogether please him. He was able to shift quickly in his emotional response from smiling to crying and from crying to smiling to achieve a desired end. At the age of 5 years, likewise, his emotional reactions are labile and versatile. He is facile in changing his emotional responses. He is highly perceptive of emotional expressions in others, and correspondingly, highly adaptive in social situations. With this emotional alertness, he shows a relatively vigorous detachment from his mother as well as affection for her. He is not given to persisting moods. We do not get the impression that his emotional characteristics have been primarily determined by his life experiences. The underlying nature of his "emotivity" at 12 weeks, at 52 weeks, and at 260 weeks seems rather constant. With altered outward configurations a certain characteristicness in emotional reactions is quite likely to persist into his later life.

Boy B presents a different constellation of characteristics. Although by no means emotionally shallow, he is by comparison less vivid, less expressive, more self-contained than Boy D. He is a sturdy, deliberate, moderately sociable, friendly child whose characteristics were evident at 1 year as well as at 5 years.

Boy B still shows motor ineptnesses and inhibitions comparable to those which he displayed in infancy. Boy D, on the other hand, has given consistent evidences of superior motor coordination from an early age in postural control, locomotion, and manual dexterity. At 20 weeks he manipulated a string of wooden beads with precocious discriminativeness; at 44, he actuated a hinged rattle with a clever screwdriver movement of the wrists; at 1 year he pulled out an electric plug in an adaptive manner. At 2 years he repeatedly inserted and reinserted electric plugs, adjusted bridge lamps, latched and unlatched doors, and operated an egg beater. The drive and deftness of his ceaseless manipulation strongly suggest in this instance mechanical insight and aptitude.

We have devoted a paragraph to motor traits because they best lend themselves to objective statement. If other traits of individuality become equally amenable to measurement and appraisal, applied psychology will be increasingly concerned with the detection of individual differences in the first year of life. There is a significant degree of internal consistency in the behavior features of the same children at 1 and at 5 years of age. This consistency seems to rest upon biological characteristicness; a characteristicness which as yet cannot be quantitatively formulated in a satisfactory manner but which is incontrovertible.

Our findings must not be overgeneralized, but they strongly indicate that certain fundamental traits of individuality, whatever their origin, exist early, persist late, and assert themselves under varying environmental conditions. This does not mean that physical and cultural environments have no influence upon the growing organism. It is suggested, however, that their influence may be properly envisaged as operating upon and subject to basic constitutional characters. The extrinsic environment impresses circumstantial and topical configurations, but a certain *naturel* is there from the beginning.

CHAPTER XIV

DEVELOPMENTAL SUPERVISION AND THE SCHOOL BEGINNER

IN THIS concluding chapter we renew an emphasis already made in the introduction: the importance of discovering and understanding the individual characteristics of children while these children are still in their earliest years. Methods such as we have outlined for the study of the individual child and for the diagnosis of defects and deviations of development serve a social purpose when they are used in a timely manner to define educational and hygienic procedures. In the preschool period of life these procedures must of necessity be highly individualized. Infants and toddlers cannot foregather in congregate groups convenient for social control. The protection of early child development requires a very personal form of developmental supervision.

A comprehensive scheme of developmental supervision pictures itself ideally as a series of safeguards with the promotion of optimal growth as the inclusive aim. Once this aim is accepted as a guiding principle, the problem of the school beginner vanishes or it takes on such an altered form that it ceases to exist. Forsooth, what is a school beginner? A six-, a five-, a four-, a three-, or a two-year-old child? And when and how should the parents prepare the child for school? And when and how should the school prepare the parents for the complicated task of rearing the child? And who can draw the line between parent education and early childhood education? These questions are all inextricably inter-related and it is for that very reason that public health and educational agencies must concern themselves with this diversified preschool terrain, which bristles with problems of social engineering.

The protection of a democratic society requires increasing attention to the welfare of children of preschool age. The White House Conference on Children in a Democracy was called by the President of the United States to strengthen the foundations of a democratic state. Four basic subjects were set up for consideration: (1) The objectives of a democratic society in relation to children; (2) The economic foundations of family life and child welfare; (3) The mental development of children and youth in present-day American life; (4) The child and community services for health, education, and social protection.

Adolescents who will presently become voters and parents are of most immediate importance in education for democracy. But any long-range view must also take into account infants and children under 6 years of age. Throughout the preschool years there is an intimate interaction between the psychologies of the child and of the parent. Democracy is a way of life which demands attitudes of tolerance and fair play. If we wish to lay the basis of such attitudes in young children we must begin with the education of adults. The adults in their own behavior must furnish the models and intimations of the democratic way. And the adults most responsible are, of course, parents and householders. For the 16,000,000 preschool children in America there is a corresponding number of fathers, mothers, grandparents, uncles, and aunts. What all these adults and their communities do with and for this great army of children will have no small influence on the evolution of our democracy.

This does not mean that one can teach democracy by direct instruction to a child of preschool age. Democracy is a mature virtue, a product of gradual growth, which embodies obedience, self-control, self-direction. For developmental reasons, however, the democratic attitudes of fair-mindedness can get a healthy start only in homes which reflect these same attitudes.

Respect for the dignity of the individual is the most fundamental component of the democratic ideal. This respect demands a greater social concern for the psychological foundations of family life and of child care. Underprivileged preschool children suffer not only in a physical sense. They suffer psychologically. They feel mental insecurity. In crowded and shiftless homes they develop anxieties and perplexities. They see sights and experience shocks from which more fortunate children are in decency spared. Innumerable households still use methods of harsh discipline: chronic scolding, shouting, terrifying threats, slapping, beating. Needless to say such inconsiderate disregard for the dignity of the individual is inconsistent with the spirit of democracy. In fact, misguided and crude forms of child management are so widespread as to constitute a public health problem, a task of preventive mental hygiene.

How can society undertake this task? By steadily widening the infant health protection which has already been initiated both through private medical practice and community measures. Having safeguarded the birth and nutrition of the infant, we should continue to supervise the course of his development up to school entrance.

There are three major areas of social control in which provisions for the welfare of the preschool child are destined to evolve with accelerated pace. These three areas are (1) Medical supervision of child development, (2) Parental and preparental education, and (3) Readaptation of the kindergarten and the nursery school.

Accelerated progress in the biological sciences and a further socialization of clinical medicine will have a profound effect upon future patterns of social control. The accumulating knowledge of the processes of child development will find expanding application. There will be increasing demands for the psychological diagnosis and understanding of individual children, whether normal, gifted, or handicapped. The protection of optimal growth will require a balanced concern for mental as well as physical welfare; and it will become increasingly important to articulate the varied efforts in the three fields of social control which have just been mentioned.

1. Medical Supervision of Child Development. The primary responsibility for protecting the life, the health, and the early development of the infant lies with the profession of medicine, and especially with pediatrics. Through private medical practice and through socialized provisions like the infant welfare center, every enlightened community provides for the periodic supervision of the child's physical growth. This supervision focuses on nutrition but is giving increasing regard to the psychological factors which underlie mental health. Development is a continuing process which can be supervised only by periodic examinations which take into account the behavior characteristics of the individual and recognize the interrelations of physical and mental welfare. The potential importance of child guidance clinics, consultation centers, and guidance nurseries in any comprehensive scheme of developmental supervision is evident.

2. Parental and Preparental Education. Adult education has come into increasing prominence as a means of social control. There are endless opportunities for the guidance of parents in the field of infant care and of child training. Children, however, differ so radically and widely and they change so rapidly during the period of their early growth that technical instruction in the particularities of child management has limited possibilities. Educational agencies can render most service by assisting parents to acquire a working philosophy of growth which will give perspective to the everyday problems of childhood.

From the standpoint of public school policy, preparental education is more basic than parental education. Adolescents should be reached by a more frank presentation of the elementary facts concerning the cycle of human growth. Animal biology, in spite of its concreteness, does not come close enough to the problems of human living. Schools and colleges could offer courses of instruction in human biology dealing more candidly with the origin, birth, physical growth, and mental growth of babies. The curriculum could also provide a practical type of psychology concerned with the laws of human nature and with the development of the child mind. Such a psychology, far from being introspective, would tend to take the adolescent out of himself and enable him ultimately to assume more objective views of the problems of parenthood. Education frankly addressed to the problems of early human development and child behavior would bear fruit in a decade, because in a few years these youths will be fathers and mothers with a more intelligent outlook upon the life cycle of a newborn infant of their own.

3. *Readaptation of the Kindergarten and Nursery School.* The problem of preschool education must be envisaged in terms of the entire span of infancy up to the sixth-year molar. We cannot educationally organize this vast domain simply by institutional expansion. We cannot multiply kindergartens and nursery schools indefinitely. We must reconstruct both of these agencies in such a way that they will reach all the people and contact the whole range of the preschool years. By the device of part-time and differential attendance, by bringing parent and child jointly into the scheme of education, by converting kindergartens and nursery schools into demonstration and guidance centers, the preschool clientele can be enormously increased without undue additions to the budget. There is no reason why the public school system, in cooperation with agencies of public health and medicine, cannot make periodic contacts with the two-year-olds, three-year-olds, and four-year-olds. These are problems of administration and of social invention. We cannot meet them if we cling too tenaciously to the patterns of attendance and regimentation of the traditional primary school.

. . . .

There is still a lamentable degree of rigidity in the prevailing regulation of school entrance. It is too much assumed that the task of the primary school is to teach reading. And sad experience has shown that mere admission to the first grade on the basis of chronological age does not insure that the child is ready for reading instruction. The result is a wide variety of conflicts between curriculum, child, teacher, and parent. This leads to maladjustments, feelings of inadequacy, misdirected teaching zeal, disappointments, and confusions. In the confusion school authorities fail to make a distinction between true reading disabilities and purely benign differences in developmental maturity and aptitude. Reading is a complex achievement, which came late in the cultural history of the race. Why should it not come with difficulty and delay for countless children who for reasons of maturity and inheritance have insufficient command of basic coordinations of eyes, hands, speech, perception, and comprehension at the age of 6 years? It takes no mean order of voluntary control for a young child simultaneously to stand on two feet, to hold a book of some weight between the fingers of a rather tiny hand, to restrain the "free" hand, to execute eye movements from left to right, pursuing narrow, closely crowded paths of printed symbols, to translate these symbols and to enunciate (with pleasing expressiveness!) "I am a gingerbread man, I am, I am. I can run from you. I can. I can." Some schools do not demand all of these performances at one time. Fortunately there is an increase of sedentary and silent reading. The psychological and neurological requirements of beginning reading, however, remain so complex that there should be a sensitive regard for underlying individual differences.

It is most significant that many of the early reading difficulties would vanish if the natural processes of maturation were given a chance to assert themselves. It is also significant that many of the graver cases of reading disability which call for clinical guidance and special therapy appear in children of high intelligence. The unsuspected frequency of such disabilities should give us pause.

The eruption of the sixth-year molar marks a transition period which accentuates inherent differences in developmental pattern. To meet these differences the induction of the preschool child into the elementary schools needs to be made more adaptive. Some cities have instituted "reading readiness" classes where slow readers and non-readers are detained and prepared until they are ready for the ordinary methods of group instruction. By individualized devices the children are given visual and language experience which naturally precede the printed page: experiences in drawing, in reading pictures, in observation, in conversation. This arrangement has had a beneficial, liberalizing effect upon the primary school. It has obliged teachers and parents to take more intelligent note of individual differences in visual and motor abilities, in speech, in social experience, and in the emotional maturity and home life of school beginners.

However, if the organization of the public school were fundamentally more flexible and more closely articulated with a supervisory hygiene of the preschool period, the problem of reading readiness would not become acute or magnified. There is too much emphasis on "homogeneous groupings" and too little utilization of the educational benefits which come from bringing children of diverse ages into close association. And there is too much emphasis on reading—at age six. The promotion of optimal growth is a more important objective.

When culture and child come into conflict it is time to be mindful of growth factors. Reading is a major cultural goal set up by society in an age which is strongly eye-minded. Important as the goal may be, it can not be realized through sheer drill and direct pressure. Concessions must be made to the nascent needs and to the patterns of individual development.

Reading as here discussed simply serves as an illustration of an important principle which applies to numberless situations where the equipment of the child and the demands of modern culture do not coincide. The child is confronted by a multitude of similar situations along the devious pathways of preschool development. The acquisition of bladder and bowel control; "habits" of eating and of sleeping; the transition from liquid to solid foods; adaptations to clothing, cleanliness, neatness, caution; table manners; right-handed handshakes; respect for possessions; cooperative play—these are only a few of an endless procession of problems.

For the child they are problems of development. The adult should regard them likewise. On a practical plane adult society must approach the problems not through authoritarian concepts of habituation, but through a philosophy which recognizes and builds on the progressive relativities of growth. In this sense, growth again proves itself a key concept for defining the tasks of child guidance.

The present volume has been designed to foster a developmental approach to the tasks of child guidance, whether these tasks relate to the everyday problems of home and nursery, or to the graver problems of a clinic. Previous chapters have detailed the gradations of growth, in order to emphasize the relative interdependencies which characterize the development of intelligence and personality. Narrow, mechanical psychometry would defeat the purpose of an individualized developmental psychology of the preschool child. The chief aim of this form of psychology is to identify and to interpret the *processes* of mental growth. An understanding of these processes provides the rationale for practical procedures in the field of parent and child guidance.

Growth is a unifying concept which rests upon the internal continuity of the whole life cycle. The problems of child guidance at school entrance, accordingly, cannot be envisaged in proper perspective except in terms of the antecedent preschool years. All growth is automatically self-conditioning. Past growth modifies present growth and both project themselves into the future. The fundamental importance of the preschool period rests upon the priority of this period.

It is the most critical epoch in the development of the individual. Death, disease, and accident then take their heaviest toll. We must remind ourselves again of the statistics which so impressively reveal the liabilities of the preschool years in the production or manifestation of defects or hearing and seeing, motor disabilities, stuttering and stammering, spastic palsies, mental deficiency, faulty attitudes, anxieties and insecurity, instabilities and distortions of personality. But assets as well as liabilities trace back to the preschool period. Temperamental traits of strength and promise, superior sensitiveness and perceptiveness, artistic talents, emotional excellence, superior poise and endurance, social adaptability, gifts of leadership, and a host of other latent and nascent powers are discernible in the preschool years.

Many liabilities and assets, however, remain concealed or imperfectly recognized because we lack the social and educational mechanisms for identifying the characteristics of children. Even in infancy there should be a more searching quest for the distinguishing features of individuality. Each infant is an individual with unique patterns and potentialities of development. Nothing less than a broad consecutive system of developmental supervision can bring into timely evidence those traits of weakness and of strength which most concern the family and the community.

For such reasons, we believe, that the next decade will witness a rapidly increasing application of medical, biometric, and psychological procedures, designed to define the assets and liabilities of the infant and young child.

22

EXAMINATION RECORDS AND ARRANGEMENTS

EXAMINATION RECORDS AND ARRANGEMENTS

§ 1. THE DEVELOPMENTAL SCHEDULES

THIS section presents the schedules of development, eleven in number, corresponding to eleven age levels from 15 months through 6 years. The source of these schedules is threefold: (1) the basic survey which cleared the ground and established a *modus operandi* was reported by Gesell in 1925 (30); (2) a more recent follow-up study of a carefully selected normative group of children (whose development during infancy had previously been studied [35,39]) supplied new and revised data for the present volume; (3) in addition, hundreds of preschool children, both normal and atypical, were examined and also re-examined in school years on the clinical service. These examinations taught us how to adapt our observations and procedures to a wide variety of conditions and vastly enriched our experience.

The normative group comprised 107 children and was a selected and homogeneous group. Only healthy subjects were included whose parents were of middle socio-economic status with respect to occupation, schooling, avocational interests and home equipment. The fathers' occupations fell within the 4.98 and 11.74 range of values listed on the Barr scale of occupational intelligence. The parents were born in the United States and the grandparents were of Northern European extraction.

The follow-up normative examinations of these children were made at 18 months, 2, 3, 4, 5 and 6 years by the staff members and one qualified graduate student[1] as follows:

Age	18 mos.	2 yrs.	3 yrs.	4 yrs.	5 yrs.	6 yrs.
Girls	21	19	20	15	33	11
Boys	20	18	16	16	27	7
Total	41	37	36	31	60	18

The voluminous examination protocols were then analyzed. While much is gained by careful control, much is also lost. No investigator completes a piece of work without wishing to do it all over again, incorporating all the things he learned the first time. Here the clinical service proved invaluable because we could modify the strictly established procedure to

---

[1] Examinations at the 18-month and 2-year levels were made by Professor Ruth W. Washburn. The examinations at the 4-year level were made by Pearl F. Gridley, Ph.D., of the National College of Education.

invite new observations and to suggest desirable revisions. Indeed, the clinical service proved to be a constant source of new ideas.

At the conclusion of the research project, the normative analysis told us a detailed and important story of the five basic age levels; our clinical experience provided data for the intermediate ages and built up a more vivid and detailed picture of the course of behavior development. The chapters dealing with the four fundamental fields of behavior describe the sources of the data, and indicate when a situation even though unstandardized is, in our judgment, valuable and revealing.

On the surface, the developmental schedules which follow appear simply to list a series of behavior items according to developmental maturity. Actually the schedules do much more than that. For each age level the schedule presents a group of items which forms a constellation of related behavior and which is in effect a thumbnail characterization of normal behavior at that age.

Application of the schedules is a simple matter of determining how well a child's behavior fits one age level constellation rather than another, by the method of direct comparison. Single items do not have age value, are not weighted, added or subtracted; the aggregate picture tells the story. There is nothing mathematical in this determination, neither is there anything mystical about it. It amounts to matching, which is neither calculation nor intuition; it is an entirely different process. Colorimetry uses the same principle.

Applying the schedules in this way does, however, require an intimate knowledge of what the constellations are, their essential characteristics, their accessory and more decorative characteristics. This implies a knowledge of much more than is presented in the schedules which give only an extracted, representative part of the total constellations. A knowledge of the course through which the development of each function must go enables an examiner to understand and to evaluate in terms of maturity all the behavior he sees, regardless of the apparent success or failure of performance. The child who piles the three formboard blocks instead of placing them in the holes is not failing a test, he is demonstrating his level of maturity; so is the child who throws all the test materials to the floor.

Matching child to schedule and arriving at a determination of maturity is simple enough when development is symmetrical in the four fields of behavior: motor, adaptive, language, and personal-social. When growth is asymmetrical, however, or when there is a great deal of scattering even within one field, the problem is less simple, though not insoluble. It is in just these instances that the psychometrically-minded would like to calculate and arrive at a compromise value; it is in just these instances that we insist that a compromise value is meaningless. If a child's maturity levels on examination are shown to be: Motor 36 months, Adaptive 42 months, Language 30 months, Personal-social 30-36 months, he is not in any way represented by an average of 34, but he is represented fairly and descriptively by the following behavior values: Motor 36 months, Adaptive 42 months, Language 30 months, Personal-social 30-36 months.

.   .   .   .

The schedules are presented on the following pages together with brief explanatory notes and reminders of the exact meaning of the items. The reader will note that an occasional item is marked (F). This designation indicates that the behavior is *focal*, in other words, peculiarly characteristic of the age at which it is placed; it is not ordinarily seen before that age and it is not seen *after* that age. The child may thus "fail" a focal item because he is not mature enough, or because he is too mature, in which latter case the "failure" becomes an indication of greater rather than lesser maturity. In all other instances failure is presumably due either to immaturity, retardation, lack of interest or cooperation, or to inappropriateness of the test.

To eliminate an enormous mass of tabular data, the normative percentage values of the behavior items, in terms of the group of children examined, have been given whenever available for the age level under consideration and for the preceding age, to give an indication of the trend and frequency of the performance. The 50 percentile has been chosen as the critical percentile. When a behavior item has been interpolated (placed between two ages on the basis of the determinations at those two ages) the percentage values of the preceding and following ages have been given. Percentages in parentheses are based on clinical cases. The clinical groups are less homogeneous than the normative cases, but consist of from twenty to thirty relatively normal children. The clinical percentages are in close agreement with the normative trends and are presented because of their indicativeness. Normative figures have been given in preference to clinical figures whenever they were available.

No percentages are given for the personal-social behavior items because of the variability of these items due to training and personality factors. These items are somewhat arbitrarily, though very liberally, assigned to the various age levels, as explained in Chapter IX. There is also a dearth of percentage values for various motor abilities, particularly at the older ages; for these items we are largely indebted to the literature, as indicated in Chapter VI.

Explanatory Notes and Reminders

The procedures for administering the test and observation items listed in the Developmental Schedule have been detailed in Part Two, Chapters VI-IX. In case of doubt the reader should consult these chapters for specific directions. The following notes are supplied for convenient reference to clarify the abbreviations of statement and to recall the details of order and method. The items are identified by the same designations which appear in the body of the volume.

15-MONTH LEVEL

(M) MOTOR			52 wks.	56 wks.	15 mos.
M-1	WALKS:	few steps, starts and stops........	26*	44	(56)
M-1	WALKS:	falls by collapse (F).............			
M-1	WALKS:	has discarded creeping...........	0	20	(54)
M-2	STAIRS:	creeps up full flight (r)...........			(48)
M-17	CUBES:	tower of 2......................	16	43	(77)
M-18	PELLET:	places in bottle.................	25	40	(78)
M-22	BOOK:	helps turn pages.................			(78)

(A) ADAPTIVE					
A-2	CUBES:	tower of 2......................	14	43	(77)
A-7	CUP AND CUBES:	6 in and out cup (F)...	0		(65)
A-20	DRAWING:	incipient imitation stroke......			(41)
A-12	FORMBOARD:	places round block........	18	38	(64)
A-12	FORMBOARD:	adapts round block promptly	19		(64)

(L) LANGUAGE					
L-2	VOCABULARY:	4–6 words or names (r)...		36	(76)
L-2	Uses JARGON (r)......................				(90)
L-1	BOOK:	pats picture (F).................			(52)
L-6	PICTURE CARD:	points to dog or own shoe			(63)

(P-S) PERSONAL-SOCIAL

    FEEDING: has discarded bottle
    FEEDING: inhibits grasp of dish on tray
    TOILET: partial toilet regulation
    TOILET: bowel control
    TOILET: indicates wet pants
    COMMUNICATION: says "ta-ta" or equivalent
    COMMUNICATION: indicates wants (points or
        vocalizes)
    PLAY: shows or offers toy to mother or examiner
    PLAY: casts objects playfully or in refusal

* The vertical columns carry percentage frequencies. Percentages based on the clinical group of cases are shown within parentheses. (F) = focal item, see p. 321; (r) reported; i = interpolated.

15 Months

MOTOR

M-1 WALKS: few steps; starts and stops
More is required than the ability to take a few steps alone. Taking a few tottering steps from one person to another, or from one chair to another, is not sufficient to score this item; the child should have enough control so that he can stop and start again without support.

M-1 WALKS: falls by collapse
Frequent falling is characteristic of early walking, and this falling is accomplished by sitting down suddenly without losing balance.

M-1 WALKS: has discarded creeping
This item implies that walking is the child's preferential method of locomotion and that if speed or efficiency is desired he will not revert to a more primitive method. Under stress of great fatigue he may, however, still occasionally creep.

M-18 PELLET: places in bottle
On command or gesture, or spontaneously. No demonstration necessary.

ADAPTIVE

A-2 CUBES: tower of two
Demonstration—the tower should stand.

A-7 CUP AND CUBES: six in and out cup
The examiner urges the child to fill the cup and to continue filling rather than emptying the cup. Consecutive cubes may even be offered the child.

A-20 DRAWING: incipient imitation stroke
Although less than half of the children of this age display this behavior, it is highly significant when seen. The item is judged not so much by the product of the crayon as by the movement made by the child in attempting to imitate the stroke. He frequently starts to respond stroke-wise and then scribbles instead.

A-12 FORMBOARD: places round block
Spontaneously or after command, pointing, or demonstration. Inserts completely.

A-12 FORMBOARD: adapts round block promptly
A large percentage of the children who can be interested in this situation will make a prompt, adaptive placement or near-placement of the round block when the formboard is rotated, though it is seldom that the performance is repeated, due to the very brief span of interest at this age.

LANGUAGE

L-1 BOOK: pats picture
Spontaneously or after examiner has pointed.

L-6 PICTURE CARD: points to dog or own shoe
In response to question, "Where is the dog—the shoe?"

PERSONAL-SOCIAL

FEEDING: Has discarded bottle
Includes night bottle.

TOILET: partial toilet regulation
Responds to regular placements on the toilet (not invariably) but does not indicate toilet needs, and does not wait to be taken to toilet if need is not correctly anticipated. Toilet "accidents" are fairly common occurrences.

TOILET: bowel control
Does not indicate toilet needs, but responds to toilet placement at a regular hour.

TOILET: indicates wet pants
By squirming, pulling at pants, fussing, etc.

COMMUNICATION: says "ta-ta" or equivalent
Spontaneously on giving or receiving an object.

PLAY: casts objects playfully or in refusal
A very characteristic pattern at this age and one which frequently interferes with examination responses. It is frequently seen in defective children who are operating at a 15-month-level.

PLAY: shows or offers toys to mother or examiner
During the examination.

18-MONTH LEVEL

(M) MOTOR			15 mos.	18 mos.
M-1	WALKS: seldom falls..............................			
M-1	WALKS: fast, runs stiffly (F).......................		(24)	(82)
M-2	STAIRS: walks up, one hand held..................			61
M-2	STAIRS: up and down unassisted, any method.......		(9)	54
M-5	SMALL CHAIR: seats self.........................		(26)	51
M-5	ADULT CHAIR: climbs into.......................		(43)	(75)
M-8	BALL: hurls.....................................			
M-9	LARGE BALL: walks into (F).....................			(53)
M-22	BOOK: turns pages 2–3 at a time.................			(45)

(A) ADAPTIVE				
A-2	CUBES: tower of 3–4............................		(27)	77
A-7	CUP AND CUBES: 10 into cup....................		(29)	60
A-8	PELLET: dumps responsively......................			65
A-16	DRAWING: scribbles spontaneously................		(12)	57
A-20	DRAWING: makes stroke imitatively...............		(10)	(52)
A-12	FORMBOARD: piles 3 (F)........................			(66)

(L) LANGUAGE				
L-2	VOCABULARY: 10 words including names (r).......		(32)	50
L-1	BOOK: looks selectively..........................		(30)	(62)
L-6	PICTURE CARDS: names or points one...........			66
L-4	BALL: names....................................			(53)
L-5	BALL: 2 directions...............................			(62)

(P-S) PERSONAL-SOCIAL

FEEDING: hands empty dish to mother

FEEDING: feeds self in part, spilling

TOILET: toilet regulated daytime

PLAY: pulls a toy

PLAY: carries or hugs doll or teddy bear

18 Months

MOTOR

M-1 WALKS: fast, runs stiffly
Two alternate items. The stiff running is best described in terms of the very upright posture that is maintained. Any leaning forward in the direction of the run would result in falling.

M-2 STAIRS: up and down unassisted, any method
Creeping or climbing up, backing or bumping down, or walking by banister or unaided. Many children of this age have no opportunity to go up and down stairs.

M-5 SMALL CHAIR: seats self
Any successful method that involves preliminary standing with back to chair. The child often peers between his legs or turns his head to assure himself that his aim is accurate, or he may squat down a little to one side of the chair and then slide over into position. Straddling the chair is more advanced.

M-5 ADULT CHAIR: climbs into
The child faces the chair, climbs up, then turns around to sit down.

M-8 BALL: hurls
As opposed to dropping with simple cast; it also implies throwing in the standing position. The younger child sits down to play ball.

M-9 LARGE BALL: walks into
After demonstration of kicking. He is not permitted to hold wall, adult's hand, etc., for support.

ADAPTIVE

A-2 CUBES: tower of three–four
He may need demonstration to begin and urging to continue. The tower should stand.

A-7 CUP AND CUBES: ten into cup
Spontaneously or with urging and demonstration.

A-8 PELLET: dumps responsively
In response to "Get it out." Hooking the pellet with the finger (rare) is an equivalent response; shaking it out is more primitive.

A-20 DRAWING: makes stroke imitatively
The stroke is imitated, without regard to direction. A stroke immediately obliterated by scribbling is a correct response in an overproductive child.

A-12 FORMBOARD: piles three
On formboard or table. This is usually the spontaneous performance when confronted with the situation.

LANGUAGE

L-1 BOOK: looks selectively
At the pictures. He may not point or name, but when asked, "Where is the dog?" etc., he definitely regards the dog.

L-5 BALL: two directions
Throwing the ball at the chair, table, or mother, is acceptable. Seating self on chair, holding ball, is not acceptable.

PERSONAL-SOCIAL

FEEDING: feeds self in part, spilling
Means part of the meal without any direct help.

TOILET: regulated, daytime
Responds to regular toilet placements. The responsibility is the mother's but she is able to keep the child dry all day with only rare "accidents." He does not indicate his toilet needs but he will wait a reasonable length of time for an opportunity to use the toilet.

21-MONTH LEVEL

(M) MOTOR		18 mos.	21 mos.	24 mos.
M-1	WALKS: squats in play (r)................			
M-2	STAIRS: walks down, hand held..........			
M-2	STAIRS: walks up, holding rail..........			
M-5	ADULT CHAIR: gets down, no help......			
M-9	LARGE BALL: kicks on demonstration.....	(25)	(56)	
M-17	CUBES: tower of 5–6....................	27	i	76
M-19	PAPER: folds once imitatively............	32	i	62

(A) ADAPTIVE				
A-2	CUBES: tower of 5–6....................	27	i	76
A-3	CUBES: imitates pushing train............	(42)	(57)	
A-11	PAPER: folds once, imitatively...........	32	i	62
A-12	FORMBOARD: places 2 or 3.............	30	i	87
A-10	PERFORMANCE BOX: inserts corner of square (F)...........................	(26)	(58)	
A-10	PERFORMANCE BOX: retrieves ball from	(21)	(56)	

(L) LANGUAGE				
L-2	VOCABULARY: 20 words (r)............	(36)	(57)	
L-2	COMBINES: 2–3 words spontaneously (r)...	(33)	(57)	
L-5	BALL: 3 directions......................	(25)	(50)	

(P-S) PERSONAL-SOCIAL

FEEDING: handles cup well, lifting, drinking, re-placing

COMMUNICATION: asks for food, toilet, drink

COMMUNICATION: echoes 2 or more last words

COMMUNICATION: pulls person to show

21 Months

MOTOR

M-1 WALKS: squats in play
Implies sufficient control and balance so that this position can be maintained for several minutes while playing on the floor or ground.

M-9 LARGE BALL: kicks on demonstration
Swings leg, foot striking the ball a sharp blow; the child is not permitted to hold the wall, etc.

M-19 PAPER: folds once imitatively
After demonstration. Creasing is not implied.

ADAPTIVE

A-2 CUBES: tower of five–six
May need demonstration to begin and urging to continue. The tower should stand.

A-3 CUBES: imitates pushing train
One or more cubes.

A-12 FORMBOARD: places two or three
In formboard, at any time during the situation.

A-10 PERFORMANCE BOX: inserts corner or square
Spontaneously or after demonstration of insertion. Does not completely insert square.

A-10 PERFORMANCE BOX: retrieves ball from
Any method such as pushing the box over, lifting and tilting the box, creeping into the box after overturning it. If the performance seems highly acci-dental, repeat. The situation cannot be used with very tall children who are able to reach the ball (rare at 21 months). This is an excellent situation in which to observe the reactions of the individual child in the face of difficulties, his persistence, ingenuity, emotional responses, etc.

LANGUAGE

L-2 COMBINES: two–three words spontaneously
Such combinations as "all gone," "big boy," "oh, dear," do not score. "Daddy go," " 'bye mama," "baby bed" are acceptable combinations.

L-5 BALL: three directions
Throwing at correct objective is acceptable. Seating self on chair holding the ball is not acceptable.

PERSONAL-SOCIAL

FEEDING: handles cup well, lifting, drinking, replacing
The younger child tilts the cup too far so that he spills profusely; he is also apt to drop or throw the cup when finished drinking.

COMMUNICATION: asks for food, toilet, drink
By gesture or word.

COMMUNICATION: echoes two or more last words
That adult has said.

COMMUNICATION: pulls person to show
For example, taking the mother's hand and leading her to the kitchen sink, as compared with standing at the sink pointing and vocalizing "uh-uh" at an earlier age.

24-MONTH LEVEL

			18 mos	*24 mos.*
(M) MOTOR				
M-1	RUNS: without falling............................		12	48
M-2	STAIRS: walks up and down alone.................			
M-9	LARGE BALL: kicks.............................			(59)
M-17	CUBES: tower of 6–7............................		20	56
M-22	BOOK: turns pages singly........................			
(A) ADAPTIVE				
A-2	CUBES: tower of 6–7............................		20	56
A-3	CUBES: aligns 2 or more, train....................		23	62
A-20	DRAWING: imitates V stroke......................		47	79
A-20	DRAWING: imitates circular stroke.................		32	59
A-28	SENTENCES: repeats 3–4 syllables.................			50
A-12	FORMBOARD: places blocks on board separately (F)		(28)	(63)
A-12	FORMBOARD: adapts in 4 trials...................		8	62
A-10	PERFORMANCE BOX: inserts square..............		29	70
(L) LANGUAGE				
L-2	SPEECH: has discarded jargon.....................			
L-2	SPEECH: 3-word sentence.........................			73
L-2	SPEECH: uses I, me, and you......................			48
L-6	PICTURE CARDS: names 3 or more................		2	57
L-6	PICTURE CARDS: identifies 5 or more.............		2	55
L-4	TEST OBJECTS: names 2..........................			(74)
L-5	BALL: 4 directions correct........................			51

(P-S) PERSONAL-SOCIAL

FEEDING: inhibits turning of spoon
TOILET: dry at night if taken up
TOILET: verbalizes toilet needs fairly consistently (r)
DRESSING: pulls on simple garment
COMMUNICATION: verbalizes immediate experiences
COMMUNICATION: refers to himself by his name
COMMUNICATION: comprehends and asks for "another"
PLAY: hands full cup of cubes to examiner
PLAY: plays with domestic mimicry (doll, teddy bear, etc.)
PLAY: parallel play predominates

24 Months

MOTOR

M-1 RUNS well
Without falling but still not very fast. Balance while hurrying.

M-2 STAIRS: walks up and down alone
May use banister.

M-9 LARGE BALL: kicks
On verbal command without demonstration. The examiner may say, "Kick it with your *foot*."

ADAPTIVE

A-2 CUBES: tower of six—seven
May need demonstration to start and urging to continue. Tower should stand.

A-3 CUBES: aligns two or more, train
In response to train demonstration.

A-12 FORMBOARD: places on board separately
Not necessarily in holes or in relation to correct holes. Usually the spontaneous response.

A-12 FORMBOARD: adapts in four trials
To rotation of the board. Trial and error or better.

A-10 PERFORMANCE BOX: inserts square
Spontaneously or after demonstration.

LANGUAGE

L-2 SPEECH: *I, me,* and *you*
Not necessarily correctly.

L-6 PICTURE CARDS: identifies five or more
By naming or pointing.

L-5 BALL: four directions correct
Throwing the ball at the correct objectives is acceptable.

PERSONAL-SOCIAL

FEEDING: inhibits turning of spoon
At least until spoon is in mouth.

TOILET: dry at night if taken up
All night.

DRESS: pulls on simple garment
Sox, mittens, pulls up pants.

COMMUNICATION: verbalizes immediate experiences
Soliloquizes on his activities as he performs them.

PLAY: plays with domestic mimicry
Puts doll to bed, covers with blankets, pretends to feed, etc.

PLAY: parallel play predominates
Plays beside another child, often engaging in the same activity, but quite separately.

30-MONTH LEVEL

(M) MOTOR		24 mos.	30 mos.	36 mos.
M-1	WALKS on tiptoe (demonstration).........			
M-4	JUMPS with both feet....................			
M-10	Tries to STAND on one foot..............			
M-17	CUBES: tower of 8......................	27	i	79
M-20	HOLDS crayon by fingers................			

(A) ADAPTIVE				
A-2	CUBES: tower of 8......................	27	i	79
A-3	CUBES: adds chimney to train...........	15	i	96
A-20	DRAWING: 2 or more strokes for cross (F)..	24	(72)	
A-20	DRAWING: imitates V and H strokes......	32	(50)	
A-14	COLOR FORMS: places 1..............	(45)	(68)	
A-12	FORMBOARD: places 3 blocks on presentation................................	(37)	57	
A-12	FORMBOARD: adapts repeatedly, error (F)	(22)	(48)	
A-27	DIGITS: repeats 2, 1 of 3 trials...........	25	i	85

(L) LANGUAGE				
L-7	FULL NAME (including r)..............		(52)	
L-6	PICTURE CARDS: Names 5.............	(17)	(43)	
L-6	PICTURE CARDS: Identifies 7..........	(17)	(67)	
L-4	TEST OBJECTS: gives use..............	(28)	(58)	

(P-S) PERSONAL-SOCIAL

COMMUNICATION: refers to self by pronoun rather than name

COMMUNICATION: shows repetitiveness in speech and other activities

PLAY: pushes a toy with good steering

PLAY: helps put things away

PLAY: can carry breakable object

30 Months

MOTOR

M-1 WALKS: on tiptoe
Demonstration—hand may be held at first.

M-4 JUMPS: with both feet
In place.

M-16 Tries to STAND on one foot
The examiner demonstrates; maintaining the pose to encourage the child to do so. The younger child refuses this situation.

M-20 HOLDS crayon by fingers
As opposed to holds in fist.

ADAPTIVE

A-2 CUBES: tower of eight
May need demonstration to start and urging to continue. The tower should stand.

A-3 CUBES: adds chimney to train
The examiner may ask, "Where is the chimney?"

A-20 DRAWING: two or more strokes for cross
Scores only if response differs from the child's response to stroke demonstration.

A-14 COLOR FORMS: places one
Round form may be demonstrated.

A-12 FORMBOARD: places three blocks on presentation
Spontaneously, or in response to "Put them in."

A-12 FORMBOARD: adapts repeatedly, error
Usually solved with error on the first rotation, but subsequent trials do not eliminate the error.

LANGUAGE

L-7 FULL NAME
Includes nickname for first name.

L-4 TEST OBJECTS: gives use
Of one or more objects. Liberal scoring, for example: "What do you do with the key?" Answer: "Door"; is acceptable.

PERSONAL-SOCIAL

COMMUNICATION: refers to self by pronoun rather than by name
May confuse *I* and *me*.

COMMUNICATION: shows repetitiveness in speech and other activities
Makes a remark over and over; tends to want things done always in the same way—ritualistic.

23

36-MONTH LEVEL

(M) MOTOR		24 mos.	30 mos.	36 mos.
M-2	STAIRS: alternates feet going up..........			
M-4	JUMPS: from bottom stair...............			
M-6	RIDES tricycle using pedals...............			
M-10	STANDS on one foot, momentary balance..			
M-12	PELLETS: 10 into bottle (within 30 sec.).....			50

(A) ADAPTIVE				
A-2	CUBES: tower of 9 (10 on 3 trials)........	9	(29)	58
A-4	CUBES: imitates bridge..................	9		80
A-9	PELLETS: 10 into bottle (within 30 sec.)...			50
A-16	DRAWING: names own drawing..........	6		77
A-18	DRAWING: names incomplete man.......			54
A-21	DRAWING: copies circle.................		(5)	86
A-20	DRAWING: imitates cross................		(5)	77
A-14	COLOR FORMS: places 3...............		(16)	(57)
A-15	GEOMETRIC FORMS: points to 4.......		(5)	54
A-12	FORMBOARD: adaptation without error or immediate correction of error...........		(24)	(59)
A-27	DIGITS: repeats 3 (1 of 3 trials)...........			59
A-28	SENTENCES: repeats 6–7 syllables........	9		61

(L) LANGUAGE				
L-1	PICTURE BOOK: gives action..........		(30)	(72)
L-2	Uses PLURALS........................		(24)	(74)
L-6	PICTURE CARDS: names 8.............		(5)	57
L-8	PICTURE: enumerates 3 objects.........		(28)	62
L-9	ACTION AGENT: 7 correct..............		(0)	50
L-10	Tells SEX............................			73
L-11	COMPREHENSION QUESTIONS A: answers 1............................			65
L-12	DIRECTIONS: obeys 2 prepositions, ball and chair.................................		(10)	(75)

(P-S) PERSONAL-SOCIAL

FEEDING: feeds self with little spilling
FEEDING: pours well from pitcher
DRESSING: puts on shoes
DRESSING: unbuttons front and side buttons
COMMUNICATION: asks questions rhetorically
COMMUNICATION: understands taking turns
COMMUNICATION: knows a few rhymes

36 Months

MOTOR

M-2 STAIRS: alternates feet going up

A foot to a step.

M-4 JUMPS: from bottom stair

Both feet.

M-10 STANDS on one foot, momentary balance

The examiner demonstrates and maintains the pose to encourage the child to do so. He may be timed by slow counting.

M-12 PELLETS: ten into bottle (within 30 sec.)

Using one hand only, one pellet at a time.

ADAPTIVE

A-2 CUBES: tower of nine (ten on three trials)

Tower should stand. May need urging to try again.

A-4 CUBES: imitates bridge

Demonstration.

A-16 DRAWING: names own drawing

Spontaneously, or in response to "What is it?"

A-18 DRAWING: names incomplete man

Calls it man, girl, bunny, Mickey Mouse, etc.

A-14 COLOR FORMS: matches three

Round form may be demonstrated.

A-15 GEOMETRIC FORMS: points to four

Direct matching not allowed.

LANGUAGE

L-1 PICTURE BOOK: gives action

In response to question, "What is . . . doing?"

PERSONAL-SOCIAL

FEEDING: pours well from pitcher

Small pitcher.

DRESSING: puts on shoes

Not necessarily on correct feet.

COMMUNICATION: asks questions rhetorically

He knows the answer; often asks a question because he wishes it to be asked of him.

42-MONTH LEVEL

		36 mos.	42 mos.	48 mos.
(M) MOTOR				
M-10	STANDS on 1 foot for 2 seconds...........			
M-11	WALKING BOARDS: walks on with both feet....................................			
M-13	DRAWING: traces diamond..............			
(A) ADAPTIVE				
A-4	CUBES: builds bridge from model.........	35	i	100
A-15	GEOMETRIC FORMS: points to 6.......	38	i	82
A-27	DIGITS: repeats 3 (2 of 3 trials)...........		i	75
A-32	WEIGHTS: gives heavy block (2 of 3 trials)..	44	i	73
(L) LANGUAGE				
L-6	PICTURE CARDS: names all............	(5)	i	
L-9	ACTION AGENT: 9 correct..............	28	i	83
L-11	COMPREHENSION QUESTIONS A: answers 2...........................	40	i	80
L-12	DIRECTIONS: obeys 3 prepositions, ball and chair.................................		i	70

(P-S) PERSONAL-SOCIAL

DRESSING: washes and dries hands or face

PLAY: associative group play taking place of parallel play

42 Months

MOTOR

M-10 STANDS on one foot for 2 sec.

The examiner demonstrates and maintains the pose to encourage the child to do so. He may be timed by slow counting.

M-11 WALKING BOARDS: walks with both feet

The younger child walks the boards with one foot on the ground, and one foot on the board.

ADAPTIVE

A-4 CUBES: builds bridge from model

No demonstration.

A-32 WEIGHTS: gives heavy block (two or three trials)

Of two, the lighter and heavier. Examiner may demonstrate lifting and testing the blocks.

LANGUAGE

L-6 PICTURE CARDS: names all without a specific question for each picture.

PERSONAL-SOCIAL

DRESSING: washes and dries hands or face

Without reminder to dry; washing or drying may not be very efficient.

PLAY: assocative group play taking place of parallel play

Several children engage in same activity with frequent cross reference and comment.

48-MONTH LEVEL

		36 mos.	48 mos.
(M) MOTOR			
M-2	STAIRS: walks down, last few steps a foot to a step...		
M-3	SKIPS on one foot..................................		
M-4	JUMPS: running or standing broad jump............		
M-8	BALL: throws overhand...........................		
M-10	STANDS on 1 foot, 4–8 seconds...................		
M-11	WALKING BOARDS: walks 6 cm. board, touching ground once to balance.........................		
M-12	PELLETS in bottle: (10 in 25 sec.)................		50
(A) ADAPTIVE			
A-5	CUBES: imitates gate.............................	6	60
A-9	PELLETS in bottle: (10 in 25 sec.).................		50
A-17	DRAWING: man with 2 parts......................	12	52
A-21	DRAWING: copies cross...........................	14	55
A-18	DRAWING: adds 3 parts incomplete man...........	0	53
A-25	DRAWING: 1 bubble, correctly placed..............		61
A-11	PAPER: folds and creases 3 times on demonstration....	36	i
A-15	GEOMETRIC FORMS: Points to 8.................	23	57
A-28	SENTENCES: repeats 1 of 3 (12, 13 syllables)........		50 .
A-19	MISSING PARTS: 1 correct.......................		52
A-23	COUNTS: with correct pointing 3 objects............		
A-32	WEIGHTS: selects heavier (3 of 3 trials).............		55
(L) LANGUAGE			
L-9	ACTION AGENT: 13 correct......................	5	58
L-14	COLOR CARD: names 1.........................		74
L-12	DIRECTIONS: obeys 4 prepositions, ball and chair...		52

(P-S) PERSONAL-SOCIAL

DRESSING: can wash and dry face and hands; brush teeth

DRESSING: dresses and undresses if supervised

DRESSING: laces shoes

DRESSING: distinguishes front and back of clothes

PLAY: plays cooperatively with other children

PLAY: builds building with blocks

DEVELOPMENTAL DETACHMENT: goes on errands outside home (without crossing street)

DEVELOPMENTAL DETACHMENT: tends to go out of prescribed bounds

48 Months

MOTOR

M-3 SKIPS: on one foot
The alternate foot takes a walking step forward.

M-4 JUMPS: running or standing broad jump
Both feet, as from one rug to another.

M-10 STANDS on one foot, 4-8 sec.
The examiner demonstrates and maintains the pose to encourage the child to do so. He may be timed by slow counting.

ADAPTIVE

A-5 CUBES: imitates gate
Demonstration. If fails, the examiner may ask, "Is it just like this one?"

A-17 DRAWING: man with two parts
As head and eyes, or head and legs.

A-18 DRAWING: adds three parts to the incomplete man
Ear may be demonstrated.

A-11 PAPER: folds and creases three times on demonstration
The creases should be sufficiently well made to leave a permanent record on the paper.

A-19 MISSING PARTS: one correct
Eye may be demonstrated.

A-23 COUNTS: with correct pointing, three objects
And answers, "How many?"

A-32 WEIGHTS: selects heavier (three of three trials)
Of two (the lighter and heavier). The examiner may demonstrate method of lifting and testing blocks.

PERSONAL-SOCIAL

DRESSING: laces shoes
Essentially correctly, but without tying.

PLAY: plays cooperatively with other children
Group play in which each child takes a part. "I'll be the mother and you be the baby," or "I'll build the walks and you fix the roof."

PLAY: builds building with blocks
Spontaneously in the cube situation. On questioning usually says it is a house, or garage, etc.

DEVELOPMENTAL DETACHMENT: tends to go out of bounds
Out of yard, also to exceed restrictions in many other ways, even in speech, "I won't."

54-MONTH LEVEL

(M) MOTOR		48 mos.	54 mos.	60 mos.
M-3	HOPS on 1 foot.........................			
M-7	ARTICULATION: no longer infantile.....	44	i	66
M-13	DRAWING: traces cross..................			

(A) ADAPTIVE				
A-5	CUBES: makes gate from model...........	23	i	75
A-21	DRAWING: copies square................			
A-25	DRAWING: 3 bubbles correct.............	11	i	75
A-15	GEOMETRIC FORMS: points to 9 of 10..	36	i	88
A-23	COUNTS: 4 objects......................	22	i	87
A-31	Makes AESTHETIC COMPARISON.....	36	i	75
A-19	MISSING PARTS: 2 correct..............	24	i	75
A-27	DIGITS: repeats 4, 1 of 3 trials............	22	i	58

(L) LANGUAGE				
L-9	ACTION AGENT: 14 correct.............	49	i	79
L-13	DEFINES in terms of use: 4 correct (F).....	26	i	77
L-11	COMPREHENSION QUESTIONS B: 1 correct.............................	27	i	

(P-S) PERSONAL-SOCIAL

COMMUNICATION: calls attention to own performance

COMMUNICATION: relates fanciful stories

COMMUNICATION: bosses and criticizes others

PLAY: shows off dramatically

54 Months

MOTOR

M-3 HOPS: on one foot
Hops forward.

ADAPTIVE

A-25 DRAWING: three bubbles correct
Correct number and placement.
A-23 COUNTS: four objects
And answers, "How many?"
A-31 Makes AESTHETIC COMPARISON
All correct.

A-19 MISSING PARTS: two correct
Eye may be demonstrated.

PERSONAL-SOCIAL

COMMUNICATION: Calls attention to own performance
"See what I did!" etc.
COMMUNICATION: Bosses and criticizes others
Other children. "He talks funny," etc.

60-MONTH LEVEL

		48 mos.	60 mos.	72 mos.
(M) MOTOR				
M-3	SKIPS using feet alternately..............			
M-10	STANDS on 1 foot more than 8 seconds....			
M-11	WALKING BOARDS: 6 cm. board, without stepping off for full length...............			
M-12	PELLETS: 10 into bottle (20 sec.).........		50	
(A) ADAPTIVE				
A-6	CUBES: builds 2 steps....................		61	
A-17	DRAWING: unmistakable man with body, arms, legs, feet, mouth, nose, eyes. (See p. 152 for individual percentages.)			
A-21	DRAWING: copies triangle...............	0	40	96
A-21	DRAWING: copies rectangle with diagonals (66 mos.)............................		48	
A-18	DRAWING: adds 7 parts incomplete man..	10	54	
A-25	DRAWING: correctly places just 1, 2, 3, 4 bubbles..............................	7	61	
A-23	COUNTS: 10 objects correctly............	5	72	
A-23	COUNTS: 12 objects correctly (66 mos.)....		42	88
A-32	WEIGHTS: not more than 1 error in 5 block test..................................	15	55	
A-24	Gives correct no. fingers separate hands.....		66	
(L) LANGUAGE				
L-15	NAMES: penny, nickle and dime..........	25	60	
L-9	ACTION AGENT: 15 correct.............	33	46	
L-14	NAMES COLORS......................	19	63	
L-8	PICTURE: some descriptive comment with enumeration.........................	25	75	
L-11	COMPREHENSION QUESTIONS B: 2 correct........·.....................	20	i	
L-16	3 COMMISSIONS........................			

(P-S) PERSONAL-SOCIAL

DRESSING: dresses and undresses without assistance
COMMUNICATION: asks meaning of words
PLAY: dresses up in clothes belonging to grownups
PLAY: can print a few letters (60–66 months)

60 Months

MOTOR

M-10 STANDS on one foot more than 8 sec.

The examiner demonstrates and holds the pose to encourage the child to do so. He may be timed by slow counting.

M-12 PELLETS: ten into bottle (20 sec.)

Using only one hand, one pellet at a time.

ADAPTIVE

A-6 CUBES: builds two steps

In response to ten-cube model of four steps.

A-18 DRAWING: adds seven parts to incomplete man

Ear may be demonstrated.

A-23 COUNTS: ten objects correctly

And answers, "How many?"

A-23 COUNTS: twelve objects correctly (66 months)

And answers, "How many?"

A-24 Gives correct NUMBER FINGERS separate hands

But not total. Not permitted to count them.

LANGUAGE

L-16 Three COMMISSIONS

In correct order.

PERSONAL-SOCIAL

PLAY: can print a few letters (60, 66 months)

Reversals acceptable.

72-MONTH LEVEL

			60 mos.	72 mos.
(M) MOTOR				
	M-4	JUMPS from height of 12″, landing on toes only......		
	M-8	ADVANCED THROWING.......................		
	M-10	STANDS on each foot alt., eyes closed...............		
	M-11	WALKING BOARDS: walks length of 4 cm. board....		
	M-13	DRAWING: copies diamond.......................	9	61
(A) ADAPTIVE				
	A-6	CUBES: builds 3 steps............................	36	67
	A-17	DRAWING: man has neck, hands on arms, clothes....		
	A-17	DRAWING: man's legs are 2-dimensional............	26	67
	A-21	DRAWING: copies diamond.......................	9	61
	A-18	DRAWING: adds 9 parts to incomplete man.........	19	50
	A-32	WEIGHTS: 5 weights, no error, best trial............	40	56
	A-19	MISSING PARTS: all correct......................	20	39
	A-27	DIGITS: 4 correct (2 of 3 trials)....................	43	67
	A-24	Gives correct no. fingers single hand, and total........	17	45
	A-26	ADDS and SUBTRACTS within five................	33	54

(L) LANGUAGE

Binet items to be used here

(P-S) PERSONAL-SOCIAL

DRESSING: ties shoe laces

COMMUNICATION: differentiates A.M. and P.M.

COMMUNICATION: knows right and left (3 of 3) or complete reversal (6 of 6)

COMMUNICATION: recites numbers up to the thirties

72 Months

MOTOR

M-4 JUMPS: from height of twelve inches, landing on toes only
Both feet.

M-10 STANDS on each foot alternately, eyes closed
Examiner demonstrates.

ADAPTIVE

A-6 CUBES: builds three steps
In response to ten-cube step model of four steps.

A-24 Gives correct number FINGERS single hand, and total
Ask: "How many on both hands altogether?"

A-26 ADDS and SUBTRACTS within 5
Answer must be correct. Give concrete problem, as, "If you had three pennies and I gave you one more penny," etc.

PERSONAL-SOCIAL

COMMUNICATION: Differentiates A.M. and P.M.
And answers question, "When does afternoon begin?"

§ 2. THE BEHAVIOR SITUATION SEQUENCES

This section deals with the problem of the best sequence for administering the test situations and, because it is neither economical nor profitable to apply all the tests pertinent to a given age to a given child, some selection in the application of test situations must also be exercised. Some of the situations recounted in Chapters VI, VII and VIII are alternates, others are concerned with the detailed investigation of a particular item of behavior, others require special apparatus or for various other reasons are not always convenient or essential in an examination. In selecting the situations which make up the Standard Situation Sequence, those situations were retained, in general, which cover a fairly wide age range, which have continuity from age to age, and which have a large representation in the developmental schedules. The list of additional situations indicates those situations which are omitted from the Standard Situation Sequence. These situations can be omitted without serious loss of items for developmental appraisal; if the examination is extended to include some of these supplementary situations, this should be done without prejudice to transitions and sustained interest.

The Standard Situation Sequence lists the situations in a suggested basic order for the age levels from 18 months through 5 years, an order which is designed to contribute to and maintain the organic continuity of the examination. Brief comment on the rationale of this order is perhaps not out of place.

The preliminary situation puts the child at ease; once that is accomplished the examiner offers tests that will be helpful in determining the age range of the child's responses. Further tests then serve to narrow this age range, to define and delimit it, exploring all fields of behavior.

At the earlier ages the *Picture Book* (15 months–3 years) is usually appealing and it can be shown at the beginning as an easy introduction to the examination as a whole. If the child is inhibited at first, the examiner can perform for him and arouse his interest, while at the same time gaining his confidence by making no demands on him. The picture book can be reintroduced toward the end of the examination if no response is obtained at the beginning.

The *Cube* situations (15 months–4 years) are introduced next. They have an almost universal appeal and the child is first permitted to do as he pleases with them, and no instructions are given until interest is aroused, or unless some comment is needed to arouse interest. The cube situation is a very useful one to give early in the examination because it covers practically the entire age range. By running rapidly through the various block-building situations the examiner can make a tentative decision as to the age range to be covered by the examination. If the child is

4 years old, for example, and successfully builds the train, bridge, and gate, the examiner will not use up valuable time and interest by giving him 2-year tests; his range will probably be 3-4-5 years. If he builds a tower of only six cubes, and fails to imitate the train and bridge, his range is more likely to be 18 months to 3 years. These indications are, of course, not infallible, and the examiner must be careful not to acquire too rigid a mental set at the outset of the examination, but should be ready to adjust the examination, as it progresses, in an upward or downward direction.

The *Cup and Cubes* (15 months–2 years) are useful in terminating the cube situation at the early ages. The young child likes to put things away. They also serve to introduce the other "putting in" situation, namely, the *Pellet and Bottle* (15 months–2 years) which itself serves to carry the child over the separation from the cubes.

The *Drawing* situations (15 months–5 years) strike a new note (at 5 years they may be the opening situations). Again we permit the child to do as he pleases before suggesting variations. And if he has just failed a block-building test, here is something he can do to his satisfaction. The series of drawing tasks is then given, progressing from the simpler to the more difficult until the upper limit of the child's ability has been determined. Here, however, strict adherence to the standard order is important: imitation-scribble, strokes, circle, cross: copying-circle, cross, square, triangle, diagonals, diamond. The circle should be given between the strokes and the cross to make the cross response more clearly adaptive. The child who cannot copy the circle is not ordinarily asked to copy the cross, but to imitate it. All these small points make for economy and efficiency in examining. At 4-5 years it is important to ask the child to "draw a man" before the Incomplete Man is presented so that his drawing will not be influenced by the latter. A hard task given out of order (the rectangle with diagonals before the square or triangle, for example) may cause a deterioration of response and the child will not do himself justice on the easier task which is well within his ability. If interest begins to flag, the *Incomplete Man* may be given later as a relief from verbal situations. The drawing situations are usually carried pretty well to the saturation point, and there are seldom any difficulties in making the transition to the

Formboard (15 months–3 years). At 15 months only the round form is given; at all the other ages, all three forms. At 18 months, however, if after a short initial trial the child is merely piling the forms on each other, etc., the square and triangle are removed. This is one of the occasions when we reverse the usual order of the easier task first.

The *Color Forms* (30 months–3 years) are presented before the *Geo-*

metric Forms (3-4-5 years) at 3 years to introduce the second situation, to make it more acceptable to the child, and also to determine readiness for the Geometric Forms. The two tests in combination are also useful in determining the ability of the child to adapt to a change in directions, from placing form on form (matching), to pointing (comparison).

The *Picture Cards* (15 months–3 years) are delayed this long in the hope that the child will now be sufficiently at ease to give verbal responses. Pointing is accepted, however, if the child does not answer. They are followed by the *Stanford Pictures* (3-4-5 years). The 3-year-old's success with the picture cards prepares him to meet the more difficult requirements of the Stanford cards.

At 3-4-5 years a series of verbal tests follows: *Action-Agent* (3-4-5 years); *Digits* (2-5 years); *Name, Sex* (3 years); *Comprehension Questions*—A (3-4 years, B (4-5 years); *Definitions* (4-5 years); *AM-PM, Right and Left, Fingers, Addition and Subtraction* (5 years), which can be relieved when it seems desirable by interspersing *Counting*—cubes (3-4 years), pennies (5 years); *Colors* (3-5 years); *Coins, Weights,* and *Missing Parts* (4-5 years). The exact order of the above listed situations is not all-important at 4 and 5 years.

The *Performance Box* (18 months–2 years) comes toward the end of the examination. Because of its size, it is arresting and it renews interest for a few minutes even if the child is beginning to become a little restless. He is permitted one or two insertions of the rod to build up a feeling of success before the square is presented. The *Test Objects* (18 months–30 months) are then presented in rapid succession, ending with the *Ball* (15 months–5 years). At this moment the child may leave the table and for the remainder of the situations he is standing or running about: *Throwing* (18 months–5 years), *Directions* with ball (18 months–2 years), *Prepositions* with ball and chair (3-4 years), *Ball in Performance Box* (18 months–2 years), *Kicking* (18 months–5 years), *Standing on one foot* (3-4-5 years). Other motor tests such as walking, stairs, chair-climbing, running tiptoe, jumping, skipping, hopping, etc., are observed incidentally or elicited informally and opportunistically; supplementary reported information is always helpful.

At the younger ages (18 months–3 years) the shift out of the room can often be facilitated by asking the child to open the door; at 5 years, the *Commissions* test terminates the examination.

STANDARD SITUATION SEQUENCE

18 months	2 years	3 years	4 years	5 years
Book	Book	Book	Cubes	Drawing
Cubes	Cubes	Cubes	spontaneous	spontaneous
spontaneous	spontaneous	spontaneous	bridge	man
tower	tower	tower	gate	letters
train	train	train	Drawing	forms
Cup and cubes	bridge	bridge	spontaneous	incomplete
Pellet and bottle	Cup and cubes	gate	man	man
Drawing	Drawing	Drawing	forms	Coins
spontaneous	spontaneous	spontaneous	incomplete	Count
scribble	strokes	man	man	Weights
strokes	circle	forms	Geometric	Action agent
circle	cross	incomplete	forms	Definitions
Formboard	Formboard	man	Picture cards,	Colors
Picture cards	Picture cards	Color forms	Stanford	Picture cards,
Performance	Digits	Geometric	Action agent	Stanford
box	Performance	forms	Digits	Missing parts
Test objects	box	Formboard	Comprehension	Digits
Ball	Test objects	Picture cards	questions	A.M.–P.M.
throwing	Ball	Picture cards,	—A	Right and left
directions	throwing	Stanford	Definitions	Fingers
performance	directions	Action agent	Comprehension	Addition and
box	performance	Digits	questions	subtraction
kicking	box	Name, sex	—B	Comprehension
Motor	kicking	Comprehension	Colors	questions
	Motor	questions	Missing parts	—B
		—A	Count	Motor
		Count	Coins	Commissions
		Colors	Weights	
		Ball	Ball	
		throwing	throwing	
		prepositions	prepositions	
		Stand 1 foot	Stand 1 foot	
		Motor	Motor	

ADDITIONAL SITUATIONS

18 months	2 years	3 years	4 years	5 years
Folds paper	Gives 1, 2, 3	Gives 1, 2, 3	Gives 1, 2, 3	Cubes
Indicates nose,	cubes	cubes	cubes	Pellets in bottle
etc.	Folds paper	Pellets in bottle	Pellets in bottle	Trace
Ball on table	Sentences	Spontaneous	Trace	Bubbles
	Ball on table	drawing	Bubbles	Geometric
	Puzzle box	Trace diamond	Fold paper	forms
		Fold paper	Goddard form-	Goddard form-
		Goddard form-	board	board
		board	Sentences	Aesthetic
		Weights	Lines	pictures
		Sentences	Orientation	Sentences
		Lines	cards	Orientation
		Orientation	Humor cards	cards
		cards	Garden maze	Humor cards
		Puzzle box	Aesthetic	Garden maze
		Kick ball	pictures	Walking boards
		Walking boards	Kick ball	V-scope
		V-scope	Walking boards	
			V-scope	

24

§ 3. THE INTERVIEW

The preliminary interview is for orientational purposes and makes no pretense of obtaining a complete account of the child. Because it usually precedes the examination, and the child is waiting, it cannot be lengthy; it should, however, include a brief recital of the child's past development and of his present abilities, his responses to daily routines, and his interests and activities. Something of his place in the family circle and the family attitude is almost sure to be gleaned.

Because the child is present, the content of the conversation is somewhat limited and excludes accounts of problems and difficulties. The younger children ordinarily do not pay much attention and probably do not understand a great deal of what is being said; care should be exercised, nonetheless. The older children do listen at intervals but they do not seem to be disturbed or made self-conscious; in fact, they often seem secretly pleased to hear their abilities recounted, particularly if the examiner shows some measure of approval and satisfaction. At 4 and at 5 years, the interview can often be arranged to follow the examination and can be conducted with the child in another room.

General Outline of Interview

(The following items are not to be used *in toto*, but selectively. They are arranged roughly in genetic sequence. See record form, § 8.)

1. Age of child (always check). Status in home, how long?
2. Motor behavior
   Age of walking; walks, falls, runs
   Seats self small chair; climbs into big chair
   Stairs, method, up-down
   Tricycle
   Skipping, jumping, etc.
   Preferred hand
3. Language behavior
   Jargon, gestures,
   Words; enumerate, or estimate vocabulary
   Joins two words; sample sentence
   Tells experiences
   Gives full name
   Songs or nursery rhymes
   Points to parts of body; knows what dog, cat say
   Simple errand, same room
   Fetch an object from another room
   Carry out two commissions, another room

4. Play behavior
    Favorite activity, toy
    Interest in picture books
    Knows pictures, points or names
    Likes story read to him, kind of story
    Doll—carry—put to bed, feed
    Dramatic play
    Imaginary playmates
    Prints a few letters

5. Domestic behavior
    Feeds self, help, control
    Toilet, regulation, day, accidents
    Asks toilet, how
    Takes responsibility toilet
    Nap and night toilet habits
    Dress, undress, lace and tie shoes, buttons
    Helps mother at home

6. Emotional behavior
    Attitude toward strangers
    Amenability to control
    Play with other children

7. Health history
    General health
    Illnesses—unusual experiences

In putting questions to the mother the examiner should refrain as much as possible from indicating a "good answer." For example, "How is he about the toilet?" is a better form than "Does he go to the toilet all by himself?" and, "What about his meals?" or "Do you feed him?" is better than "Does he feed himself?" "Does he still take a nap?" permits the mother to say "No" without feeling she has managed things badly or being tempted to conceal what she imagines to be a deviation from the clinic's standards. Direct questions become more or less necessary, of course, if the mother does not respond adequately to more general questions.

Unless the mother has come in for advice about behavior difficulties, in which case she is told that they will be discussed with her privately, it is generally wise not to suggest problems to the mother by questioning. We have found that the question, "Is he a good boy—do you have any trouble with him?" is a very revealing one. The usual response is, "Yes, he's a good boy. Of course, like all children he's stubborn (or naughty, etc.) sometimes, but he's really no trouble." This is probably a tolerant, sensible mother. The mother who says, "He's perfect, he's an angel—he's too good," is either doting, has an unusually submissive child, or may even have a retarded child. The mother who says sarcastically, "It depends on what you mean by 'good'—" or who begins a recital of woes, is in need of guidance, and the discussion of the problems is deferred until a more appropriate occasion. The mother who says, "Well, yes, but I wanted to ask you about such and such," is also probably a sensible mother; at least she has been able to formulate her problem unemotionally. Specific questions such as does he have temper tantrums, does he suck his thumb, etc., are not asked. Information of that sort will be volunteered when the mother is ready to ask for help and it is best to wait these natural developments.

The results of the preliminary interview and of the examination determine the need for further interviews. At the conclusion of the session, if the child's development is satisfactory, the mother may be so informed; otherwise, she is asked to come in for a second interview. In giving a mother the results of a developmental examination, we are particularly careful not to give it in terms of D.Q. or I.Q., as these terms are so often misunderstood or abused by the laity. The normal child is described as "normal," the superior child as "normal, bright," the retarded child in terms of his maturity level and its prognostic significance.

When guidance problems are involved, the preliminary interview and the developmental examination are but the first steps in a diagnostic and therapeutic process which will probably include more prolonged observation of the child and numerous interviews of a very different character. The general purpose of the "problem" interview is not to analyze the problem as such but to enable the mother to see for herself the problem in its proper relationship to the child's development, personality, and environment, and to understand and meet realistically the developmental course of the difficulty.

§ 4. RECORDING THE EXAMINATION

To derive the fullest possible value from an examination, it should be skillfully administered and so recorded that it will be available and fruitful for later reference and comparison. Ideally the recording should be complete and should include not only the responses to specific test situations but also the child's irrelevant remarks and behavior, his general demeanor in adjusting to the examination, his references to his mother, *how* as well as *what* he responds, his methods of evading or refusing, facial expressions and so forth. Complete recording requires the presence of an individual whose sole duty it is to record the child's behavior. In this case the recorder is concealed behind a one-way-vision screen and makes a minute record of the child's performance. The recorder should be a trained person, able to record quickly (in shorthand or abbreviated long hand) and able to record selectively. This implies a knowledge of what constitutes unexpected as well as expected behavior and significant deviations. The examiner should be on the alert to make the child's remarks clear to the recorder (by repeating them) as most children speak very softly. The presence of a competent recorder frees the examiner from the necessity of interrupting the flow of the examination to make her own notes.

If the examiner is to record as well as administer the examination, notes must be reduced to a minimum. A check or a word now and then, recorded as unobtrusively as possible, is all that can be done without disturbing the examination, particularly at the younger age levels. The examiner has to deal with the distraction her writing causes, the child perhaps demanding her pencil, or "What are you doing?" She also faces the possibility that in moments of stress, behavior will go unrecorded and perhaps be irrevocably lost. Simple explanations as, "I'm writing," "This is mine—here are your toys," suffice in most cases. If the recording threatens the success of the examination, notes had better be abandoned at the time and later made from memory.

It is possible for an examiner to train herself to retain a fairly complete memory picture of the whole examination behavior, though some details will inevitably be lost. Notes should be made immediately after the examination before the picture fades, and a more complete account written or dictated from the notes as soon as possible after the child has left the clinic. The actual labor of formulating this account will assist the examiner in defining her characterization of the child.

Other examiners may prefer simply to score the child's performance on the developmental schedules, either during the examination or immediately afterward, and record in detail only a sample of the behavior, or an episode illustrating the typical patterns of attention, or emotion, or performance.

§ 5. EXAMINATION SETUP AND EQUIPMENT

For the proper conduct of an examination, two or preferably three rooms and a conveniently located bathroom are needed. A simple arrangement is pictured in Plate XX. First there should be a reception room. In this room the examiner and the child make their first acquaintance; the examiner may talk with the mother; and friends and relatives who may have come along may wait. The room need not be large, but it should be comfortably and cheerfully furnished, contain chairs enough for all, including a small one for the child, and some magazines and a book or two. It should not be well stocked with toys, though there may be some in reserve, because we wish the child to be quite ready to leave this room for his examination.

The examining room should be unfurnished except for essentials. Walls can be attractive without being gaily decorated. A small room seems to induce more intimate rapport, a large room to be an invitation to wander, explore, or even romp. The furniture consists of the examining table and chair for the child, chairs for the mother and examiner, and a cabinet containing the test materials. The arrangement of the furniture depends a little on the size and shape of the room. If the child's chair is placed with its back to the wall, the table before it, the mother's chair to the right, the examiner's chair and cabinet to the left, when the child is seated he has the room before him but he is more or less enclosed. He does not feel penned in and he can see the door that leads out, but access to the room is not quite free and the arrangement quite subtly suggests that he keep his place.

This arrangement, with the child flanked by the mother on one side and the examiner on the other, has several advantages over other possible arrangements. The one disadvantage that must be acknowledged is that the examiner is not always able to see everything the child does; the right hand may at times be out of sight and the child can turn toward his mother and his face will not be seen. On the other hand, the child may need to exclude the examiner from the scene to feel at ease, and it is advantageous if he can do this without being under the necessity of leaving the table. The examiner can retreat or emerge, be a large or a small factor in the picture, without changing her position. The one precaution the examiner must keep in mind is not to interfere with activities of the left hand by her manner of presenting materials from the left.

Any other position, particularly vis-à-vis is less desirable. It hampers the direct view of the recorder and observers. Moreover the examiner thereby becomes too dominating a figure and tends to embarrass or inhibit the child by watching him too intently.

The child's chair and table are low and suited to his size. The mother's chair is an ordinary adult chair and elevates her slightly above the field of action. The examiner's chair is low, putting her nearer the child's level. The best cabinet is closed, as toys laid out on open shelves invite the child to get up, investigate, help himself, or tease for something he sees. A small chest or cabinet of drawers is ideal, as opening a drawer to get a toy does not reveal what is yet in store. Large test objects can be quite successfully concealed on the floor behind the cabinet. Anything else in the room is only diverting. The radiator is usually ignored by the child, but we have found as insignificant an item as an electric outlet in the wall to be distracting on occasion.

The third room is the observation room. It adjoins the examining room and permits observers to watch the examination through a one-way-vision screen which can be installed in a connecting door. If the examination is to be recorded, the recorder is also behind the screen. More and more commonly the father also comes with the child, and provision can easily be made for him to watch the examination if an observation room or alcove is available. Students and social workers can also take advantage of this opportunity to observe the child under relatively controlled and standard conditions.

§ 6. ONE-WAY-VISION OBSERVATION

Seeing is believing. This is the central maxim of visual education. The one-way-vision screen is a device which permits an unseen observer to see. It enables him to see many things which he could not otherwise see at all. It brings him closer to the realities of child behavior because it removes the distorting and the disturbing influences of the observer. It must therefore be considered not merely as a laboratory gadget but as an adaptable technique which has many practical uses both for controlled and naturalistic observation and for educational demonstrations. The one-way-vision screen[1] is a contrivance which combines intimacy of observation with detachment.

The principle of the one-way screen is relatively simple. Perhaps you have had an experience like this: You walked down a sunny path of a garden; you opened the screen door of a porch located at the end of the path; to your surprise you found in the shadow of the porch someone whom you had not noticed at all while you were in the garden. Yet all the while this person could see you plainly. To construct a one-way-vision booth one must imitate these conditions. The observer must be in a partial darkness; light should not stream directly through the screen. The observer's station should also be carpeted to absorb sound and light. The surface of the screen which faces upon the field of observation is

---

[1] Our own experience with the one-way screen began with the photographic recording dome as described elsewhere (31; 36; see also Halverson, H. M.: *American Journal of Psychology*, 1928, *40*, 126-128). The dome is a hemispherical structure 12 feet in diameter, large enough to house a crib which is located in the universal focus of cameras mounted on two of the curved ribs. In the construction of the dome, especially of the exterior, we had the benefit of suggestions and technical advice from Professor Raymond Dodge. To secure both ventilation and visibility the dome was encased in ordinary 16 mm. wire netting, painted white on its interior surface. This feature, in combination with the curvatures of the dome and the diffused interior illumination, produced a very gratifying degree of one-way-vision for the observers posted in the darkened laboratory without. A modified arrangement was later installed in the guidance nursery. Since then we have experimented with different methods of heightening the one-way transparency, under varying conditions.

painted white to produce a diffuse dazzle which makes the screen appear opaque. Thus the screen is transparent in one direction only.

This simple screen-door principle is illustrated in actual application in the arrangement pictured in Plate XX. At (12) is shown an ordinary door which has been converted into a one-way-vision device by cutting out the solid panel and inserting an ordinary 16-mesh wire screen. (The best procedure for the processing of this screen will be detailed at the end of this section.) The door can be made opaque by closing the wooden panel which drops down on a hinge. It serves for one-way vision when Room 7 is darkened by the drawing of shades and curtains over the window. This panel gives upon Examination Room 15 and brings the observer within a few feet of the child and the examiner, and enables him to observe the slightest movements and to hear the vocalizations and conversation. The oblong panel (14) is similarly constructed. It gives upon the examining room and, being at eye-level, it permits either prolonged or casual observation from the darkened hallway. This accessory arrangement has proved convenient in the course of clinical work because it offers more or less brief glimpses of an examination with a minimum of disturbance and pre-arrangement.

The large observation panel (12) in the pictured location is doubly convenient because it can be made to serve in either direction. The observation room can be converted into an examining room. It is the examining room which is then darkened in accordance with the one-way-vision principle already outlined.

When favorable lighting conditions prevail, this basic screen arrangement can be enlarged and diversified for a variety of purposes as pictured in Plate XXI. This plate shows the general arrangements of the Guidance Nursery at the Yale Clinic of Child Development. Six different types or adaptations will be briefly described. An expansive screen (1) serves for a commodious room which accommodates thirty stools of graduated heights (1a), so that a group of students may assemble amphitheatre-wise for observation of activities and demonstrations in the main nursery. An offset provides close-up observation of the children in the kitchen unit (2). The screen at (3) is part of another large observation alcove which was incorporated into an ordinary nursery room by erecting a thin partition which reaches from floor to ceiling. The wainscoting of this partition was decorated with murals as described below.

Screen 4 is a very simple arrangement which merely consists of French doors which are veiled with moderately heavy, small-mesh, curtain netting, partially concealing the observers who may look out upon the playground.

Screen 5 serves the small observation booth which is strategically placed in one corner of the large nursery unit for individual observers. We have found this small booth particularly useful for parents in connection with parent-guidance work.

In addition to the standard screen (5) this room is equipped with a transparent one-way-vision mirror (6) which is set as a panel five feet from the floor between the booth and the bathroom. (Miroir diaphane "Argus." Bte. France. Etranger.) From the bathroom this panel functions and looks entirely like an ordinary mirror, although quite diaphanous from the booth. It, however, does not transmit conversation. Similar observation booths are provided for parents in connection with examining rooms.

The advantages of one-way observation by parents deserves special mention. The mother of a problem child may be so deeply and emotionally involved in her problem that she cannot see it objectively. She is invited to watch her child from the observation booth in the nursery. Here the one-way screen often works a quiet miracle. The simple intervention of the transparent barrier of the screen creates a new perspective, a wholesome shift toward psychological detachment and objectivity. Seeing is believing. She begins to see in a new light. This is an efficacious form of visual education. It reduces the necessity of verbal explanation or of exhortation. We have talked less to parents since one-way-vision screens were installed.

A few hospitals have installed one-way-vision facilities to aid in the demonstration of patients. The advantages for psychiatric demonstration, as well as for observation, are obvious. Not only does the screen create conditions otherwise unobtainable, but it tends to accentuate visual impressions. Like an etching or a miniature model, it tends to vivify the configuration of phenomena.

The teacher in training benefits from similar forms of one-way observation. One-way screen arrangements have been successfully used for demonstrations of schoolroom activities and teaching methods at elementary grade levels. Such arrangements also have many possibilities in connection with public museums and other forms of educational exposition. Periscopes, concealed balconies, single-vision mirrors, and one-way glass all have their special uses, but the simplicity and flexibility of the one-way screen and its permeability to air, sound, and light give it peculiar advantages. Fortunately these advantages can be realized with relatively slight expenditure of funds and of ingenuity.

It should be emphasized that concealment is a subsidiary or negative value of one-way-vision. The screen was not designed for spying, but for positive educational and scientific controls of observation. Rather one would emphasize that one-way-vision protects the privacy of the children and, on occasions, the privacy of their attendants and their parents. The invisibility of the observers serves to make the observation more serious and purposeful. It also tends to enhance the import of the observed behavior. The status of the infant, and of the young child as well, seems to gain thereby. His individuality is perceived in new perspective.

PREPARATION OF ONE-WAY-VISION SCREENS

Ordinary 16-mesh wire screen can be used. Thin white enamel paint may be applied with painter's brush in the regular manner, if done with care so as not to clog the mesh. The paint should dry between the several coats. No. 30 wire cloth has definite advantages, particularly if casein paint instead of ordinary enamel is used. The casein paint should be thinned down with water to the consistency of thin cream and then applied with an air brush. At intervals, the air brush should be used to force air only through the screen in order to blow out any excess paint which may have clogged the mesh. This process is repeated four or five times. Casein paint dries rapidly and the successive coats may be applied in the course of one day.

It is best to apply the paint before the screens are permanently mounted. If the screens are already in position, an absorbent barrier should be placed behind the screen to collect the transmitted paint spray.

The location of the observers' station is of critical importance. The station should be as dark as possible. Enough light for ordinary recording purposes will in any event enter through the screen. Ideally the observation station should be located on the window side of the room. Care should be taken so that direct light from windows or from lamps will not strike directly through the screens. Such direct rays of light tend to reveal the observer's eye glasses and light-colored objects. Invisibility is increased by wearing dark clothes. The efficiency of the one-way-vision screen is also increased if the room upon which the screen gives is illuminated by indirect rather than direct lighting.

The walls of the observation station should be painted black or midnight blue. Dark curtains draped on the walls and thick carpeting on the floor serve to silence sounds inadvertently made by the observers. Placement of plate glass behind the screen excludes sound but usually interferes with ventilation. Strict silence is an extremely important rule. Our injunction to the observer who enters the station for the first time is, "Be absolutely quiet. The children can hear you even though they cannot see you."

When lighting conditions are unfavorable, special adaptations may be experimentally tried. Two screens, one behind the other, sometimes bring about a desired increase of invisibility. In some instances we have camouflaged the one-way-vision screen and made it attractive by painting a mural on the exterior surface (3b). Such a mural should avoid the color blue as much as possible because of the marked degree of absorption. A light cumulus cloud effect can be superimposed on a white screen as shown in 3b, Plate XXI. A mural proves psychologically most effective when placed immediately below the screen. Plate XXI 3b and d show an engaging mural prepared by Lois Maloy. It is needless to point out the preschool motif in this mural. Placed next to the floor at the child's eye level this mural serves to divert his attention away from the screen itself. Under favorable conditions, however, even the unembellished screen comes to be accepted as a normal part of the child's environment and, if no mysterious noises emerge from behind its concealment, the screen serves a permanent function in the economy of the study of child behavior. One-way-vision adds to the intimacy, the piquancy, and objectivity of observation.

§ 7. EXAMINATION MATERIALS

Many of the test situations can be administered with simple and improvised materials. It is important, however, to observe the detailed specifications in most of the items. These specifications are detailed below and may be read in connection with the illustrations which appear in Chapter V, Plates XVIII and XIX.

Record forms and the developmental test materials in part or in whole are procurable at cost price through the Psychological Corporation, 522 Fifth Avenue, New York City.

BALL (large): White rubber, red and green stripes encircling middle. Diameter 15 cm. (SR 4526, Seamless Rubber Company, New Haven, Conn.)

BALL (small): White rubber, red and green stripes encircling middle. Diameter 6 cm. (SR 4560, Seamless Rubber Company, New Haven, Conn.)

BOTTLE: Glass, 7 cm. in height, 2 cm. diameter at opening. (Plate XVIII, i)

BOY BLOWING BUBBLES: Green, letter-size paper with picture of boy blowing bubbles. (Plate XIX, e)

COLOR FORMS: Five red forms pasted on white card 8.5 x 11 inches. *Circle:* 5 cm. in diameter (upper right); *square:* 5 cm. (upper left); *triangle:* 6.5 cm. (lower left); *semicircle:* 8 cm. in diameter (lower right); *Maltese cross:* 7 cm. in length and 2.5 cm. in width of arms center. Five red cardboard shapes of corresponding size and shape. (Plate XIX, h)

COPY OF FORMS: White cards 8 x 5 inches with following forms outlined in black in center of card: *Circle:* diameter 8 cm.; *cross:* lines at rectangles, 7.5 cm.; *square:* 7 cm.; *triangle:* equilateral, 9.5 cm.; *diamond:* (horizontal) 5.5 cm. each side, top angle 125°; *diagonal:* rectangle 10 x 6.5 cm. with two diagonals and a perpendicular to center of each side. (Plate XIX, c)

CRAYON: Red lumber (Eberhard Faber No. 836). (Plate XVIII, j)

CUBES: Ten white wood, painted red. 2.5 cm. square. (Plate XVIII, g)

CUP: White enamel with black handle. 9.5 cm. in diameter at top; 6 cm. deep. Size 9. (Plate XVIII, h)

FORMBOARD AND FORMS (Gesell): Half-inch board 36 x 16 cm., painted dark green. Three holes cut equidistant from each other and from edges of the board from left to right as follows: *Circle:* diameter 8.7 cm.; *equilateral triangle:* 9.3 cm.; *square:* 7.5 cm. Three white wooden forms to fit holes, each 2 cm. thick: *Circle:* diameter 8.5 cm.; *equilateral triangle:* 9 cm.; *square:* 7.3 cm. (Plate XVIII, k)

GARDEN MAZE: Sheet of paper, letter-size, with shaded area to indicate garden and heavy double lines to indicate path. (Plate XIX, g)

GODDARD FORMBOARD AND FORMS: .75-inch board, 18 x 12.5 inches, painted dark brown. Ten forms, including the circle, triangle, square of the size used in the Gesell Formboard. Other forms are of the same relative size. (C. H. Stoelting Co., Chicago, Ill.) (Plate XIII, m,n,o)

HUMOR CARD: Picture of man fishing up a shoe. (Plate XIX, f)

INCOMPLETE MAN: Green, letter-size paper with incomplete drawing of man. (Plate XIX, d)

ORIENTATION CARDS (Castner): Three cards (5 x 8 inches) each having a row of seven pictures. Center picture in each case is drawn larger and with heavier lines than others in the row. Other pictures represent common objects of relatively neutral interest value. All pictures are of symmetrical form. (Plate XIX, i)

PAPER: Green letter-size Hammermill bond No. 16. (Plate XVIII, j)

PELLETS: White or pink, sugar, flat on one side, convex on other. Diameter 8 mm. (Cachous, Bradley-Smith Co., New Haven, Conn.) (Plate XVIII, i)

PERFORMANCE BOX, ROD AND SQUARE: Wooden box, painted green. Length 38 cm., width 24.7 cm., height 17.6 cm. Open only at one end. Ends 24.7 x 17.6 cm. Top of box is 38 x 24.7 cm. 8 cm. from closed end of box is rectangular hole 2.5 x 7.6, short side of rectangle parallel to long side of box. 18 cm. from closed end of box is round hole, diameter 2 cm. At 27.5 cm. from closed end is rectangular hole 3.2 x 2 cm., long side of hole parallel to long side of top of box. Measurements for placement of holes are made from closed end of box to nearest side of hole. The geometric center of all holes is on a line which bisects the top lengthwise. Use with performance box round, wooden *rod* painted red: length 10 cm., diameter 1 cm. Also the white *square* wooden form 2 cm. thick, 7.3 cm. across used in Gesell Formboard. (Plate XVIII, l)

PICTURE BOOK: Goosey Gander. (No. 613, Sam'l Gabriel Sons Co., New York.) (Plate XVIII, f)

PICTURE CARDS (Gesell): (1) White card 5.75 x 5.25 inches, divided by black lines into four equal rectangles: each rectangle contains a drawing. Drawings are of: cup, shoe, dog, and house. (Plate XIX, a)   (2) White card, 5.75 x 5.25 inches, divided by black lines into six equal rectangles: each rectangle contains a drawing. Drawings of: flag, clock, star, leaf, basket, book. (Plate XIX, b)

PORTEUS PATH-TRACING TESTS: Green sheet, letter-size, with first three Porteus maze tests reproduced on it (diamond, cross, and path).

PUZZLE BOX AND BALL: Puzzle box is 2.5 x 3.5 x 1.5 inches. An opening at the top 1.5 inches square allows a bright-colored ball to project slightly. The box is fastened by a cord attached at one end. At its free end a loop passes through a ring at the center of the bottom of the box, and a small wooden stick is slipped through the loop. In order to get the ball, three steps are necessary: (1) the bar must be slipped from the loop; (2) the loop must be pulled through the ring; and (3) the cover must be lifted from the box. The cover is the same depth as the box. (Plate XVIII, m)

ROD: A square stick 15 inches long, 1.5 cm. through, for getting ball from table.

TEST OBJECTS: Six objects: pencil, penny, shoe, key, closed pocket knife, and ball.

V-SCOPE: A truncated cardboard cone 9.5 inches long, with both large and small ends open. Cone is constructed of two pieces of cardboard, and lies flat until opened by subject's pressing inward with both hands. Also a series of 10 small white cards (3 x 5 inches) each bearing the picture of a simple and familiar object such as flower, house, cup, etc. (See ref. 89)

WALKING BOARDS: Three boards: 2, 4, and 6 cm. wide, 250 cm. long, and 10 cm. high. Small square platform at each end so that the child can stand level with the board to start and can balance both feet at end before stepping down.

In addition to the above, certain material of the Binet intelligence scale may be used, as described by Terman (see ref. 121).

LINES: White card with two horizontal black lines in the center: one line 2.25 inches; one 1.75 inches.

WEIGHTS: Two black one-inch cubes, weighted. One weighs 3 grams, one 15 grams. Or five weights: 3, 6, 9, 12 and 15 grams each.

MISSING PARTS: White card with four figures drawn on it—some feature or part of the body omitted from each figure. (See ref. 8, fig. 6, p. 29)

KUHLMANN-TERMAN GEOMETRIC FORMS: White card with 10 geometric forms in outline. Forms are in 3 rows, 4 in each of the first two rows and one on each end of the third row. (See line drawing in text, p. 166)

PICTURE CARDS: Dutch, canoe, post-office, and parlor scenes.

COLORS: Card with 4 bright-colored rectangles symmetrically placed. First rectangle colored red, second yellow, third blue, and fourth green.

AESTHETIC COMPARISON: Card showing 3 pairs of women's faces, one of each pair of faces pretty, the other ugly. (See ref. 8, fig. 5, p. 23)

§ 8. RECORD FORMS

In this section are presented four record forms, the Introductory Report, the Preliminary Interview, the Developmental Schedule, and the Summary Face Sheet. These forms, properly filled out and accompanied by the child's drawings, would represent a minimum examination record; in a re-examination, a second Introductory Report would be unnecessary. A more complete case report would include physical measurements, the findings on physical examination, the behavior day, and a detailed account of the child's responses during the examination.

1. *The Introductory Report* should be completely filled out by the person requesting the examination of the child and returned to the Clinic before an appointment for examination is made. The information furnished by this report enables the child to be routed to the examiner most interested in the problem, and enables the appointment to be made at the time which does not interfere with the child's naps or mealtimes. Most preschool children are best examined in the morning.

The examiner should never assume that all the pertinent information regarding a child has been included in this report; it is well to check many points, particularly birth date and age, and to ask the parent or attendant to expand on some of the details. The name and address of the attending physician is requested so that a firsthand report can be obtained if necessary, and a report of any previous examination can be secured and included in the record.

2. *The Interview Record* is discussed in full in § 3. This form is filled out by the examiner in as much detail as possible and incorporated in the record.

3. *The Developmental Schedule.* The Developmental Schedules are given in full in § 1. A sample record form is included here. The items are checked as + or − in the first left-hand column; individual examiners may devise other symbols to represent near-success, superior performance, low-grade performance, etc., which may be indicated in the second left-hand column. The dotted lines at the right provide space for notes and comments or for a brief description of the performance. In each field of behavior space is provided for undesignated extra items.

In scoring a child's performance on examination, several adjacent age levels should be rated, until the aggregate of + signs changes to an aggregate of − signs. Each field of behavior is then considered separately. An example follows.

If the child earns a full complement of + signs at the 3-year level in the motor field, his maturity level in the motor field is 3 years. If he has a full complement of + signs at 3 years, and one or two at 42 months in the adaptive field, his maturity level in the adaptive field is 3 + years; if he has an almost full complement of + signs at 3 years in the language field but one or two − signs, his maturity level in the field of language is 3 − years. If his + and − signs are almost equally divided between 30 and 36 months in the field of personal-social behavior, his maturity level in the personal-social field is 30-36 months. To obviate over-simplification

(*Text continued on page 366*)

INTRODUCTORY REPORT—PRESCHOOL AND INFANT

This report should be filled out completely by teacher, parent, doctor, or social worker, and returned to the Clinical Secretary prior to the date of the appointment. Additional and more detailed information bearing on the problem should accompany this report.

Name of child   Street address   Phone
    Age   City
By whom referred   Present date
Social worker

Name	Birth date	Nat'l	Occupation	Education	Nat'l of grandparents
Father..........	....	....	....	....	....
Mother.........	....	....	....	....	....

	Name	Birth date	School grade
Brothers and Sisters			

BIRTH HISTORY: Date of birth.............   Verified?............
Birth weight.......... Term: premature ...... wks.; postmature ...... wks.; full...... Complications during pregnancy:
Delivery: Physician (name and address).......................................
Home or hospital (name and address)..
Duration of labor
    (Details—normal, precipitate, difficult, version, instrumental):
Condition at birth (cried immediately, cyanotic, resuscitated, etc.):
Condition during first month (feeding difficulties, convulsions, crying, etc.):
HEALTH HISTORY: (List illnesses with dates. Give date and summary of last physical examination.)

DEVELOPMENTAL HISTORY: Sat unsupported at ...... mo.; walked alone at ...... mo.; began to name objects (ball, etc.) at ...... mo.; trained to toilet at ...... mo.; held own cup at ...... mo.; fed self with spoon at ...... mo. Further details:

REASON FOR REFERRING TO CLINIC:

(All *the information called for on this report is* important. *Please do not fail to fill in the other side of this sheet.*)

(Reverse side of Introductory Report)

FAMILY HISTORY: (Note any exceptional or significant facts in regard to parents, home conditions, relatives, background.)

FOSTER HOME: Has child been in foster home?　　　In an institution?
(Give details including *names* of foster parents and *dates* of placement.)

SOCIAL HISTORY: (Home and foster home conditions, treatment of child, opportunities for play with other children same age, etc.)

CHILD'S BEHAVIOR CHARACTERISTICS: (Mother or foster mother's description of child's outstanding personality traits.)

BEHAVIOR DAY: (Time of sleeping, feeding, playing, bathing, toilet, etc.) When, during the day, does the child's longest and happiest play period occur?

Are there any problems with regard to feeding, sleeping, play, etc.?

Has there been a previous psychological examination?　　　By whom?
　　　　　　　　　　　　　　　　　　　　　　　　　　　　Address

This report was filled out by...............
Please state relationship to child.................

SUPPLEMENTARY BEHAVIOR INTERVIEW

Name................ Age........ Date............ CCD No...............
Informant: Duration of foster placement:
  Relationship to child:

Motor behavior (include handedness and manner of manipulation of objects)

Language behavior (include gestures)

Play behavior (include toys)

Domestic behavior (feeding, dressing, toilet, cooperation)

Emotional behavior (dependency, management, playmates, specific behavior deviations)

Health history

DEVELOPMENTAL RECORDING SCHEDULE

			Examiner
Name	Age	Date	Case No.

MOTOR   24 months

———Runs without falling..

———Stairs: walks up and down alone..................................

———Large ball: kicks...

———Cubes: tower of 6–7..

———Book: turns pages singly...

——— ....

——— ....

ADAPTIVE

———Cubes: tower of 6–7..

———Cubes: aligns 2 or more, train....................................

———Drawing: imitates V stroke.......................................

———Drawing: imitates circular stroke.................................

———Sentences: repeats 3–4 syllables..................................

———Formboard: places blocks on board separately (F)................

———Formboard: adapts in 4 trials....................................

———Performance box: inserts square..................................

——— ....

——— ....

LANGUAGE

———Speech: has discarded jargon.....................................

———Speech: 3-word sentence..

———Speech: uses I, me, and you......................................

———Picture cards: names 3 or more...................................

———Picture cards: identifies 5 or more...............................

———Test objects: names 2..

———Ball: 4 directions correct..

——— ....

——— ....

PERSONAL-SOCIAL

———Feeding: inhibits turning of spoon................................

———Toilet: dry at night if taken up..................................

———Toilet: verbalizes toilet needs fairly consistently (r).............

———Dressing: pulls on simple garment................................

———Communication: verbalizes immediate experiences.................

———Communication: refers to himself by his name....................

———Communication: comprehends and asks for "another"..............

———Play: hands full cup of cubes to examiner........................

———Play: plays with domestic mimicry (doll, teddy-bear, etc.)........

———Play: parallel play predominates.................................

——— ....

——— ....

Summary Face Sheet

YALE CLINIC OF CHILD DEVELOPMENT

Name   Birth date   Date   Exam. No.   Case No.
              Age   Recorder   Examiner   Med. No.

Physical deviations: Laterality:
Social deviations:
Behavior deviations:

	Low	Medium	High	
Gross motor.....				Weeks/Months
Fine motor......				
Adaptive........				
Language.......				
Personal-social...				
....				
....				
....				
General outlook..				

File items:
Classification: Follow-up:

Characteristic performance:
Level:

_____	Gross motor
_____	Fine motor
_____	Adaptive
_____	Language
_____	Personal-social
_____	
_____	

General Summary and Characterization:

Predictive Items and Recommendations:

it is best to indicate the range of distribution when there is definite unevenness in performance.

4. *The Summary Face Sheet.* As its title indicates, this sheet is used to summarize the case: the history, the present findings, the predictions and recommendations. Space is provided for a note on significant deviations in the physical make-up of the child, in his social history or status, or in his behavior. His characteristic performance is briefly described, and the maturity levels in the various fields of behavior may be given numerically in the column at the left, or checked in profile in the grid provided above, either in weeks of development or months of development.

The general summary and characterization should include a description of the child's appearance, his adjustment to the examiner and the examination, comments on the symmetry or asymmetry of his performance, and an appraisal of the child in terms of the examination and in terms of his problem. The parent-child relation should also be described. Sample characterizations are given in Chapter XIII, together with a full discussion of their purpose and value.

Under the heading Predictive Items and Recommendations, the examiner records the plan of treatment or disposition of the case. It is also well to include for later reference a check statement covering prediction or prognosis.

§ 9. ILLUSTRATIVE CASE MATERIALS

The developmental examination procedures outlined in the present volume have been used over a period of years in the diagnostic and advisory service of the Yale Clinic of Child Development. Case studies have been reported in journals and in previous publications, especially the following: *Infancy and Human Growth* (31), *Biographies of Child Development* (40), and *Feeding Behavior of Infants* (38).

The first mentioned volume presented the mental growth curves of thirty-three infants and young children whose behavior development was repeatedly appraised by clinical examinations. We have followed the subsequent careers of thirty of these children over a period of from ten to fifteen years. These cases are reported in a volume entitled *The Biographies of Child Development* which also reports individual studies of behavior growth of fifty-one additional children. The volume on feeding behavior deals with the developmental aspects of nutrition and the regulation of feeding and related personal-social behavior.

The following citations to the two latter volumes call attention to a wide range of illustrative material. To the general reader these references will supply concrete examples of the diagnostic procedures in practical application. The references to the *Biographies* may be considered an integral and vital part of the present book. They take the place of over-

frequent qualifications and parenthetical discussions of exceptional behavior. To the student and examiner the illustrative case materials may
furnish suggestions as to the critical evaluation of the behavior characteristics elicited by individual examinations and by the longer range
developmental studies covering a period of years.

CHAPTER VI. MOTOR DEVELOPMENT

Gesell et al: *Biographies of Child Development*

Motor acceleration in infancy (§ 5, p. 29 ff.).
Motor complications in a case of birth injury, with a discussion of the motor basis
of mental growth (§ 17, p. 57 ff.).
General superiority, with ordinary motor development (§ 10, p. 43 f.).
Early motor retardation, with subsequent compensatory development (§ 14,
p. 49 ff.).
Motor characteristics in a case of pubertas praecox (§ 22, p. 76 ff.).
Motor superiority, case illustrating (§ 29, p. 123 ff.).
Motor complications (§ 50, p. 207 ff.).
Laterality: Laterality in relation to language retardation (§ 31, p. 131 and § 32,
p. 132 ff.); Laterality in the prediction of reading difficulty (§ 34, p. 153 f.
and § 35-39, p. 156 ff.); Laterality in cases of delayed behavior integration
(§ 40, p. 175); Laterality in a case of marked developmental fluctuation
(§ 47, p. 195 ff.).

CHAPTER VII. ADAPTIVE BEHAVIOR

Gesell et al: *Biographies of Child Development*

Superiority, illustrated by specific responses in adaptive and other fields (§ 5,
p. 29 ff.).
Subnormal growth trends (§ 16, p. 54 ff.).
Characteristics of adaptive and other behavior in a case of birth injury (§ 17,
p. 57 ff.).
Behavior characteristics in a treated cretin (§ 23, p. 87 ff.).
Descriptive account of response to adaptive items below 12 months (§ 45,
p. 189 ff.).
Retarded development in a case of premature birth (§ 24, p. 91 ff.).
    Of the numerous references throughout the *Biographies* to drawing behavior,
the following will be found of particular interest. Starred references include
illustrative reproductions of children's drawings.
Drawing behavior (*§ 8, p. 36 ff.; *§ 22, p. 76 ff.; *§ 28, p. 118 ff.; *§ 34,
p. 149 ff.; § 35-39, p. 156 ff.).

CHAPTER VIII. LANGUAGE BEHAVIOR

Gesell et al: *Biographies of Child Development*

A case showing superiority in language development from 1 to 16 years (§ 7,
p. 34 f.).

Discussion of the clinical interpretation of language behavior (§ 8, p. 36 ff.).

Superior command of language and ideas, with examples (§ 9, p. 41 ff.).

Description of language complications in a case of birth injury (§ 17, p. 57 ff.).

General discussion of early retardation in language, with detailed presentation of two cases (§ 31-33, pp. 129-146).

Clinical prediction of reading difficulty and reading readiness (§ 34-39, pp. 149-169).

CHAPTER IX. PERSONAL-SOCIAL BEHAVIOR

Gesell et al: *Biographies of Child Development*

Consistent personality picture, from 1 to 15 years (§ 3, p. 21 ff.).

Personality as an early indicator of superior potentiality (§ 8, p. 36 ff.).

Personal-social characteristics in a case of borderline intelligence (§ 16, p. 54 ff.).

Personality factors in a birth injury case (§ 17, p. 57 ff.).

Personal-social behavior in relation to prematurity of birth (§ 24, p. 99).

Personality in relation to language retardation (§ 31-33, p. 129 ff.).

Personality in relation to reading readiness (§ 34, p. 154; § 35-39, p. 156 ff.).

Personality as a complicating factor in preschool examinations (§ 40, p. 174 f.).

Cases illustrating personality complications (§ 43, p. 183 ff.; § 46, p. 193 ff.; § 47, p. 195 ff.).

Personality in a case of birth injury (§ 61, p. 246 ff.).

Continuity of personality picture despite severe disease trauma (§ 65, p. 254 ff.).

Unusually favorable personality picture in a case of hydrocephalus (§ 67, p. 260 ff.).

General discussion of personal-social individuality (pp. 303-309).

Play behavior (§ 61, p. 245 ff.; § 67, p. 260 f.; § 70, p. 267 ff.).

Gesell and Ilg: *Feeding Behavior of Infants*

Eating Behavior

Mechanics of feeding (Chapter IV, pp. 24-35).

Breast and bottle behavior (Chapter VI, pp. 49-55).

Cup behavior (Chapter VII, pp. 56-59).

Spoon behavior up to 3 years (Chapter VII, pp. 60-65).

Photographic delineations of feeding behavior in the first 2 years (Chapter IX, pp. 66-89).

Individualization in the supervision of infant feeding (Chapter X, pp. 93-107).

Indicators of behavior maturity with respect to the first 2 years (pp. 142-144).

Case data on eating behavior (pp. 153-156; 158-161; 163-166; 169-172).

Sleeping Behavior

Sleeping schedules of individual children (pp. 94-100, 153, 158, 163, 169).

Sleeping and feeding charts of individual children during the first 2 years (pp. 95, 97, 154, 159, 164, 170).

Developmental Detachment
Increasing abilities for self help (Chapter XI, pp. 108-120, 131).
Adult-infant relationship (pp. 132-135).
Case data on adult-infant relationship (pp. 157, 162, 167, 173).

Elimination
Bowel and bladder control (pp. 124-131).
Case histories discussing (pp. 156, 161, 167, 172).

CHAPTER X. THE PHILOSOPHY OF THE DEVELOPMENTAL EXAMINATION

Gesell et al.: *Biographies of Child Development*

See Chapter IV. The Appraisal of Growth Characteristics (pp. 102-109).

CHAPTER XII. CLINICAL ADAPTATIONS TO ATYPICAL CONDITIONS

Gesell et al.: *Biographies of Child Development*

See Chapter III. Comparative Studies of Early and Later Development in Thirty Infants, pp. 13-101: A. Normal and retarded development, pp. 14-28; B. Acceleration and superiority of equipment, pp. 29-43; C. Atypical and pseudo-atypical growth complexes, pp. 44-56; D. The tendency toward optimum in growth, pp. 57-67; E. Physical asymmetry, pp. 68-72; F. Glandular and nutritional factors in mental growth, pp. 73-90; G. Prematurity and postmaturity, pp. 91-101, 224.
See also Chapter V. Individual Studies of Behavior Growth, pp. 113-302; H. Superior mental endowment, pp. 113-126; I. Language problems, pp. 127-146; J. Irregularities in early mental development, pp. 171-210; N. Physical complications, pp. 239-270; O. Foster care and child adoption, pp. 273-302.

CHAPTER XIII. INDIVIDUALITY AND ITS CHARACTERIZATION

Gesell et al.: *Biographies of Child Development*

See Chapter VI. The Individuality of Growth Careers, pp. 303-309.

§ 10. SELECTED REFERENCES

References which are referred to in the text are designated by number in parentheses.

1. Allport, Gordon W. *Personality: a psychological interpretation*. New York: Henry Holt, 1938, xiv + 587.
2. Ames, Louise B. "The sequential patterning of prone progression in the human infant," *Genet. Psychol. Monogr.*, 1937, *19*, 409-460
3. Andrus, R. "Tentative inventory of the habits of children from two to four years of age." New York: *Teach. Coll. Contr.*, Teachers Coll., Columbia Univ., 1924, No. 160.

4. Baldwin, Bird T., & Stecher, Lorle I. *The psychology of the preschool child.* New York: D. Appleton & Co., 1927, 305.
5. Barker, M. "Preliminary report on the social-material activities of children," *Child Develpm. Monogr.* No. 3. New York: Teachers College, 1930, p. 69.
6. Bayley, Nancy. "The development of motor abilities during the first three years," *Monogr. Soc. Res. Child Develpm.*, 1935, No. 1, p. 26.
7. Biber, Barbara. "Children's drawings from lines to pictures," *Cooperative School Pamphlet No. 6.* New York: Bureau of Educational Experiments, 1934, 43.
8. Binet, Alfred & Simon, Th. "Le développement de l'intelligence chez les enfants," *L'Année Psychologique*, 1908, xiv, 1-94.
9. ———. "La mesure du développement de l'intelligence chez les jeunes enfants," *Societé pour l'étude psychologique de l'enfant.* Paris, 1925, xxviii + 66 + xxv.
10. Bott, E. A., Blatz, W. E., Chant, Nellie, & Bott, Helen. "Observation and training of fundamental habits in young children," *Genet. Psychol. Monogr.*, July, 1928, 4, 1, 161.
11. Brandner, Margarete. Der Umgang des Kleinkindes mit Würfeln bis zu den Frühesten Formen des Bauens. In Das Bilderisch Gestaltende Kind, Herausgegeben von Felix Krueger und Hans Volkelt. Munchen: C. H. Beck'Sche Verlagsbuchhandlung, 1939, 217.
12. Buehler, Charlotte & Hetzer, Hildegarde. *Testing children's development from birth to school age* (Trans. by Henry Beaumont). New York: Farrar & Rinehart, 1935, 191.
13. Burnside, Lenoir H. "Coordination in the locomotion of infants," *Genet. Psychol. Monogr.*, 1927, 2, 5, 279-372.
14. Cameron, Norman. "Individual and social factors in the development of graphic symbolization," *J. Psychol.*, 1938, 5, 165-184.
15. Castner, Burton M. "Prediction of reading disability prior to first grade entrance," *Amer. J. Orthopsychiat.*, Oct., 1935, 5, 375-387.
16. ———. "Handedness and eyedness of children referred to a guidance clinic," *Psychol. Rec.*, 1939, 3, 8, 99-112.
17. ———. "The clinical file as an index of research material." (In preparation)
18. Courtney, D. M., & Johnson, B. J. "Skill in progressive movements of children," *Child Develpm.*, 1930, 1, 4, 345-347.
19. Cunningham, Bess V. "An experiment in measuring gross motor development of infants and young children," *J. educ. Psychol.*, 1927, 18, 458-464.
20. Dennis, Wayne. "Laterality of function in early infancy under controlled developmental conditions," *Child Develpm.*, 1935, 6, 242-252.
21. Descoeudres, Alice. Le développement de l'enfant de deux à sept ans. Paris: Delachaux et Niestlé, S.A., 1921, 232-282.
22. Dewey, Evelyn. *Behavior development in infants.* New York: Columbia Univ. Press, 1935, viii + 321.
23. Ding, E. "Night terrors in children," *Ztschr. f. Kinderforsch.*, 1937, 46, 283-296.

24. Enders, Abbie C. "A study of the laughter of the preschool child in the Merrill-Palmer School," Papers, Michigan Acad. Sci., Arts, & Letters, 1927, *8*, 341-356.
25. Eng, Helga Kristine. *Experimental investigations into the emotional life of the child compared with that of the adult.* London, New York: M. Milford, Oxford Univ. Press, 1925, vi + 243.
26. Feldman, M. W. *Antenatal and postnatal child physiology.* New York: Longmans, Green & Co., 1920.
27. Foster, Josephine C. & Headley, Neith E. *Education in the kindergarten.* New York: American Book, 1936, xiii + 368.
28. Foster, Josephine C. & Mattson, Marion L. *Nursery school education.* New York: D. Appleton-Century, 1939, xii + 361.
29. Gates, G. S. "An experimental study of the growth of social perception," *J. educ. Psychol.,* 1923, *14*, 449-461.
30. Gesell, Arnold. *The mental growth of the preschool child. A psychological outline of normal development from birth to the sixth year, including a system of developmental diagnosis.* New York: Macmillan, 1925, vii + 447.
31. ——. *Infancy and human growth.* New York: Macmillan, 1928, xvii + 418.
32. ——. *The guidance of mental growth in infant and child.* New York: Macmillan, 1930, ix + 322.
33. ——. "Reciprocal interweaving in neuro-motor development. A principle of spiral organization shown in the patterning of infant behavior," *J. comp. Neurol.,* 1939, *70*, 2, 161-180.
34. —— & Lord, Elizabeth E. "A psychological comparison of nursery-school children from homes of low and high economic status," *Ped. Sem.,* 1927, *35*, 339-356.
35. —— & Thompson, Helen. *Infant behavior: its genesis and growth.* New York: McGraw-Hill, 1934, viii + 343.
36. —— et al. *An atlas of infant behavior: a systematic delineation of the forms and early growth of human behavior patterns,* illustrated by 3,200 action photographs, in two volumes. New Haven: Yale Univ. Press, 1934, 922.
37. —— (assisted by Louise B. Ames). "Early evidences of individuality in the human infant," *Sci. Mon.,* Sept., 1937, xlv, 217-228.
38. —— & Ilg, Frances L. *Feeding behavior of infants.* Philadelphia: Lippincott, 1937, ix + 201.
39. —— & Thompson, Helen. *The psychology of early growth.* New York: Macmillan, 1938, ix + 290.
40. ——, Amatruda, Catherine S., Castner, Burton M. & Thompson, Helen. *Biographies of child development. The mental growth careers of eighty-four infants and children.* New York: Paul B. Hoeber, Inc., Medical Book Dept. of Harper & Brothers, 1939, xvii + 328.
41. Giesecke, M. "The genesis of hand preference," *Monogr. Soc. Res. Child Develpm.,* 1936, *1*, 5, 102.
42. Goddard, H. H. "The formboard as a measure of intellectual development in children," *Train. Sch. Bull.,* 1912, *9*, 49-52.

43. Goodenough, F. L. "Resistant behavior of infants and children," *J. exper. Psychol.*, 1925, *8*, 209-224.

44. ——. *Measurement of intelligence by drawings.* Chicago: World Book Co., 1926, ix + 177.

45. ——. *The Kuhlmann-Binet tests for children of preschool age. A critical study and evaluation.* Minneapolis: Univ. Minn. Press, 1928, 146.

46. ——. "The emotional behavior of young children during mental tests," *J. juv. Res.*, 1929, *13*, 204-219.

47. ——. *Anger in young children.* (Monograph series No. 9) Minneapolis: Univ. Minn. Press, 1930, 278.

48. ——. *Developmental psychology. An introduction to the study of human behavior.* New York: D. Appleton-Century Co., 1934, xvii + 619.

49. —— & Anderson, John E. *Experimental child study.* New York: The Century Co., 1931, xii + 546.

50. ——, Foster, J. C. & Van Wangenen, M. J. *Minnesota preschool scale.* (Manual Form A) Minneapolis, Philadelphia: Educ. Test Bureau, Inc., 1932.

51. Gridley, Pearl F. "Graphic representation of a man by four-year-old children in nine prescribed drawing situations," *Genet. Psychol. Monogr.*, 1938, *20*, 183-350.

52. Hattwick, L. A. "Sex differences in behavior of nursery school children," *Child Develpm.*, 1937, *8*, 343-355.

53. —— & Sanders, M. K. "Age differences in behavior at the nursery school level," *Child Develpm.*, 1938, *9*, 27-47.

54. ——. *Some suggestions for guidance of nursery school children.* Chicago: W.P.A. Nursery Schools of Chicago, 1938, 39.

55. Hetzer, Hildegarde. "Entwicklungsbedingte Erziehungsschwierigkeiten," *Zeitschr. f. pädagogische Psychol.*, 1929, *30*. Leipzig: Quelle & Meyer. (Scheibner, Stern, Fischer)

56. Hetzel, v. Georg. "Äussere Körperform," *Handbuch der Anatomie des Kindes*, 1938, *1*, 479-524.

57. Heubner, O. "Über Zeitfolgen in der psychischen Entwicklung des Säuglings und des jungen Kindes," *Ergeb. d. inn. Med. u. Kinderhk.*, 1918, *16*, 1-31.

58. Hicks, J. A. "The acquisition of motor skill in young children. A study of the effects of practice in throwing at a moving target," *Child Develpm.*, 1930, *1*, 2, 90-103.

59. Holbrook, S. M. *A psychological study of a group of three-year-old children.* M. A. Thesis, Yale University, 1922.

60. Hooker, Davenport. "The origin of the grasping movement in man," *Proc. Amer. Philos. Soc.*, 1938, *79*, 579-606.

61. Hulson, Eva Leah. "An analysis of the free play of ten four-year-old children through consecutive observations," *J. juv. Res.*, 1930, *14*, 188-208.

62. Jaffa, Adele. *The California preschool mental scale.* Syllabus Series, No. 251. Berkeley: Univ. Calif. Press, 1934, 66.

63. Jenkins, Lulu Marie. "A comparative study of motor achievements of children of five, six, and seven years of age," *Teach. Coll. Contr. Educ.* No. 414, 1930, x + 54.

64. Jersild, Arthur T. & Bienstock, Sylvia F. "A study of children's ability to sing," *J. educ. Psychol.*, 1934, *25*, 481-503.

65. Johnson, Buford J. *Mental growth of children in relation to the rate of growth in bodily development.* New York: E. P. Dutton, 1925, xix + 160.

66. —— & Courtney, D. M. "Tower building," *Child Develpm.*, 1931, *2*, 2, 161.

67. ——. *Child psychology.* Baltimore, Md.: Charles C. Thomas, 1932, xii + 439.

68. Jones, Harold Ellis. "Dextrality as a function of age," *J. exper. Psychol.*, 1931, *14*, 125-143.

69. Johnson, Harriet M. *Children in the nursery school.* New York: John Day, 1934, xx + 325.

70. Jones, Mary C. & Burks, Barbara S. "Personality development in childhood," *Monogr. Soc. Res. Child Develpm.*, 1936, *1*, No. 4, 1-205.

71. Jones, Vernon A. "A study of children's ability to note similarities and differences," *J. educ. Psychol.*, 1925, *16*, 253-260.

72. Kearney, I. *The mental and educational status of a group of kindergarten children.* M. A. Thesis, Yale University, 1923.

73. Kenderdine, Margaret. "Laughter in the pre-school child," *Child Develpm.*, Sept., 1921, *2*, 228-230.

74. Knox, A. A. "A scale based on the work at Ellis Island for estimating mental defect," *J. Amer. Med. Assn.*, March, 1914, *lxii*, 741-747.

75. Kuhlmann, F. *A handbook of mental tests.* A further revision and extension of the Binet Simon scale. Baltimore, Md.: Warwick and York, 1922, 208.

76. ——. *Tests of mental development: A complete scale for individual examination.* Minneapolis, Minn.: Educational Test Bureau, 1939, xi + 314.

77. Krötzsch, W. *Rhythms und Form in der freien Kindererziehung.* Leipzig: Haase, 1917.

78. Levy, David M. & Tulchin, Simon H. "The resistant behavior of infants and children during mental tests," *J. exper. Psychol.*, 1923, *6*, 304; 1925, *8*, 209-224.

79. Lewin, Kurt. *A dynamic theory of personality.* Selected papers. New York and London: McGraw-Hill, 1935, ix + 286.

80. Little, N. F. & Williams, H. M. "An analytical scale of language achievement," *Univ. Ia. Stud. Child Welfare*, 1937, *13*, (No. 2) 47-48; 88-94.

81. Lowenfeld, Viktor. *The nature of creative activity.* New York: Harcourt, Brace, 1939, xvii + 272.

82. McCarthy, D. A. *The language development of the preschool child.* Minneapolis: Univ. Minn. Press, 1930, xiii + 174.

83. McCaskill, Carra Lou & Wellman, Beth L. "A study of common motor achievements at the preschool ages," *Child Develpm.*, 1938, *9*, No. 2, 141-150.

84. McGinnis, Esther. "The acquisition and interference of motor habits in young children," *Genet, Psychol. Monogr.*, 6, 3, 1929, 203-311.
85. McGinnis, John M. "Eye-movements and optic nystagmus in early infancy," *Genet. Psychol. Monogr.*, 1930, 8, 4, 321-430.
86. Meier, Norman C., Daniels, Parmely Clark, Jasper, Constance C. and others. "Studies in the psychology of art," *Psychol. Monogr.* 1933, No. 45, ix + 188.
87. Mengert, Ida G. "A preliminary study of the reactions of two-year-old children to each other when paired in a semi-controlled situation," *J. Genet. Psychol.*, Sept., 1931, 39, 3, 393-398.
88. Meyer, Edith. "Comprehension of spatial relations in preschool children," *J. genet Psychol.* (In press)
89. Miles, W. R. "Ocular dominance demonstrated by unconscious sighting," *J. exp. Psychol.*, 1929, 12, 113-126.
90. Mitchell, Lucy Sprague. *Here and now story book.* New York: Dutton, 1921, 366.
91. Muntz, Leonard. *A study of individual differences in two-year-old children.* M. A. Thesis, Yale University, 1921.
92. Murchison, Carl (ed.). *A handbook of child psychology.* Worcester, Mass.: Clark Univ. Press. 1931, xii + 711.
93. ———. *A handbook of child psychology,* Second Edition, revised. Worcester, Mass.: Clark Univ. Press, 1933, xii + 956.
94. Murphy, Gardner & Murphy, Lois Barclay. *Experimental social psychology.* New York: Harper & Brothers, 1931, ix + 709.
95. Newhall, S. M. "Identification by young children of differently oriented visual forms," *Child Develpm.*, 1937, 8, 105-111.
96. Nice, M. M. "Ambidexterity and delayed speech development," *Ped. Sem.*, 1918, 25, 141-162.
97. ———. "On the size of vocabularies," *Amer. Speech,* 1926-1927, 2, 1-7.
98. Olsen, Willard C. "Problem tendencies in children." Minneapolis: Univ. Minn. Press, *Institute Child. Welf. Monogr.*, 1930, No. 3, pp. 92.
99. Oseretzky, N. "Methods of investigation of psychomotor activity," *Beik. z. Zsch. f. angew. Psychol.*, 1931, No. 57, pp. 162.
100. Parten, Mildred. "Social participation among pre-school children," *J. abnorm. (soc.) Psychol.*, 27, 1932-33, 243-269.
101. Piaget, Jean. *The language and thought of the child.* New York: Harcourt, Brace, 1926, xxiii + 246.
102. ———. *Judgment and reasoning in the child.* New York: Harcourt, Brace, 1928, viii + 260.
103. ———. *The child's conception of physical causality.* New York: Harcourt, Brace, 1930.
104. Pintner, Rudolf & Paterson, Donald G. *A scale of performance tests.* New York: D. Appleton & Co., 1923, ix + 218.
105. Porteus, S. D. *Porteus tests: The Vineland revision.* Publ. of the Training School at Vineland, N. J. 1919, No. 16.

106. ——. *Guide to Porteus maze test.* Publ. of the Training School at Vineland, N. J., 1924, No. 25, pp. 35.

107. Reynolds, Martha M. "Negativism of pre-school children." New York: *Teach. Coll. Contr. Educ.*, No. 288, 1928, viii + 126.

108. Rice, Charlotte. "Excellence of production and types of movements in drawing," *Child Develpm.*, 1930, *1*, 1, 1-14.

109. ——. "The orientation of plane figures as a factor in their perception by children," *Child Develpm.*, 1930, *1*, 2, 111-143.

110. Rouma, G. *Le langage graphique de l'enfant.* Paris: Alcan, 1913, 284.

111. Sherbon, Florence Brown. *The child. His origin, development and care.* New York: McGraw-Hill Book Co., 1934, xix + 707.

112. Shirley, Mary M. *The first two years.* Vol. I. Minneapolis: Univ. Minn. Press, 1931, xv + 227.

113. Smith, M. E. "An investigation of the development of the sentence and the extent of vocabulary in young children," *Univ. Ia. Stud.*, 1926, *3*, No. 5, 92.

114. ——, Lecker, G., Dunlap, J. W., & Cureton, E. E. "The effects of race, sex, and environment on the age at which children walk," *J. genet. Psychol.*, 1930, *38*, 489-498.

115. Stern, William (trans. by Anna Barwell) (Rev. ed.). *Psychology of early childhood up to the sixth year of age.* New York: Holt, 1930, 612.

116. Stoddard, George D. & Wellman, Beth L. *Child psychology.* New York: Macmillan, 1934, xii + 419.

117. Stutsman, Rachel. "Performance tests for children of preschool age," *Genet. Psychol. Monogr.*, 1926, *1*, 1, 1-67.

118. ——. *Mental measurement of preschool children, with a guide for the administration of the Merrill-Palmer scale of mental tests.* New York: World Book Co., 1931, x + 368.

119. Sweet, C., Watson, R. G., & Stafford, H. E. "Physiologic changes in posture during the first six years of life," *J. Amer. Med. Ass.*, 1928, *91*, 1519-1520.

120. Sylvester, R. H. "The form board test," *Psychol. Monogr.*, 1913, *15*, No. 4, 1-56.

121. Terman, Lewis M. *The measurement of intelligence.* Boston: Houghton Mifflin Co., 1916, xviii + 361.

122. —— & Merrill, Maud. *Measuring intelligence. A guide to the administration of the new revised Stanford-Binet tests of intelligence.* Boston: Houghton Mifflin, 1937, xi + 461.

123. Thomas, D. S., et al. "Some new techniques for studying social behavior," *Child Develpm. Monogr.* No. 1. New York: Columbia Univ. Press, 1929, pp. 213.

124. Thompson, Helen. "Spontaneous play activities of five-year-old children," Paper presented before Amer. Psychol. Ass., Dartmouth Univ., Hanover, N. H. *Psychol. Bull.*, 1936, *33*, 9, 751. (Abs.)

125. ——. "The dynamics of activity drives in young children." Paper presented at XIe Congrès International de Psychologie, Paris. Publ. in

Onzième Congrès International de Psychologie, Paris, 1937. Paris: 1938, p. 470.

126. Town, C. H. "Analytic study of a group of five- to six-year-old children," *Univ. Ia. Stud. Child Welf.*, 1921, *1*, No. 4, 1-87.

127. Updegraff, Ruth. "Preferential handedness in young children," *J. exp. Educ.*, 1932-1933, *1*, 134-139.

128. ——, et al. *Practice in preschool education.* New York: McGraw-Hill, 1938, xvi + 408.

129. ——, et al. "Studies in preschool education, I." *Univ. Ia. Stud. Child Welf.*, 1938, *14*, 283.

130. Vincent, E. L. "Some suggestions for approaching children and their parents," Part I. *J. Pediat.*, 1937, *11*, 697-742.

131. Washburn, Ruth W. "A scheme for grading the reactions of children in a new social situation," *J. genet. Psychol.*, 1932, *40*, 1, 84-99.

132. Wellman, Beth. "The development of motor coordination in young children," *Univ. Ia. Stud. Child Welf.*, 1926, *3*, No. 4, 93.

133. ——. "Significant factors in the motor coordination of young children," *Psychol. Bull.*, 1928, *25*, 178-179.

134. ——. "Physical growth and motor development and their relation to mental development in children," in *Handbook of child psychology*, Carl Murchison, ed. Worcester, Mass.: Clark Univ. Press, 1931, 242-277.

135. Whipple, Guy M. *Manual of mental and physical tests.* Baltimore: Warwick & York, 1924, xvi + 367.

136. Wild, M. R. "The behavior pattern of throwing and some observations concerning its course of development in children," *Res. Quart. Amer. Ass. for Health & Physical Educ.*, 1938, 3, 20-24.

137. Williams, Harold M., Silvers, Clement H., & Hattwick, Melvin J. "The measurement of musical development, II," *Univ. Ia. Stud. Child Welf.*, 1935, *11*, No. 2, 100.

138. ——. "A qualitative analysis of the erroneous speech sound substitutions of preschool children," *Univ. Ia. Stud. Child Welf.*, 1937, *13*, 19-32.

139. ——. "An analytical study of language achievement in preschool children," *Univ. Ia. Stud. Child Welf.*, 1937, *13*, 7-18.

140. Wolff, L. V. "Development of the human foot as an organ of locomotion," *Amer. J. Dis. Children*, 1929, *37*, 1212-1220.

141. Woolley, Helen T., & Cleveland, Elizabeth. "Performance tests for three-, four-, and five-year-old children," *J. exp. Psychol.*, 1923, *6*, 58-68.

142. *Yale films of child development.* Ten unit films and two feature length films, 35 and 16 mm. sound scored. For full bibliography see Gesell & Thompson (39, 238-240).

INDEX

Action-Agent test, 202, 203, 223-228, 286
  characteristic forms of response, 225
    table of, 224
  genetic gradations, 227
  procedure, 223
  responses to,
    table of correct, 224, 228
  scoring, 224
  sex differences in, 227-228
Adaptations to atypical exam. conditions, 281-295, 369
Adaptive behavior, 14, 19, 21, 22, 25, 27, 30, 35, 42, 47, 53, 108-188
  defined, 108
  expressive of individuality, 297
  illustration of, Plates XII, XIII
  illustrative case materials, 367
  in individuality characterization, 297, 299-302, 305
  schedules, 322-342
    explanatory notes for, 323-343
  situations, 108-188
  types of,
    block building, 109-120
    comparative judgment, 180-185
    drawing, 137-169
    form
      adaptation, 120-129
      discrimination, 129-137
    immediate memory, 175-180
    number concepts, 169-175
    problem solving, 186-188
  See also Behavior situations, adaptive.
  See also specific situations as **Bridge** building, Cube play, etc.
Aesthetic
  behavior, 254-258
    developmental sequences, 254-258
    discussion of, 258
    individual differences in, 258
    See also Block play, Music, Painting, etc.
  comparison, 182, 183, 237
    behavior trends, 182
    procedure, 182
    scoring, 182
    sex differences, 182

Aesthetic—(*Continued*)
  procedure—(*Continued*)
    significance of, 182
    table of behavior, 183
Age levels in
  months,
    1-4 months, 246
    8-9 months, 246
    12-18 months, 71, 190, 191
    15 months, 26, 68, 110, 113, 114, 122, 123, 126, 211, 219, 242, 244, 245, 247-249, 251, 252, 258, 270, 303
      developmental schedule, 322, 323
    18 months, 29-40, 68, 71, 77, 78, 81, 83, 85, 89, 92, 94, 110, 113, 116, 122, 124, 126-128, 132, 140, 158-160, 186, 191-195, 211, 213, 214, 216, 217, 219, 242, 244, 245, 248, 249, 251, 254, 258-260, 269-273, 277
      developmental schedule, 324, 325
      illustrated, Plate IV
    18-24 months, 68, 71
    21 months, 72, 127, 217, 219, 242, 244, 245, 247, 249, 259
      developmental schedule, 326, 327
    24 months. *See* Two years.
    30 months, 72, 135, 194-200, 216, 244, 245, 247, 249, 259
      developmental schedule, 330, 331
      See also 2½ years.
    36 months. *See* Three years.
    42 months, 211, 246
      developmental schedule, 334, 335
    48 months. *See* Four years.
    54 months,
      developmental schedule, 338-339
    60 months. *See* Five years.
    72 months. *See* Six years.
  weeks,
    1-4 weeks. *See* Neonate.
    4 weeks, 18-20
    12 weeks, 76, 77
    16 weeks, 20-22, 67, 68, 70, 76
    16-28 weeks, 13, 67
    20 weeks, 68, 70, 76, 77
    24 weeks, 76, 77

26